The Wave
Book Four

OTHER BOOKS BY LAURA KNIGHT JADCZYK

Amazing Grace – An Autobiography of the Soul

The Secret History of the World and How to Get Out Alive

The Occult Significance of 9/11

The High Strangeness of Dimensions, Densities, and the Process of Alien Abduction

The Wave

Book Four

Laura Knight-Jadczyk

Red Pill Press
2005

Table of Contents

A Short Introduction

Those readers who have read *The Wave* online know that it is almost a thousand pages of text. Thus, we have decided to split it up into separate volumes to make it easier to handle, to read, and even to print.

Volumes 2, 3, 4, and 5 do not contain the introductory materials that have been included in Volume 1, and thus this volume begins with the continuation of *The Wave*, where we left off in Volume 3.

The introduction to the series on the website says:

> The Wave is a term used to describe a Macro-cosmic Quantum Wave Collapse producing both a physical and a "metaphysical" change to the Earth's cosmic environment theorized to be statistically probable sometime in the early 21st century. This event is variously described by other sources as the planetary shift to 4th density, shift of the ages, harvest, etc., and is most often placed around the end of 2012. The subject of The Wave begins with a UFO abduction account, a transcript of an actual hypnotic regression session, that refers to a global cataclysmic change.

> This series of articles, written by Laura Knight-Jadczyk, demonstrates the unique nature of the Cassiopaean Experiment. In her skillful collecting of the pieces of the puzzle from throughout the transcripts, in-depth research, personal experiences, weaving them into a finished product, Laura brings added depth and dimension to the original transmissions. Laura presents what the Cassiopaeans - We are *you* in the future - have to say about the eventuality of The Wave - *from* the future - including an exploration of the limitations of man's present estate, in cognitive, biological, historical and ontological terms.

The fact is, in the past three years, we have made much progress in our understanding of the Wave and our relationship to it. I will be adding material to the end of this book version of the series that will not appear on the website, and that will finally bring us to a conclusion to *The Wave*. Whether or not that conclusion is correct remains to be seen.

I don't think we have very long to wait to find out.

Chapter 29

Stripped to the Bone
Or The Shamanic Initiation
Of The Knighted Ones:
Technicians of Ecstasy

Service to Self and Service to Others

The Nexus Seven write in *Top Secret/Demon*:

"The notions of Service-to-Self and Service-to-Others in popular use in channeled Ufology today are outrageous, but apt simplifications of the real intricacies of the matter. As the definitions change of exactly what 'self' encompasses, these notions map across a wide variety of different orientations, and it is appropriate to introduce the dialectic, the triad pattern that is really involved beyond the dualistic notion. Although merely extending the differentiating metaphor into three classes is hardly as far as it can be taken."

In this remark, The Nexus Seven make it clear that they are falling under the influence of the "damping effect" of the STS deceptions. There is no clearer understanding of the reality of Creation than to grasp the concept of Being vs. Nonbeing, Creation vs. Entropy. That's the bottom line. The One that *is* Two in One. It is only in the dynamic between them that there even *is* a "Third Man". The Third Man is the Created Cosmos: the matter of Entropic, sleeping consciousness enlivened with Creative, Awakening consciousness.

Q: (L) But, just a clue: how does thought become matter?

A: Bilaterally. Dual emergence.

Q: (L) Emergence into what and what?

A: Not "into what and what", but rather, "from what and to what".

Q: (L) What emerges from what?

A: The beginning emerges from the end, and vice versa.

Q: (L) And what is the beginning and what is the end?

A: Union with the One. 7th density, i.e.: all that is, and is not.

The *two fundamentals of all that is*. The most important concept of all to grasp in order to know how to "grow" or "ascend" to higher realms.

The thing is, since it is a "cycle", this means that not everyone is "ready" at any one time! Those who *are* ready have a profound sense of "mission". And for some, that "mission" is to assist those who are *very close* to awakening to be able to do so. But, even those with a "mission" must awaken to it:

Q: (L) But, just exactly what is the mission?

A: You are awakening to it just fine, thank you!

Q: (L) Are you saying that all this constant discussing and taking things apart and talking about them and thinking about all these things is actually getting us somewhere?

A: Absolutely!!!!

Q: (L) Is some mode of sharing this information we are receiving part of this "mission"?

A: When you have learned, you have energized yourself. Lead by the hand? No way, Jose!

Q: (L) So, we have to make that choice ourselves. Okay, we discussed a name that would sort of symbolize this mission and we came up with - and who knows how - Aurora to symbolize the dawn, waking up... that sort of thing. Where in the world did this come from?

A: Refer to the previous answer.

Q: (L) So, we have to choose everything here. And there are no comments?

A: No need, you are doing just fine by yourselves.

Q: (S) What did you expect them to say? "Atta girl!?" [Laughter] Will we be able to find some way to support this mission?

A: We are not going to answer that, as it would violate level one directive.

Q: (L) What is a "level one directive"?

A: Refer to last answer.

Q: (L) Well, fine! I want to know! Is there some place that gives out orders up there?

A: You will know when it is right, and not before!

Q: (L) I want you guys to know that I sometimes feel a wee tiny bit like a pawn on a chessboard!

A: You should, you inhabit 3rd density STS environment.

Q: (L) I was at least hoping that if I was a pawn, that some of the players were good guys. Is that asking too much?

A: Yes. The "Good guys" don't play chess.

Q: (L) But there have been so many strange events, so many synchronous events. Is that the good guys helping or the bad guys leading me astray?

A: Neither. It is Nature running its course.

Q: (L) Okay. One of the sensations I have experienced is that I have had it up to the eyebrows with the negative energies and experiences of 3rd density, and I have thought lately that this feeling of having had enough, in an absolute sense, is one of the primary motivators for wanting to find one's way out of this trap we are in. I want out of it. Is this part of this "nature" as you call it?

A: Yes. When you see the futility of the limitations of 3rd density life, it means you are ready to graduate. Notice those who wallow in it.

Q: (L) Some people obviously wallow in extreme materiality. And there seems to be another kind that is more subtle, which has to do with saying that you want to grow and become enlightened, and yet such a person is unable to pierce the veil of their own illusions about how to become enlightened, and then they wallow in the illusion that they are really making progress...

A: Wallowing takes many forms. More often, the sign of wallowing is someone who does not feel alienated by the obvious traps and limitations of 3rd density.

So, we know that the obvious traps and limitations of 3rd density produce a "sense of alienation" in the person who is in the process of awakening.

But then, awakening is not precisely the same thing as "growing to fit" 4th density. We know we have to awaken in order to choose our polarity/orientation, but then comes the matter of amplification through Forced Oscillation.

And it is in this matter of choosing orientation and amplification that the terms of Service to Others and Service to Self become the most important ideas presented to humans in the present time. They are *not*, "outrageous, but apt simplifications of the real intricacies of the matter", as the Nexus Seven suggest.

In practical terms, how do we "grow stronger" in our polarity? If it is to be of the Service to Others alignment, isn't it just necessary to give? Isn't that the only key? And don't the Service to Self polarized beings just take?

Well, it IS that simple, and it is more complex.

From one perspective, it would seem that the most accepting and loving thing to do would be to love *all* - to surround all those of the Service to Self alignment with Love and Light so that they would be enclosed and permeated with this love which would then transform them to the Service to Others alignment.

But note immediately that, in these terms, the sending of love is intended to *change*, to *transform*, to *deny free will*. And thus, by simply doing this, one is aligning with the very Orientation that seeks to deny Free Will, i.e. STS. The result is that the very love energy being sent IS Service to Self Forced Oscillation!

And what will it then do? It will *amplify* the STS frequency in the person or situation it is being sent to transform. It will do the opposite of what is wanted, but exactly what is intended.

Service to Self seeks to dominate and take all to stuff in its black hole of fear. To send love (or to give anything) with the intention of changing, transforming, or making anything different than what it is, is to seek *domination.*

For the Service to Others polarity to allow itself to be manipulated by deceptive teachings of "sending love and light to transform the world", amounts to the ipso facto acceptance of dominance. The damping of its own frequency, the loss of amplitude.

Service to Others seeks to give *all* of self to others. But, because the chief thing it wishes to give is Free Will, it only gives when *asked*.

Sounds like a marriage made in Heaven, yes? One side wants to take; one side wants to give. Go for it, right?

The idea that those of the STO frequency must not give without being asked is a subtle thing. The concept inherent in "asking" is that of willing exchange. The asking is the giving of the one who asks. The response is the giving of the one who is asked. If there is anything in either of them that expects any change *other* than the explicit asking and giving, the interaction falls into STS and not STO.

However, if one can ask, and one can give without expectation of any change of any kind in the receiver, the STO dynamic is operational.

If there is even a hidden motive that anything will be changed by the exchange, the result is damping of the STO frequency.

When you give in response to manipulation, which is a domination dynamic, you are also giving from a position of STS, which is further Self-damping to STO orientation and amplifying to STS. And then, on top of self-damping, you are losing energy, because there is no willing exchange!

The end result of giving Love energy to the STS polarity is to gradually deplete the STO polarity in the self as well as in the grander scheme of things, and eventually, to deprive all those of that polarity from shared, symbiotic sustenance. One has then, by default, become part of the STS hierarchy and has lost any usefulness in terms of Service to Others. And if you are seeking to polarize in the STO mode, you must gain energy by alignment and amplification to move OUT of the STS realm into an STO dynamic where all give to each other and there is multiplication of force in the act, rather than depletion.

Another way of saying it is that the true object of the STO dynamic is to give to God in the role of the *creative* or *free will function*; to establish frequency resonance in this dynamic.

The true object of the STS dynamic is to give to God in the role of Death and the Destroyer - the Thought of Non-being, to deny Free Will to Create or BE.

The STS side wants to give enslavement. The STO side must refuse in order to retain their strength and purity and ability to actualize Free Will for ALL.

The essence of Creation is the fact that, beneath the empirical, observable "real world" is the realm of potentials and our physical world is manifested out of the underlying potentialities by our perspective. The "gift of Free Will" of the Creator is our ability to *choose* our perspective. We can choose "living water" that becomes "a spring of water welling up continually within", to "eternal life/creation", or we can choose the water from the "well of Jacob the supplanter", which will leave us thirsty again and again. And it is in this choice that we come to the remark of Don Juan; "... As awareness reaches levels higher than the toes, tremendous maneuvers of perception become a matter of course".

Such a choice is a "maneuver of perception", though it is only in retrospect that I can even say this. I was as ignorant of what was happening to me as a person could be.

Further maneuvers of perception amount to the ability to make every choice based on "seeing the unseen". Every time we choose, based on knowledge/love, rather than chemical/emotional love or assumption/wishful thinking love, we are giving a push to the swing of amplifying our Frequency Resonance Vibration. And such amplification increases our polarization and we "grow".

The problem is, in the beginning, when we begin to use discipline to try to "see the unseen", we are like a blind man stumbling through a maze. We are Theseus in the lair of the Minotaur, guided only by the thread of

Ariadne. Our ability to perceive the Noumenal world, the activities of 4th density, requires great attention, great discipline, and an ability to "face with serenity odds that are not included in our expectations". We have to learn the art of "facing infinity without flinching". And it is this process that the Cassiopaeans are facilitating. What they tell us about the Noumenal world, the 4th density realm, is not supposed to terrify us in the end, it is supposed to wake us up to the odds that are facing us that are *not* according to our expectations.

And, as we begin to learn to really *see*, we begin to make some experimental choices based on what we are seeing. Some of them work, some of them don't. We adjust our course gradually, learning what amplifies our polarity and what damps our polarity.

I recently received some correspondence from members of the Group who have been experimenting with "awakening" and "seeing the meanings behind the reality" as outlined by the Cassiopaeans. One of them wrote:

> "One thing I am finally realizing in spite of decades of religious and social training to the contrary, is that we all have only one decision to make, just one. At any specific moment, we are all faced with the opportunity to invoke an STS or an STO approach to the specific lesson at hand. By placing focus on this specific choice of the moment instead of fretting about a lifetime of 'wrong' choices and carrying the weight of redemption/salvation via an outside source who demands that you pay them money so they will 'speak nicely about you to their lord in an afterlife', coupled with the Cassiopaean's insistence that there is no 'right or wrong', just lessons, makes the 'task' of being an STO candidate sooooooo much easier..."

And another member of the Group responded:

> "Doesn't it seem like a choice made in the present moment that brings deep clarity and understanding of a lesson, changes the nature of all choices ever made?
>
> And that is the essence of the matter. A choice made in the present moment - *any* present moment - excluding all the outside influences, with ONLY the consideration of whether it *allows* Free Will to all involved, changes the nature of all choices ever made!"

Every choice that supports Free Will for any being, whether that being is using their Free Will to choose to deny free will to either themselves or others, to the extent Free Will is maintained for all involved, is a choice *for* Free Will at the deepest levels of existence. But notice the key: to support Free Will of others to choose and fully experience their own path - and that does *not* mean to support the choice they have made by participating in their lesson! To participate in the choice of orientation of another is to make it your own. It can then act as a damper to your own amplification.

This means that the ability to support Free Will in others, which lies in the STO pathway, *must* remain pure and must *not* be subsumed into the STS alignment, or Free Will for all could cease to exist in our present reality, which would create an imbalance of such awesome proportions, that I shudder to consider the consequences. In fact, it could even be said that learning the true dynamics of Service to Others and Free Will in the cadres of those who have the internal inclination, and to begin to practice it, might considerably ameliorate any predicted cataclysms. One thing that is certain, however, to continue to violate Free Will by all the "Love and Light" efforts to change the world, to "transform the darkness into light" will result in nothing but worsening conditions on our planet by the very fact that they amplify the STS polarity.

It is for God, for *all* - including the Service to Self polarity - which the STO candidates must refuse to support and sustain and feed those of the STS orientation. If you feed the STS polarity, it grows stronger (and it has already been in charge here for over 300,000 years!) and the STO presence will grow weaker, which will erode Free Will for all.

So, we return again to the peeling of the onion of illusion, the constant hammering of the point that you are asleep, the shocking of your sensibilities over and over again with the idea that unless you awaken, your position is hopeless - you are "food for the gods". By taking away every hope and dream of outside salvation you ever thought you could cling to, I am stripping your bones bare. Not only am I stripping your bones, I am boiling your flesh. And, to those who are truly *asking*, it is an essential function I am performing for you. It is the Shamanic Initiation. You cannot be "reborn" unless you die. And, "unless a man be born again", he can have no "eternal life".

In the broadest sense, the human being who has mastery over his own life is a Shaman. And those of you who resist this process most strenuously are most likely the ones with the greatest Shamanic capacity. Will is will. It just needs to be married to knowledge.

It has been observed that the desire of the human being to enter into ecstatic contact with the Divine is in direct conflict with the fear of being obliged to renounce the simple human condition. We can see, from our discussion above, that this is, essentially, the conflict between Service to Others and Service to Self. The work to gather the knowledge and become humble and face the deep inner truth about the self is the price, and not everyone is able to pay it. And this is the human dilemma. There is nothing cozier than to be a human being. We can live forever behind veils of illusion, suffering our blindness, and dying in our ignorance; and, until some aspect of that human has had its fill of suffering and death, there will be no desire to venture into the unknown to seek the cure for the human disease. Only the soul that is ready for this definitive journey is willing to risk the soul chilling fear of traveling into the enchanted forest of the Cosmos, in order to experience the unspeakable joy of finding the Grail - the choice for Free Will Service to Others that serves *all*.

A Shaman is, as Eliade describes, a **Technician of Ecstasy**. This is an essential qualification and/or result of contact with the Divine. More than that, in order to be in direct contact with the Divine, the human being must be able to "see the unseen". This **Seeing** is the capacity of human beings to enlarge their perceptual field until they are capable of assessing not only outer appearances, but also the essence of everything in order to access the level of being that enables them to make choices that are capable of initiating a new causal series.

Of course, problems arise when an individual attempts to be a Shaman without knowledge. A recent correspondent sent us some information about a popular channeled source that claims to be teaching a new perspective on physics.

"Dear Ark and Laura,

I don't know much about Scalar Waves, certainly not enough to know whether or not the below site's information on Scalar Waves is useful, but I pass the information along to you. I have heard Anna Hayes speak on the Jeff Rense radio show, and she made a good impression as an apparently calm and knowledgeable person."

J***

Ark went to the site in question and began to read. After a period of study, he responded as follows:

Hi J***,

While reading:

"Dimensions are interwoven layers of scalar waves that serve to direct the flow of consciousness/energy into multiple patterns of refraction through which the hologram of matter density, linear time and manifest objectification of reality can be experienced. Dimensions exist in precise relationship to each other creating a 90-degree difference in Angular Rotation of Particle Spin between dimensional bands. Scalar Waves are points of Standing Waves, composed of quantities of consciousness, that emanate out of fixed points of vibration which form ultra-micro-particle units called Partiki, Partika and Particum. Scalar Waves exist within a fixed Scalar Field that forms the Universal Unified Field of consciousness/energy. Fixed scalar waves appear to move due to a perpetual action of internal fission and fusion, through which series of scalar standing wave points 'flash on and off' creating perpetual rhythms of motion called 'flash-line sequences' through which continual manifestation and de-manifestation of matter occurs."

I can't help thinking that it is a pity that a person that evidently knows nothing about waves, dimensions, particle spin, etc. chooses to "TEACH" others on these subjects. But, on the other hand, creating more confusion is what the Lizzies must have on their mind. And they seem to be successful. On the other hand, we are in a Free Will Universe - it is up to each person to choose the path and the "teacher". Thanks for the link - it helps me.

Best,

ark.

As it happened, Ark's response was also sent to a promoter of the above channeling who then responded:

Hi:

One doesn't need to know anything on a specific topic when the information isn't coming from oneself but from a higher source.

Love, Light, and Joy

Dee Finney

Aside from the fact that actually reading that nonsense is an energy drain, such a perspective does *not* resonate with the Cassiopaean information in which independent study and gaining of knowledge is urged as the only means by which we can be protected from being led into "traps". Ark replied:

Dear Dee,

"Sure, but to check whether the information comes from a higher source or lower source, it is always necessary first to check whether the information makes any sense or is just a mumbo-jumbo. There are lot of dead dudes and other entities that are more than ready to pour all kinds of nonsense into our heads.

Real research is *always* necessary. How else can we know we are not being disinformed? You must never *rely* on what the entities tell you. You always have to check and keep critical! Unless you *want* to live in an illusion. Many people do.

Best,

Ark"

Anyone can be a channel. It takes knowledge and *will* to be able to *choose* to do the work to access expanded states of consciousness.

One of the hardest things for anyone to acknowledge is their own susceptibility to suggestion, manipulation and external control. No one wants to admit that their awareness can be manipulated. Yet, without exception, all of the Mystery Teachings tell us that the first order of business in expanding awareness is to overcome the hypnosis, or "sleep state" in which man exists. And, without exception, all of the Mystery Teachings tell us that this is so formidable a task that only one in ten thousand can achieve it!

Think about this for a moment. Nine thousand, nine hundred ninety-nine people will react to this statement by thinking: "I am the one in ten thousand!" The Great Masters will tell you that if you think this, then you are *not*!

It is the one who realizes that all of his perceptions must be minutely scrutinized, doubted, tested, examined and challenged who has the smallest hope of escaping the hypnosis!! And, to realize this is but the first in a long series of steps to awakening. And, remember, awakening is not the same thing as seeing! Many can see in expanded awareness, but immediately go back to sleep and what they saw is interpreted by the standards of the "hypnotic sleep state" of ordinary awareness. This is what happens to most of those who claim to channel with no need to "check their sources"! And, as Ark wrote, "to check whether the information comes from a higher source or lower source, it is always necessary first to check whether the information makes any sense or is just a mumbo-jumbo. ...real research is always necessary. ... you must never RELY on what the entities tell you. ...unless you *want* to live in an illusion".

And, from my perspective, the main reason such "seers" do not doubt, test, examine and challenge their so-called "guides" is due purely and simply to ego. They have been told that they are "special" or "chosen" or are the "messenger" of this or that "council" or the "heavenly host" or whatever, and it is far easier and more comfortable to believe this, and the further instruction that, "all you need to do is listen to us!", than to exert the enormous efforts required to acknowledge, and extirpate the ego's weaknesses, the chief one being, of course, susceptibility to manipulation by forces far more devious than the human mind can fathom.

Don Juan says that Seers must be paragons of virtue by their will and intent in order to override the nearly invincible laxness of the human condition and programming. To say, "One doesn't need to know anything on a specific topic when the information isn't coming from oneself but from a higher source", is so astonishing an example of this laxness and manipulation that it is difficult to understand how a person can write it without being immediately assaulted by the insanity of such a view!

"One of the necessary conditions of learning to truly SEE is to be able to bring the mind to focus on anything with uncommon force and clarity. Yet, what is learned during these periods of focus is usually unavailable to normal recall." [Castaneda, **The Fire From Within**, 1984]]

Obviously, great polarized strength is necessary here. *Seeing* is to witness the unknown and to glimpse the unknowable. The unknown is veiled from man but is within the reach of man's reason if he is sufficiently polarized and amplified! The unknowable is the indescribable, the unthinkable, and the unrealizable. It is something that may never be known to us in our human state, but seers who are in the grip of laxness and programming don't let *that* stop them!

"...There have certainly been attempts to imbue the [ineffable unknown] with attributes [it] does not have. But that always happens when impressionable people learn to perform acts that require great sobriety. Seers come in all sizes and shapes. ...There are scores of imbeciles who become seers. Seers are human beings full of foibles, or rather, human beings full of foibles are capable of becoming seers. ...The characteristic of miserable seers is that they are willing to forget the wonder of the world. **They become overwhelmed by the fact that they see and believe that it is their genius that counts**. A seer must be a paragon in order to override the nearly invincible laxness of our human condition. More important than seeing itself is what seers do with what they see."[1]

Apparently the effort required to bring this learning to normal consciousness is staggering and impossible for most people because they have no "vessel of knowledge" prepared to receive it. He further tells us, and this is corroborated in other teachings, that to interact with the unknown, but that which is ultimately within the reach of knowing through great work, is energizing, exhilarating and fulfilling even when it is also full of apprehension and fear. It seems that one of the effects of enlargement of the perceptual field is a combination of sheer joy combined with a frightening feeling of sadness and longing. This is apparently because a full field of awareness includes all the opposites in perfect balance.

But, even on the level of the unknown that is ultimately accessible to human perception, Seers who truly See often go to pieces on finding out that existence is incomprehensibly complex and that our normal awareness distorts all and perverts with its limitations. Don Juan remarked that:

"In the life of warriors it was extremely natural to be sad for no overt reason. ...Whenever the boundaries of the known are broken, a mere glimpse of the eternity outside is enough to disrupt the coziness of our

---

[1] Castaneda, *The Fire From Within*, 1984]

controlled awareness. The resulting melancholy is sometimes so intense that it can bring about death. ...The best way to get rid of melancholy is to make fun of it."[2]

But, to interact with the unknowable is to become drained or confused, open to oppression and possession. The bodies of such seers lose tone, their reasoning becomes flawed, and their sobriety wanders aimlessly. The Cassiopaeans have said:

"A: The bottom line is this: You are occupying 3rd density. You are by nature, STS. You can be an STO candidate, but you are *not* STO until you are on 4th density. You will *never* grasp the meaning of these attempted conceptualizations until you are at 4th and above."

To make this point a little clearer, let me add that, before the "Fall", human beings were 3rd density STO, which means that they were *aligned* with 4th density STO. We have already discussed what this reality must have been like in terms of the megalith builders who were able, by their interaction with Celestial forces, to manifest all that was needed without assault on the environment of Earth.

Don Juan tells us that the Seers of ancient times were, "men capable of inconceivable deeds. They were powerful sorcerers, somber and driven, who unraveled the secrets", of existence at our level. They were able to, "influence and victimize people by fixating their awareness on whatever they chose". This is an important key in terms of Frequency Resonance Vibration that cannot be overstressed.

There are two positions in the study and understanding of awareness: Sorcerers vs. The Warrior Who Sees. They Both practice the same Seeing; the difference is Intent. The Sorcerer practices to control others. The Warrior practices to become Free.

The Cassiopaeans designate these two positions as "Service to Others", and "Service to Self". Those who wish to control others are Serving Self; those who wish to become free and help others who wish to become free are Serving Others.

Shaman is another way to describe the Warrior who practices to be free. A Shaman is not a magician or a sorcerer although he *can* play those roles if he chooses. He is not a healer, though he can play that role also. A Shaman is far more; he is a psychopomp, a priest, a mystic and a poet. Shamanism is *not* a religion, it is a function, a role, a magico-religious phenomenon specific to certain individuals who have *ecstatic capacity* permitting "magical flight" to higher realms, descent into the underworld to battle dark forces, mastery over fire, matter, time and space.

---

[2] Castaneda, 1984

Unfortunately, as Don Juan noted, in the present time, the Shamanic acts are acts of great laxity, distortion and aberration.

The word "shaman" comes to us through Russian from the Tungusic *saman*. The word is derived from the Pali *samana*, (Sanskrit *sramana*), through the Chinese *sha-men* (a transcription of the Pali word).

The word shaman, may be related to Sarman. According to John G. Bennett[3], *Sarmoung* or *Sarman*:

"The pronunciation is the same for either spelling and the word can be assigned to old Persian. It does, in fact, appear in some of the Pahlawi texts...

The word can be interpreted in three ways. It is the word for bee, which has always been a symbol of those who collect the precious 'honey' of traditional wisdom and preserve it for further generations.

A collection of legends, well known in Armenian and Syrian circles with the title of *The Bees*, was revised by Mar Salamon, a Nestorian Archimandrite in the thirteenth century. *The Bees* refers to a mysterious power transmitted from the time of Zoroaster and made manifest in the time of Christ."

'Man' in Persian means 'the quality transmitted by heredity and hence a distinguished family or race. It can be the repository of an heirloom or tradition. The word sar means head, both literally and in the sense of principal or chief. The combination sarman would thus mean the chief repository of the tradition...'

And still another possible meaning of the word sarman is... *literally, those whose heads have been purified.*"[4]

Those whose heads have been purified! What an interesting idea! Especially when you consider the concept of Frequency Resonance Vibration and Orientation/Polarization.

We already suspect that these ideas are far older than Zoroaster. And for those who have supposed that the concept of the shaman was stimulated by Buddhism, I will point out that other studies have shown that, even before the intrusion of Buddhism into Central Asia, there was the cult of *Buga*, god of the sky, a celestial worship that antedates Sun and Moon worship.

The central theme of Shamanism is the "ascent to the sky" and/or the "descent" to the underworld. In the former, the practitioner experiences

---

[3] I generally hold Bennett's ideas somewhat suspect because he was one of Gurdjieff's students who seems to have missed many of the main points of what Gurdjieff was trying to say and do..

[4] John G. Bennett, *Gurdjieff: Making of A New World*

Ecstasy, in the latter, he battles demons that threaten the well being of humanity. There are studies that suggest evidence of the earliest practices is in the cave paintings of Lascaux with the many representations of the bird, the tutelary spirits, and the ecstatic experience (ca. 25,000 B.C.). Animal skulls and bones found in the sites of the European Paleolithic period (before 50,000 - ca. 30,000 BC) have been interpreted as evidence of Shamanic practice.

The "ecstatic experience" is the primary phenomenon of Shamanism, and it is this ecstasy that can be seen as the act of merging with the celestial beings. Merging results in Forced Oscillation that changes Frequency. Continued interaction with Celestial beings is a form of Frequency Resonance Vibration.

The idea that there was a time when man was directly in contact with the Celestial Beings is at the root of the myths of the Golden Age that have been redacted to the Grail stories of the 11th and 12th centuries. During this paradisical time, it is suggested that communications between heaven and earth were easy and accessible to everyone. Myths tell us of a time when the "gods withdrew" from mankind. As a result of some "happening", i.e. "The Fall", the communications were broken off and the Celestial Beings withdrew to the highest heavens.

This is exactly what the Cassiopaeans have told us regarding our former alignment with 4th density STO and our present alignment with 4th density STS, and which we have examined to some extent in earlier sections of the present work.

However, the myths also tell us that there were still those certain people who were able to "ascend" and commune with the gods on the behalf of their tribe or family. Through them, contact was maintained with the "guiding spirits" of the group. The beliefs and practices of the present day shamans are a survival of a profoundly modified and even corrupted and degenerated remnant of this archaic technology of concrete communications between heaven and earth.

And, again, the Cassiopaeans suggested this perspective, which was confirmed in later studies. But we will come to that later.

The shaman, in his ability to achieve the ecstatic state inaccessible to the rest of mankind, was regarded as a privileged being. More than this, the myths tell us of the First Shamans who were sent to earth by the Celestial Beings to *defend* human beings against the "negative gods" who had taken over the rule of mankind. It was the task of the First Shamans to activate, in their own bodies, a sort of "transducer" of cosmic energy for the benefit of their tribe. This was expressed as the concept of the "world tree", which became the "axis" or the Pole of the World and later the "royal bloodlines".

It does seem to be true that there is a specific relationship between this function and certain "bloodlines". But, as with everything that has been provided to help mankind, this concept has been co-opted by the forces seeking to keep mankind in darkness and ignorance. The true and ancient bloodlines of the First Shamans have been obscured and hidden by the false trail of the invented genealogies of the Hebrew Old Testament. These trails supposedly lead to certain branches of present day European royal and/or noble families, which seek to establish a counterfeit "kingship" that has garnered a great deal of attention in recent times.

In this present time, there are indications that Cosmic changes of monumental proportions are "in the wind". There are also indications that a particular "time element" is involved, and all the forces of darkness seek to deceive and obfuscate at levels never before achieved in order to distract, confuse, dilute and defuse the abilities of those who may be the bearers of the "circuits of change" for all humanity.

The Sufis have kept the "Technician of Ecstasy" concept alive in their tradition of the "Poles of the World". The *kutub* or *q'tub* (pole of his time) is an appointed being, entirely spiritual of nature, who acts as a divine agent of a sphere at a certain period in time. Each *kutub* has under him four *awtads* (supports) and a number of *abdals* (substitutes), who aid him in his work of preserving and maintaining the world. The interesting thing about this idea is that the individual who occupies the position does not even have to be aware of it! His life, his existence, even his very physiology, is a function of higher realities extruded into the realm of man. That this has a very great deal to do with "bloodlines", as promulgated in recent times is true, but not necessarily in the ways suggested. Again, we will come to that soon enough.

Q: (L) But isn't the nature of a person determined by their soul and not the physical body?

A: Partially, remember, aural profile and karmic reference merges with physical structure.

Q: (L) So you are saying that particular genetic conditions are a physical reflection of a spiritual orientation? That the soul must match itself to the genetics, even if only in potential?

A: Yes, precisely.

Q: (L) So a person's potential for spiritual advancement or unfoldment is, to a great extent, dependent upon their genes?

A: Natural process marries with systematic construct when present.
[Cassiopaeans]

As I am going through the text, preparing it for publication, I see so many things that were clues to things yet to come even from the time of writing The Wave. You could say that the experiences that resulted from publishing this material were initiatic in a very significant way. It's one thing to be a mystic in private, it is altogether another thing to put your knowledge to work, to exist in that state where your understanding leads to action.

In the present time, it seems that those with the "bloodline" are awakening. It is no longer feasible to be a "Pole of the World" who is asleep, because, as we will soon examine, there are some very serious matters of choice and action that may be incumbent upon the awakened Shaman. The first order of business seems to be to awaken and accumulate strength of polarity.

Shamans are born *and* made. That is to say, they are *born to be made*, but the making is their choice. And, from what I have been able to determine, the choice may be one that is made at a different level than the conscious, 3rd density linear experience. Those who have made the choice at the higher levels, and then have negated the choice at this level because they are not able to relinquish their ordinary life, pay a very high price, indeed.

A shaman stands out because of certain characteristics of "religious crisis". They are different from other people because of the *intensity of their religious experiences*. In ancient times, it was the task of the Shamanic elite to be the "Specialist of the Soul", to guard the soul of the tribe because only he could *see the unseen* and know the form and destiny of the Group Soul. But, before he acquired his ability, he was often an ordinary citizen, or even the offspring of a shaman with no seeming vocation (considering that the ability is reputed to be inherited, though not necessarily represented in each generation.)

At some point in his life, however, the shaman has an experience that *separates* him from the rest of humanity. The Native American "vision quest" is a survival of the archaic understanding of the natural initiation of the shaman who is "called" to his vocation by the gods.

A deep study of the matter reveals that those who seek the magico-religious powers via the vision quest when they have not been called spontaneously from within by their own questing nature and feeling of responsibility for humanity, generally become the Dark Shamans, or sorcerers; those who, through a systematic study, obtain the powers deliberately for their own advantage. (Again, Don Juan's distinction between the Sorcerer and the Warrior who practices to be Free.)

The true Shamanic initiation comes by dreams, ecstatic trances combined with extensive study and hard work: intentional suffering. A shaman is expected to not only pass through certain initiatory ordeals, but he/she must also be deeply educated in order to be able to fully evaluate the experiences and challenges that he/she will face. Unfortunately, until now, there have been precious few who have traveled the path of the Shaman, including the practice of the attendant skills of "battling demons", who could teach or advise a course of study for the Awakening Shaman. In my own case, over thirty years of study, twenty years of work as a hypnotherapist and exorcist, and the years of "calling to the universe" that constitute the Cassiopaean Experiment stand as an example of how the process might manifest in the present day.

The future shaman is traditionally thought to exhibit certain exceptional traits from childhood. He is often very nervous and even sickly in some ways. (In some cultures, epilepsy is considered a "mark" of the shaman, though this is a later corrupt perception of the ecstatic state.) It has been noted that shamans, as children, are often *morbidly sensitive*, have weak hearts, disordered digestion, and are subject to *vertigo*. There are those who would consider such symptoms to be incipient mental illness, but the fact is that extensive studies have shown that the so-called hallucinations or visions consist of elements that follow a *particular model* that is consistent from culture to culture, from age to age, and is composed of an amazingly rich theoretical content. It could even be said that persons who "go mad", are "failed shamans" who have failed either because of a flaw in the transmission of the genetics, or because of environmental factors. At the same time, there are many more myths of failed Shamanic heroes than of successful ones, so the warnings of what can happen have long been in place. Mircea Eliade remarks that:

> "... The mentally ill patient proves to be an unsuccessful mystic or, better, the caricature of a mystic. His experience is without religious content, even if it appears to resemble a religious experience, just as an act of autoeroticism arrives at the same physiological result as a sexual act properly speaking (seminal emission), yet at the same time is but a caricature of the latter because it is without the concrete presence of the partner."[5]

Well, that's a pretty interesting analogy! It even suggests to us the idea that one who attempts to activate a Shamanic inheritance within the STS framework of Wishful Thinking, has an "illusory" partner as in the above-

---

[5] Eliade, *Shamanism*, 1964

described activity, with similar results. In other words, Sorcery is like masturbation: the practitioner satisfies himself, but his act does no one else any good. And, by the same token, a Shaman who operates without knowledge is like the proverbial "three minute egg": he gets everybody all excited, and then leaves them hanging! In both cases, such an individual has satisfied only themselves, and it could be said that, in the latter case, it is actually worse because another individual has been used for that satisfaction.

But, such amusing vulgarities aside (even if they *do* make the point remarkably well) the thing about the shaman is that he/she is not just a sick person, he is a sick person who has been *cured*, or who has succeeded in curing himself!! This point can't be overemphasized! Those who aspire to mysticism, to the Shamanic path, and who still remain frail or sickly in physical, material or spiritual terms, may not yet have been presented with the initiation, or, if they have, may have failed to pass. The possibility of achieving the Shamanic powers for Service to Self also exists, so great care has to be used in trying to "see the unseen".

In many cases, the "election" of the shaman manifests through a fairly serious illness which can only be cured by the "ascent to the sky". After the ecstatic vision of initiation, the shaman feels *much* better! After the response to the calling of the gods, the shaman shows a more than normally healthy constitution; they are able to achieve immense concentration beyond the capacity of ordinary men; they can sustain exhausting efforts and, most importantly, they are able to "keep a cool head" in the face of experiences that would terrify and break an ordinary person.

Another point that should be emphasized is that the Shaman must be able to be in full control of himself even when in the ecstatic state! (Trance channeling with no memory of what transpired is *not* the activity of a Shaman!) This ability to "walk in two worlds simultaneously" demonstrates an extraordinary nervous constitution. It has been said that the Siberian shamans show no sign of mental disintegration well into old age; their memories and powers of self-control are *well* above average.

Don Juan calls this state being "impeccable". This idea is also reflected in the archaic systems of the Yakut, where the shaman must be "serious, possess tact, be able to communicate effectively with all people; above all, he must not be presumptuous, proud, ill-tempered". The true shaman emanates an inner force that is conscious, yet *never offensive*. At the same time, it should be noted that a true shaman might evoke very negative responses from those who are under the domination of the STS polarity.

Getting back to the infirmities, nervous disorders, illness of crisis and so forth that are the "signs of election", it is also noted that, sometimes an accident, a fall, a blow on the head, or being hit by lightning are the signs from the environment that the shaman has been elected. But, being "called" is not the same as being "chosen", or, more precisely, choosing. "Many are called; few choose to respond."

This choosing is a process. And it is a process of struggle and pain and suffering because, in the end, what is being killed is the ego.

I have taken you, the reader, through many of the stages of this process vicariously, and I know that it is affecting you in many of the same ways it affected me, judging by the mail I have received. Many of you have been through some of the stages of initiation already. Many of you are struggling with the process of death of the ego and striving for rebirth as the Shaman - he whose head has been purified. In any case, many of you know that this can be a process of many years and many stages, sometimes including many illnesses, many accidents, and many assaults to the physical body as well as the soul.

The pivotal initiation of the Shaman occurs after a long period of "preparation". In retrospect, I can see this was the process, but as I was going through it, I had no idea that this was what was happening. I was just struggling through the illnesses, the accidents, the suffering, the trials, the tribulations, the lessons and so forth that seemed to just be the path of my life in generic terms. I didn't see them as tests, or that they manifested in my life as the "call". It was only *after* the "choice" that I began to make the discoveries that explained the process of my life, and which I am now sharing with you.

For many of you, reading these pages has had a similar effect - initiatory - though the present series was not begun with that intention. It just, more or less, took over and began to "write itself". So, for those that want "just the facts, ma'am!" I apologize. I'm not going to change it, but I acknowledge your right to want something different.

Returning to my "descent into Hell" and the sensation of being "stripped of everything", yes, there had been other steps in the process, other choices, visions and experiences. But none of them were like the moment of being completely stripped to the bone of *all belief in anything and everything I ever held as true*, including all my beliefs and illusions about my personal life and relationships and my very self!

The pathology of the Shamanic path seems to be part of the means of reaching the "condition" to be initiated. But, at the same time, they are often the means of the initiation itself. They have a physiological effect that amounts to a transformation of the ordinary individual into a technician of the sacred.

(But, if such an experience is not followed by a period of theoretical and practical instruction, the shaman becomes a tool for those forces that would use the Shamanic function to further enslave mankind as we have already noted.)

Now, the experience that transforms the shaman is constituted of the well-known religious elements of *suffering, death and resurrection*. One of the earliest representations of these elements is in the Sumerian story of the descent of Ishtar/Inanna into the Underworld to save her son-lover, Tammuz. She had to pass through Seven "gates of Hell" and, at each door or gate, she was stripped of another article of her attire because she could only enter the Underworld Naked. While she was in the underworld, the earth and its inhabitants suffered loss of creative vigor. After she had accomplished her mission, fertility was restored.

The most well known variation of this story is the myth of Persephone/Kore, the daughter of Demeter, who was kidnapped by Hades/Pluto. In her grief for her daughter, Demeter denied fertility to the earth. An agreement to have her daughter with her for part of the year, resulted in the manifestation of seasons. We can see that this represents a very ancient account of the cyclical nature of time. But, even more, we can now see that it is a Shamanic tale of descent of the "daughter" of the Greater Soul unit into 3rd density where it is entrapped by the forces of darkness, and the searching of Demeter for her daughter is the calling of the higher self to the Shamanic path. And, of course, we also note that in the Sumerian versions, it was the separation of the goddess from her consort, which would indicate the separation of the dual energies and the hemispheres of the brain that we have already discussed.

The Shamanic visions represent the descent as dismemberment of the body, flaying of the flesh from the bones, being boiled in a cauldron, and then being reassembled by the gods and/or goddesses. This, too, is well represented in myth and legend, including the myth of Jesus: Suffering, death, and resurrection.

A Yakut shaman, Sofron Zateyev, states that during this visionary initiation, the future shaman "dies" and lies in the yurt for *three days* without eating or drinking. ...

Pyotr Ivanov gives further details. In the vision, the candidate's limbs are removed and disjointed with an iron hook; the bones are cleaned, the flesh scraped, the body fluids thrown away, and the eyes torn from their sockets. After this operation all the bones are gathered up and fastened together *with iron.*

According to a third shaman, Timofei Romanov, the visionary dismemberment lasts from three to seven days; during all that time the candidate remains like a dead man, scarcely breathing, in a solitary place.[6]

According to another Yakut account, the evil spirits carry the future shaman's soul to the underworld and there shut it up in a house for three years (only one year for those who will become lesser shamans). Here the shaman undergoes his initiation. The spirits cut off his head, which they set aside (for the candidate must watch his dismemberment with his own eyes), and cut him into small pieces, which are then distributed to the spirits of the various diseases. Only by undergoing such an ordeal will the future shaman gain the power to cure. His bones are then covered with new flesh, and in some cases he is also given new blood.

According to another account, the "devils" keep the candidate's soul until he has learned all of their wisdom. During all this time the candidate lies sick. There is also a recurring motif of a giant bird that "hatches shamans" in the branches of the World Tree which is an allusion to an "Avian bloodline" that is opposed to a Reptilian heritage. The following excerpts are from the available accounts obtained in field research and should be read with the awareness that we have now entered a world of pure symbolism:

"...The candidate ...came upon a naked man working a bellows. On the fire was a caldron "as big as half the earth." The naked man saw him and caught him with a huge pair of tongs. The novice had time to think, "I am dead!" The man cut off his head, chopped his body into bits, and put everything in the caldron. There he boiled his body for three years.

There were also *three anvils*, and the naked man *forged the candidate's head* on the third, which was the one on which the best shamans were forged. ...

The blacksmith then fished the candidate's bones out of a river in which they were floating, put them together, and covered them with flesh again. ...

He forged his head and taught him how to read the letters that are inside it. He changed his eyes; and that is why, when he *shamanizes*, he *does not see with his bodily eyes* but with his mystical eyes. He pierced his ears, making him able to understand the language of plants.

...The Tungus shaman Ivan Cholko states that a future shaman must fall ill and have his body cut in pieces and his blood drunk by the evil spirits. These throw his head into a caldron where it is melted with certain metal pieces that will later form part of his ritual costume.

---

[6] Eliade, 1964

...Before becoming a shaman the candidate must be sick for a long time; the souls of his shaman ancestors then surround him, torture him, strike him, cut his body with knives, and so on. During this operation the future shaman remains inanimate; his face and hands are blue, his heart scarcely beats.

...A Teleut woman became a shamaness after having a vision in which unknown men cut her body to bits and cooked it in a pot. According to the traditions of the Altain shamans, the spirits of their ancestors eat their flesh, drink their blood, open their bellies and so on.

...In South America as in Australia or Siberia both spontaneous vocation and the quest for initiation involve either a mysterious illness or a more or less symbolic ritual of mystical death, sometimes suggested by a dismemberment of the body and renewal of the organs.

...They cut his head open, take out his brains, wash and restore them, to give him a *clear mind* to penetrate into the mysteries of evil spirits, and the intricacies of disease; they insert gold dust into his eyes to give him keenness and strength of sight powerful enough to see the soul wherever it may have wandered; they plant barbed hooks on the tips of his fingers to enable him to seize the soul and hold it fast; and lastly they *pierce his heart with an arrow* to make him tenderhearted, and full of sympathy with the sick and suffering.

...If the alleged reason for the renewal of the organs (conferring better sight, tenderheartedness, etc.) is authentic, it indicates that *the original meaning of the rite has been forgotten.*

...Then the master obtains the disciple's "lighting" or "enlightenment", for [this] consists of *a mysterious light which the shaman suddenly feels in his body,* inside his head, within the brain, an inexplicable searchlight, a *luminous fire,* which enables him to see in the dark, both literally and metaphorically speaking, for he can now, even with closed eyes, see through darkness and perceive things and coming events which are hidden from others...

The candidate obtains this *mystical light* after long hours of waiting, sitting on a bench in his hut... When he experiences it for the first time "it is as if the house in which he is suddenly rises; he sees far ahead of him, through mountains, exactly as if the earth were one great plain, and his eyes could reach to the end of the earth. Nothing is hidden from him any longer; not only can he see things far, far away, but he can also discover souls, stolen souls, which are either kept concealed in far, strange lands or have been taken up or down to the Land of the Dead.

...The experience of *inner light* that determines the career of the Iglulik shaman is familiar to a number of higher mysticisms. In the Upanishads, the "inner light" defines the essence of the *atman.* In yogic techniques, especially those of the Buddhist schools, light of different colors indicates the success of particular meditations. Similarly, the Tibetan Book of the Dead accords great importance to the light in which, it appears, the dying man's soul is bathed during his mortal throes and immediately after death; a man's destiny after death (deliverance or reincarnation) depends on the firmness with which he chooses the immaculate light.

...The essential elements of this mystical vision are the being divested of flesh. ...In all these cases reduction to the skeleton indicates a passing beyond the profane human condition and, hence, a deliverance from it.

...Bone represents the very source of life. To reduce oneself to the skeleton condition is equivalent to reentering the womb for a complete renewal, a mystical rebirth. ...It is an expression of the will to transcend the profane, individual condition, and to attain a transtemporal perspective.

...The myth of renewal by fire, cooking, or dismemberment has continued to haunt men even outside the spiritual horizon of shamanism. ...

The myth of rejuvenation by dismemberment and cooking has been handed down in Siberian, Central Asian, and European folklore, the role of the blacksmith being played by Jesus or other saints."[7]

I would like to add that these same ideas of death and re-birth are well represented in Alchemical literature as the various processes of "chemical transmutation". As we have quoted already:

In order to respect the principle of hermetism adopted by the Tradition, we must understand that esoteric teachings are given in a sibylline form.

St Isaac the Syrian points out that: The Holy Scriptures say many things by using words in a different sense from their original meaning. Sometimes bodily attributes are applied to the soul, and conversely, attributes of the soul are applied to the body. The Scriptures do not make any distinction here. However, enlightened men understand.

A couple of important things to note are the ideas that the candidate must be "under the control" of demons or beings that torture and torment him in order that he may learn their wisdom, and that this process confers greater "powers" on the initiate. A present day experience that is so similar to this initiation is the Alien Abduction scenario. Unfortunately, just as was reported among the Shamanic stories of "failed initiates" or those who chose the "dark path", there are many who have embraced the tormentors and become possessed by them to one extent or another. In a deeper sense, we can observe that the very fact of our existence in the STS Third density reality - the World Inside the Devil - constitutes an initiation over many, many incarnations. We must suffer the lies before we can perceive the truth!

---

[7] Eliade, *Shamanism*, 1964

So now, perhaps, the reader can see what I am doing. I am sharing with you the knowledge of the process of initiation which many of you have experienced with no context; I am assisting those who have asked, in the process of being stripped to the bone; of suffering, dying and, hopefully, being resurrected; of becoming a Shaman; of becoming one whose head has been purified.

All of what follows from here on out must be understood to apply *only* to those who have accepted the *call*. If your life has not followed the Shamanic pattern, none of the following can be construed to apply to you. If, on the other hand, you do think that your call is to be "one whose head has been purified", then you should study a great deal more until you arrive at your own "initiation", at which point *your* choices will be clear to *you*. But, for the sake of those who are already "there", the following remarks are being made as generalities to be applied *only* if or when they "fit".

As I said, after the "initiation" that I passed through in my "descent" into Hell, the world changed for me in profound ways. The profundity of the change was at a level I could not fully fathom in my consciousness, but it bore fruit almost immediately. My view of all my relationships, all my actions and interactions with the world changed in incalculable ways. I could literally "see the unseen" dynamics of every exchange between myself and other people in all situations. And by seeing, I was able to choose that reaction that was truly expressive of Unconditional Love, of Truth, of ultimate Beauty in Cosmic terms. I no longer saw with my human eyes nor was I ruled by my human emotions. This does *not* mean that I did not feel them! But I had already made a choice of the greatest magnitude in terms of putting aside all human egoic need for comfort and illusion, and I was simply not able to ever view anything the same way again.

Certainly, I have come under intense criticism from various quarters because making the choice to have no close relationships based on lies, or that permit lying, makes it imperative that such relationships either be corrected, and if that is not possible, relegated to a distance.

One of the first acts of application of this new state of being was, as I have chronicled, the reordering of my personal life which included divorcing my husband and bringing to a halt all manipulative interactions between myself and my children, close friends and associates.

Many people saw these actions as "unfeeling" or a certain "coldness" or lack of love and caring. But, the *Truth* is I knew that as long as I participated in these dynamics, I was *feeding* the Service to Self forces. I understood my position: that I needed to gain strength. I also knew that I needed to be strong in my polarization for the sake of others, not just those immediately in my life. It wasn't easy. It was the hardest thing I ever did. I was devastated at the thought of hurting anyone. But, I also realized from looking back over my life that I was particularly vulnerable to having people placed close to me who were there for the express purpose of draining my life force, because it was very potent, and by manipulating me to give in the STS dynamic. I was a powerful feeding machine to amplify those energies!

I also understood that those who are *not* awake are completely subject to engaging in this type of manipulation even subconsciously. More than this, I understood that I must battle for the souls of those I loved and that this could even mean saying "no" to them literally, or spiritually, so as not to amplify the STS frequency in them. I knew that if I continued to act as their buffer, I was making it almost impossible for them to overcome their own predatorial natures. Such a price was so high that I couldn't bear to consider it. That value took precedence over my own "human emotions" that sought only ease and peace and to "make things nice".

Yes, I realize the love that I felt for my children which made me think that we could or would travel into the higher levels together might be a trap, but at least I knew for sure that, if it was their soul choice, they needed to wake up and do it fast, and they would *never* do it with me there allowing myself to be manipulated into giving amplification to their STS tendencies! I understood that it was *not* love to do anything that prevents another from learning a lesson that they are here to learn, no matter how hard it is to watch when someone you love is suffering.[8] You must love another as they *are* in order to be able to allow them to learn their own lessons, and this is the bitterest lesson of all for the human part of one who chooses to serve others in the Cosmic sense.

That does not mean I stopped being kind or giving, nor does it mean that I stopped being a parent and imposing necessary discipline that is part of the parent-child soul agreement, it simply means that I knew that if I was "acting a certain way" to persuade someone to fulfill my idea of how they should be, without considering their choices and lessons, that I was not helping them. I also knew that if I allowed them to manipulate me by intimations that it would produce some result favorable to me, it was the *wrong* reason to do it. I also knew that when they did things that required a disciplinary response, they were *asking* me to discipline. Most asking takes place in action, not words!

---

[8] Do not misunderstand me, I do not mean standing by when someone is sick, or needs help for any real reason in the course of daily life.

In the case of my ex-husband, I realized that, by continuing to support him emotionally in his choices which, most of the time, if not *all* of the time, happened to be in direct opposition to my own, as well as opposed to the well being of the family, I was either expecting this support to "convert him" to my view, or I was simply giving up my free will. I understood that his choices were his and fully worthy of his pursuit. They just weren't mine. And, by the same token, *my* choices were not his and he had made that clear so that I could no longer be angry when he behaved in passive aggressive ways about things I wanted or needed, making it clear that he only did things for me grudgingly, and to "keep the peace". Not only that, I understood that, by his behavior, he was *asking* me to release him. Even if it was neither conscious nor part of his social and religious programming. At a very deep soul level, he was being guided to behave in ways that were subtle, yet definitely asking for release. To refuse such asking, would *not* be Love!

In the case of the husband and wife relationship, this is a most difficult thing to assess because it is a relationship based on commitment to similar goals and ideals and intimate interactions of assimilation and identification with one another. When you fully realize that the giving of energy to the Service to Self alignment in *any* respect is to help it grow while you are diminishing your own possibilities of increasing the Service to Others dynamic, you are faced with very difficult choices at the most intimate level. And, it is actually *in* and *through* these choices and their activation that you are marrying your knowledge to your will! If you perceive, make the correct choices for true STO dynamic, implementation will powerfully amplify your Frequency! The closer the relationship, and the harder it is to *do* it, to overcome the illusions of programming, the more profound the effect it can have on the amplification!

In terms of a marriage partner, yes, of course, you can still have similar goals of raising your children, of paying your bills, of building a nest egg for retirement. Can't we say that "Serving Others" might constitute "giving of support" to such mundane human pursuits while the other aspects of our lives, our spiritual pursuits, are kept separate? Not only that, but when one looks at divorce, one is looking at possibly losing one's own financial/physical/emotional support system which may be detrimental especially when children are involved, so isn't that very Self Serving?

In the case of a marriage, this is where the rubber hits the road in terms of applying one's knowledge and choices. It all depends on your idea of what marriage is supposed to be and what your life goals are, and whether or not they can harmonize.

For most of us, marriage constitutes a commitment to support and sustain another person physically, emotionally and financially "for better or for worse, for richer or for poorer, in sickness and in health, until death do us part".

Note the key words: "support and sustain."

Now, if it becomes clear that the marriage partner is at a level or position on the "learning cycle" that is different from the individual who is "waking up", what is the level of responsibility? One might think that it is their responsibility to stay in the marriage because they simply *are* married or committed. In this case one then has to think very carefully about the term "*response* - ability".

How are you going to respond to a person who makes choices to act as "food" in the Service to Self hierarchy? How are you going to respond to a person who is still "lost in the illusion" that he has free will and the power to choose his destiny, and is completely unaware of the forces that dominate our world? How are you going to support a person who makes choices to *not* expand his or her knowledge base to the same extent that you have, a person who is content to stay in the locked room and doesn't care that it may be locked. He or she has not even arrived at the point of checking the door! If you have left your own "locked room", are you then going to move into the locked room of another person?

Well, you can continue to support them, in which case your energy amplifies their own STS frequency AND feeds the STS dynamic *through* them.

Okay. That's cool. You can think that this is something you are willing to do as an act of Love and Giving because Loving and Giving are your ideals. But there is something far more important here and that is: if, at the soul level, they have set up lessons so as to be eventually brought to a crossroads, a choice, your continued support and sustenance prolongs the period of time it will take them to do it! It may even be that, by your support, the individual will not learn what they incarnated to learn in this life and will be obliged to do a whole additional life (or more than one), over again. If you are trying to "save" them you are doing far more harm than good.

I am reminded of a case Edgar Cayce dealt with. Seems that a couple had a baby and obtained a reading for the child shortly after birth. They were told how special the child was and how many lessons he was going to learn, and what great things he would do as a consequence.

His parents only heard the "special" and "great things" part and ignored the "lessons" part. They began a lifetime of protecting the boy so that he would be ready to do his great work. Every time there was a problem, they stepped in and "fixed" it or helped him find the way out, and so on and so on.

Then, in his early 20s, the boy was killed in an auto accident.The parents were devastated. They went to Cayce and asked him, "why? He was so special, you told us he had a great work to do"! Cayce gave them another reading that pointed out the fact that the boy had a "life plan" before he was born, and that included getting some karma out of the way and learning some specific things by making certain mistakes and having to pay for them. It was all set up in a graduated way so that he would never have to deal with more than his skills could handle at any one time.

However, due to the interference of the parents, it was clearly seen by his higher self that the lessons were not being learned, that the parents were not being truly loving toward the "soul and its plan", and in order to prevent more and greater karma, (as well as to get the lesson out of the way in the most expeditious way possible so that, at least, he would have time to return quickly for the next stage of his series of life plans), he would have to "check out".

Naturally, reading about this was quite a revelation to me. I began to understand my relationship with my children in a very different way. I also began to think of the lessons that my kids had to learn as blessings even though some of them were very hard for me to live through, standing by and doing nothing to help. It's like watching a kid learn to ride a bicycle, and watching them fall again and again, and not rushing over every time to pick them up. Instead, you smile and help them to see the scrapes and bruises as badges of victory even though you want to pack them in cotton wool.

On the soul level, this is much more difficult because the lessons can be quite painful.

A friend of mine recently wrote to me about a clue he was given about this very matter:

> "I don't think that we can `save` anybody *but* we can help many others in *saving themselves* (well, I guess you could call that a form of saving if you want, it's only semantics).
>
> When I went to sleep last night, I sort of asked: if there is anything to us `saving` others, show me how it's done. And I had this dream, just before waking up... Basically, I was facing someone of the `other camp`, we were in a sort of fight/discussion, until he said: please, release me, help me out of this. It was said in all honesty, sincerely. Then, `something` of me or something `came out` of me, sort of melted with this individual and *he changed completely, in a sort of morphing way. very strange*!!!"

And the key was in what the soul of the other was crying: *please release me*! And this is, indeed, the way! To release that soul to enter fully into the lessons they have chosen without your interference or support except to Love them *as they arE* and to give to them only when they truly *ask*, without manipulation. The something that "came out" and "melted with the individual" was this Unconditional Love that allowed them to *be* as they are, at their level, fully and completely so that they could *grow* out of it! He "gave free will" and discontinued his feeding of the *sts* frequency, thereby releasing the soul to change in its own way and time!

So, in the Cosmic scheme of things, which is *true* Love and Giving? To support and sustain a person in lies and illusion with all the attendant "food" that is implicit in the marriage relationship, to continue to amplify their STS frequency, or to *release* them to lessons - the giving of what is truly appropriate to their actions which demonstrate clearly what the soul is asking - that may eventually facilitate their own growth and/or initiation, if not in this life, in the next?

Of course, the question then becomes: can you withdraw support from the dynamic and still support the person? The fact is, in terms of soul choices, it is impossible to *intimately* support a person who is aligned to a certain soul choice without also supporting that person's choices. In other words, how can you "sleep" with someone who has different goals than your own? Each time you do, an energy transfer takes place, and it amounts to your energy going to feed their goals, so you might as well decide that the goals are your own, because certainly, your energy is advancing them.

But, it is here that a very hard look has to be taken at the self to inquire *why* you would want to continue to support and sustain a person who is part of a dynamic that you have chosen *not* to feed any longer? (Again, I repeat that what I am saying here is *only* for those who have taken the step toward full initiation!)

Are you staying in the relationship because of financial considerations? Is it "for the children"? Or because you don't see how you could continue your path of learning without the financial backing of the marriage? If it is for financial considerations relating to yourself, it is easy to see that *you* are the vampire. You are offering an "illusion" of love and support in order to obtain something that *you* want or need. If you are staying for the sake of the children, you need to be very careful how you think this is going to benefit them.

In the first place, at some soul level these children are learning by observing and experiencing. If they observe and experience a vampire dynamic between their parents and themselves, that is what they will grow up to emulate in their own lives

Is that what you want for your children? That they should marry for financial considerations? Or that they should marry someone who does not really love them for themselves, but then find that they have to stay in the marriage "for the sake of the children", further perpetuating the dynamic to the next generation? Is that what you want for your children and your children's children? Can you look at your own life and say, with deepest honesty, that this is what you would want for someone you love very much?

In another sense, if you are in a relationship where there is "feeding" going on, one or both of the marriage partners is going to *have* to obtain energy from somewhere, and the most likely sources are going to be the children. Is *that* what you want?

Another key is, can you stay in the relationship without *expectation* of *anything* being changed or made better by your presence and/or support?

The essential thing about the STO Shamanic path is to give only when *asked*. And then, to give *all* that is asked. Most love relationships consist of one person asking another (implicitly or explicitly) to give them their "ideal partner". This may have nothing at all to do with who the person really is. And certainly, most relationship partners will try to fulfill this role, at least for a time. But when the energy of pretending to be something you are not runs out, what is left? An even deeper issue is: what if the pretense of who or what you are is so programmed into you by the role you were taught to play by your own upbringing, and you find one day that this just isn't you, but you can't stop doing it because if you stop, you have no idea what you would do.

In any event, *giving* only when *asked* pretty much excludes giving to those of the STS orientation because they *never* ask! They manipulate, they demand, they beg, they even ask with their words but not their actions. And so, the only real thing a person seeking STO alignment can give to one who is still firmly embedded in the STS path is a "*No*".

This issue of "asking" is a thing you can often only see by *seeing the unseen*. Perhaps one way to think about it would be that you could tell if someone is really "asking" if there is *no anticipation* on their part that you will give to them what they are asking! And, there is no condition placed upon *you* as to whether or not you say yes or no. In other words, if you say "no", (because you cannot say yes for whatever reason) you are certain that there will be no break or decline in your relations. And the same thing applies to the self. If you "ask", are you really asking? Or, is there some string attached such as "if you love me you will say yes", or "see what I have done for you; now it's your turn", whether implied or not?

Boris Mouravieff[9] has written extensively on this subject and I will quote some of his material here that comes at the problem from a slightly different angle:

> "Homo Sapiens lives immersed in his everyday life to a point where he forgets himself and forgets where he is going; yet, without feeling it, he knows that death cuts off everything.
>
> How can we explain that the intellectual who has made marvelous discoveries and the technocrat who has exploited them have left outside the field of their investigations the ending of our lives? How can we explain that a science which attempts everything and claims everything nevertheless remains indifferent to the enigma revealed by the question of death? How can we explain why Science, instead of uniting its efforts with its older sister religion to resolve the problems of Being - which is also the problem of death - has in fact opposed her?
>
> Whether a man dies in bed or aboard an interplanetary ship, the human condition has not changed in the slightest.
>
> Happiness? But we are taught that happiness lasts only as long as the Illusion lasts... and what is this Illusion? Nobody knows. But it submerges us.
>
> If we only knew what Illusion is, we would then know the opposite: what Truth is. This Truth would liberate us from slavery."

---

[9] Boris Mouravieff's trilogy *Gnosis* is an attempt to recover and describe, in terms understandable to modern man, a particular Tradition handed down over the centuries, in a sometimes broken line, but one that still exists today in the Eastern Orthodox Church. This tradition could be said to be the Christian equivalent of Yoga, Zen, and the other inner traditions of the far Eastern religions, disciplines, which have each existed as specializations within the religion of which they are a part.

It is not one man's system or invention, but has its roots far back in the history of Christianity - whose roots lie in certain statements of St. Paul, and perhaps even of Christ himself. Their development can be traced first through formative figures of the early churches, and it clearly relates to the doctrines expressed in the key texts of Eastern spirituality such as the *Philokalia.*

It clearly relates the oral tradition known as the **Royal Way** that survives to this day in the main centers of monasticism in the Eastern church. But it does not claim to be a work of Orthodox theology, nor to reinterpret Orthodox doctrine.

Mouravieff admits that the survival of this tradition within the church is tenuous, that the doctrine does not appear to survive in full or has not been collected together in full. Monks on Athos admit the existence of the Tradition but say that it has never been fully spelled out in writing. The importance of Mouravieff's work is the effort he has made to collect that dispersed information and to make it accessible in practical form.

This last remark seems to me to be important. Very often people write to me and say that the C's material is too "scary" and that we talk too much about the "illusion" why aren't we talking about positive things or concentrating on "escaping" or whatever.

Well, the fact seems to be that what Mouravieff has said above is the key: If we cannot map the illusion, we have no hope of getting out of it. It is in mapping the illusion that we are able to distinguish between what Mouravieff calls the "A" influences and the "B" influences. We call it seeing the Theological Reality behind the Matrix. Mouravieff points out that the more we "collect" or "perceive" the "B" influences, and act on them, the more we "magnetize". And naturally, *see*ing the "A" influences, or discerning the lies of our reality, consists in an ongoing series of "shocks" that seem to be necessary to change our center of gravity.

The point is that it seems that until a person fully *sees* the illusion - the layers and layers of it - they have no hope of becoming free of it. Until we are trained, step by step, to discern the lies from the truth, we have no internal consistency and are subject to the whims of the Control System at every turn. And it seems to be that this patient, time-consuming, taking apart of our reality and extracting the Truth/"B" influences is what literally "grows" the soul.

Many people simply can't do it. They can't stand the bloody mess of the birth of the higher self which takes place on the bodies of all the sacred cows that were held so close for so long. They want to hear nice stories about how their breathing and spinning tetrahedrons are going to just fix them right up. They want to hear how the "Guardian Alliance" is going to help us out of the soup. They want to hear how the Zetas are warning us that we are in danger of being smacked by a rogue planet and if we ask real nice, we might get a seat on the airlift out.

As Mouravieff has just said: "If we only knew what Illusion is, we would then know the opposite: what Truth is. This Truth would liberate us from slavery."

And it seems that the only way we have of discovering Truth in this reality, is to first of all strip away all the lies. And Lord! There's a raft of them! Now, back to Mouravieff:

> "What strikes us from the very beginning is that man confuses moral progress with technical progress, so that the development of science continues in dangerous isolation.
>
> The brilliant progress that has come from technology has changed nothing essential in the human condition, and will change nothing, because it operates only in the field of everyday events. For this reason it touches the

inner life of man only superficially. Yet from very ancient times it has been known that the essential is found within man, not outside him.

Humanity has arrived at an important turning point in its history. The Cartesian spirit which destroyed scholastic philosophy is now in turn being left behind. The logic of history demands a new spirit. The divorce between traditional knowledge, of which religion is a trustee, and acquired knowledge, the fruit of science, threatens to make sterile our civilization.

Yet it is an aberration to believe that Science by its very nature is opposed to [spirit], and it must also be firmly stressed that [spirit] does not include any tendency opposed to Science. On the contrary, the [mystics] foresaw the prodigious development of Science.

The celebrated formula of St. Paul: *Faith, Hope and Love,* summarizes a vast programme of evolution for human knowledge. If we examine this formula in relation to its context we see that the first two terms are temporary, while the third is permanent. [...] It was appropriate to the epoch in which it was expressed, and its significance has had to evolve with time. [...] Science and knowledge are called on to replace Faith and Hope, which defined the limits of what was accessible to the mentality of the epoch when he taught - have since then known extraordinary development.

He therefore adds: 'Now that I have become a man, I have put away childish things.'

This is how the passage from Faith to Knowledge is described. [Faith being appropriate to that time, Science replacing Faith in our time.]

St. Paul then specifies that this last, although necessary in evolution, is NOT a final state, as it is incomplete by nature. He adds that 'When that which is perfect is come, that which is incomplete disappears'.

The perfect is Love, which unites in itself the accomplishment of all virtues, of all prophecies, of all mysteries, and of all Knowledge.

It is by the joint efforts of traditional science, based on Revelation, and of acquired Science, the domain of positive knowledge, that is, on 'Faith and Hope', that one can hope to fulfill the programme traced out by St. Paul, and finally attain Love in its integral meaning."

Mouravieff talks about the degrading of women to "living merchandise" and how Jesus (as a Gnostic teacher) taught "reciprocal choice in love" which established the idea of "romance" between men and women. I have already noted that this seems to be philosophy of the "Golden Age", transmitted down through the ages via Archaic Shamanism, the Eleusinian Rites, and then later the True Teachings of Jesus, not to be confused with the Egyptian mythical overlay that is known as Christianity today.

"Reciprocal choice in love" is certainly a theme of the Grail stories with their emphasis on romance - on "platonic love" and so on - and it has long been a mystery as to what, precisely, this allegory was supposed to convey. If what Mouravieff is saying is true, then it will all begin to make perfect sense, even including the possible survival of the Cathar teachings in the Grail stories and the lays of the minstrels and Troubadours, etc. Mouravieff writes:

"The romance, by which Christian society expressed the principle of reciprocal choice, reached its climax in the Middle Ages. In spite of the decline it has known since then, and in spite of a current tendency to return to regressive forms of relations between the sexes, it still remains the avowed ideal of our society.

Is it not exact, then, to speak of the death of romance? A revolution is occurring silently which will replace the free romance, distinctive mark of the Christian era, with the singular romance characteristic of the Holy Spirit. Liberated from servitude to procreation, this romance of tomorrow is called on to cement the indissoluble union between two strictly polar beings, a union which will assure their integration in the bosom of the Absolute. As St. Paul says:

'Nevertheless, neither is the woman without the man, nor man without the woman in the Lord.'

The vision of such a romance has haunted the highest minds for thousands of years. We find it in platonic love, the basis of the singular romance in the myths of Androgyne man; of Orpheus and Eurydice; of Pygmalion and Galatea... This is the aspiration of the human heart, which cries in secrecy because of its great loneliness. This romance forms the essential aim of esoteric work. Here is that love which will unite man to that being who is unique for him, the Sister-Wife, the glory of man, as he will be the glory of God. Having entered into the light of Tabor, no longer two, but one drinking at the fount of true Love, the transfigurer: the conqueror of Death.

Love is the Alpha and Omega of life. All else has only secondary significance.

Man is born with the Alpha. It is the intention of the present work to show the path which leads towards the Omega.

When we ask someone who lives under this constant pressure of contemporary life to turn his mental vision towards himself, he generally answers that he has not enough time left to undertake such practices. ... If he acquiesces, he will in most cases say that he sees nothing: Fog; Obscurity. In less common cases, the observer reports that he perceives something which he cannot define because it changes all the time.

This last observation is correct. Everything is in fact continually changing within us. A minor external shock, agreeable or disagreeable, happy or unhappy, is sufficient to give our inner content a quite different appearance.

If we follow up this interior observation, this introspection, without prejudice, we will soon note that our "I" of which we are so consistently proud, is not always the same self: the "I" changes.

As this impression becomes more defined we begin to become more aware that it is not a single being who lives within us but several, each having his own tastes, his own aspirations, and each trying to attain his own ends.

If we proceed with this experience, we will soon be able to distinguish three currents with that perpetually moving life: that of the vegetative life of the instincts, so to speak; that of the animal life of the feelings; and lastly that of human life in the proper sense of the term, characterized by thought and speech.

It is as though there were three beings within us, all entangled together in an extraordinary way.

So we come to appreciate the value of introspection as a method of practical work which permits us to know ourselves and enter into ourselves.

The inner content of man is analogous to a vase full of iron filings in a state of mixture as a result of mechanical action. Every shock received by the vase causes displacement of the particles of iron filings. Thus real life remains hidden from the human being due to the constant changes occurring in his inner life.

Even so, as we shall see later, this senseless and dangerous situation can be modified in a beneficial way. But this requires work; conscientious and sustained effort. Introspection carried out relentlessly results in enhanced internal sensibility. This improved sensibility in its turn intensifies the amplitude and frequency of movement whenever the iron filings are disturbed. As a result, shocks that previously were not noticed will now provoke vivid reactions. These movements, because of their continuous amplification, can create friction between particles of iron so intense that we may one day feel the interior fire igniting within us.

The fire must not remain a harmless flare-up. Nor is it enough that the fire smolders dormant under the ashes. A live and ardent fire once lit must be carefully kept alight by the will to refine and cultivate sensitiveness. If it continues in this way, our state can change: the heat of the flame will start a process of fusion within us.

...A live and ardent fire, once lit must be carefully kept alight by the will to refine and cultivate sensitiveness. If it continues in this way, our state can change: the heat of the flame will start a process of fusion within us.

From this point on the inner content will no longer behave like a heap of iron filings: it will form a block. Then further shocks will no longer provoke interior change in man as they did previously. Having reached this point he will have acquired a firmness; he will remain himself in the midst of the tempests to which life may expose him.

To reach this state, we must from the beginning rid ourselves of all illusions about ourselves, no matter how dearly held; an illusion - if it is tolerated at the start - will grow en route, so that suffering and additional effort will be necessary in order to rid ourselves of it at a later date.

As long as man has not reached the point of fusion, his life will be in effect a factitious existence, as he himself will change from moment to moment. Since these changes will occur as a result of external shocks which he can almost never foresee, it will also be impossible for him to predict in advance the exact way he will change internally. thus he will live subject to events as they occur, always preoccupied by constantly "patching up". He will in fact progress toward the unknown, at the mercy of chance. This state of things is the principal law under whose authority he leads his illusory existence.

Esoteric science indicates the possibilities and the means of freeing oneself from this law.

But to begin effectively in this way, one must first clearly see the situation as it is.

To live in the True, with all lies excluded, is the prerogative of the Cycle of the Spirit: Light without shadow.

We speak here about certain human beings who have attained or who are about to attain the Second Birth. The text leaves no room for ambiguity:

Lie not to one another: seeing that you have put off the old man with his doings and have put on the new man, that is being renewed until the knowledge after the image of God: where there cannot be Greek and Jew, circumcised and uncircumcised, barbarian, Scythian, slave and freeman; but Christ is all and in all.

This is only addressed to those who are on the Way in their relations between themselves.

He who reaches Love would not know how to lie. But to triumph over lies requires an esoteric culture which is inaccessible to ordinary man.

This highlights the important problem of lying.

The struggle against lying is long and drawn out. It is first of all a struggle against ourselves, against our spontaneous tendencies, and against that mechanicalness that makes us revert constantly to lying.

Useless lies to others are far less harmful than lying to oneself - and easier to master and heal. Lying to oneself sometimes takes on finely shaded forms that necessitate total and sustained attention, together with methodical and persistent efforts.

to eliminate useless lying to others does not demand continual effort: one must simply watch to see that it does not slip into conversation. At the moment when it is on our lips a simple effort of attention is sufficient to stop it. That is why in struggling for truth, it is recommended to begin with this type of lie.

But, we easily understand that lying to oneself, or the struggle against this kind of lie, is not perceptible from the exterior.

When we stop lying uselessly, this will also be unnoticed by those around us. One can say that in practice, the struggle against these two categories of lies does not alter man's relations with other men in any way, although it is very effective for the person who undertakes it. We can therefore begin it without delay, as long as we do it discreetly so as not to draw attention to ourselves, and so do not provoke increasing pressure from the General Law [of accident and mechanicalness which will try to circumvent these efforts; i.e. The Predator's mind/Matrix.]

[...] As for efforts at suppressing lies to oneself, they entail quite different and important consequences. Such lies grow deep roots. In this domain, paradoxical situations sometimes arise, some of them of such psychological subtlety that it is difficult to draw them out of the shade.

Here we must mention the question of marriages where one of the partners, having realized that this union is an error, persists in trying to convince him or herself of the contrary. If he is of an affectionate nature, he will redouble his amiability towards his partner as if truly toward his polar "other". The absurdity of the situation reaches its limits if the other partner reacts by adopting a corresponding attitude - without any sincere or spontaneous glow of tenderness.

The danger from the esoteric point of view is that, by mere force of habit, such a situation takes on for one of the partners, or even for both of them, the value of true love. this kind of lying to oneself can go on for dozens of years with people who are amiable and of good faith, and they entail tragic disillusions in the end.

The man who starts to struggle against lying to himself must be forewarned of these difficulties, and of the possible collapse of some or all his greatest values.

All should know that true esoteric work only begins after the individual has passed through a general bankruptcy and has had his gods helplessly thrown to the ground.

We have indicated the absolute necessity for anyone who aspires to esoteric development to cure himself as soon as possible of this deep-rooted habit of lying to himself.

We shall now look at this problem from another angle: that of the objective results which man obtains when he is able to stop lying.

This work takes time, demands the courage to face disillusion, and needs self-confidence and faith in the self. As the seeker advances, he feels a new sentiment.

He will sometimes feel bitter regret as his beautiful dreams vanish, but at the same time he will feel himself more and more liberated.

His growing sincerity towards himself will establish an atmosphere of truth in his inner life. The law proclaimed "you shall know the truth, and the truth shall set you free" will apply to him in its fullness.

The word "free" was deliberately chosen to contrast a state of slavery.

After each operation of inner purification, painful though it may be, the seeker will feel more and more fully a profound gratitude for being freed from this absurd slavery.

Having reached a certain stage in internal liberation, the individual will understand the full value of the magical power expressed in the word Freedom.

The acquisition of Inner Freedom is the *sine qua non* condition of further success in esoteric work.

This elimination of lying to the self enables one to observe the work of the lower centers in the self objectively. This observation is commenced from this "command post" of impartial observation and judgment of the individual who has overcome the lies to the self.

When our interior world is thus purified by these rays of the "B", when we have ceased to lie to ourselves, how then are we to act towards others?

This problem is far from easy.

It is written: 'the kingdom of heaven is forced, and it is the violent men who hold it.'

If we remember that the kingdom of heaven is within, and NOT outside us, then we begin to understand that some force or even violence must be employed *internally* to retake our own fortress.

This is very often necessary to eliminate the roots of Illusion within us, the mother of lies to ourselves.

Thus we see that the test at the fourth step is decisive. Until lying stops, man drags along the defects of his past: lying, weakness, self-pity, inner compromise.

Generally, it takes time, the opportunity and the possibility to rid himself of his *baggage* before committing himself to the fourth step is met. Many individuals, because of the weight of their past, waste time and allow many opportunities which present themselves to go by.

But, on the fourth step, the balance sheet must be drawn up and accounts settled. Man, *poor and naked,* is accepted at the second Threshold, but only on condition that he is consistent and pure.

The essential is that he be consistent, meaning that he contains within himself true Love, which can only be revealed by the cessation of lying to the self.

Everything false within him will be burned by the flames of this blazing sword.

All of these steps happen more or less together in many combinations. They are distributed unequally according to different personalities, and driven by the force of our Desire to be free.

In stepping onto the Staircase, to approach and then cross the Second Threshold, man adopts a new attitude towards himself: from this point on, he takes his fate in his own hands.

During later development, the Individuality becomes progressively integrated with the higher cosmos. [...]

The life of man is a film. It is certainly difficult for our Cartesian minds to grasp this concept. Our three-dimensional minds are badly adapted to ideas and facts which touch on the domain of the eternal.

Incomprehensible as it may seem, our life is truly a film produced in accordance with a script. This film goes on continuously, without ever stopping, in such a way that, at the time of his death, man is born again. What seems absurd is that he is born in the same place, at the same date where he was born before, and of the same parents. So the film goes on again. Each human being, then, is born with his own particular film. this represents the field of action in which man is called to apply his conscious efforts.

The repetition of the film is not reincarnation, although these two notions are often confused. Exterior man, who lives in the system of the Future-Past cannot embrace in a single moment the ensemble of his film, nor even the part that contains his immediate future. To do so, he would need to enlarge the slot of his Present.

It thus happens to him that, faced with certain events, he will feel that he has already seen or lived those events. Some see in such phenomena the proof of so called reincarnation. In reality, phenomena of this sort are the result of a casual and temporary surge of fine energies in the organism: the slot of the individual Present then enlarges for a few moment, and some significant facts of the immediate future slip into the waking consciousness. In this way, the impression is created of a return of another time. In a certain way this is true, although the impression of having lived before is only caused by mechanical unfolding of the film.

By reincarnation, we must understand a phenomenon of a very different order. Although the theoretical film revolves integrally on the plane of possibilities, meaning in eternity, the film of the exterior man clings to the plane of realization, that is, of Time, but only to the extent strictly necessary to satisfy the ends of the Ray of Creation.

True reincarnation, on the other hand, occurs entirely in time, and belongs integrally to the domain of the Real, well understood as part of the broader frame of Manifestation. The human personality is not a reality in the proper sense of the word, but a possibility. It plays a role in the film to which it is attached, from which it will not disappear until the moment of the Second Birth. At that moment, it will cease to be a Personality. Because of its indestructible union with the real "I", it will be transfigured, and so it will become an Individuality. As long as man lives in the wilderness, self-satisfied and immersed in lies and illusions, the film will unfold with mechanical inflexibility, and the Personality will remain entirely unchanged.

These circumstances start to change the moment man crossed the first Threshold. This passage can be compared to the conception of the future Individuality. The Staircase symbolizes the period of gestation, and the crossing of the second Threshold represents the second Birth, the birth of Individuality. As man becomes more and more integrated with his "I", growing his Individuality, he becomes progressively integrated with the Cosmos and acquires "gifts" appropriate to his individual nature. Simultaneously, he progressively participates in real, objective existence, which finally characterizes his being.

This is liberation from the bonds of the film.

It is only at this point of evolution that true individual reincarnation becomes possible.

True reincarnation is not mechanical; it is done consciously, generally to accomplish a mission.[...]

It is important to grasp clearly the difference which exists between the film, a mixture of possibilities, and reincarnation in time, which belongs to the domain of the Real, and to understand the meaning of this difference.

At the time of the second Birth, that is to say, by crossing the Second Threshold, man escapes his bondage to the film, and enters the domain of redemption. He is then admitted into the sacred brotherhood of living Beings. These beings are an unshakable force: those who are part of it are no longer subject to illness or sorrow. Death loses its hold over them. They have overcome the world.

In theory, the film in which man is born and in which he lives can go on until the end of the world, on condition that he is happy, satisfied with himself, attributing his virtues to himself, and blaming others for his mistakes and misfortunes. Properly speaking, this kind of existence cannot be considered as human; it could be described as anthropoid. This term is justified in the sense that exterior man, immersed in self-satisfaction, represents the crowning achievement of millions of years of evolution of the species from its animal ancestors, yet from the point of view of esoteric evolution, he is a possibility which has not yet been realized.

If we envisage the problem of esoteric evolution from the point of view of the film and the different parts man can play in it, it is clear that this kind of evolution is impossible as long as the film can always be considered as turning in the same circle. People who perform in such a film are those we have called anthropoids, puppets, the dead who, in the words of Jesus, 'believe themselves to be alive'.

Esoteric evolution starts when man, by his conscious efforts, proves capable of breaking the circle and transforming it into an ascending spiral. The spiral represents an intermediate state between the position where the human Personality is found to be trapped in the film, which revolves mechanically in a way hardly separated from the eternal plane, and that of the perfect, free Individuality, who is able, if need arises, to reincarnate consciously in Time.

This is an intermediate state in this sense, that the film definitely departs from the plane of the eternal, from the plane of possibilities. The curve of life, which for exterior man does not in practice differ from a circle, transforms itself into a spiral and does not end - as it did previously - almost at its point of departure: the distance between these two points now marks a definite progression in Time.

The film in the form of a spiral belongs to human beings who climb the staircase. Complete disengagement of the film is produced at the moment of crossing the second threshold. If man is able to do that successfully during a single life, so breaking the circle for the very first time, he does not return to it. Such a case is very rare: it is the lot of the just.

Generally, this liberation requires several lives; several revolutions of the spiral. As a general rule, each revolution occurs in Time, and consequently can appear to be a reincarnation. In reality, it is nothing but a return to exterior life. A pseudo-reincarnation like this is neither conscious nor personal: it is the actors in the film who return, and they do not remember any previous experiences.

However, a change is possible as soon as the conscious efforts of man increase the effect of the Time factor by enlarging perception of the Present. In a film which unfolds in a spiral in this way, the contents of the play change; they change in two ways: first in each life, that is, during each revolution, and also from spiral to spiral. The composition of the cast, the circumstances, and the scenery all change. Two elements however remain permanent: first, the general aim, to reach and cross the second Threshold; then the absolute condition for crossing this Threshold, that all the karmic debts which have been accumulated in the present life, as well as during previous spirals, must be neutralized and liquidated.

Before the Second Threshold, every drama must be played out to its denouement. The work is hard and difficult because man constantly makes mistakes.

The attentive reader has already understood that following the spiral, or climbing the Staircase, is reserved for human beings who have already absorbed a certain quantity of "B" influences and who thus possess a more or less developed magnetic center. This does not guarantee that they will make no more errors.

It is true that from the time man first mounts the Staircase he is watched, especially if he makes sincere and considerable efforts. The Esoteric Brotherhood offers him a helping hand. Certain meetings, a play of favorable circumstances, are the forms taken by this help. This assistance does not, however, free him of the need to work on himself and to go on making conscious efforts. In addition, it must be said that often the proffered help is not used, because man does not listen to the advice given, or because he does not grasp the meaning of the favorable circumstances and the possibilities of progress which open before him. He is still more than half a creature of the domain of Illusion, he continues to take frequent impulsive decisions, and often turns against his own avowed aims.

It must be understood that as long as a man has not attained and crossed the Second Threshold, he will have to start all over again. He will restart every spiral in the wilderness, he will once again have to discern the Cosmic Solar influences, cross the First Threshold, and climb the Staircase step by step. It is true that no conscious effort is ever lost, but the experience acquired in one spiral only appears in the next in the form of innate personal aptitudes, or vague recollections of people in the cast.

We should know that, at the end of a spiral (incarnation), a comparison is made between the film as it was conceived at the time of birth and what it has become at the time of death. The balance sheet between these two states is drawn up, as in accounting, by listing assets and liabilities, followed by a profit/loss statement. This will show the result of the elapsed life objectively.

This balance sheet furnishes the basic elements for composing the film at the start of the following spiral.

If we could avoid all errors and complications in this new experience, produced as a result of free movements, esoteric evolution would then occur in a harmonious rising curve.

Generally, this is not the case. Man most often comes to this idea of evolution after he has already complicated the film to which he belongs.

But true evolution cannot occur except on the basis of the original film - after all artificially added elements have been eliminated. The latter is conditional on a return to the PURITY of the centers, especially the emotional center which - at least at the start - is the sole receptacle of Cosmic Solar influences.[…]

The heart must therefore be pure, and if not already pure, it must be purified. This is the sine qua non condition of success.

All the discussion of lying in all its aspects is given to emphasize the absolute need for purifying the heart, and for beginning to re-educate the emotional center in a positive direction. [Remember, the emotions are represented by the horse pulling the coach.]

This necessity explains the meaning of the words of Jesus: 'Except you turn, and become as little children, you shall in no wise enter into the kingdom of heaven'."

This refers specifically to the emotional life. Many have interpreted this as a restriction on the development of the intellect. This is a huge mistake. Intelligence and intellect must be developed and stimulated. The admonition to "become as little children" only points to the need for purity of the centers, *not* the idea of keeping them in a primitive state.

"Paul wrote: 'Brothers, be not children in that which concerns judgment, be children in what concerns malice, but as to judgment, be fully grown men'.

[...]Once the First Threshold is crossed, *esoteric work will begin to reveal the true meaning of the film*. Man must proceed with an impartial analysis of its contents: the role that each of the actors plays in it - and the value of this role - must be passed through a sieve.

Gradually, *as this stripping work progresses*, the positive or negative character of different roles emerges more and more clearly. After this, inappropriate elements tend to disappear from the scene.

At the end of this analysis, the film will contain only a reduced number of actors. but all of them are organically bound together, and with the hero, by the contents of the play, as it was conceived from the beginning of these experiences... which are pursued by the real 'I' through centuries or even millennia. The play must then be played out to its resolution or denouement.

The basic task of man, once he has crossed the first Threshold, is to shelter himself from the karmic influences which are the effects of errors committed in his free movements, either in the present life or in the past. In the past, workers used to go to some monastery or hermitage where they were able to concentrate on introspective work. In the present, our times require energetic and rapid methods.

Our last question is to examine the method whereby the Staircase between the two Thresholds can be climbed more quickly, while we remain and work in the contemporary world.

This means exists: it is to work as a couple. However, for this esoteric work to be completed successfully by two people, it is essential that the two beings - man and woman - are integrally polar.

In the 'long path', by successive elimination based on long and minute analysis of his film, and after new errors and new failures, man may end by finding his legitimate spouse, a fully integral polar being with whom to unite himself.

In the 'short path', man must begin by a conscious search for his polar being. If found, they can work together on the film which - in its origin - is common to them both.

A man alone is incomplete. But just where he is weak, his polar being is strong. together, they form an integral being: their union leads to the fusion of their Personalities and a faster crystallization of their complete subtle bodies, united into a common second Birth.

This is the redemption of 'original sin'.

The system of films is conceived in such a way that polar beings will necessarily meet in life, in certain cases more than once. Only the confused ties contracted in this life by each of them, as a result of their free movements, combined with the karmic consequences of one or more previous experiences, can divert the man or woman from the *only* being with whom they could from a Micro cosmos.

If there were no karmic debt, everything would go wonderfully: two young people would meet in the most favorable family and social atmosphere, and their union would represent a true fairy-tale. But this is not reality.

Obeying the principle of Imperfection, and moved by the action of the General Law, the two predestined beings will commit errors. Deeply buried in lies, they do not generally know how to appreciate the gift they are given. Often, they do not even recognize each other.

If this is the case, then an agonizing question is put: is there one or more means to detect our polar being, and if so, what are these means?

To meet that person, to do so without recognition, to let our polar being pass by, is the worst mistake we could possibly make: because we would remain in our factitious life, without light.

Must not everything be sacrificed in favor of a union which is the only chance of our life: the promise of return to paradise lost?

Nevertheless we should beware of the last trap, one we can fall into just at the moment when ineffable happiness seems to smile upon us.

We have just said: all must be sacrificed; we have not said: all must be broken.

If, having recognized one another, the two polar beings triumph over this last ordeal or test, often the most painful, the new life, will open in front of them, as they are then called to be One on earth and in heaven."

The essential thing to know is that Service to Others is the path of spiritual love, which is entirely distinct from the love of the world and self-love. The whole secret of True Magic lies within the laws of the divine proximity. As you grow closer to Love as God the creator expresses it, you grow closer to God. And God loves everything exactly as it is. That is *why* it *is*!

There are other, deeper and crucial considerations in this matter of relationships.

At this point, in order to clarify the matter, I am going to insert information that was received and researched *after* the original *Wave* Series was written.

In *Book III* of his *Gnosis*, Boris Mouravieff discusses what he calls "pre-adamic humanity" and "adamic humanity". Here are some excerpts of what Mouravieff has to say:

"In the first volume of *Gnosis*, we already referred several times to the coexistence of two essentially different races: one of *Men*, and another of *Anthropoids*. We must emphasize the fact that from the esoteric point of view the latter term has no derogatory meaning.

...The Scriptures contain more than one reference to the coexistence on our planet of these two humanities – which are now alike in form but unlike in essence. We can even say that the whole dramatic history of humanity, from the fall of Adam until today, not excluding the prospect of the new era, is overshadowed by the coexistence of these two human races whose separation will occur only at the Last Judgment. [10]

...The human tares, the anthropoid race, are the descendants of pre-adamic humanity. The principal difference between contemporary pre-adamic man and adamic man – a difference which is not perceived by the senses – is that the former does not possess the developed higher centers that exist in the latter which, although they have been cut off from his waking consciousness since the Fall, offer him a real possibility of esoteric evolution. Apart from this, the two races are similar: they have the same lower centers the same structure of the Personality and the same physical body, although more often than not this is stronger in the pre-adamic man than in the adamic; regarding beauty, we must not forget that

---

[10] Mouravieff, Boris, *Gnosis, Volume III*, translated and edited by Robin Amis, (Robertsbridge, UK: Praxis Institute Press 1993) p. 107.

pre-adamic man and woman were created by God on the sixth day, in His image and after His likeness, and that the daughters of this race were beautiful. [11]

By identifying himself with the 'I' of his Personality, Adam lost consciousness of his real 'I' and fell from the Eden that was his original condition into the same condition as the pre-adamics... The two humanities, coming from two different creative processes, later mingled on the level of organic life on Earth... From then on, the coexistence of these two human types, and the competition, which was the result of this, became the norm...we can see that throughout the centuries, even in our own day, adamics in their post-fall condition, have been and are generally in an inferior position to the pre-adamics.

...For the moment we will restrict ourselves to repeating that contemporary adamic man, having lost contact with his higher centers and therefore with his real 'I', appears practically the same as his pre-adamic counterpart. However, unlike the latter, he still has his higher centers, which ensure that he has the possibility of following the way of esoteric evolution. *At present*, pre-adamic man is deprived of this possibility, but it will be given to him if adamic humanity develops, as it should during the era of the Holy Spirit." [12]

Quoting and paraphrasing Mouravieff further:

"The Era of the Holy Spirit has two faces - one of Paradise regained and the other a Deluge of Fire... We can even say that the whole dramatic history of humanity, from the fall of Adam until today, not excluding the prospect of the New Era, is overshadowed by the coexistence of these two human races whose separation will occur only at the Last Judgment. It is to this that Jesus referred in parables when he spoke to the crowds, but described in clear terms for the benefit of his disciples; the most noteworthy description is the parable of the tares and the good seed, on which he made the following commentary:

He that soweth the good seed is the Son of man: the field is the world: the good seed are the children of the kingdom: but the tares are the children of the wicked one: the enemy that sowed them is the devil: the harvest is the end of the world...

The coexistence of a race of Anthropoids and a race of Men, confirmed here, is necessary from the point of view of the General Law, to maintain uninterrupted the stability in movement of organic life on earth. It is also necessary because of the principle of equilibrium. The first race is a counterbalance, which allows the race of Men to pursue its esoteric evolution. Jesus confirmed this when he spoke about the End in the following terms:

---

[11] Ibid., pp. 108-109.
[12] Ibid., p. 129.

Then, shall two be in the field; one shall be taken, and the other left. Two women shall be grinding at the mill; the one shall be taken, and the other left.

Tares grow without having to be cultivated. Good seed, on the other hand, demands a great deal of care if it is to bear fruit.

Pre-adamic man was never an Individuality. Created as a Personality on the 6th day (symbolically speaking), he is deprived of every possibility of direct, 'individual individuation' - if one may put it thus - for his existence was placed under the law of collective Individuation, which is governed by [the Thought Center of Non-being] with the aid of a whole hierarchy of spirits who are subject to its authority.

Pre-Adamic man does not reincarnate. Not having any individualized element in himself, he is born and dies but he does not incarnate, and consequently he cannot reincarnate. The individualization of pre-adamics is collective, and is directed in groups by certain spirits of the hierarchy. This does not, however, prevent pre-adamics from entering the evolutionary field that forms the experiences of adamic man in great numbers, and since adamic man suffers from a lack of discernment because of his corrupt state, this disturbs and slows his evolution.

Because of the Principle of Equilibrium, humanity on this earth is divided into two equal parts - adamics and pre-adamics. The equilibrium between them is automatically adjusted to follow fluctuations of the incarnations of adamic souls. However, if the adamic race, by casting its pearls to the swine, denies its divine nature to an inadmissible degree, this balance will be broken in favor of the tares. In the parable of the talents, Jesus foresaw this possibility of such a degeneration - where the servant buried the one talent entrusted to him and, on returning it to his master without having made it multiply, was told: 'Thou wicked and slothful servant ... and cast ye the unprofitable servant into outer darkness: there shall be weeping and gnashing of teeth.' There is no need to emphasize the esoteric meaning here...

When the two humanities were created, they were placed under different authorities. The Fall necessitated special measures and thus the *Staircase* was provided. From that point on, Adamic man was subjected to the law of birth and death and kept only a dim consciousness of his higher self in spite of the almost complete obstruction of his channel of communication with the higher centers, which still exist in him. This gives him the possibility of a choice. If he hears the *Voice of the Master*, the higher intellect, and resolutely steps onto the Staircase, and if he reaches the Fourth Step and resists the Trial by Fire, then, when he crosses the Second Threshold, he will be welcomed as a Prodigal son... it is an event that will be understood only by those who have accomplished it.

If the adamic humanity, en masse, abandons the combat that leads to restoration of their former estate - Ascension - and if this desertion goes beyond the tolerances of balance, the good seed can be progressively stifled by the tares. The world will then head straight into catastrophe - which this time will take the form of a Deluge of Fire.

If the equilibrium, which is already in jeopardy, were to be reestablished, then with the integral and simultaneous incarnation of adamic souls, the Time of Transition would enable Adamic man to enter the Era of the Holy Spirit [– a reality where one was in constant touch with the Creative Principle, 4th density.] Then would follow a thousand years consecrated to the perfecting of the TWO races, and after a second millennium, the reign of the Androgyne, the Last Judgment would definitively separate the tares from the good seed. At this point, Adamic man would begin an even higher evolution, and would at last attain the Pleroma, [6th density.] At this point, and only at this point, will the Tares of the present time cease to be tares and be promoted to the ranks of "good seed." They would begin their own long, evolutionary course that the adamics have already achieved. Then they, in their turn, will receive the higher centers of consciousness which, given them in potential, would be the talents they must make fruitful.

At this point, the Adamics *who degenerated into pre-adamics*, would also have the possibility of taking up their abandoned evolution again while an equal number of the most able pre-adamics would receive the talents that were initially given to the former and this would help them leap forward on the road of esoteric evolution. They may be compared with gifted, hardworking students who get a double promotion while the incapable and lazy ones do another year in the same class.

Meanwhile, the two races are totally mixed: not only nations, but even families can be, and generally are, composed of both human types. This state of things is the belated result of transgressing the Biblical prohibition against mixed marriages.

The dominant position of the pre-adamics that is a result of the esoteric failure of the adamics is now creating a critical situation of unprecedented gravity. *The remainder of the Time of transition offers the last chance for humanity to reestablish the threatened equilibrium and so avoid a general cataclysm.*

If we do not take this opportunity, the tradition of 'Solomon' will finally overcome the tradition of 'David/Perseus.' Then, deflected from the goals of Ascension, and even going beyond the limits of what is necessary and useful to feed the Matrix, the false prophets and their followers, thinking that they are right, will hurl pre-adamic humanity - the children of this world - against the adamics - the children of light - and will provoke a final frightful and useless struggle.

If this should happen, if the adamic humanity does not manage to quell the revolt against the Love of the Son, a resistance that would ensure victory, the balance will finally be broken, and humanity will be destroyed in the Deluge of Fire."

Mouravieff's description of the "Fall" of the Adamic race also follows the same lines as the description given to us from the Cassiopaeans where we see that this is a symbolic version of the "Fall" of our consciousness unit. In the following excerpt, note that our term "Lizzies" is a short-hand notation for those theorized denizens of hyperdimensional realities whose "essence" is "read" as reptilian:

08-28-99

Q: Well, this is one of the problems I am dealing with in trying to write this history of mankind. As I understand it, or as I am trying to figure it out from the literature, prior to the 'Fall in Eden,' mankind lived in a 4th density state. Is that correct?

A: Semi/sort of.

Q: Please be more specific.

A: 4th density in another realm, such as time/space continuum, etc.

Q: Okay, so this realm changed, as a part of the cycle; various choices were made: the human race went through the door after the 'gold,' so to speak, and became aligned with the Lizzies after the 'female energy' consorted with the wrong side, so to speak. This is what you have said. This resulted in a number of effects: the breaking up of the DNA, the burning off of the first ten factors of DNA, the separation of the hemispheres of the brain...

A: Only reason for this: you play in the dirt, you're gonna get dirty.

Q: (T) What were we before the "Fall"?

A: 3rd density STO.[13]

Q: (T) We are STS at this point because of what happened then?

A: Yes.

[...]

Q: (T) We were 3rd density STO at that time. Was this after the battle that had transpired? In other words, were we, as a 3rd density race, literally on our own at that point, as opposed to before?

A: Was battle.

Q: (L) The battle was in us?

---

[13] The Cassiopaeans use the terms Service to Others (STO) and Service to Self (STS) to describe the manifestations of the two basic principles. STO describes the state of living according to the Creative Principle; STS describes the state of living according to the Entropic Principle. Much of our work in this life is to understand these two basic principles, aligning yourself with one or the other.

A: Through you.

Q: (T) The battle was through us as to whether we would walk through this doorway... (L) The battle was fought through us, we were literally the battleground. (T) Was the battle over whether or not we walked through that door?

A: Close.

Q: (T) Okay, we were STO at that point. You have said before that on this density we have the choice of being STS or STO.

A: Oh Terry, the battle is always there, it's "when" you choose that counts!

[...]

Q: (T) This must tie into why the [aliens] keep telling people that they have given their consent for abduction and so forth. We were STO and now we are STS.

A: Yes, ... "When" you went for the gold, you said "Hello" to the Lizards and all that that implies.

Q: (T) ...By going for the gold, we became STS beings because going for the gold was STS.

A: Yes.

Q: (T) And, in doing so, we ended up aligning ourselves with the 4th density Lizard Beings...

A: Yes.

Q: (T) Because they are 4th density beings and they have a lot more abilities than we at 3rd density...

A: You used to be aligned with 4th density STO.

Q: (T) And we were 3rd density STO. But, by going for the gold we aligned ourselves with 4th density STS.

A: Yes.

Q: (T) And by doing so we gave 4th density STS permission to do whatever they wish with us?

A: Close.

Q: (T) So, when they tell us that we gave them permission to abduct us, it is this they are referring to?

A: Close.

Q: (J) Go back to what they said before: "Free will could not be abridged if you had not obliged". (T) We, as the human race, used our free will to switch from STO to STS. (L) So, at some level we have chosen the mess we are in and that is the Super Ancient Legend of the Fallen Angel,

Lucifer. That is us. We fell by falling into that door, so to speak, going after the pot of gold, and when we fell through the door, the serpent bit us!

A: But this is a repeating syndrome.

Q: (L) Is it a repeating syndrome just for the human race or is it a repeating syndrome throughout all of creation?

A: It is the latter.

The adamic race with its full set of DNA, with its connection to the higher centers in place and functioning, is what the C's describe here as 3D density STO living in a "semi/sort of" 4D state aligned with 4D STO. That sounds very much like a "Golden Age" when man "walked with the gods".

In making the choice to experience greater physicality, the consciousness unit fractures and "Falls" from the STO state, loses its connection with the higher centers, and finds itself more or less at the same level as the pre-adamic race, those who have no possibility of reaching the higher centers because the DNA hardware isn't in place. However, because this new 3D STS existence was not the "natural habitat" for a body with the potential to reach the higher centers, the fallen race is at a disadvantage compared to the pre-adamics.

Q: In Book III of his *Gnosis*, Mouravieff discusses what he calls "pre-Adamic humanity" and "Adamic humanity". As I read this I could see that the thing I was struggling to understand in terms of psychopathy as discussed in the *Adventures Series*,[14] was exactly what Mouravieff was describing. However, he was using the Bible to explain it, and that just didn't quite work. Nevertheless, the basic idea is that pre-Adamic human types basically have no "soul", nor any possibility of growing one. This is certainly shocking, but there have been many recent scholarly discussions of this matter based on what seems to be clinical evidence that, indeed, there are human beings who are just "mechanical" and have no "inner" or "higher self" at all. Gurdjieff talked about this and so did Castaneda. Are Mouravieff's ideas about the two basic TYPES of humans - as far as they go- accurate.

A: Indeed, though again, there is a "Biblical Gloss". The pre-Adamic types are "organic" portals between levels of density.

This, of course, raises the issue of whether or not trying to "help" or "save" such individuals is a waste of time. This is a major clue as to why the early Christians were charged with holding a "vile superstition" and "hatred of humanity".

---

[14] http://www.cassiopaea.org/cass/adventureindex.htm

Q: Is it a waste of time to try to help or "save" such individuals?

A: Pretty much. Most of them are very efficient machines. The ones that you have identified as psychopaths are "failures". The best ones *cannot be discerned except by long and careful observation.*

Q: Have any of us ever encountered one of these "organic portals" and if so, can you identify one for the sake of instruction.

A: If you consider that the population is equally distributed, then you will understand that in an ordinary "souled" person's life, that person will encounter half as many organic portals as souled individuals. BUT, when someone is in the process of "growing" and strengthening the soul, *the Control System will seek to insert even more "units" into that person's life.* Now, think of all the people you have ever met and particularly those with whom you have been, or are, intimate. Which half of this number would YOU designate as being organic portals? Hard to tell, eh?

Q: (B) Is this the original meaning of the "pollution of the bloodline"?

A: Yes.

This certainly gave a whole new meaning to the experiences I have described in the *Adventures series* published on our website. It also became clear that the work of discerning these "organic portals" from souled human beings is *crucial* to the so-called "ascension" process. Without the basic understanding of conservation and transformation of energies, there is no possibility of making any progress in such a pursuit. This means that the understanding of Organic Portals vis a vis human beings of the "bloodline" (diffused though it may be throughout all of humanity), is the deepest and most crucial of esoteric secrets.

During the session quoted above, one of the attendees stated that there was a member of her family who she was certain was one of these "organic portals". The C's jumped to respond:

A: Now, do not start labeling without due consideration. Remember that very often the individual who displays contradictory behavior may be a souled being in struggle.

Q: (L) I would say that the chief thing they are saying is that the really good ones - you could never tell except by long observation. The one key we discovered from studying psychopaths was that their actions do not match their words. But what if that is a symptom of just being weak and having no will? (A) How can I know if I have a soul?

A: Do you ever hurt for another?

Q: (V) I think they are talking about empathy. These soulless humans simply don't care what happens to another person. If another person is in pain or misery, they don't know how to care.

A: The only pain they experience is "withdrawal" of "food" or comfort, or what they want. They are also masters of twisting perception of others so as to seem to be empathetic. But, in general, such actions are simply to retain control.

Q: (A) What does having a soul or not having a soul have to do with bloodline?

A: Genetics marry with soul if present.

Q: Do "organic portals" go to fifth density when they die?

A: Only temporarily until the "second death".

Q: (V) What is the "origin" of these organic portal human types? In the scheme of creation, where did they come from?

A: They were originally part of the bridge between 2nd density and 3rd density. Review transcripts on the subject of short wave cycles and long wave cycles.

Ark had been reading the transcripts and noted that the C's had said that sleep was necessary for human beings because it was a period of "rest and recharging". They had also said that the *soul* rests while the body is sleeping. So, the next logical question was "what source of energy was tapped to recharge both the body and the soul"?

A: The question needs to be separated. What happens to a souled individual is different from an organic portal unit.

At this point, we stopped and discussed the possibility that the life force energy that is embodied in Organic Portals must be something like the soul pool that is theorized to exist for flora and fauna. This would, of course, explain the striking and inexplicable similarity of psychopaths, that is so well defined, that they differ from one another only in the way that different species of trees are different in the overall class of "Tree-ness" So, we divided the question and asked first:

Q: ... where does the energy come from that recharges Organic Portals.

A: The pool you have described.

Q: Does the recharging of the souled being come from a similar pool, only maybe the "human" pool?

A: No - it recharges from the so-called sexual center which is a higher center of creative energy. During sleep, the emotional center, not being blocked by the lower intellectual center and the moving center, transduces the energy from the sexual center. It is also the time during which the higher emotional and intellectual centers can rest from the "drain" of the lower centers' interaction with those pesky organic portals so much loved by the lower centers. This respite alone is sufficient to make a difference.

But, more than that, the energy of the sexual center is also more available to the other higher centers.

Q: From where does the so-called "sexual center" get *its* energy?

A: The sexual center is in direct contact with 7th density in its "feminine" creative thought of "Thou, I Love". The "outbreath" of "God in the relief of constriction". Pulsation. Unstable Gravity Waves.

Q: Do the "centers" as described by Mouravieff relate at all to the idea of "chakras".

A: Quite closely. In an individual of the organic variety, the so-called higher chakras are "produced in effect" by stealing that energy from souled beings. This is what gives them the ability to emulate souled beings. The souled being, in effect, perceives a mirror of their own soul when they ascribe "soul qualities" to such beings.

Q: Is this a correspondence that starts at the basal chakra which relates to the sexual center as described by Mouravieff?

A: No. The "sexual center" corresponds to the solar plexus. Lower moving center - basal chakra. Lower emotional - sexual chakra. Lower intellectual - throat chakra. Higher emotional - heart chakra. Higher intellectual - crown chakra

Q: (V) What about the so-called seventh, or "third eye" chakra?

A: Seer. The union of the heart and intellectual higher centers. This would "close the circuit" in the "shepherd's crook" configuration.

Q: (V) What about the many ideas about 12 chakras, and so forth, that are currently being taught by many new age sources?

A: There are no such. This is a corrupted conceptualization based on the false belief that the activation of the physical endocrine system is the same as the creation and fusion of the magnetic center. The higher centers are only "seated" by being "magnetized". And this more or less "External" [unseated] condition of the Higher Centers has been perceived by some individuals and later joined to the perceived "seating" locations, in potential. This has led to "cross conceptualization" based on assumption!

Q: Are the levels of initiation and levels of the staircase as presented by Mouravieff fairly accurate?

A: Yes, but different levels accessed in other so-called lives can relieve the intensity of some levels in "another" life.

Summing Up

And so it is, according to the most ancient secret tradition, there are two types of humans on our planet. In the above quoted session, the

Cassiopaeans confirmed that, once the Biblical gloss was removed, Mouravieff's description was accurate. The most important thing about the Cassiopaean comments is, however, that they were able to deepen our understanding by situating the pre-adamic race within hyperdimensional reality and the Matrix control system. Let's look at four points they raised:

- The pre-adamic race serve as portals between levels of density.

- They are "very efficient machines", and "The best ones cannot be discerned except by long and careful observation".

- They steal energy from souled beings so as to emulate them.

- They make-up one-half of humanity.

One-half of humanity. Stealing energy from souled beings. Think about it. Sure does sound like what most people would consider a "vile superstition" and a "hatred of humanity". Not just then, but now as well.

But *if it is true*, it explains why the teachings of Jesus say what they do. It also explains why it had to be covered up. Because, *if it is true*, it means that the two races have been interbreeding for a very, very long time.

Intermixing of the Races

It is extremely important to understand that the two races have been interbreeding for thousands, if not tens of thousands of years. It is impossible to look at the races on the earth today, the red, the white, the black, or the yellow, and argue that one or the other is this "pre-adamic" and soulless race. We cannot speak of groups, nations, tribes, or peoples who are members of the "soulless" race as a group. The DNA of the two races is completely mixed, and this is the real meaning of the pollution of the bloodline. Only those with the appropriate genetic makeup are actually able to accommodate a soul and therefore pursue esoteric work, which means that no color or ethnic group is either excluded or has an advantage.

Consider this further: According to the ancient tradition revealed by Mouravieff, the DNA of these two races is so mixed that both can be found *within the same families*. Jesus pointed out that he would turn a husband against his wife, a child against the parent, and so on. And we now begin to really understand what this might have meant, again, assuming this information to be accurate.

We wish to insist on this point so that the hard of thinking will not take this idea and use it to underpin any racist attitudes. The two races are so intermingled that it is a question of the individual genetics of each person on the planet. This is suggested in these comments from the Cassiopaeans:

Q: (L) I want to get back on my question that you have not answered... I want to know who, exactly, and why, exactly, genetically engineered the Semitic people, and why there is such an adversarial attitude between them and the Celts and Aryans.

A: It is not just between the Jews and Celts, if you will take notice. **Besides, it is the individual aural profile that counts and not groupings or classifications.** But, to answer your question: there are many reasons both from *on and off the planet*....

Q: (L) So, the creation of the Germanic "Master Race" was what they were going after, to create this "breeding ground"?

A: Yes.

Q: (L) And, getting rid of the Jews was significant? Couldn't a Germanic master race be created without destroying another group?

A: No.

Q: Why?

A: Because of 4th density prior encoding mission destiny profile.

Q: (L) What does that mean?

A: This means encoding to activate after elevation to 4th density, thus if not eliminated, negates Nephalim domination and absorption. Jews were prior encoded to carry out mission after conversion, *though on individual basis*....

You will notice that the C's are pointing us in the direction of individuals and away from groups. It is not "groupings or classifications", it is the "individual aura profile". And this coincides with Mouravieff's statements on the issue as he remarks here:

"...But the mixing of chromosomes was already an accomplished fact, so that the hormonal symmetry of the adamics has naturally diminished through the generations until it has become stabilized at the point it has now reached. ... certain indications in the Gospel lead us to believe that the two human races that coexist on the earth are *numerically equal*..." (p. 130)

We repeat: The DNA of these two races is so mixed that both can be found within the same families. Your brother, sister, mother, father, daughter or son. Not somebody "other" across the world or across the street worshipping a different god or with a different skin color. It may be somebody you live with every day of your life, and if so, they have but one reason to be here, to drain, distract and deflect souled beings from evolving. And it is important also to note that this cannot be "conscious". Such individuals are as little aware that they do *not* have "higher centers" as those who do except, perhaps, that the latter may feel something is "missing" in their lives.

The way back to the activation of the DNA necessary to attain the contact with the higher centers is not through genetic manipulation, which is seeing the question through the lens of Matrix influences. The way back is through the ancient spiritual science, the real work of the alchemists, which through the heating of the crucible, the neo-cortex, rewires the brain so that the ancient and broken connection with the higher centers can be reestablished. It is the fusing of the "magnetic center", the "birth of the holy child", the real "I". This is natural "genetic modification" in terms of enhancing the feedback loop between the Thought Center of Being rather than the Thought Center of non-being. Big difference.

Q: (A) Which part of a human extends into 4th density?

A: That which is affected by pituitary gland.

Q: (L) And what is that?

A: Psychic.

Q: (A) Are there some particular DNA sequences that facilitate transmission between densities?

A: Addition of strands.

Q: (L) How do you get added strands?

A: You don't get, you receive.

Q: (L) Where are they received from?

A: Interaction with upcoming wave, if vibration is aligned.

Q: (L) How do you know if this is happening?

A: Psycho-physiological changes manifest. […] STO tends to do the process within the natural flow of things. STS seeks to alter creation processes to fit their ends.

OPs and the Big Picture

That there exists a soulless race, now numbering close to 3 billion inhabitants of this planet, certainly helps explain why the Earth is in its current state. That this soulless race are portals used by the 4D STS to maintain their control over us further explains the depth of the manipulations and why it was essential to cover up the teachings of the man we now call Jesus, but who the Cassiopaeans have said was actually named Jesinavarah. Organic Portals are the terminal connections of the geographic overseer sub-units of the Thought Centers of non-being. It is through our relationships with them that we feed and maintain the Matrix.

Organic portals are generic vehicles or portals, in human form, open for use by a variety of forces, which is why they make excellent matrix puppets. It just so happens that they're being used now by 4D STS to control 3D STS / 4D STO candidates through "clapper" and "vampire" functions - keeping us locked into a behavioral pattern matching the orchestrated norm, and being physically close to us to sap our energies and to keep us from having enough "escape velocity" to remove ourselves from the Matrix Control System's tug, via development of our magnetic centers.

Thus we see that the "natural" function of the OP, of imitation of the soul energy, assumes a specific character with the STS development stream of collecting the soul energy of souled individuals in order to pass it along the feeding chain to 4D STS. The principal role of the OP is now to prevent the genuine seeker from advancing along the Way. This is clear when we look at the following:

OPs collect soul energy from souled individuals.

This energy is transmitted to 4D STS.

OPs are intermixed in families with souled individuals.

When a souled individual makes the commitment to the "work", he or she needs to learn to conserve the soul energy, for without it the work cannot be done.

When one makes a commitment to the "work", one comes under attack.

This "attack" comes from those closest to you: family and friends.

The Cassiopaeans said, "*But*, when someone is in the process of 'growing' and strengthening the soul, *the Control System will seek to insert even more 'units' into that person's life*".

So in many ways, the actual work of learning to adjust the lens of one's view of reality involves *learning to discern the true nature of the seeker's relationships* in order to conserve energy from the OPs in the reality so that the seeker can accumulate enough energy to grow and strengthen the connection to the soul. Mouravieff makes this clear when he makes the following comments about understanding the "film" of your life:

> "In theory, the *film* in which a man is born and in which he lives can go on until the end of the world, on condition that he is happy, satisfied with himself, attributing his virtues to himself, and blaming others for his mistakes and misfortunes. Properly speaking, this kind of existence cannot be considered as human; it could be described as *anthropoid*. This term is justified in the sense that *exterior* man, immersed in self-satisfaction, represents the crowning achievement of millions of years of evolution of the species from its animal ancestors, yet, from the point of

view of esoteric evolution, he is a possibility which has not yet been realized.

> If we envisage the problem of esoteric evolution from the point of view of the *film* and the different parts man can play in it, it is clear that this kind of evolution is impossible as long as the *film* can always be considered as running in the same circle. People who perform in such a *film* are those we have called *anthropoids*, puppets, the *dead* who, in the words of Jesus, 'believe themselves to be alive'. Esoteric evolution starts when man, by his conscious efforts, proves capable of breaking the circle and transforming it into an ascending spiral." (Book I, pp 234-5)

But to do this, those secondary roles, those filled by the puppets, the Organic Portals, must be eliminated from the *film*.

> "As we have just said, man most often comes to this idea of evolution after he has already complicated the *film* to which he belongs. But true evolution cannot occur except *on the basis of the original film* – after all the artificially added elements have been eliminated. The latter is conditional on a return to the purity of the centers, especially the emotional center which – at least at the start – is the sole receptacle of spiritual influences, and seat of the *magnetic center*. The heart must therefore be pure, and if it is not already pure it must be purified. This is the *sine qua non* condition of success." (Book I, p. 238)

And, as we now know, the heart cannot be purified without great knowledge which leads to perspicacity. Painful though it may seem to be, among those "artificially added elements" which need to be eliminated from our lives are the Organic Portals.

This suggests to us the possibility that the figure around which the Jesus legend was wrapped was presenting a teaching that denied everything that all of the other religions promoted. Such a concept denies the value of sacrifice to the gods; it denies the value of appeasing the gods, honoring the gods, praying to the gods, expecting to be saved by or cleansed from sin by any of the gods. It places the important lesson squarely upon the human being as described in the Parable of the Prodigal Son. It describes the son as going to a Far Country. It describes the "Fall" as "a famine in the country". It tells us how the Prodigal Son went to a "resident of the Far Country" to ask for help. We can easily see that this resident represents the God of this world in his three monotheistic permutations. And what did the God do? Sent the Prodigal Son to live with the pigs. And there we see the clear explication of the Organic Portals in our lives. And we also understand the use of the term in the saying: do not cast your pearls before swine lest they turn and rend you in pieces. And speaking of pearls, we begin to understand the reason that the "pearl" was used as the metaphor for the magnetic center "buried" in a field and the necessity to sell all you own to obtain the field with the pearl of great price. A pearl is formed over time, layer after layer, around a seed, a kernel, a grain of sand that is an "irritant". In this world, souled beings ARE irritants, but in this world they have the possibility of "growing a soul", and ascending.

If we just learn to "make nice and get along" and suffer as nobly as possible and forgive and forget while maintaining close "feeding relationships" with Organic Portals, then we are wasting our time. Forgiveness and understanding are, certainly, important. But what is most important is to not use such as a pretext to prolong the feeding relationship. The big problem is: discerning the difference between the children of the Kingdom of Heaven and the children of a "lesser god".

 As we have already noted, *before* the Fall, those human beings with higher centers had access to communication with the higher densities via the "Maidens of the Wells", or the union between the right and left hemispheres of the brain and alignment with the 4th density STO. Because of their alignment, their frequency, and the lack of STS dampers, it was a simple matter to amplify Frequency Resonance Vibration.

After the Fall, it seems that a specific genetic variation was somatically induced by the incarnation of certain higher density beings who "gave their blood" for the "redemption of man". That is to say that they changed the body and DNA by Forced Oscillation. It is likely that this was done through the female incarnations because of the role of the mitochondrial DNA, but I don't want to get ahead of myself here, so we will leave that for the moment.

 Nevertheless, the presence of this DNA, depending upon the terms of recombination, makes it very likely that there are literally millions of carriers of this bloodline/Shamanic ability on the earth today. And it is for all of *you* that these pages are being written.

What strikes me as particularly fiendish is the way Christianity has co-opted, twisted and perverted the teaching. Christians certainly teach their followers about separating themselves from "sinners", but their version of those from whom they must be separated is based entirely on human judgements of what is or is not "sinful", based on their religious creed. On the other hand, the doctrine of Gnosis suggests that we view all others as potentially having the higher centers, real human empathy, and it is only when we begin to act, based on those higher principles, that we find ourselves being attacked, or attempts made to vector us away from the path to gnosis.

Don't expect people to understand you when you begin to assess your lessons and your relationships and to act on those assessments. The more a person becomes assimilated to the Service to Others orientation, the more effective his choices become, but, at the same time, to others his existence becomes incomprehensible and even a threat.

Now, it is pretty easy to practice these terms when giving to strangers or associates that are not intimately involved in your life. It's a lot harder to do it in close, personal relationships! But that is where it is most essential for the Shaman!

The reason for this is the particular role the Shaman plays in the Cosmic dynamics of all times, and most especially the present - that of the Spiritual Warrior.

> "...Shamanism is important not only for the place that it holds in the history of mysticism. The shamans have played an essential role in the defense of the psychic integrity of the community. They are preeminently the *antidemonic champions*; they combat not only demons and disease, but also the black magicians.

> The exemplary figure of the shaman champion is the mythical founder of *Na-khi* shamanism, the tireless slayer of demons. The military elements that are of great importance in certain types of Asian shamanism are accounted for by the requirements of *war against the demons*, the true enemies of humanity. In a general way, it can be said that shamanism defends life, health, fertility, the world of 'light', against death, diseases, sterility, disaster, and the world of 'darkness'."[15]

The fundamental and universal function of the Shaman is to have the force necessary for what we call the struggle against "the powers of evil". This does *not* mean going and dukeing it out with a demon or arguing over which channeled information is right or wrong or praying for World Peace or sending Love and Light to war-torn Bosnia. It doesn't mean doing spirit release or exorcism (though it could include such things in certain circumstances).

What it *does* mean is the constant and ever present need to sustain a very particular Frequency Resonance. What the Shaman represents is a "Pole of the World", through which the energies of Creation can be transduced into 3rd density. They are required to manifest in their bodies certain frequencies that can only be developed in relationships where the life force of the Shaman is *enhanced* by the interaction, not drained.

The "battling of demons" is clearly a clue that the STO Shaman must amplify the STO frequency and avoid amplification of the STS dynamic. That is where the true battle is being fought.

---

[15] Eliade, 1964, op. cit.

In the stories of the ancient Shamans of great power, it is often noted that, if they become a Shaman at a point in their life when they have a spouse and family, very often the Shaman is given a new *spirit spouse* whose most important function is to prepare *special food* for the Shaman so that he/she can do the special work. Sometimes this spirit spouse was an *actual second wife* or husband, who moved in with the family. In cultures where Shamanism was understood, if the original wife was not *suitable*, she at least understood the necessity for a special wife to fulfill the function of *feeding the shaman*. Of course, there are some stories of first wives who did *not* take well to having a second wife, even if it was only a spirit and not embodied in another woman, and the result was generally a conflict that ended in the death of the first wife. (Or husband if the shaman was a woman.) One suspects that this idea is at the root of the many ancient myths of the battles of brothers over a woman, or a "sacrifice" such as the story of Cain and Abel.

The point of this is not *necessarily* that it tells us something in a literal sense, but that it is symbolic of the Shaman's spiritual need to interact with beings that engage in an STO dynamic of mutual giving rather than manipulation and draining. A conclusion could be drawn that the STO Shaman must be in direct interaction, on an intimate level, only with someone who is *like* him or her in the sense Mouravieff has described it. In such a case their energies will exchange, commutate, and expand from the interaction. They will "push each other's swing". They will set up a Frequency Resonance Vibration between them that is so powerful that they will naturally "grow".

Of course we know by now that the forces of entropy that we suspect can be quite conscious, and may inhabit hyperdimensional space, will bring forward many of their own candidates for this intimate interaction who are *not* alike for the purpose of making sure that the Shaman never gains sufficient strength. At the same time, it is also possible that the presence of such persons in the Shaman's life *can* serve the all-important function of assisting in the "breaking down" and stripping of the flesh from the bones in preparation for the initiation. But, once the initiation has occurred, it is *crucial* for the Shaman to *act* in order to immediately strengthen his polarity. It is better to be in *no* relationship than to be in one that both drains and damps the self and feeds and amplifies the STS frequency.

And by acting based on the subtle clues in his environment, including his own body, his ability to *see* grows as well. And when his ability to see increases, he is better able to make choices, based on seeing the unseen, that act in a beneficial way for the entire STO polarity. The more the

Shaman exercises Free Will and ensures the Freedom of Will of others, the more available the energy of Free Will becomes to the entire planet. And this has a huge implication: the more Free Will is available, the more the STS domination will *naturally decrease*! The fewer people who are "available" for feeding, the less the STS orientation can grow!

The Shaman is a *specialist in the sacred*. They are able to *see* the spirits, to *go up into the sky* (interact with STO hyperdimensional realities) and meet the gods, to *descend to the underworld* (perceive STS hyperdimensional realities) and fight the demons, sickness, and death.

The shaman's essential role in the defense of the psychic integrity of the community depends above all on his ability to *see* what is hidden and invisible to the rest and to bring back direct and *reliable* information from the supernatural worlds.

Regarding this *See*ing, the problem has been defined in more modern terms by Donald Hoffman, a Cognitive scientist at the University of California, Irvine. Hoffman is the author of *"Visual Intelligence"*. He writes in response to a question as to what he believes that he cannot prove:

> "I believe that consciousness and its contents are all that exists. Space-time, matter and fields never were the fundamental denizens of the universe but have always been, from their beginning, among the humbler contents of consciousness, dependent on it for their very being.
>
> The world of our daily experience - the world of tables, chairs, stars and people, with their attendant shapes, smells, feels and sounds - is a species-specific user interface to a realm far more complex, a realm whose essential character is conscious. It is unlikely that the contents of our interface in any way resemble that realm.
>
> Indeed the usefulness of an interface requires, in general, that they do not. For the point of an interface, such as the Windows interface on a computer, is simplification and ease of use. We click icons because this is quicker and less prone to error than editing megabytes of software or toggling voltages in circuits.
>
> Evolutionary pressures dictate that our species-specific interface, this world of our daily experience, should itself be a radical simplification, selected not for the exhaustive depiction of truth but for the mutable pragmatics of survival.
>
> If this is right, if consciousness is fundamental, then we should not be surprised that, despite centuries of effort by the most brilliant of minds, there is as yet no physicalist theory of consciousness, no theory that explains how mindless matter or energy or fields could be, or cause, conscious experience."

There is an astonishing likeness between the accounts of Shamanic ecstasies and certain epic themes in archaic oral literature. The shaman's adventures in the other world, the ordeals that he undergoes in his ecstatic descents below, and ascents above to the sky, suggest the adventures of the heroes of the great myths and epics from Gilgamesh to Perseus, from Odysseus to Perceval. It is extremely likely that most of the motifs, as well as the characters, images, and clichés of these myths and stories are of ecstatic origin. In this sense, they become essential for study to those following the Shamanic path because they are, in all likelihood, narratives of shamans describing their journeys and adventures in the superhuman worlds.

> "We have termed the ecstatic experience a 'primary phenomenon' because we see no reason whatever for regarding it as the result of a particular historical moment, that is, as produced by a certain form of civilization. Rather, we would consider it fundamental in the human condition, and hence known to the whole of archaic humanity; what changed and was modified with the different forms of culture and religion were the interpretation and the evaluation of the ecstatic experience.
>
> What, then, was the historico-religious situation in Central and North Asia, where, later on, shamanism crystallized as an autonomous and specific complex?
>
> Everywhere in those lands, and from the earliest times, we find documents for the existence of a Supreme Being of celestial structure, who also corresponds morphologically to all the other Supreme Beings of the archaic religions. The symbolism of ascent, with all the rites and myths dependent on it, must be connected with celestial Supreme Beings; we know that 'height' was sacred as such, that many supreme gods of archaic peoples are called "He on high", "He of the Sky", or simply 'Sky'. This symbolism of ascent and height retains its value even after the 'withdrawal' of the celestial Supreme Beings... Hence we must conceive of Asiatic shamanism as an archaic technique of ecstasy whose original underlying ideology - belief in a celestial Supreme Being with whom it was possible to have direct relations by ascending into the sky - was constantly being transformed by a long series of exotic contributions culminating in the *invasion* of Buddhism.
>
> The concept of mystical death, furthermore, encouraged increasingly regular relations with the ancestral souls and the 'spirits', relations that ended in possession.
>
> The phenomenology of the trance underwent many changes and corruptions, due in large part to confusion as to the precise nature of ecstasy. Yet all these innovations and corruptions did not succeed in eliminating the possibility of the true Shamanic ecstasy; and we have been

able to find examples of genuine mystical experiences of the shamans, taking the form of 'spiritual' ascents...

More than once we have discerned in the Shamanic experience a 'nostalgia for paradise...'."[16]

We return again to the question: in practical terms, What are we supposed to *do*? Let's look at something we have brought up before and see if we cannot find a clue here:

A: First, some blockbuster stuff for the Knighted ones... Look upon a detailed map, and reflect, remember lonely journeys from long ago, and begin to unlock shattering mysteries, which will lead to revelations opening the door to the greatest learning burst yet!!

Q: You said "knighted ones", as though there were some significance to the name...

A: Discover...

Q: Is there some genetic engineering here?

A: No, not in the sense you are thinking. But, all are in some sense. [...]

Q: (L) Well, what I *really* want to know is *why* have we had all of these *crazy* things happen in our lives, and all of these people ranged all around us seemingly placed there, or manipulated deliberately to affect us negatively. I mean, am I wrong, or is this not a *very* unusual and crazy situation?

A: Why do you think?

Q: Well, I have no idea!

A: Because you are of the extremely rare and few who have the abilities to put the puzzle together.

Q: So, what are we supposed to do? (TK) Discover.

A: **Yes**.

Now, even though the remark was made to me and my brother, and even considering the fact that our patronymic is Knight, the real question is: What is it to be "Knighted"? We already know that, in certain terms the whole concept of the Knight possibly is derived from the Shamanic function. And, if that is the case, how many more "Knighted Ones" are there?

The Hero of the Grail Quest is Perceval, the "Desired Knight". He was also known as the "Widow's Son", which also happens to be. an appellation of Horus the Younger, Isis being the Widow of Osiris. The story of Isis and Osiris we can easily see is a variation of the story of

---

[16] Eliade, 1964, op. cit.

Demeter and Persephone and Ishtar/Inanna descending into the underworld to save her son-lover Tammuz/Dumuzi.

Perceval united many pagan and Christian myths but it is also evident that the Christian mythos was a redaction of the ancient Shamanic path. Perceval was sent to "cure the world's ills" and to "restore the Waste Land to fertility". He was hidden, like most "divine children", and raised in obscurity, but the question we are most concerned with is Why "Perceval"? If we consider that all the names and descriptions in the Grail stories are clues, which it is evident they are, then we must think that the name of the central character is one of the biggest clues.

When we look into the name Perceval, we find the first thing that we notice is its similarity to Persephone. It is thought that the name was derived from the name of the Welsh demigod Peredur or Paladrhir whose name meant "Spearman with a Long Shaft".[17] (Don't laugh! There's more to this than meets the eye!) This has often been compared to an ancient appellation of Osiris, which was "Mummy with a Long Member". So, it has been assumed that Perceval means "He Who Pierces the Valley", in terms of sexual connotation.

I gave this matter a great deal of thought at one point and I just wasn't satisfied with these explanations. I was puzzling over it one day and doing some searching on the Internet for any clues I could find, when it began to thunder outside. As I was hurrying to turn off and unplug my equipment (after losing two modems to lightning), a *tremendous* bolt of lightning struck practically right outside my window. I instantly thought about my dog that is *terrified* of lightning. "Poor Percy", I thought... and instantly I realized the origin of Perceval. You see, my dog's name is Perseus.

So, I began to think of Perseus and compare the stories in dynamic terms. You see, there are more stories of *failed* heroes than there are of successful ones, but Perceval and Perseus were *successful* heroes In fact, Perseus is about the most successful hero in all of epic and mythical history! He not only cut off the head of the Gorgon *and* killed the Sea Monster, he saved the damsel in distress, married her, and was "Raised to the stars". Perseus was the epitome of the hero who Frees the Maidens of the Wells. By his marriage with Andromeda he achieved the Shamanic ability of using the power of the head of Medusa to "balance the realm" by turning to stone all those who oppressed the people. Notice the all-important point that the Shamanic Knight, Perseus did not "fight" anyone;

---

[17] If you think about it, the many icthyphallic representations of great heros may simply represent the fact that they were "united" to their "polar mate". The phallus may have an altogether spiritual connotation according to the "Rule of the Sybils".

he merely held up the head of the Gorgon and those who were "tuned" to it, turned to stone.

Q: [In terms of the Quest, the Search for the Grail], what is the meaning of 'The Widow's Son'? The implication?

A: Stalks path of wisdom incarnate. Perceval was knighted in the court of seven.

Q: The court of seven what?

A: Swords points signify crystal transmitter of truth beholden.

***

Q: (L) In studying the myths of the Golden Age, I have found that the 'Seven Sages' are supposed to be the original Celestial powers that were the benefactors of mankind before the Fall. You once said that Perceval was 'knighted in the Court of Seven' and that the swords' points signify 'crystal transmitter of truth beholden'. Do these seven sages relate to this 'Court of Seven' that you mentioned?

A: Close.

Q: (L) When you said 'swords points signify crystal transmitter of truth beholden', could you elaborate on that remark?

A: Has celestial meaning.

Q: (L) Who was worshipped by the people who built Stonehenge?

A: Complicated. Spirit, stars, energy.

***

Q: In reading the Celtic legends, I discovered that Cassiopaea was part of a Triple Goddess construct along with Andromeda and Danae, Danu, or Don, as in **Tuatha de Danaan**, or the court of the goddess Danu. So, in other words, the supreme goddess of the Celts was Cassiopaea. Rhys states it explicitly. Cassiopaea is found in the zodiacal area of Aries, the 'lamb', where Cepheus the 'rock' and 'king' is also found, as well as Perseus, 'he who breaks' - with one of the stars in his foot being called 'breaker of rocks'. The representation is of Perseus overcoming the serpent, and the ancient Celtic engravings of the horned god show him gripping two serpents by the throat. I would like to understand the symbology here...

A: You are on the right track.

Q: What is the symbology of the 'breaking of rocks', as in the alchemical texts, as well as related to Perseus as 'he who breaks'?

A: Occurs at a time when rocks break, as in the electromagnetic impulses that emanate from earthbound rocks when sheared by tectonic forces, **and**

**much more importantly, the possible utilization of said forces
whether naturally or otherwise induced.**

Q: I have a few questions on the subject of Cassiopaea. On several
occasions you have described Cassiopaea or the Cassiopaeans, the unified
thought form light beings that transmit through Cassiopaea, as being the
'front line of the universe's system of natural balance'. On another
occasion you said that Isis was a 'vanguard'. Now, it seems to me that
something that is at the front line is also a vanguard - that the definitions
are interchangeable, or similar. In reading through all the various myths
and legends, it occurs to me that the similarity between the imagery of
Queen Cassiopaea and Isis is quite striking. What is the relationship
between Queen Cassiopaea, archetypally speaking, and Isis?

A: Subliminal. For those who "see the unseen".

Q: The other thing I noticed about the word 'Isis' is that it can be slightly
altered to make 'I Zeus'. And, Perseus can be 'per Zeus' and Persia can be
made to say 'per ziu'. One of the oldest etymological roots for the word
'God' is 'ziu' from which we get 'deu'. These all represent the English
translation of 'for God', with Perceval being 'per ziu val' or 'strong for
God'. Could you comment on these relationships?

A: Interconnected by trilingual learning curve.

Q: I also noticed that the word 'Osiris' could also be slightly modified to
say 'of Sirius'. Comment, please.

A: Sirius was regarded highly in your "past".

Q: What was the foundation of this regard for Sirius?

A: "From whence cometh, is seen that which knows no limitation."

Q: Could you elaborate on that?

A: Could, but will not.

Q: Why?

A: Because you can!

***

Q: In the same vein, I have noticed that there are two classes of arachnids.
There are scorpions and there are spiders. The zodiac was changed by
taking the pincers away from the Scorpion and creating out of them the
sign of Libra. This image was one of a woman holding a balance scales,
usually blindfolded. This was done within recorded history, but

was probably formalized through the occult traditions of Kaballah. Now,
in trying to figure out who has on what color hat, if there is such a thing, I
have come to a tentative conclusion that the spider, or spinner of webs, is
the Rosicrucian encampment, and that the Scorpion represents the seeker
of wisdom... because, in fact, the word for Scorpio comes from the same

root as that which means to pierce or unveil. Therefore, the Scorpion is also Perseus, per Ziu, or 'for God'. And the Rosicrucians are the 'other', so to speak. Can you elaborate on this for me? Or comment?

A: What a tangled web we spin, when we must not let you in.

***

Q: Okay. Tracking the Triple Goddess back to the oldest references, we get to KaliMa. There are all kinds of derivations of this name, but the thing that strikes me is the relationship to the goddess Kell, or Kella, as well as to the word kell, Celts, and how this might be transformed into the word 'Cassiopaea'. Can you comment on this?

A: Do not the Celts like "kelly" green?!?

Q: Yes. So. What does 'green' have to do with it?

A: Keep searching... learning is accomplished thusly, and learning is fun!

Q: Okay. The three aspects of the goddess: in the story of Perseus, there was Cassiopaea/Danae, Andromeda, and Medusa... the three aspects, the mother, the virgin, and the crone. But, in this story, Perseus manages to cut the head off the crone. In other stories, the crone always manages to win. Is there any particular reason why Perseus cuts off the head of Medusa? Was this transposed? Was the Medusa merely another aspect of the goddess or was it something else?

A: Serpentine.

Q: What about serpentine? Representative of the serpent race or the Lizzies?

A: Eden.

Q: Ah. Medusa represents the Fall. The new standard of limitation. The alignment with the Reptoids.

Q: In the oldest religions, it is the Goddess, the Mother, and the endless sea of potential of unassumed experience that was the Goddess. It was a celestial concept before it was reduced to an earth concept. There was unconditional love in the beginning. But then, the patriarchal view twisted it and it became violent and ugly and restrictive. And, from the patriarchal view came the 'redeeming son' when before, it was the redemption of the Goddess' blood. So, what I want to know is: what happened to create the patriarchal system? How was the Goddess suppressed?

A: All has been distorted and suppressed, so why not this?

Q: You once mentioned 'Greek Enforcers' who wrote the New Testament. Where did these Greek Enforcers come from?

A: Order of Thelon.

Q: On another occasion you called the Nephilim 'enforcers'. Is there any relation between this order of Thelon and the Nephilim?

A: Maybe...

Q: Where is the headquarters of this group?

A: Sicinthos.

Q: Never heard of it. Okay. Next question: the White Mare Goddess image that prefigured the Omega symbol, what is the relationship of the White Mare to the symbolism of the knight? The knight on the horse is repeatedly used in alchemical symbolism.

A: Rites.

Q: One of the rites in question is that the making of the knight involves touching both shoulders with the end of a sword, which is actually a symbolic beheading. Why is the knight symbolically beheaded?

A: Blast open limitations of encasing spirit in body.

We should notice in this last remark that the "knighting" is very probably a survival of the "head of the shaman being forged on an anvil".

Q: When I post material on the web site, there are many who resonate to the material. I have been of the opinion that Unified Thought Form beings such as you describe yourselves, must relate to a very large group as represented in this density. I know that we are dealing with limiting terms. But, when you say "we are *you* in the future", does this apply to people who *choose* the Cassiopaean option?

A: Maybe it is best to say it applies to those who recognize the application.

Q: So, if they recognize it, if they know it is them, they are part of it. (A) But, thinking in nonlinear terms, its up to us to work to make this precise. You are asking this question which implies that the answer exists. But, exactly what the answer is may be it is not yet chosen, and it is up to us to make it this way.

A: Lodestar is a clue for you.

Q: I guess that means a guiding star of some sort. A lodestone is magnetic, it is where the compass points so that you can find your direction. Okay, in the myth, Cassiopaea, Danae, and Athena work together to enable Perseus to cut off the head of the Gorgon and kill the sea monster and rescue Andromeda. Of all the mythical heroes, Perseus stands out because he was *successful*. He went on the quest, he succeeded in the mission, and he freed the maiden in distress, killed a slew of Lizzie types, balanced the situation in his environment, and then even lived happily ever after. He didn't lose his reason, he didn't fail... it is about the only really successful myth. He *did* it. And did it well.

A: A quest is successfully followed one step at a time. No need to gauge the staircase.

Q: The only point I was trying to make was that maybe the only reason for the Cassiopaean connection, maybe even for the term "Cassiopaea", is that it is the archetype of the function...

A: That is good.

Q: In this other book here, there is a Celtic word that pops up: 'pryf'. What is pryf?

A: Soul.

Q: The book says here that there is a need for someone of a certain bloodline to come along and 'free the dragon spawn'. 'None other than she can bring the pryf up from the deep no matter how they may make the serpents squirm. If she can hold her place in the gates of time'. What are they talking about here; bringing up the dragon spawn, and how does that relate to soul?

A: You cannot see?

Q: It also says that this person with this bloodline, that it is the duty of this person to create a bridge between man and the gods, to open the doorways of time. Can you comment on that?

A: These questions have explanations which are readily apparent.

Q: Well, before, when I asked a question, you said that I would get my answer from the 'trees'. This book is all about 'trees', in one way or another - ancient Druids and so forth. Was that clue given so that I would notice these things in this particular book even though it is fiction?

A: Certainly.

Now, put this last most interesting item together with the symbology of the 'breaking of rocks', related to Perseus as 'he who breaks' and we might think that, at some point in the not too distant future, at a time when "rocks break, as in the electromagnetic impulses that emanate from earthbound rocks when sheared by tectonic forces", the role of the Shaman in the times ahead of us is "the possible utilization of said forces whether naturally or otherwise induced" to produce a "wormhole" to a different reality that can be traversed *in the body*.

So, perhaps we have some better idea of the function of the Shaman-Knight... the Knighted Ones: Incarnations of the archetype of Perseus, a "child of the God" in the sense of being an offspring of the Thought Centers of STO, the hero who cut off the head of the Gorgon, who freed the spirit of limitations, those of a particular Frequency Resonance Vibration of sufficient strength and purity to be able to create a bridge between man and the gods, to open the doorways of time.

Not a bad day's work, I think!

Chapter 30

The 3-5 Code:
The Journey From Jerusalem
To Oak Island Via the Pyrenees

Now it is time to return to an important series of clues given by the Cassiopaeans regarding what we call the "3-5 Code". It is so complicated a story that I have despaired of ever being able to convey it without confusing the reader, but I am going to try. I do ask that you please understand that there were so many "threads" being followed at any given time that in all that has been written thus far, I have been separating them out and following them one at a time even though much was either happening simultaneously or at the very least, overlapped in time. But, at least we are now getting into some really fun things.

As the reader already knows, the subject of the 3-5 Code was first brought up on 11-11-95. There have been a lot of people asking about this strange occurrence of these double 11's and I hope to be able to provide some clues to solving that mystery as we go along. But, we will be diverting on several lateral themes as we proceed before coming back to the Code, proper, and we start with this frequent need to divert right at the very beginning here.

You see, the whole problem really started with the issue of Jesus. Even though I already had experience with the fact that invoking the "name of Jesus" really had little (if any) effect whatsoever on the occasions that I had worked with exorcism type activities, (and this was troubling, to say the least!), I was still in the mode of the standard Fundamentalist New Age belief that determining the attitude or teachings about Jesus from any given channeled source would be helpful in determining the "orientation" of that source and could save you from a lot of problems further down the road.

Like most "New Age Elders", I was still measuring everything by the standard of Edgar Cayce. So, we were asking our "Jesus Questions" as a sort of "test" for the Cassiopaeans.

Q: (L) Who was Jesus of Nazareth?

A: Advanced spirit.

Q: (L) Was Jesus an individual who had psychic or unusual powers from birth?

A: Close.

Q: (L) Did he have an awareness from the earliest times of his life that he was in some way special or chosen?

A: yes.

Q: (L) Was Jesus born from an immaculate conception; that is did his mother not have sex with a man in order to conceive him?

A: No.

Q: (L) She did have sex with a man in order to conceive him, is that correct?

A: Yes.

Q: (L) Who was the man with whom she had sex to Conceive Jesus?

A: Tonatha.

Q: (L) And who was this individual, Tonatha?

A: Acquaintance.

Q: (L) Was he selected for some reason to be the biological father of Jesus by other beings or powers.

A: Close.

Q: (L) Can you give us any details about him? What was his lineage, where did he come from, etc?

A: He was a member of the White Sect.

Q: (L) What is the white sect?

A: AKA Aryans. [This one slipped right by me.]

Q: (L) Was Mary a member of the Essene group?

A: Yes.

Q: (L) Was this man also a member of the Essenes?

A: No.

Q: (L) And this person, Tonatha, was chosen to be the biological father of Jesus?

A: Yes.

Q: (L) Why did Mary not marry him? [Laura the eternal romantic!]

A: Feelings were extremely transient. Influenced by telepathic suggestion. Hypnotized level 1.

Q: (L) What date, counting backwards in our calendrical system, was Jesus born on?

A: 01 06 minus 14.

Q: (L) What time of day was he born?

A: 6 am.

Q: (L) Was there any unusual celestial event in terms of star or planet alignments at that time?

A: No.

Q: (L) Was there an event where the Magi came to present gifts?

A: Close.

Q: (L) Who was it that came to present him gifts?

A: 3 prophets.

Q: (L) What country did these prophets come from?

A: Iran. Also known as Persia. [The "Persian connection" later proves to be VERY significant!]

Q: (L) What was the "star" that indicated to the prophets...

A: Spaceship.

Q: (L) What kind of space ship?

A: Mother.

Q: (L) Where did this mothership come from?

A: Other realm.

Q: (L) Does that mean other realm as in dimension or density?

A: Yes.

Q: (L) Do we know of these other realms or densities as other star systems or planets?

A: Partly.

Q: (L) Jesus grew up to the age of twelve, at which point he was bar Mitzvahed. Is that correct?

A: He was bar Mitzvahed at the age of 10. Aramaic rite.

Q: (L) Did Jesus, during the course of his growing up years travel to other countries and study under other masters?

A: No.

Q: (L) Where did he receive his teaching or training?

A: Channeled to him.

Q: (L) Did he at any point in his life travel to India?

A: No. [This surprised us as *many* channeled sources have claimed this to be so.]

Q: (L) Did he travel to Egypt and undergo an initiation in the Great Pyramid?

A: No. [This also was a surprise in contradiction to our expectations as it was part of the "New Age" dogma!]

Q: (L) He lived his entire life in Palestine? [I was somewhat incredulous!]

A: Near. In that general area. The Bible is not entirely accurate.

Q: (L) When Jesus attended the marriage at Cana, whose wedding was it?

A: Did not happen.

Q: (L) Did Jesus feed thousands of people with a few loaves and fishes?

A: No.

Q: (L) Are you saying that all the miracles of the Bible are myths?

A: Remember this is corrupted information altered after the fact for purposes of political and economic gain and control.

Q: (L) Tell us what Jesus really did.

A: He taught spiritual truths to those starving for them.

Q: (L) And what was the basis of these spiritual truths?

A: Channeled information from higher sources.

Q: (L) What is the truth that Jesus taught?

A: That all men are loved by the creator and are *one* with same.

Q: (L) Did he perform any miracles?

A: Some.

Q: (L) Can you tell us about one or two of them?

A: Healing.

Q: (L) Was he able to literally heal with the touch of his hand?

A: Yes.

Q: (L) Did he perform exorcisms?

A: Close.

Q: (L) Is Reiki the method he used to heal, or something similar?

A: Yes.

Q: (L) Is there any way to enhance the Reiki energy to make it powerful enough that one could do in a very short time what now takes quite a while? [As it seems apparent that Jesus did.]

A: Yes.

Q: (L) What can one do to enhance the Reiki energy?

A: Attain lofty spiritual purity.

Q: (L) Are the only miracles he did healing?

A: No.

Q: (L) What other kinds of miracles did he do?

A: Telekinesis.

Q: (L) Did he walk on water?

A: No.

Q: (L) Did he turn water into wine?

A: No.

Q: (L) Are these all just stories?

A: Yes.

Q: (L) What is the purpose of the stories?

A: Control.

Q: (L) Was Jesus crucified?

A: No.

Q: (L) Was somebody crucified on a cross and represented to be Jesus?

A: No.

Q: There was no crucifixion and no resurrection after three days? Is that correct?

A: Close.

Q: (L) Okay, what is the truth on that matter?

A: He spent 96 hours in a comatose state in a cave near Jerusalem. When he awoke, he prophesied to his disciples and then exited the cave. 27,000 people had assembled because of mother ship appearance and he was taken up in a beam of light.

Q: (L) When did he go into this sleep state? Did he just go in one day and go to bed and go to sleep and then a ship came and picked him up?

A: Close.

Q: (L) So he appeared to his followers to have died?

A: They thought this.

Q: (L) Did he get up and say anything to anybody before he left on the ship?

A: Yes.

Q: (L) Did he come back to life... so to speak?

A: Yes.

Q: (L) And then he told them things he had seen in his extended meditative sleep, is that what happened?

A: Close.

Q: (L) Okay, what happened?

A: Told prophecies then proclaimed eventual return.

Q: (L) Was this information he got during this period of 'extended sleep'?

A: Yes.

Q: (L) How long was he asleep, or in this state of semi-death?

A: 96 hours.

Q: (L) And then, a ship arrived and took him away, is that correct?

A: Yes. Upon pillar of light.

Q: (L) Is there any special power or advantage in praying in the name of Jesus?

A: Yes.

Q: (L) Well, if he didn't die and release his spirit into the earth plane, how is this power conferred?

A: Prayers go to him.

Q: (L) And what does he do when he hears the prayers?

A: Determines their necessity against background of individual soul development.

Q: (L) You say that when a person prays to Jesus that he makes some sort of a decision, is that correct?

A: Yes.

Q: (L) Well, how can he do that when millions of people are praying to him simultaneously?

A: Soul division.

Q: (L) What do you mean by soul division?

A: Self explanatory.

Q: (L) Do you mean soul division as in cellular meiosis where a cell splits and replicates itself?

A: No.

Q: (L) Does Jesus' soul divide?

A: Yes.

Q: (L) How many times does it divide?

A: Endlessly as a projection of consciousness.

Q: (L) And what happens to this piece of soul that is divided or projected?

A: Is not a piece of a soul.

Q: (L) What is it?

A: It is a replication.

Q: (L) Is each replication exactly identical to the original?

A: Yes. And no.

Q: (L) In what way is the replicated soul different from the original?

A: Not able to give individual attention.

Q: (L) Are any of us able to replicate in this manner if we so desire?

A: Could if in same circumstance. The way the process works is thus: When Jesus left the earth plane, he went into another dimension or density of reality, whereupon all "rules" regarding the awareness of time and space are entirely different from the way they are perceived in your reality. A "Time warp cocoon, if you will. At this point in space time his soul which was/is still in the physical realm, was placed in a state of something akin to suspended animation and a sort of advanced form of unconsciousness. From that point to the present his soul has been replicated from a state of this unconsciousness in order that all who call upon him or need to be with him or need to speak to him can do so on an individual basis. His soul can be replicated ad infinitum--as many times as needed. The replication process produces a state of hyper- consciousness in each and every version of the soul consciousness.

Q: (L) So, you are saying that Jesus is in a state of suspension, voluntarily, in another plane of existence, having chosen to give up his life on this plane in order to continuously generate replications of his **soul pattern** for other people to call upon for assistance? A sort of "template generator"?

A: Yes. Precisely.

Q: (L) If one calls upon him more than once, does one get a double dose?

A: Define.

Q: (L) If one repeatedly calls upon Jesus does one get repeated replications or additional strength, power or whatever?

A: No. Once one has truly made the connection, that's all that's needed.

Q: (L) This is an interesting concept. Has any other soul volunteered to perform this work?

A: Yes. 12 at the present "time".

Q: (L) Can you name any of the others?

✓ A: Buddha. Moses. Shintanhilmoon. Nagaillikiga. Others, varying
degrees. Jesus is the strongest currently.

On the one hand, what the Cassiopaeans were saying about Jesus was "comforting" in that it explained a certain template "availability" that seemed to many to be very real, while at the same time returning the responsibility for soul evolution, or Free Will, to the individual; on the other hand, they were saying clearly and unequivocally that there was NO *crucifixion* upon which "salvation by grace" was predicated!

Was Jesus crucified? Well, it is on this point that millions of people believe that they are "saved". So, it is a pretty big issue! The thing is, the "fruits" of this doctrine tend to demonstrate an exclusionary Us against Them mode of thinking that brings us back to the issue of Free Will - are we choosing because the choice is weighted, or the *only* good choice, or do we actually have *free* will?

As we have already noted, the idea of any "only way a man can be saved" is Nazi Spirituality. Nevertheless, the explanation seemed to be that there certainly was an awesome event of *some* sort that followed a period of mysterious initiation and that this was the event that was later "mythicized" into the Crucifixion story that followed the general lines of all the "suffering savior" religions of history. I didn't know what to think about this.

It was not too long afterward that I came across the following passage in Manly Hall's exhaustive compendium, *The Secret Teachings of All Ages:*

"According to popular conception, Jesus was crucified during the thirty-third year of His life and in the third year of His ministry following his baptism.

About AD 180, St. Irenaeus, Bishop of Lyons, one of the most eminent of the ante-Nicene theologians, wrote *Against Heresies*, an attack on the doctrines of the Gnostics. In this work, Irenaeus declared upon the authority of the Apostles themselves that Jesus lived to old age. To quote:

'They, however, that they may establish their false opinion regarding that which is written, maintain that He preached for one year only, and then suffered in the twelfth month. [In speaking thus], they are forgetful of their own disadvantage, destroying His whole work, and robbing Him of that age which is both more necessary and more honourable than any other, that *more advanced age*, I mean, during which also as a teacher He excelled all others.

For how could He have had His disciples, if He did not teach? And how could He have taught unless He had reached the age of a Master?

For when He came to be baptised, He had not yet completed His thirtieth year, but was beginning to be about thirty years of age; and, *according to these men*, He preached only one year reckoning from His baptism. [*according to these men - heretics*] On completing His thirtieth year He suffered, being in fact still a young man, and who had by no means attained to advanced age.'

Now, that the first stage of early life embraces thirty years, and that this extends onward to the fortieth year, every one will admit; but from the fortieth and fiftieth year a man begins to decline towards *old age*, which Our Lord possessed while He still fulfilled the office of a Teacher, even as the Gospel and all the elders testify; those who were conversant in Asia with John, the disciple of the Lord, affirming that John conveyed to them that information. And He remained among them up to the time of Trajan. Some of them, moreover, saw not only John, but the other apostles also, and heard the very same account from them, and bear testimony as to the validity of the statement.

Whom then should we rather believe? Whether such men as these or Ptolemaeus, who never saw the apostles, and who never even in his dreams attained to the slightest trace of an apostle?"[18]

Well, obviously, this "Gospel" that Irenaeus refers to as testifying that Jesus did not suffer and die has disappeared! But, commenting on the foregoing passage of Irenaeus, theologian Godfrey Higgins remarks that it has fortunately escaped the hands of those destroyers who have attempted to render the Gospel narratives consistent by deleting all such statements. He also notes that the doctrine of the crucifixion was a *vexata questio* among Christians even during the second century.

"The evidence of Irenaeus, " he says, "cannot be touched. On every principle of sound criticism, and of the doctrine of probabilities, it is unimpeachable."[19]

Manly Hall adds these remarks:

"It should further be noted that Irenaeus prepared this statement to contradict another apparently current in his time to the effect that the ministry of Jesus lasted but one year.

Of all the early Fathers, Irenaeus, writing within eighty years after the death of St. John the Evangelist, should have had reasonably accurate information.

If the disciples themselves related that *Jesus lived to advanced age* in the body, why has the mysterious number 33 been arbitrarily chosen to symbolize the duration of his life? Were the incidents in the life of Jesus

---

[18] Manly Hall's *Secret Teachings of All Ages*, op. cit.
[19] *Anacalypsis*, Godfrey Higgins, London, 1836, quoted by Manly P. Hall

purposely altered so that His actions would fit more closely into the pattern established by the numerous Savior-Gods who preceded him?"[20]

Aside from the issues of what the Cassiopaeans had said about Jesus - and this confirmation by no less than one of the early church fathers, St. Irenaeus, here is one of our mysteries, the number 33, making an appearance right in the Bible. But that was only the first of many. Manly Hall discusses the issue of numbers and secret ciphers:

"The use of ciphers has long been recognized as indispensable in military and diplomatic circles, but the modern world has overlooked the important role played by cryptography in literature and philosophy.

If the art of deciphering cryptograms could be made popular, it would result in the discovery of much hitherto unsuspected wisdom possessed by both ancient and medieval philosophers. It would prove that many apparently verbose and rambling authors were wordy for the sake of concealing words.

Ciphers are hidden in the most subtle manner: they may be concealed in the watermark of the paper upon which a book is printed; they may be bound into the covers of ancient books; they may be hidden under imperfect pagination; they may be extracted from the first letters of words or the first words of sentences; they may be artfully concealed in mathematical equations or in apparently unintelligible characters; they may be extracted from the jargon of clowns or revealed by heat as having been written in sympathetic ink; they may be word ciphers, letter ciphers, or apparently ambiguous statements whose meaning could be understood only by repeated careful readings; they may be discovered in the elaborately illuminated initial letters of early books or they may be revealed by a process of counting words or letters.

If those interested in Freemason research would give serious consideration to this subject, they might find in books and manuscripts of the sixteenth and seventeenth centuries the information necessary to bridge the gap in Masonic history that now exists between the Mysteries of the ancient world and the Craft Masonry of the last three centuries.

The arcana of the ancient Mysteries were never revealed to the profane except through the media of symbols. Symbolism fulfilled the dual office of concealing the sacred truths from the uninitiated and revealing them to those qualified to understand the symbols.

Forms are the symbols of formless divine principles; symbolism is the language of Nature. With reverence the wise *pierce the veil* and with clearer vision contemplate the reality; but the ignorant, unable to distinguish between the false and the true, behold a universe of symbols.

---

[20] Hall, 1928, 1988, op. cit.

It may well be said of Nature - the Great Mother - that she is ever tracing strange characters upon the surface of things, but only to her eldest and wisest sons as a reward for their faith and devotion does she reveal the cryptic alphabet, which is the key to the import of these tracings.

...Only recently an intricate cipher of Roger Bacon's has been unraveled, revealing the fact that this early scientist was well versed in the cellular theory. Lecturing before the American Philosophical Society, Dr. William Romaine Newbold, who translated the cipher manuscript of the friar, declared: 'There are drawings which so accurately portray the actual appearance of certain objects that it is difficult to resist the inference that Bacon had seen them with the microscope.

...These are spermatozoa, the body cells and the seminiferous tubes, the ova, with their nuclei distinctly indicated. There are nine large drawings of which one at least bears considerable resemblance to a certain stage of development of a fertilized cell.' [See **Review of Reviews**, July, 1921]

...The most famous of all literal cryptograms is the famous biliteral cipher described by Sir Francis Bacon in his *De Augmentis Scientiarum*. Lord Bacon originated the system while still a young man residing in Paris.

The biliteral cipher requires the use of two styles of type, one an ordinary face and the other specially cut. The differences between the two fonts are in many cases so minute that it requires a powerful magnifying glass to detect them.

...Lord Bacon is believed to have had two Roman alphabets specially prepared in which the differences were so trivial that it is almost impossible for experts to distinguish them.

A careful inspection of the first four "Shakespeare" folios discloses the use throughout the volumes of several styles of type differing in minute but distinguishable details.

It is possible that all the "Shakespeare" folios contain ciphers running through the text. These ciphers may have been added to the original plays, which are much longer in the folios than in the original quartos, full scenes having been added in some instances.

The biliteral cipher was not confined to the writings of Bacon and "Shakespeare", however, but appears in many books published during Lord Bacon's lifetime and for nearly a century after his death. In referring to the biliteral cipher, Lord Bacon terms it *omnia per omnia*. The cipher may run through an entire book and be placed therein at the time of printing *without the knowledge of the original author*, for it does not necessitate the changing of either words or punctuation.

It is possible that this cipher was inserted for political purposes into many documents and volumes published during the seventeenth century. It is well known that ciphers were used for the same reason *as early as the Council of Nicea*.

...Many cryptograms have been produced in which numbers in various sequences are substituted for letters, words, or even complete thoughts.

The reading of numerical ciphers usually depends upon the possession of specially arranged tables of correspondences. The numerical cryptograms of the Old Testament are so complicated that only a few scholars versed in rabbinical lore have ever sought to unravel their mysteries.

...The most simple numerical cipher is that in which the letters of the alphabet are exchanged for numbers in ordinary sequence...

...Authors sometimes based their cryptograms upon the numerical value of their own names; for example, Sir Francis Bacon repeatedly used the cryptic number 33 - the numerical equivalent of his name."[21]

Somewhere along the way I read that all of the manuscripts of the different books of the Bible that were being translated under the patronage of King James, were deposited into the care of Sir Francis Bacon by the many translators involved in the project. Apparently he had them in his possession for a year, but there are no reports as to what he was doing with them. It was suggested that the fact that Jesus went from age 30, when he began his ministry of one year, to the age of 33 at his crucifixion at the end of this one year, was a "signature" of Lord Bacon. It would sure be interesting to have an original copy of the first edition of the King James Version of the Bible to peruse for possible coded information!

Later I came across the suggestion that the "coded signature" of Lord Bacon in the New Testament was evidence that there was a Masonic conspiracy involved in the production of the Jesus myth. Bacon was also thought to have been in on the formation of the Rosicrucians, and others suggested that he had died the "philosopher's death". That is to say that he achieved the "great work" of alchemy which bestows upon its successful students the gift of immortality, and that a log or box of rocks was buried in his place. Supposedly, those who "fake their deaths" in this manner leave some sort of "clue" as to what really happened, and the clue that Lord Bacon had achieved the great work was in the fact that he died from *eating a spoiled rooster* - the rooster being an ancient symbol of alchemy.

After the "funeral", the new Master Alchemist, who now has supernatural powers, takes his place among the order of those who have already "ascended" into this "new state of being", and can thereafter appear and disappear at will to those who are ready to receive deeper instruction, having proved themselves worthy by their labor, will and intent.

---

[21] Hall, Jubilee Edition, *The Secret Teachings of All Ages*,1988

All of this was very interesting to me, and I read and reread books on alchemy, theories about the supposed ciphers encoded in the works of Shakespeare, purported to be a pseudonym for either Lord Bacon himself, or a cabal of alchemists whose project was to preserve their secrets for subsequent generations to decode.

In the meantime, I read many works, both pro and con, about the Masonic "conspiracies" to take over the world and how the number 33 repeatedly appears whenever they have a "hand" in something. It was suggested that even the death of JFK was part of the Masonic plan to rule the world - or, at the very least, control it from behind the scenes - and everywhere I looked there were folks making this or that wild claim or conjecture about the repeated appearance of the number 33.

In the present time we have the claims of David Icke that the death of Princess Diana was a "Masonic Sacrifice", and that all of the members of European nobility are secret Masons, shape-shifting Reptilian beings with bloody appetites.

Meanwhile, the Masons and Shriners build children's hospitals, do good works in general, and there are few people who don't have a Mason or two in the family tree, including yours truly.

Well, with all the confusion, with all the "proofs" going one way and another, it was difficult to sort it all out and decide just "who was on first" here! No sooner would I become convinced that the Masons were the most evil bunch on the planet, with designs on the freedoms of everyone, than I would come across an article or book that claimed exactly the opposite with exactly as much "proof". Somewhere along the way I came across a pamphlet that claimed that the New Testament was written by a "rich and powerful aristocratic Roman family, the Calpunius Pisos", and that all the books therein were written between the years 70 and 140 A.D. This pamphlet claimed that there was an "inner circle" of those who knew this and that the group included "Boccaccio, Bacon AKA Shakespeare, Cervantes, Rabelais, Tolstoy, Milton, Spenser, Tennyson, Thackeray, Kipling, Stevenson, Poe, Oleson, Browning, Noyes, Lewis Carroll, A. Conan Doyle, Verne, Baum, Tolkien, ad infinitum".

I have to admit that their evidence was very compelling! One thing that this pamphlet demonstrated was that the number *22* was the code for "Christos" and the number 19 was the "code" for "Piso". The number 24, by their interpretation, was the code for "Jesus". Whoever these folks were, they were seeing coded messages in everything from steamship ads to Dick Tracy cartoon strips!

Around this point in time, a friend had picked up a book in a used book stall at a flea market and, knowing of my interests in anything that was about ancient mysteries, especially the Flood of Noah, brought the book over to me. It was entitled *Lost Survivors of the Deluge*, by Gerd von Hassler and translated from the German by Martin Ebon. You sure wouldn't expect to find anything about Jesus in there, now would you? But, we need to remember the reputed remark of Jesus that the "end of the age" would be "as in the days of Noah", so somehow; the two things were intertwined in my mind. As I was just reading along, I came to the following passage and the hair on my head began to stand on end:

"In the Bible it says: 'And it came to pass, when men began to multiply on the face of the earth, and daughters were born unto them, that the Sons of God saw the daughters of men that they were fair; and they took them wives of all which they chose. And the Lord said, My spirit shall not always strive with man, for that he also is flesh: yet his days shall be but a hundred and twenty years. With this Divine dictum, the golden times, when gods and their direct offspring lived to be 900 years old, and more, came to an end.'

For hundreds of years, these lines have troubled religious scholars, because direct and literal translations specifically yields the term 'Sons of God', as pursuing human maidens. Accordingly, some 2,000 years were devoted to many an inspired and convoluted explanation, in order to come to terms with a notion that fits neither the concepts of the Bible, nor that of a heavenly Divine Creator, but had to be given an appropriate interpretation."

"This is a fact [since the Deluge] we have lost godlike Near-Immortality and all the efforts to intensify the quality of the divine blood through incest - as both the Inca Emperors and the Pharaohs attempted - had to fail. [...] The Divine Blood had been diluted. But God had desired the equality of the divine with the human. The Bible tells us:

And God said, let us make man in our image, after our likeness...

'Let us make man in our image' is but one of the somewhat dictatorial decisions of democratic majorities within a family of gods, to be found in all the world's myths.

This brings us to the crucial question. It is, indeed, so vital and controversial that St. Boniface, when he presented it to the Frisians during his missionary journey on June 5, 754, was put to death by the sword! Today, we may ask such a question without facing the sword; it is: Just what is the name of the God-Creator? What is the name of the god who governed the earth even before the Deluge; this God of Gods, rightly called Father of the Gods, and thus Father of all Mankind?

To put it even more simply: If a highly developed civilization existed more than 10,000 year ago, governing the world's then populated regions, and if the God-King was able to aid his contemporaries in surviving the Deluge catastrophe, surely the name of this ruler must have been handed down to later generations of survivors; who was he?

We know from the *Epic of Gilgamesh*, of the horrible Enlil, who was responsible for the Deluge. The other gods did not think highly of him, but feared him a good deal. His influence never extended beyond Mesopotamia.

His antagonist, Shamash, the Sun God, enjoyed greater prestige. He remains, notably in Asia even today, a figure of magical power, the epitome of the shaman.

But even the early Egyptians called their Sun God by a different name, Ra. This need not mean much, because Plato tells us that the Egyptians had even then developed a unique and high level of civilization hostile toward the unknown earlier culture.

The Egyptian term 'Ra' was integrated into the language of early Peru, where we encounter the annual sun festival Rami or Raymi. But this adaptation undoubtedly dates back only to the period following the Deluge, as does the word 'Wotan'.

This enables us to draw a firm dividing line: we are able to eliminate all gods who emerged from the post-Deluge civilizations as creators of cultures, builders of cities, magicians or agronomists.

The ONE God for whom we search has to be the father - or even ancestor - of this post-Deluge generation of gods.

Just as Tuisto, father of Mannus, was the ancestor of Germanic culture.

Tuisto? Can that be accurate? Or did Tacitus fail to understand the name correctly?

The curious linking of the darkest and lightest vowel in our language brings back a curious association.

Of course! It is Tiu, the god whom the early Germans recalled when they made up the calendar and named one day of the week after him: Tuesday. Otherwise he has been overshadowed by the ever-present Wotan-Odin, as the highest Ruler of the Heavens.

This replacement took place, at the latest, during the *Volkerwanderung*, the Great Migration that caused a gigantic upheaval of populations on the Eurasian land mass. We may even assume that, just because Tiu (or Ziu) was removed heavenward, the very vigorous Wotan managed to take his place in human imagination and thought. It was a fate that Wotan experienced himself later on, when missionaries cut down the very oaks that had been dedicated to his divine presence.

Tiu-Ziu was just as much one of the Aesir as Wotan had been. And the Aesir had even managed to infiltrate the antagonist worlds of Egypt and Mesopotamia, representing the sun and divine wisdom. [...]

I do think, however, that our search for the original name of the primal Creator-God should not get bogged down in such minute details. The survivors of the Deluge of whom we learn from the Bible and the earlier Gilgamesh Epic and other traditions, were themselves survivors of the earlier world of gods. [...]

Over thousands of years, they passed on a handful of names. No doubt, precisely how much and what one name or another had originally meant may simply have been forgotten over the long, long years.

If we concentrate on the godlike of God Ziu, we discover the following points:

▶ *Zius* was the highest god of northern Europe

▶ As *Zeus*, he was the highest god of ancient Greece

▶ As *Jupiter* (Iu-Pitar = Tius-Pater) he was the Father God of ancient Rome

▶ As *Deus* (from which we derive 'Deity') he was the basic concept of the heavenly, the only Deity in the Latin liturgy of the Church, and the God in all Romance languages, (as well as in the word 'theology')

▶ As *Ometeotle* (again, 'theology' is closely related) he was the highest god of the Mayan culture.

▶ As *Cinteotl* and God of Corn he is equivalent to *Quetzalcoatl*, the WHITE GOD

▶ As *TONATIUH*, he was the Sun God, who provided the Aztecs with a sort of Valhalla for their war dead.

▶ As *Xiuhtecutli*, he was the Fire God of ancient Mexico.

▶ As *Tirawa-Atius*, the highest divinity of the Pawnee, he was credited with populating the world with 'giants'.

▶ As *Tieholtsodi*, the monster who caused the Deluge and ruled all waters, he exists in the traditions of the Navajos

▶ As *Szeu-kha*, he is the son of the Creator-God whom the Pima Indians knew as floating above the Deluge

▶ As the falcon *Tiuh-Tiuh* of the Guatemaltec Indians he mixed the blood of a snake with that of a tapir, kneaded it with corn-flour and 'thus created the flesh of man'. This tribe says that it came from *Tulan*, the Place of the Sun, *across the sea.*

All of this narrows down to one conclusion - which nevertheless is not definitive - and that is: our old Tuesday God, *Tiu*, was a divine Ruler-God in primeval times and his name imprinted itself so deeply into human memory that it has survived thousands upon thousands of years."[22]

What was the name the Cassiopaeans gave to the real man behind the Jesus myth?

Tonatha.

✳ Amazingly similar to Tonatiuh.

At the very moment that I encountered this little clue, I was contemplating the evidence as to whether or not alchemists were able to actually achieve the "Great Work" and "immortality" and how this might relate to Jesus. And so, the question that emerged from that study was whether or not the Cassiopaeans had given us a clue - in this alleged "real name" of Jesus - to an actual Sect that had members who might be thousands of years old. Now that I had found this strange collection of the "names of god", I began to wonder if, by giving us this name, the Cassiopaeans were telling us that such an *immortal* was the actual biological father of Jesus?

What this amounted to was an interesting thread relating to the "bloodline" of Jesus. Where will it ultimately lead? Who and what was this "Tonatha" who bears one of the oldest names of God?

Let me point out that this particular bit of information from the Cassiopaeans - this name, of which we were completely ignorant at the time - later connected to information that went back into the mists before recorded history. Yes, it is true that this was information that was known in some circles before we received it, (or Von Hassler wouldn't have been writing about it), but it was definitely *unknown to us* in any way.

Does this prove that the Cassiopaeans are actually who and what they say they are?

No. But, if nothing else, it demonstrates a "connection" to SOME source, even if only the universal consciousness or "akashic records".

Meanwhile, we were given some clues in another direction that ended up connecting to all of this in a bizarre way, so we have to pause and go in another direction for a moment. (I warned you this was going to be complicated!)

I first heard about Oak Island when I was just a kid. My grandfather subscribed to several magazines, one of which (I think it was "*Argosy*") published an article on the "Oak Island Mystery". I was completely fascinated by this account and it stayed in the back of my mind for many years.

---

[22] Von Hassler, 1976]

After the Cassiopaeans came along, as I have described before, I was like a kid in a candy store. It was fun to go through my many books and just ask question after question about all the things that were mysterious in our world. In a sense, it was a sort of "test" just to see *what* they would say about these things, and I had no particular attachment to their remarks because, in many cases, there was no way to validate them. In terms of "Mysteries", one theory was about as good as another. I was initially just curious to get a *lot* of material to analyze later, so I was jumping through things in a quick and haphazard way. I didn't know what an editing headache I was creating for myself. Heck, I had no idea what an impact the Cassiopaeans were going to have on my life! We didn't even record the first half dozen or so sessions because we didn't think it was that important!

But, before we get to the Cassiopaean comments on the Oak Island Mystery, I believe it would be useful to briefly recapitulate what is presently known about it.

The Oak Island Mystery

Oak Island is situated off the coast of Nova Scotia, and it is thought that the name of the island relates to the many oak trees that formerly dotted the small speck of land. There are a couple of residents who have built homes there, and in recent times, a causeway was built which effectively makes it no longer an island, but a peninsula.

As is the case with other "Legends", there are a number of *apocalyptic* [23]versions of the "discovery" on Oak Island.

One version of the story tells us that, in 1795, a few young lads rowed over to the island to explore as part of an "adventure game" or on a dare. They were attracted to the "mystery" of the island because it was claimed by the local Indians to be haunted due to the fact that strange lights had reportedly been seen there.

Knowing how such stories get told and retold, it is likely that the island was considered to be haunted by the locals, and dangerously so. A Chester woman whose mother had been one of the earliest settlers reported that once when the fires and lights had been observed, a boatload of men who had gone to investigate had disappeared without a trace. This is quite similar to urban myths of today.

---

[23] There is no record of the pit on Oak Island before a newspaper article in 1862, and the stone with the indecipherable inscriptions, allegedly discovered in the pit in 1804, and then lost, does not appear in any work until 1970.

Whatever version of the story is told, the names of the three boys were Daniel McGinnis, John Smith, and Anthony Vaughn. As to what the boys "discovered", again there are some variations. It was a large oak tree with either a "large ship's pulley" hanging from an overhanging branch, or the "burn marks" on the branch that looked as though a heavy load had been suspended from a rope at that point. Details about the vegetation either being cleared away, or new growth in an area under and around the tree occur in different versions.

The boys apparently decided that they had discovered where pirates had buried treasure, so they went off to fetch digging tools to recover whatever must be buried there. They dug a circular shaft 13 feet in diameter and, according to the basic story found strange things - barriers - at various levels: at 4 feet, flagstones; at 10 feet, a platform of solid oak; at 20 feet another oak platform, and at 30 feet, still another oak platform.

Obviously, three boys weren't going to dig that much. Apparently, after the initial discoveries that something mysterious was indeed indicated, they had sought help from some men of the community. But it was all in vain because the hole suddenly filled with water just at the point when they thought they were going to get to the treasure. Nine years went by. In 1804, Simeon Lynds formed a "treasure hunting syndicate and digging resumed. At 40 feet, another layer of Oak covered with putty was found. Then there was a layer of charcoal. At 50 feet there was another oak platform sealed with coconut fiber. At 60, 70 and 80 feet, oak platforms; at 90 feet, a flat stone was reportedly found that measured 3 x 1 feet. The stone was said to not be native to the areas and had "strange markings" on it.

The story about the stone is rather confusing. It was said to have been installed at the back of a fireplace for a number of years. It was later "recovered" and exhibited to raise money for more digging. A Professor of languages claimed to have "cracked the code" and translated the markings to say "10 feet below, 2 million pounds". Someone else who saw the stone in the early years of this century remembered that when he saw it, there were no "strange markings". It seems to have disappeared.

At 98 feet, water began to pour in, apparently channeled to the pit through a series of stone-lined, coconut fiber filled conduits that act as "wicks". In 1849, a new syndicate was formed that bored 5 holes. They found that at the 98-foot level, there was a spruce platform 5 inches thick. This was followed by a 12-inch space, then 4 inches of oak, and then 22 inches of drilling brought up bits of metal. Also retrieved were 3 metal links of a chain.

Following that event, which excited the drillers because it was claimed that the chain was gold and "looked ancient", (though I have never read an account by anyone who had actually SEEN it - it was always hearsay), the drillers kept going and encountered 8 inches of oak, another 22 inches of metal; 4 inches of oak; 6 inches of spruce; then 7 feet of clay and nothing else. At one point, it was reported that a James Pitblado found and pocketed something off the drill, but there is no firm idea as to whether this really happened, and if so, what the item was.

In 1859, another attempt was made. This was when the conduits were discovered that repeatedly filled the pit with water. The discovery of the flood tunnels convinced this horde of idiots that there was a fabulous treasure. They reasoned that it was inconceivable that anyone would go to that much trouble to conceal ordinary treasure! Of course, the more logical reason would be to think that it was never meant to be dug up and therefore, could NOT be treasure!

In 1865, still another attempt. This gang tunneled beside the original shaft, into it sideways, built a dam against the water, and so forth. Failure.

In 1894, a new gang dynamited the flood tunnel! They lowered a pipe into the pit and at 126 feet, they struck iron. They drilled past the obstruction and, at 151 feet, hit *cement*! Drilling further, after 2 more inches, they encountered 5 inches of oak and then "large metal objects", then "loose metal", and then more "large metal objects".

Sounds to me like there was some kind of big machine buried down there and they were just tearing it apart with their drills! There were attempts in 1931, and in 1963, a hole 80 feet wide and 130 feet deep was dug. Nothing.

In the 1990s, a submarine TV camera revealed what *looked like* three chests and a severed hand. Divers were lowered to a depth of 235 feet, but found nothing. A good question to ask here is: what would a severed hand be doing down there? The bodies of the several people who have died during the 200 years of attempts to excavate this pit were all completely recovered. In any event, the lighting of the film was bad; there was nothing to provide scale. What was seen as a "chest" could have been a piece of wood a few inches square. The only thing this film did was more or less prove that there *was* a pit of some kind, but whether or not it existed prior to all the digging, it's hard to say.

Now, what seems to me to be the obvious questions are: why would someone who buries a "treasure" leave such things as a "marker stone", or a depression in the ground, marks on a tree, and other obvious signs of concealing said treasure? Doesn't make a lot of sense, does it?

All the stories, legends, assumptions, beliefs and "wishful thinking" have been generated by treasure hunters who have an agenda: to get money to dig to get more money! Then, there are the folks who have linked this mystery to the Legends of the Holy Grail, the Ark of the Covenant, and so on. There are no artifacts in existence that have been validated reliably, and the site itself has been so obliterated by greed that no self-respecting archaeologist would even dream of attempting to sort out the mess!

With all the books and articles and supposed investigations, there is a dark shadow of greed and avarice hiding the facts of the matter. We can wishfully think all we want, but that doesn't make a story true - as it is told, that is. And that is the crux of the matter. Where there is smoke, there is likely to be some fire, even if only a little! And, there are real questions about Oak Island that beg answers.

The first question is, naturally, was there ever a mystery to begin with? Since there exists no "hard evidence" of a pit on Oak Island before a newspaper article in 1862, can we rely on this first reportage as being even remotely accurate? One assumes, of course, that there was some sort of evidence to justify the article, and that it was checked.

If the initial discovery took place in 1795, that means 67 years had passed before the telling. As we review the story, we see that an awful lot of effort was claimed to have been exerted during that 67 years.

In considering the story about the boys who made the discovery, 67 years is not too long for there to be people with living memory of the events able to tell about it, so we can't discard it on that account.

A major effort was claimed to have been undertaken in 1859, three years before the subject was publicized, and it seems that the 1865 and 1894 efforts would not have been attempted if there was not some evidence "on the ground", so to say, that something was there.

Thus it seems that, based on this last consideration, that there is a good probability that there is something to the story. So, let's move on to the next questions.

IF there was an original pit, as described, who dug it? Who had the capabilities to dig it? Was it a storage chamber? If so, *what* was stored in it? If it was not a storage chamber, what other explanations can there be for the apparent original disturbance of the landscape? How, at this late date, would it be possible to sort through all the lies and confusion?

How do we explain the burn marks/pulley on the tree and the cannon shot reportedly found during the original dig? Is this evidence of pirates and treasure? Or an ammo dump? But, if it was that, why go to such extreme measures to make the materials almost impossible to access in a rapid manner? That doesn't make sense. And, if it was a practical joke perpetrated by some young boys, it is certainly one of the most elaborate and long lived pranks in history!

We find ourselves in the presence of a very great mystery that has defied two hundred years of brawn and brain to solve! Now, with so great a host of words already spent on the subject, notwithstanding that the mystery has never been solved in any concrete and verifiable way, what more could I add to the matter without further muddying the waters?

I can only add the Cassiopaean commentary, and many things that were learned as a result of these clues.

The first time we discussed the Oak Island mystery with the Cassiopaeans, it actually was a sort of afterthought question to a somewhat similar mystery. I had just read an account in an old *Fate* magazine that goes as follows:

> "Hidden deep within a Czech mountain is an ancient shaft and tower seemingly built by advanced technology but older than the bones of extinct beasts..."

The author, Antonin T. Horak, wrote down the cave exploration adventure of a member of the Czech resistance, which occurred in October of 1944, during WWII. Mr. Horak stated that the account was confirmed by friends of his in Czechoslovakia in 1965. The story was first printed in the March 1965 issue of *National Speleological Society* in an attempt to interest other speleologists in mounting an expedition. The captain of the Slovak Resistance who told the story for the speleology magazine, was apparently hidden in this cave, along with a companion who was wounded, by a farmer near the villages of Plavince and Lubocna at 49.2 N 20.7 degrees E. The farmer's name was Slavek.

> "Slavek moved rocks in the cranny and opened a low cleft, the entrance to this roomy grotto. Placing Martin (the wounded companion) in a niche, we were astonished to see Slavek become ceremonious: he crossed himself, each of us, the grotto, and with a deep bow, its back wall where a hole came to my attention. ...Slavek begged me not to go further into his cave. ...He told me that only once, with his father and grandfather, had he been in this cave; that it was a huge maze, full of pits which they never wanted to fathom, pockets of poisonous air and 'certainly haunted'."

Well, needless to say, our captain was very curious and decided to investigate the cave that could make an illiterate farmer/shepherd so superstitious.

"I started my cave tour with rifle, lantern, torches, pick. After a not too devious nor dangerous walk and some squeezings, always taking the easiest and marking side passages,

I came, after about one and one-half hours into a long level passage, and at is end a barrel sized hole. Crawling through and still kneeling, I froze in amazement. There stood something like a large, black silo, framed in white. ...

I thought that this is a bizarre natural wall or curtain of black salt, or ice, or lava. But I became perplexed, then awestruck, when I saw that it was a seemingly manmade structure which reaches into the rocks on all sides.

Beautifully, cylindrically curved, it indicated a huge body with a diameter of about 25 meters. Where this structure and the rocks meet, large stalagmites and stalactites formed that glittering white frame.

The wall is uniformly blue-blackish; its material seems to combine properties of steel, flint, and rubber. The pick made no marks and bounced off vigorously.

Even the thought of a tower-sized artifact embedded in rock in the middle of an obscure mountain, in a wild region where not even legend knows about ruins or mining industry, overgrown with age-old cave deposits, is bewildering. The fact is appalling.

Not immediately discernible, a crack in the wall appears from below about 20 to 25 cm wide, tapers off and disappears into the cave's ceiling two to five cm wide. Its insides, right and left, are pitch black and have fist-sized, sharp valleys and crests. The crack's bottom is a rather smooth trough of yellow sandstone and drops very steeply into the wall.

I threw a lighted torch through; it fell and extinguished with loud cracklings and hissings as if a white-hot ploughshare were dropped into a bucket. Driven to explore and believing myself thin enough to get through this upside down keyhole, I went in."

He got stuck and had to get himself unstuck, and so he gave up and went back to his companion.

Returning on Oct. 24, 1944... (The notes are from a journal) the Captain tried to get through again. He took off all his clothes and covered himself with "sheep fat" and managed, after some difficulty, to get inside the tower. He found himself in a curved black shaft.

The Captain had come with plenty of lights - torches, lanterns etc. - and said that all the light together did not reach the ceiling. According to the journal, he leaves and comes back the next day, smears himself with sheep fat again, and goes back through the crack.

At this visit, the Captain started shooting his gun upward which nearly blew his eardrums out because of the acoustics, but he didn't hear an impact. Then, he fired at the walls themselves, somewhat above, and noted blue-green sparks and dancing flames. He started digging in the floor and found *fossilized* animal teeth.

Returning again, on October 26, the Captain took a pole to make the lantern go higher, but still was not able to see the ceiling. At this point, his companion died, and he was free to rejoin his unit and that was the end of the story.

Needless to say, this tidbit about an artificial structure made out of unknown material, that was so old a mountain had "grown" around it really piqued my curiosity. Who or *what* in the world, could be responsible for such a thing? So, I asked:

> Q: (L) In one of my *Fate* magazines over there I read a story about a fellow who discovered an enormous structure in a cave when he was hiding there during WW II. A shaft in the Tatra Mountains in Czechoslovakia. What was this thing this man found in this cave?
>
> A: Magnesium wall made by Lizard beings. Constructed 309448 years ago. It was part of a base. It was buried during cataclysms.

Well, that answered that! Couldn't be verified, for sure, but, the word "buried" triggered a thought about my recent reading about Oak Island, so why not just settle this whole Oak Island thing at once!? I didn't have to believe what the C's said about it, but since nobody else really had a good explanation, another one wouldn't hurt! I didn't know that I was getting ready to open a can of worms!

> Q: (L) What is buried on Oak Island?
>
> A: Regenerator.
>
> Q: (L) What is a regenerator?
>
> A: Remolecularizer.
>
> Q: (L) Who put it there?
>
> A: Lizard beings.
>
> Q: (L) When did they put it there?
>
> A: 10,000 years ago, approximately.
>
> Q: (L) Do they use it from time to time?
>
> A: No. [We didn't ask if anyone ELSE used it!]
>
> Q: (L) Does it still work?
>
> A: It could.
>
> Q: (T) What is the purpose of a remolecularizer?
>
> A: Regenerate matter.

Q: (L) Such as physical bodies?

A: Yes.

Q: (L) So, you just go and stand next to it or inside it or whatever and it regenerates you?

A: Any matter.

Q: (L) Well, that would be a really handy thing to have in the barn. Is there any way to get it out of there?

A: Maybe. Are you planning an expedition?

Q: (L) No, we're just being nosy. How deep is it buried?

A: Deep.

Q: (T) Well, we can send it in to a treasure hunter's magazine and give somebody an idea of how far they have to go. (L) Yeah, tell them what it is and they will go whole hog for it. (T) Yeah. It's a regenerator. "What?" Well, it's a remolecularizer. What's wrong with you? Where have you been? You never wanted to be regenerated? You, too, can be a Time Lord! (L) Amaze your friends, confound your enemies, you can hypnotize any woman from a distance by the power of your... [Chorus] *regenerator*! (T) Wow! Look at the size of his Regenerator! [Much laughter] Thank you.

A: Good Night.

As you can see, it was late and we were all getting a little silly. Little did we know that this was going to get serious!

A few months later, I was reading over the above text and decided I wanted to ask a bit more about it. The C's had already talked about <u>Transdimensional Atomic Remolecularization</u> as the mode of time travel as well as the technology used for moving between densities and dimensions. They had mentioned that "remolecularization" was the mode of assembly of 3rd density matter from 4th density and higher "thought" transduced via the effects of supernovae, so, I just assumed that TDARM was also what was buried at Oak Island:

Q: (L) When I was reading our little bit about Oak Island the other day, I noticed that we never followed up on certain things. Could we ask on that now?

A: Yes.

Q: (L) Okay, you said at that time that a Transdimensional Atomic Remolecularizer was buried at Oak Island. Is that correct?

A: Yes. [So, my assumption was on target.]

Q: (L) Who buried it there?

A: Learn. [Note that they had previously answered that the Lizard Beings did, but now were suggesting that there was more to this issue than met the eye.]

Q: (L) Well, we are getting ready to learn because you are going to teach us, is that correct?

A: You already have tools.

Q: (L) What do you mean we already have tools?

A: We are trying to teach you to use your most precious commodity.

Q: (L) And that is, of course, our minds?

A: You betcha!

We were, for the first time, facing questions that we had to investigate on our own. As time has gone by, I have learned that this type of question - ones that we have to figure out - seem to be related to our "destined" mission. That may be only my own assumption and may have no basis in fact, but as the clues begin to fit together, the reader can make his or her own assessment.

I did some more reading on the subject of Oak Island in order to discover there was any way that what the Cassiopaeans were saying could be true. The more I read from different sources, the more confused I got. There were lies, manipulations, corruption of information and artifacts, and evidence of incredible greed on all sides of this story. Seems that everybody who had anything to do with it was *sure* that there was a ton of money buried there and they would do about anything to be the one to dig it up. The result was a complete *mess*. I decided that I was *never* going to make any sense out of this Oak Island business!

Q: (L) Okay. What I read about Oak Island was that there were legends of lights being seen there prior to 1703. [Remember that 1795 is when the boys rowed to the island and discovered the rope marks on the sawed off tree limb and the depression in the ground.]

A: Yes.

Q: (L) Prior to 1703 would put the burial of whatever is there at least prior to that time. Were those lights that were seen and reported by the local natives, the lights of craft of other beings other than the humans of this planet?

A: Electromagnetic profile.

Q: (L) The thing that was noticed when the kids who discovered the pit first visited the Island in 1795, was that a limb was sawed off of a tree over the depression and there were marks of a rope as though pulleys had been utilized. (T) If someone more advanced than humans dug the pit, they wouldn't have used chain hoists and pulleys. (L) That is what I am getting at. So, if there was evidence of this kind of stuff on the tree, it would seem to indicate that somebody had been doing something there who was a little more human or limited in their technology, is that correct?

A: Yes.

Q: (L) At the same time, my thought is that, it is beyond human technology to have *produced that pit at that point in history*. That's pretty evident from the diagrams of the structure.

A: Beyond *known* technology.

Q: (L) And yet humans may have been involved in digging something up from the evidence of the pulley activity.

A: Bingo. Some humans have always communed with "higher" powers. We are speaking of conscious communion in this and other instances.

Q: (L) Okay, there was conscious communion between humans and other powers in the building of this pit. What group of humans was this?

A: It's fun learn.

Q: (J) How about pirates?

A: No.

Q: (L) Indians?

A: Keep going, network.

Q: (L) There were the French and the English. How about the Vikings? (F) No, the Vikings were 600 years before that. (T) Well, we don't know how long ago the apparent pit was dug. (L) When was the pit dug that relates directly to the rope burns on the tree?

A: 1500s. Nationality is not issue.

Q: (T) Well, this remolecularizer was dug up sometime in the middle of the 1500s. Somebody was told to dig there by higher powers.

A: Access sect information.

Q: (L) So, it could have been a religious group.

A: Now, who claimed communion, Laura has in memory banks from absorption of mass reading practice.

I had to admit that I was drawing a blank. I just couldn't think of any "sect" that was wandering around in North America in the 1500's that would have that kind of "conscious communion" with higher powers. Notice that the term "higher powers" was placed in quotes by the C's, and they also said originally that the device was buried by "Lizard beings". The same origin was given for the magnesium wall in Europe. My suggestion that humans may have been involved in digging something up from the pit was met with an affirmative answer, and it was this group that we were now discussing, not necessarily the group that buried the thing.

The question then is: are we looking for a group claiming communion that are wearing white hats, or black hats? Was the item buried by Lizard beings after being stolen? Or did it belong to them? It seemed to me that there was a clear distinction between those who buried something on Oak Island and those who were digging there in the 1500s. Or maybe not.

Q: (F) Was there a sect from that era that claimed communion?

A: Yes.

Q: [At this point I was really shooting in the dark.] (L) Maybe it had something to do with the people that later became known as the Cajuns, a French religious sect that was living there... Acadians is what they were... and they called the area Acadia... Was it the Cajuns?[24]

A: Maybe.[25]

Q: (L) Now, this article says that it would have taken a hundred men working every day for six months to dig this pit...

A: No.

Q: (L) The article also says that it must have been dug in 1780... [This article did not take into account the reports of strange lights on the island prior to 1703.]

A: No.

Q: (L) When they drilled into the pit, some bits of gold came up and a piece of parchment and maybe some other odds and ends. What were these?

A: Alchemy.

With this answer, the C's gave us the most important clue to many great mysteries, though we didn't know it at the time. Whatever had been hidden there had something to do with alchemy, and if that was the case, did it mean that it had been stolen and concealed by "Lizard beings" and their cohorts, or did it belong to them in the first place? My guess was that if it belonged to them, there would be no need for them to hide it so thoroughly. The only reason I could think of for such actions was that whatever it was, it was something that they could not use - or destroy - for some reason, but wanted to prevent anyone else from using it.

Q: (L) If these people were involved in doing this, why did they do it?

A: Instructed to do it.

---

[24] Meaning, of course, the French settlers who later became the Cajuns.
[25] Now, we know that "maybe" is only a "you're getting warm but still off the mark" hint.

Q: (L) They were instructed by the higher powers they were in contact with, correct?

A: Yes.

Q: (L) What did they intend to do with it? Did someone intend to come back for it at some point in time?

A: No.

Now, the most *obvious* question of all was *not* asked: If it had been buried there by Lizzies 10,000 years ago, and these guys were instructed about it, and dug it up, and then reburied it, *what* did they dig it up to *do* with it in the 1500's? Or, did they fail to dig it up at all?

Q: (T) Is it buried there in that location for a specific reason?

A: Sure.

Q: (T) Does the location itself have something to do with the purpose of it?

A: Magnetic.

Q: (T) Are there other ones buried on the planet?

A: Yes.

Q: (T) Are they aligned to each other on the planet in some kind of geometric pattern?

A: Maybe.

Q: (T) Do they all work together?

A: Maybe.

Q: (J) Can you tell us where some of the other ones are?

A: Use mind. That is what it is there for.

Q: (T) We are using our minds. And, we are talking to you about this. We are friendly.

A: Shortcut city.

Q: (T) Yeah! That's what it is all about. We are still third density! If we use...

A: It's not nice to fool Mother Cassiopaea!

Q: [Laughter] (T) If we were to follow the coordinates where this thing is buried, would it lead us to others?

A: Try it and see.

Q: (L) Okay. I want to get back to the function of this thing. You say it is buried not to be dug up. It is actually buried to stay there? Is that correct?

A: Yes.

Q: (L) Then that explains a lot of things about the way it was buried. There was supposedly found, at a certain level, a rock with carving on it. It was destroyed through carelessness. I am curious as to what this said. Can you access this and tell us what it said?

A: Measure marker.

Q: (J) Could it be possible that this device was somehow related to the crystal pyramid of Atlantis?

A: In a small sense.

Q: (J) Did the pyramid have anything to do with powering this device?

A: Yes.

Q: (L) Is this device continuously operational?

A: No.

Q: (L) What stimulates it to go into operation? That is, assuming it does.

A: Magnetic anomalies.

Q: (J) Is it affected by earthquakes?

A: Can be.

Q: (L) Are these magnetic anomalies ones that occur naturally on the planet?

A: Both.

Q: (L) So, they can occur naturally on the planet or they can be generated or stimulated by some other source?

A: Yes.

Q: (J) Is this device a doorway for entry into this dimension?

A: Can be used as such.

Q: (T) Is it a stand-alone machine or is it to be used in conjunction with others?

A: Either.

Q: (T) Are they positioned in such a way if something small happens only a couple of them kick in, but if something large happens, as many as necessary?

A: Okay.

Q: (L) Who owns it? Who built it?

A: Answer for yourself, and enough, already on this subject!!!!

Q: (J) I think I just heard a door slam!

Well, aside from the fact that I was asking a dumb question, considering that they had already told us that the Reptoids had built it and put it there originally, I guess you can see from our attempts to begin to learn to think - to *really* think - that it was a definite struggle. Working to get rid of assumptions and allow the creative thinking process to flow was a lot of *work*. But, not nearly as much work as I had ahead of me based on just a few clues.

In the end, the clues about "sect", "Acadia" and "alchemy", and the time period of the 1500's that had been given were all I had to go on. So I hit the books again. I realized that just the normally available resources were not going to get me where I wanted to go, so I began to look for links to alchemy, and links to links. I made lists of names and dates and obscure references and began to follow them. There was a *lot* of material.

I obtained obscure alchemical texts full of strange coded messages and bizarre pictures that were supposed to "reveal" something to those who had the insight to understand. It apparently wasn't me, and I struggled day after day to try to divine some meaning from these lunatic descriptions of experiments with sexual overtones, most of which proclaimed at the beginning that the truth was going to be given plainly!

Nowadays, our materialistic science derides alchemists as misguided mystics who followed a dream of discovering a substance that could transform base metals into gold. Yes, they admit that much scientific discovery was accomplished in these pursuits, but they toss out the objective of the alchemists as just a pipe dream.

Nevertheless, there are interesting stories there, some so deeply curious that the mind cannot grapple with the implications, and they are immediately discarded as too fantastic for serious consideration. I want to recount a few of them here so that the reader who is not familiar with the literature might be sufficiently intrigued to do research on his/her own.

But first, a short discussion of the "Philosopher's Stone". This is the goal of the Alchemist; a fabled substance that can not only transmute metals into gold, but can heal any illness, banish all sickness from a person's life, and confer an extended lifespan, if not immortality, on the body. At least, that is how it is described. That may or may not be a "cover story". The stories of the "philosopher's stone" may, in fact, describe the 4th density state of existence.

It was thought that, by a lengthy process of purification, one could extract from various *minerals* the "natural principle" that supposedly caused gold to "grow" in the earth. In an anonymous 17th Century alchemical text, The *Sophic Hydrolith*, this process is described as "purging [the mineral] of all that is thick, nebulous, opaque and dark", and what would be left would be a mercurial "water of the Sun", which had a pleasant, penetrating odor, and was very volatile.

Part of this liquid is put aside, and the rest is then mixed with a twelfth of its weight of "the *divinely endowed body of gold*", (ordinary gold won't do because it is defiled by daily use). This mixture then forms a solid amalgam, which is heated for a week. It is then dissolved in some of the mercurial water in an egg-shaped phial. Then, the remaining mercurial water is added gradually, in seven portions; the phial is sealed, and kept at such a temperature as will hatch an egg.

After 40 days, the phial's contents will be black; after seven more days, small grainy bodies like fish eyes are supposed to appear. Then 'the "Philosopher's Stone" begins to make its appearance: first reddish in color; then white, green and yellow like a peacock's tail then dazzling white; and later a deep glowing red. Finally, "the revivified body is quickened, perfected and glorified" and appears in a beautiful purple.

This and many similarly obscure and crazy sounding texts are the bulk of Alchemical Literature. But, we have to remember one thing: these texts were written in CODE: the code of the Sybils.

> "In order to respect the principle of hermetism adopted by the Tradition, we must understand that esoteric teachings are given in a sibylline form.
>
> St Isaac the Syrian points out that: The Holy Scriptures say many things by using words in a different sense from their original meaning. Sometimes bodily attributes are applied to the soul, and conversely, attributes of the soul are applied to the body. The Scriptures do not make any distinction here. However, enlightened men understand."

And:

> "By invigorating the Organs the Soul uses for communicating with exterior objects, the Soul must a acquire greater powers not only for conception but also for retention, and therefore if we wish to obtain still more knowledge, the organs and secret springs of physical life must be wonderfully strengthened and invigorated.
>
> The Soul must acquire new powers for conceiving and retaining..."

It seems rather clear to me that these instructions had absolutely nothing to do with anything *outside* of the body! But, what they did actually describe, I hadn't a clue.

Nevertheless, I persisted in reading many texts of this kind and searching for clues there and in the stories of the alchemists themselves. It was in reading the anecdotes about so-called Alchemists that I became convinced that there was, indeed, something very mysterious going on here. For example: In 1666, Johann Friedrich Schweitzer, physician to the Prince of Orange, writes of having been visited by a stranger who was

> "...of a mean stature, a little long face, with a few small pock holes, and most black hair, not at all curled, a beardless chin, about three or four and forty years of age (as I guessed), and born in North Holland."

Before I finish the story, it needs to be pointed out that Dr. Schweitzer, who was the author of several medical and botanical books, was a careful and objective observer and was a colleague of the philosopher, Baruch Spinoza. Schweitzer was a trained scientific observer, a reputable medical man, and not given to fraud or practical jokes. And yet, what I am about to describe is, in modern understanding, impossible. In fact, it was his accomplishments that "attracted" the strange man, or so the manuscript says:

> "After salutations ended, this new Guest, with great Reverence, asked, whether he might have freedom to come to me; because for the Pyrotechnick Art sake, he could not, nor was he willing to pass by the Door of my house; adding, that he had not only thought to have made use of some Friend to come to me, but had also read some of my little Treatises, especially that, which I published, against D. Digbies Sympathetick Powder, in which I discovered my doubt of the true Philosophick Mystery.
>
> Therefore, this occasion being taken, he asked me, whether I could believe, that place was given to such a Mystery in the things of Nature, by the benefit of which a Physician might be able to cure all Diseases universally, unless the Sick already had a defect either of the Lungs, or Liver, or of any like noble Member?
>
> To which I answered. Such a remedy is exceedingly necessary for a Physician, but no man knows what and how great are the Secrets yet hidden in Nature, nor did I ever in all my Life see such an Adept Man, although I have read and perused many things, touching the verity of this thing, or Art, in the Writings of Philosophers. I also enquired of him, whether he (speaking of the Universal Medicine) were not a Physician?
>
> But he answered by denyal, professed, that he was no other than a Melter of Orichalcum, and that in the Flower of his years, he had known many things, from his Friend, rare to the Sight, and especially the way of Extracting Medicinal Arcanums by the force of Fire, and that for this very cause, he was a Lover of this so noble Science of Medicine.
>
> Moreover, long after other discourses, touching Experiments in Metals, made by the violence of Fire, Elias the Artist spake to me thus; Do you not know the Highest Secret, when it is offered to your sight, viz. the Stone of Phylosophers, you having read in the Writings of many Chymists most excellent, touching the Substance, Colour, and strange effect of the same?

I answered, not at all; except what I have read in Paracelsus, Helmont,
Basilius, Sandivogius, and like Books of Adept Phylosophers extant.
Nevertheless, I think, I am not able to know the Phylosophick Matter,
whether it be true, or not, although I should see it present before me."

Essentially, after something of an "examination", Schweitzer was asked
whether he would recognize the "Philosopher's Stone" if he saw it. The
stranger - "Elias the Artist" - then took out of his pocket a small ivory box
that held

"...three ponderous pieces or small lumps... each about the bigness of a
small walnut, transparent, of a pale brimstone colour."

The stranger told Schweitzer that this was the very substance sought for
so long by the Alchemists.

Schweitzer held one of the pieces in his hand and asked the stranger if
he could have just a small piece. The man refused, but Schweitzer
managed to steal a small bit by scraping it with his fingernail.

The visitor left after promising to return in three weeks time to show
Dr. Schweitzer some "curious arts in the fire".

As soon as he was gone, Dr. Schweitzer ran to his laboratory where he
melted some lead in a crucible and added the tiny piece of stone. But, the
metal did NOT turn into gold as he anticipated. Instead, "almost the whole
mass of lead flew away, and the remainder turned into a mere glassy
earth".

Three weeks later, the mysterious stranger was at his door again. They
conversed, and for a long time the man refused to allow Dr. Schweitzer to
see his stones again, but, at last,

"...he gave me a crumb as big as a grape or turnip seed, saying, receive
this small parcel of the greatest treasure of the world, which truly few
kings or princes have ever known or seen."

Schweitzer must have been a whiner because he recounts that he
protested that this was not sufficient to transmute as much as four grains of
lead into gold. At this, the stranger took the piece back, cut it in half, and
flung one part in the fire, saying, "it is yet sufficient for thee!"

At this point, Schweitzer confessed his theft from the previous visit, and
described how the substance had behaved with his molten lead. The
stranger began to laugh and told him:

"You could no more dexterously play the Thief, than apply the Tincture. I
wonder, that you, so expert in the Fire, do no better understand the fuming
Nature of Lead. For if you had wrapped your Theft in yellow Wax, that it
might have been conserved from the Fume of Lead, then it would so have
penetrated into the Lead, as to have transmuted the same into Gold."

The discussion continues, during the course of which the stranger tells Schweitzer:

> "The true writings of Philosophers are only understood by the truly Adept. Therefore, touching the Time, they would write nothing certain; yea, I say, no Lover of this Art, can find the Art of preparing this Mystery in his whole Life, *without the Communication of some true Adept Man*. In this respect, and for this Cause, I advise you, my Friend, because you have seen the true Matter of the true Work, not to forget your self, and thirsting after the perfection of this Art, to cast away your own Goods; for you can never find it out. [...]

> For unless you know the thing, from the beginning of the Work to the end, you know nothing thereof. Indeed I have told you enough, yet you are ignorant how the Stone of Philosophers is made, and again, how the Glassy Seal of Hermes is broaken, in which Sol gives forth Splendor from his Metallick Rayes, wonderfully coloured, and in which Speculum, the Eyes of Narcissus behold Metals transmutable, and from which Rayes the Adept gather their fire, by the help of which, Volatile Metals are fixed into most fixed Gold, or Silver."

The strange man leaves at this point in the story and promises to return the next morning to show Schweitzer the correct way to perform the transmutation but:

> "The next day he came not, nor ever since. Only he sent an excuse at half an hour past nine that morning, by reason of his great business, and promised to come at three in the afternoon, but never came, nor have I heard of him since; whereupon I began to doubt of the whole matter.

> Nevertheless late that night my wife... came soliciting and vexing me to make experiment... saying to me, unless this be done, I shall have no rest nor sleep all this night...

> She being so earnest, I commanded a fire to be made - thinking, alas, now is this man (though so divine in discourse) found guilty of falsehood...

> My wife wrapped the said matter in wax, and I cut half an ounce of six drams of old lead, and put into a crucible in the fire, which being melted, my wife put in the said Medicine made up in a small pill or button, which presently made such a hissing and bubbling in its perfect operation, that within a quarter of an hour all the mass of lead was transmuted into the ... finest gold."

Baruch Spinoza, who lived nearby, came the next day to examine this gold and was convinced that Schweitzer was telling the truth. The Assay Master of the province, a Mr. Porelius, tested the metal and pronounced it genuine; and Mr. Buectel, the silversmith, subjected it to further test that confirmed that it was gold.

What occurs to me when I read this story is the fact that Schweitzer, in spite of his great learning, did not have the "right stuff", and his attempt at purloining a bit of the "stone" was his downfall. Recall this:

"Like attracts like.

When a candidate has developed virtue and integrity acceptable to the adepts, they will appear to him and reveal those parts of the secret processes which cannot be discovered without such help.

Those who cannot progress to a certain point with their own intelligence are not qualified to be entrusted with the secrets which can subject to their will the elemental forces of Nature."

It seems rather clear that Schweitzer was being tested and that he failed the test.

The testimony of these men survives to this day.[26] Now, either ALL of them are lying, or Dr. Schweitzer really did have a strange experience exactly as he describes it.

The interesting thing is that other people have described similar visitations by strange men who proclaim to them the truth of the alchemical process, demonstrate it, and then mysteriously disappear. It has happened in widely enough separated places and times to suggest that it is not a collusive fraud or a delusion. Twenty years before Schweitzer's meeting with the mysterious stranger, Jan Baptiste van Helmont, responsible for several important scientific discoveries, was the first man to realize that there were other gases than air, actually having invented the term "gas", wrote:

"For truly I have divers times seen it [The Philosopher's Stone], and handled it with my hands, but it was of colour such as is in Saffron in its powder, yet weighty, and shining like unto powdered glass.

There was once given unto me one fourth part of one grain [16 milligrams]... I projected [it] upon eighty ounces [227 grams] of quicksilver [mercury] made hot in a crucible; and straight-away all the quicksilver, with a certain degree of noise, stood still from flowing, and being congealed, settled like unto a yellow lump; but after pouring it out, the bellows blowing, there were found eight ounces and a little less than eleven grains of the purest gold."

Sir Isaac Newton studied alchemy until his death, remaining convinced that the possibility of transmutation existed.

The great philosophers and mathematicians, Descartes and Leibnitz, both were convinced that transmutation was a reality. Even Robert Boyle,

---

[26] John Frederick Helvetius. *The Golden Calf, Which the World Adores, and Desires*, London 1670.

who wrote a book entitled *The Sceptical Chymist*, was sure until the end of his life, that transmutation was possible!

Why? These men were scientists. And, the argument that their ideas or observations were less scientific than those of the present day simply does not stand up to scrutiny.

As noted, alchemists were rumored at various times to have gained immortality, and one of these was Nicolas Flamel. Flamel was a poor scribe, or scrivener and copyist. The story goes that, in 1357 he bought an old illuminated book...

> "The cover of it was of brass, well bound, all engraven with letters of strange figures... This I know that I could not read them nor were they either Latin of French letters... As to the matter that was written within, it was engraved (as I suppose) with an iron pencil or graver upon... bark leaves, and curiously coloured..."

Reportedly, the first page was written in golden letters that said *Abraham the Jew, Priest, Prince, Levite, Astrologer and Philosopher, to the Nation of the Jews dispersed by the Wrath of God in France, wisheth Health*. So, quite rightly, Flamel referred to the manuscript as the *Book of Abraham the Jew*. The dedication was followed by curses upon anyone who was not either a priest or a Jew reading the book. But, Flamel was a scribe, which he must have imagined exempted him from these curses, so he read the book.

The purpose of the book was avowedly to give assistance to the dispersed Jews by teaching them to transmute lead into gold so that they could pay their taxes to the hated Roman government. The instructions were clear and easy, but only described the latter part of the process. The instructions for the beginning were said to be in the illustrations given on the 4th and 5th leaves of the book. Flamel remarked that, although these were well executed,

> "...Yet by that could no man ever have been able to understand it without being well skilled in their Qabalah, which is a series of old traditions, and also to have been well studied in their books."

As the story goes, Flamel tried for 21 years to find someone who could explain these pictures to him. Finally, his wife urged him to go to Spain and seek out a rabbi or other learned Jew who might assist him. He made the famous pilgrimage to the shrine of St. James at Compostela, carrying with him carefully made copies of the book. After his devotions at the shrine, he went to the city of Leon in northern Spain where he met a certain "Master Canches", a Jewish physician. When this man saw the illustrations, he was "ravished with great astonishment and joy", upon recognizing them as parts of a book that had long been believed to have been destroyed. He declared his intention to return with Flamel to France, but he died on the trip at Orleans. Flamel returned to Paris alone. But, apparently, the old Jew must have told him something for he wrote:

> "I had now the prima materia, the first principles, yet not their first preparation, which is a thing most difficult, above all things in the world... Finally, I found that which I desired, which I also knew by the strong scent and odour thereof. Having this, I easily accomplished the Mastery... The fist time that I made projection [transmutation] was upon Mercury, whereof I turned half a pound, or thereabouts, into pure silver, better than that of the Mine, as I myself assayed, and made others assay many times. This was upon a Monday, the 17th of January about noon, in my home, Perrenelle [his wife] only being present, in the year of the restoring of mankind 1382."

Note this date of January 17th, as it will come up numerous times! Several months later Flamel did his first transmutation into gold. Is this just a story? Well, what IS true and can be verified is that Nicolas and Perenelle Flamel endowed "fourteen hospitals, three chapels and seven churches, in the city of Paris, all of which we had built from the ground, and enriched with great gifts and revenues, with many reparations in their churchyards". "We also have done at Boulogne about as much as we have done at Paris, not to speak of the charitable acts which we both did to particular poor people, principally widows and orphans."

After Flamel's death in 1419 the rumours began. Hoping that they could find something hidden in one of his houses, people searched them again and again until one of them was completely destroyed.

There were stories that Nicolas and Perenelle were still alive. Supposedly, she had gone to Switzerland and he buried a log in her grave, and then another log was buried at his own funeral.

In the intervening centuries, the stories persist that Flamel and Perenelle defeated death. The 17th century traveler, Paul Lucas, while traveling in Asia Minor, met a Turkish philosopher who told him, "true philosophers had had the secret of prolonging life for anything up to a thousand years..."

Lucas said, "At last I took the liberty of naming the celebrated Flamel, who, it was said, possessed the Philosopher's Stone, yet was certainly dead.

He smiled at my simplicity, and asked with an air of mirth: Do you really believe this? No, no, my friend, Flamel is still living; neither he nor his wife has yet tasted death. It is not above three years since I left both... in India; he is one of my best friends."

In 1761, Flamel and his wife were reported to have been seen attending the opera in Paris.

Well, there is an issue here regarding the supposed clue about "Abraham the Jew" which *seems* to point us in the direction of a Jewish fraternity of alchemists or keepers of secrets. I don't want to go off on that thread here and now because it would add so much complexity to the issues that we might never find our way through the maze. But, to ease the mind of the reader, I will make a few remarks about this here. It's curious that Eugene Canseliet, in his preface to the Second Edition of Fulcanelli's *Le Mystere des Cathedrales*, apparently upon the instruction of the master alchemist, emphasized so dramatically the difference between kabbala and Cabala saying:

> "...This book has restored to light the phonetic cabala, whose principles and application had been completely lost. After this detailed and precise elucidation and after the brief treatment of it, which I gave in connection with the centaur, the man-horse of Plessis-Bourre, in **Deux Logis Alchimiques, this mother tongue need never be confused with the Jewish Kabbala.** Though never spoken, the phonetic cabala, this **forceful idiom**, is easily understood and it is the **instinct** or **voice of nature.** By contrast, the Jewish Kabbala is full of transpositions, inversions, substitutions and calculations, as arbitrary as they are abstruse. This is why it is important to distinguish between the two words, CABALA and KABBALA in order to use them knowledgeably. Cabala derives from cadallhz or from the Latin caballus, a horse; kabbala is from the Hebrew Kabbalah, which means tradition. Finally, figurative meanings like **coterie, underhand dealing** or **intrigue**, developed in modern usage by analogy, should be ignored so as to reserve for the noun **cabala** the only significance which can be assured for it."

Now, the curious bringing in of the terms "coterie", "underhand dealing" and "intrigue" in conjunction with what he has just remarked about Kabbalah meaning "tradition", and Cabala being "horse", is a most curious juxtaposition of words. It almost seems that Fulcanelli is telling us that the Kaballah, or the tradition is a red herring. Fulcanelli himself makes a curious remark in *The Dwellings of the Philosophers*:

> "Alchemy is obscure, only because it is hidden. The philosophers who wanted to transmit the exposition of their doctrine and the fruit of their labors to posterity took great care not to divulge the art by presenting it under a common form, so that the layman could not misuse it. ...That the philosophers had no other means at their disposal to **steal from the ones what they wanted to expose to the others**, but this confusion of metaphors, of diverse symbols, this prolixity of terms, of capricious formulas traced by the flow of the pen, expressed in clear language for the use of the greedy or the foolish..."

The point of this short aside is this: don't assume anything about Jews, Masons, or any other group when trying to solve the mystery. Nearly everything we come across will be obscured. And, when it is right out in plain view, it will be even more difficult to see!

Getting back to our purported alchemists, we come now to the year 1745 in which Prince Charles Edward Stuart, known as the "Young Pretender", staged his Jacobite rebellion in an attempt to regain the British throne for his father the "Old Pretender".

The Jacobite cause, for all intents and purposes, had been crushed at the battle of Culloden in April of that year, yet there was a constant fear by the British government that the Jacobites were still plotting with their French sympathizers, and being French and in London was, at that time, a liability. This "spy fever" resulted in the arrest of many Frenchmen on trumped up charges, and most of them were later released, but it was a dangerous time for Gallic visitors!

In November of that year, one Frenchman was arrested and accused of having pro-Jacobite letters in his possession. He became very indignant and claimed that the correspondence had been "planted" on him. Considering the mood of the time, it is quite surprising that he was believed and released! Horace Walpole, English author and Member of Parliament, wrote a letter about this incident to Sir Horace Mann on December 9, 1745 saying:

> "The other day they seized an odd man who goes by the name of Count Saint-Germain. He has been here these two years, and will not tell who he is or whence, but professes that he does not go by his right name. He sings and plays on the violin wonderfully, is mad and not very sensible."

This is one of the few "authentic", on the scene comments about one of the most mysterious characters of the 18th century.

Another acquaintance of the "Count Saint-Germain, Count Warnstedt, described Saint-Germain as, "the completest charlatan, fool, rattle-pate, windbag and swindler".

Yet, his last patron said that Saint-Germain was "perhaps one of the greatest sages who ever lived".

Clearly this was one of those people you either love or hate!

Saint-Germain first comes to our attention in the fashionable circles of Vienna in about 1740, where he made a stir by flaunting the fashion of the day by wearing black all the time! Everybody else was into bright colors, satins and laces, ornate patterns and designs; and along comes Saint-Germain with his somber black outfits set off by glittering diamonds on his fingers, shoe buckles, and snuff box!

What an attention getter! If you want to stand out in a roomful of robins, cardinals and blue jays, just be a blackbird!

He also had the habit of carrying handfuls of loose diamonds in his pockets instead of cash!

So, there he is, garnering attention to himself in this bizarre way, and naturally he makes the acquaintance of the local leaders of fashion, Counts Zabor and Lobkowitz who introduce him to the French Marshal de Belle Isle.

Well, it seems that the Marshal was seriously under-the-weather, but his illness is not recorded so we can't evaluate the claims that Saint-Germain cured him, but nevertheless, the Marshal was so grateful he took Saint-Germain to Paris with him and set him up with apartments and a laboratory.

The details of the Count's life in Paris are pretty well known, and it is there that the rumors began. There is an account by a "Countess de B___" (a nom de plume, it seems, so we have to hold the information somewhat suspect), who wrote in her memoirs, *Chroniques de l'oeil de boeuf*, that, when she met the Count at a soiree given by the aged Countess von Georgy, whose late husband had been Ambassador to Venice in the 1670's, that the old Countess remembered Saint-Germain from her days in Venice.

So, the old girl asked the Count if his father had been there at the time. He replied no, but *he* had! Well, the man that Countess von Georgy had known was at least 45 years old *then*, at least 50 years ago, which appeared to be the age of the man standing before her!

The Count smiled and said, "I am very old". "But then you must be nearly 100 years old", the Countess exclaimed. "That is not impossible", the Count replied. He then related some details that convinced the old lady that it was really *him* she knew in Venice.

The Countess exclaimed, "I am already convinced. You are a most extraordinary man, a devil!"

"For pity's sake!", cried Saint-Germain in a loud voice heard all around the room. "No such names!" He began to tremble all over and left the room immediately.

A pretty dramatic introduction to society, don't you think? But, was it real, or the ploy of a very clever con artist? Did he deliberately choose to adopt the name of someone long dead, about whom he may have already known a great deal, and then did he set out to deceive and con in a manner well known to us in the present time? Was he a snake oil salesman or a true man of mystery?

In any event, that was the beginning of the "legend", and many more stories of a similar nature spread through society like wildfire.

Saint-Germain apparently fed the fires with hints that he had known the "Holy Family" intimately and had been invited to the marriage feast at Cana where Jesus turned water into wine, and dropped casually the remark that he "had always known that Christ would meet a bad end". According to him, he had been very fond of Anne, the mother of the Virgin Mary, and had even proposed her canonization at the Council of Nicaea in AD 325!

What a guy! A line for every occasion!

Pretty soon the Count had Louis XV and his mistress, Madame de Pompadour, eating out of his hand, and it certainly *could* be true that he was a French spy in England when he was arrested there, because he later did handle some sticky business for the credulous king of France.

In 1760, Louis sent Saint-Germain to the Hague as his personal representative to arrange a loan with Austria that was supposed to help finance the Seven Years' war against England.

But, while in Holland, the Count had a falling out with his friend Casanova, who was also a diplomat at The Hague. Casanova tried hard to discredit Saint-Germain in public, but without success.

One has to wonder just what it was that Casanova discovered or came to think about Saint-Germain at this time?

In any event, Saint-Germain was making other enemies. One of these enemies was the Duc de Choiseul, King Louis' Foreign Minister. The Duc discovered that Saint-Germain had been scoping out the possibilities of arranging a peace between England and France.

Now, that doesn't sound like a bad plan at all, but the Duc managed to convince the King that this was a dire betrayal, and the Count had to flee to England and then back to Holland.

In Holland, the Count lived under the name Count Surmont, and he worked to raise money to set up laboratories in which he made paint and dyes and engaged in his alchemical experiments.

By all accounts, he was successful in *some* sense, because he disappeared from Holland with 100,000 guilders!

He next shows up in Belgium as the "Marquis de Monferrat". He set up another laboratory with "other people's money" before disappearing again. (Are we beginning to see a pattern here?)

For a number of years, Saint-Germain's activities continued to be reported from various parts of Europe and, in 1768 he popped up in the court of Catherine the Great. Turkey had just declared war on Russia, and Saint-Germain promoted himself as a valuable diplomat because of his status as an "insider" in French politics.

Pretty soon he was the adviser of Count Alexei Orlov, head of the Russian Imperial Forces. Orlov made him a high-ranking officer of the Russian Army and Saint-Germain acquired an English alias, "General Welldone".

His successes in Russia could have enabled him to retire on his laurels, but he didn't. In 1774 he appeared in Nuremberg seeking money from the Margrave of Brandenburg, Charles Alexander. His ostensible alias at this point (apparently he was no longer satisfied with being either a Count or a Marquis) was Prince Rakoczy of Transylvania!

Naturally, the Margrave of Brandenburg was impressed when Count Orlov visited Nuremburg on a state visit and embraced "the Prince" warmly. But later, when the Margrave did a little investigating, he discovered that the *real* Prince Rakoczy was indubitably dead and that this counterfeit Prince was, in fact, only Count Saint-Germain!

Saint-Germain did not deny the charges, but apparently he felt that it was now time to move on.

The Duc de Choiseul, Saint-Germain's old enemy, had claimed that the Count was in the employ of Frederick the Great. But, that was probably not true because, at this point, Saint-Germain wrote to Frederick begging for patronage. Frederick ignored him, which is peculiar if he *had* been in the employ of the Prussian king as de Choiseul thought. But, never to be discouraged as is the case with many con men who can never quite figure out when to quit, Saint-Germain went to Leipzig and presented himself to Prince Frederick Augustus of Brunswick as a Freemason of the fourth grade!

Now, Frederick Augustus just happened to be the Grand Master of the Prussian Masonic Lodges, so this was *really* a stupid move on the part of Saint-Germain since it turned out that he was *not* a Mason! But, it is true of the pattern of all con men... their egos eventually prove to be their downfall!

The Prince challenged Saint-Germain because he did not know the secret signals and sent him away as a fraud.

In 1779, Saint-Germain was an old man in his 60's who continued to claim to be vastly older. He must have learned to subdue his ego somewhat because, at Eckenforde in Schleswig, Germany, he was able to charm Prince Charles of Hesse-Cassel. At this point, part of his scam included being a mystic, for he is recorded as having told Prince Charles:

"Be the torch of the world. If your light is that only of a planet, you will
be as nothing in the sight of God. I reserve for you a splendour, of which

the solar glory is a shadow. You shall guide the course of the stars, and those who rule Empires shall be guided by you."

Sounds rather like the buildup to another con job! Nothing like feeding the ego of the "mark" before slipping away with all his money! In this case, it didn't work. Prince Charles made no mark on history and on February 27, 1784, Saint-Germain died at Prince Charles' home on Eckenforde. He was buried locally and the Prince erected a stone that said:

"He who called himself the Comte de Saint-Germain and Welldone of whom there is no other information, has been buried in this church."

And then, the Prince burned all of the Count's papers, "lest they be misinterpreted".

Supposedly there is evidence that the Count did *not* die, and many occultists claim he is still alive for these past two centuries!

The mystery of Saint-Germain is mostly due to the uncertainty surrounding his origins. One source says that he was born in 1710 in San Germano, son of a tax collector. Eliphas Levi, the 19th century occultist said that Saint-Germain was born in Lentmeritz in Bohemia, and was the bastard son of a nobleman who was also a Rosicrucian. The first theory is more likely to be correct.

It *is* known that he had a genuine gift for languages and could speak French, German, English, Dutch and Russian fluently. He also claimed that he was fluent in Chinese, Hindu and Persian, but there was no one about to test him on those.

We note that Horace Walpole said that he was a wonderful violinist and singer and painter, though none of his purported art has been known to have survived. Supposedly, he was able to paint jewels that glittered in a very lifelike way.

There is also a great deal of anecdotal evidence that Saint-Germain was an expert jeweler - he claimed to have studied the art with the Shah of Persia! In any event, he is reported to have repaired a flawed diamond for Louis XV, who was very pleased with the result.

Saint-Germain also was said to have had an extensive knowledge of chemistry in all its branches at the time, and the many laboratories that he set up with borrowed money were all designed to produce brighter and better pigments and dyes and also for alchemical studies.

Then, there was his reputation as a healer. Not only did he allegedly cure the Marshal de Belle Isle, he also was supposed to have cured a friend of Madame de Pompadour of mushroom poisoning.

Saint-Germain *never* ate in company, which appears to have been part of his plan to focus attention on himself. He could sit at a table where everyone else was gorging on the most amazing array of delectable dishes, and eat and drink nothing. Casanova wrote:

"Instead of eating, he talked from the beginning of the meal to the end, and I followed his example in one respect as I did not eat, but listened to him with the greatest attention. It may safely be said that as a conversationalist he was unequaled."

I can certainly think of a couple of individuals about whom I could say the same thing. In both cases, they most certainly were psychopaths.

Colin Wilson, author of *The Occult*, thought that Saint-Germain must have been a vegetarian.

So, in the end, the *real* mystery, aside from his origins, but the two may be connected, is *where* did Saint-Germain get all his specialized knowledge?

Of course, as we have noted here, not all who met Saint-Germain were impressed by his talents. Casanova was entertained by him, but nevertheless thought that he was a fraud and a charlatan. He wrote:

"This extraordinary man, intended by nature to be *the king of impostors and quacks*, would say in an easy, assured manner that he was three hundred years old, that he knew the secret of the Universal Medicine, that he possessed a mastery over nature, that he could melt diamonds, professing himself capable of forming, out of 10 or 12 small diamonds, one of the finest water... All this, he said, was a mere trifle to him.

Notwithstanding his boastings, his barefaced lies, and his manifold eccentricities, I cannot say I found him offensive. In spite of my knowledge of what he was and in spite of my own feelings, I thought him an astonishing man..."

I have to say that I thought the same thing about the two psychopaths I knew with similar talents.

Count Alvensleben, a Prussian Ambassador to the Court at Dresden, wrote in 1777:

"He is a highly gifted man with a very alert mind, but completely without judgment, and he has only gained his singular reputation by the lowest and basest flattery of which a man is capable, as well as by his outstanding eloquence, especially if one lets oneself be carried away by the fervour and the enthusiasm with which he can express himself. Inordinate vanity is the mainspring driving his whole mechanism."

The ambassador's remark that Germain was "without judgment" is interesting as this is the very symptom that emerges again and again in cases of psychopathy studied by Hervey Cleckley and written about in his book *The Mask of Sanity*.

It sounds like an easy thing to dismiss Saint Germain out of hand. But, in the case of the Count, we have a little problem: just which of the stories are really about *him*?

The plot thickens!

It seems that Berthold Volz, in the 1920's, did some deep research on the subject and discovered, or so it is claimed, that the Duc de Choiseul, who was overwhelmingly jealous of the Count, hired *a look-alike impostor* to go about as the Count, exaggerating and playing the fool in order to place the Count in a bad light.

Or is this just another story, either wishful thinking or deliberately designed to perpetuate the legend? Are we getting familiar with this "bait and switch" routine yet?

Supposedly, Saint-Germain foretold the outbreak of the French Revolution to Marie Antoinette who purportedly wrote in her diary that she regretted that she did not heed his advice. I haven't seen it, so I can't vouch for it. But, in my opinion, it wouldn't be too hard a thing to predict, considering the political climate of the time!

It was said that Saint-Germain appeared in Wilhelmsbad in 1785, a year after he was supposed to have died, and he was accompanied by the magician Cagliostro, the hypnotist Anton Mesmer, and the "unknown philosopher", Louis Claude de St. Martin[27]. But it is hearsay and may be designed to create a link between the Martinists and Saint-Germain.

Saint-Germain was alleged to have gone to Sweden in 1789 to warn King Gustavus III of danger. Next he visited his friend, diarist Mademoiselle d'Adhemar, who said he still looked like he was only 46 years old! Apparently, he told her that she would see him five more times, and she claimed this was, in fact, the case. Supposedly the last visit was the night before the murder of the Duc de Berri in 1820.

Again, we find this to be unsupported by evidence.

Napoleon III ordered a commission to investigate the life and activities of Saint-Germain, but the findings were destroyed in a fire at the Hotel de Ville in Paris in 1871 - which many people think is beyond coincidence.

---

[27] According to the Martinist Order: St Martin was born in 1743 and was trained for the legal profession but he bought himself a commission in the French Army and was stationed in Bordeaux. It was in Bordeaux he encountered Scottish Rite Freemasonry, was Initiated but eventually he became disappointed with their system and he subsequently resigned and broke all contacts with it. Shortly afterwards he became fully involved with a mystic stream or Tradition that had included such names as Court de Gebelin, Benjamin Franklin the American statesman and the English Nobleman, Sir Francis Dashwood. He travelled widely and following an invitation from the Golitzin family in Russia he went there and was Initiated into the Lineage that now runs through the British Martinist Order.

My thought would be that the only reason to destroy such a report would be if it had proved the Count to be a fraud. The result of this fire is that the legend is enabled to live on. Therefore, it is likely that the report would have made some difference in the legend, such as putting it to rest as a fraud. Had it been helpful to the legend, it would not have changed what is *already the case,* which is that people believe that Saint-Germain was something of a supernatural being. Thus, its destruction, if engineered, must only have been to protect the status quo.

One of the next threads of the legend was gathered into the hands of Helena Blavatsky who claimed that Saint-Germain was one of the "hidden masters" along with Christ, Buddha, Appollonius of Tyana, Christian Rosencreutz, Francis Bacon and others.

A group of Theosophists traveled to Paris after WWII where they were told they would meet the Count; he never showed up.

In 1972, a Frenchman named Richard Chanfray was interviewed on French television. He claimed to be Saint-Germain and, supposedly, in front of television cameras, transmuted lead into gold on a camp stove!

Lest we forget the more recent "communications" of the count to the head of the Church Universal and Triumphant, Elizabeth Clare Prophet.

In the end, on the subject of Saint-Germain, we find lies and confusion. But, by now, we are getting used to it and are learning to think in different ways. If Saint-Germain was a fraud we have to think somewhat carefully about those who claim him as their "connection" to things esoteric!

During the 19th and 20th centuries, alchemy lost favor with the rise of experimental science. The time was that of such stellar names as Lavoisier, Priestley and Davy.

Dalton's atomic theory, and a host of discoveries in chemistry and physics, made it clear to all "legitimate" scientists that alchemy was only "mystical" and, at best, a harmless pastime of no scientific value.

Organizations such as the Golden Dawn and Ordo Templi Orientis devised corrupted mixtures of snippets of alchemy and oriental philosophy, stirred in with the western European magical traditions, but these were clearly distorted imitations composed mostly of wishful thinking.

When one deeply studies the so-called "adepts" of these "systems", one is confronted again and again with the archetype of the "failed magician" so that one can only shake the head and remember the warning of the great alchemists that those who do not develop within themselves the "special state" that is required for the "Great Work", only disaster can result.

There is no doubt in my mind that such groups dabble in "alchemy" of a sort, or "magick" of another, and there is no doubt that they may, in fact, "conjure" connections to sources of "power" on occasion. But, overall, a survey of what can be learned about them tends to point in the direction of much wishful thinking or even the possibility of domination by the forces of darkness in the guise of "angels of light".

Nevertheless, in 1919, British physicist Ernest Rutherford announced that he had achieved a successful transmutation of one element into another: nitrogen to oxygen! Admittedly, his procedures and results in no way resembled the work of the alchemists; but, what he had done was refute the insistence of most scientists of the day that transmutation was impossible. In fact, it became known that radioactive elements gradually "decay", giving off radiation and producing "daughter elements" which then decay even further. For instance one such chain starts with uranium and the end product is lead.

So, the question became, can the process be reversed? Or, if you start with another element, what might you end up with?

Franz Tausend was a 36 year-old chemical worker in Munich who had a theory about the structure of the elements that was a strange mixture of Pythagoreanism and modern chemistry. He published a pamphlet entitled, "180 elements, their atomic weight, and their incorporation in a system of harmonic periods". He thought that every atom had a frequency of vibration characteristic of that element, related to the weight of the atom's nucleus and the grouping of the electrons around it. This part of his idea was shown to be basically correct by later research. However, Tausend further suggested that matter could be "orchestrated" by adding the right substance to the element, thereby changing its vibration frequency, in which case, it would become a different element.

As it happened, at about the same time, Adolf Hitler was sent to prison for attempting to organize an armed uprising.

One of Hitler's cohorts was General Erich Ludendorff, but Ludendorff was acquitted of the charges and ran for president of Germany the following year. He was defeated by Hindenburg, so he turned his mind to raising money for the nascent Nazi party. He heard rumors that a certain Tausend had transmuted base metals into gold, and he formed a group, including numerous industrialists, to investigate this process.

Tausend gave instructions that they should purchase iron oxide and quartz, which were melted together in a crucible.

A German merchant and member of this group, named Stremmel, took the crucible to his hotel bedroom for the night so that it could not be tampered with. The next morning, Tausend heated the crucible in his electric furnace in the presence of his patrons, and then added a small quantity of white powder to the molten mass. It was allowed to cool, and then, when it was broken open, a gold nugget weighing 7 grams was inside.

Ludendorff, to say the least, was ecstatic. He set about forming a company called "Company 164". Investment money poured in and within a year the general had diverted some 400,000 marks into Nazi Party funds. Then, in December, 1926, he resigned, leaving Tausend to handle all the debts.

Tausend managed to continue raising money and on June 16, 1928, supposedly made 25 ounces of gold in a single operation. This enabled him to issue a series of "share certificates" worth 22 pounds each (10 kilograms of gold).

A year later, when no more gold had been produced, Tausend was arrested for fraud, tried, found guilty, and sentenced to four years in prison. Nevertheless, while waiting for trial, he was able to perform a transmutation under strict supervision, in the Munich Mint. This was submitted to the court as evidence that no fraud had taken place, but it was contested and did not save him from prison.

In the same year that Tausend was convicted, a Polish engineer name Dunikovski announced in Paris that he had discovered a new kind of radiation, which would transmute quartz into gold. The mineral, spread on copper plates, was melted by an electric discharge at 110,000 volts, and was then irradiated with these new "z-rays".

Investors poured two million francs into Dunikovski's project, but, within a few months, when no gold appeared, he was also tried and found guilty of fraud.

After two years in prison, Dunikovski's lawyer obtained an early release, and he went with his family to Italy where he again began to experiment. Rumors soon started that he was supporting himself by the occasional sale of lumps of gold. His lawyer, accompanied by the eminent chemist, Albert Bonn, went to see him. What was discovered was that the quartz being used by Dunikovski (and presumably by Tausend as well) already contained minute quantities of gold. The gold could be extracted by a usual process, producing about 10 parts per million, but Dunikovski's technique produced almost 100 times as much. Nevertheless, he was only dealing with small quantities of gold because his equipment could only handle small quantities of quartz.

Dunikovski claimed that his process accelerated the natural growth of "embryonic" gold within the quartz. He gave a demonstration before an invited group of scientists, which attracted considerable attention. An Anglo-French syndicate formed to bring sand from Africa and treat it in a big new laboratory on the south coast of England, but W.W.II started at about this time and Dunikovski disappeared. It was rumored that he was "co-opted" by the Germans and manufactured gold for them to bolster their failing economy - but there is no proof.

Since WWII, there have been and still are, many practitioners of alchemy. Much of this activity has been centered in France, including Eugene Canseliet who was a pupil of the mysterious Fulcanelli mentioned above.

In studying alchemy and the history of alchemy and all related books I could find, I came finally to Fulcanelli and the mention of him in the book *Morning of the Magicians* by Pauwels and Bergier.[28]

Bergier claimed that in June of 1937 - eight years before the first atom-bomb test in New Mexico - that he was approached by an impressive but mysterious stranger. The man asked Bergier to pass on a message to the noted physicist Andre Helbronner, for whom Bergier was then working. The man said that he felt it was his duty to warn orthodox scientists of the danger of nuclear energy. He said that the alchemists of bygone times - and previous civilizations - had obtained such secret knowledge and it had destroyed them. The mysterious stranger said that he really had no hope that his warning would be heeded, but felt that he ought to give it anyway. Jacques Bergier remained convinced until the day he died that the stranger was Fulcanelli.

As the story goes, the American Office for Strategic Services, the forerunner of the CIA, made an intensive search for Fulcanelli at the end of the war. He was never found.

The argument against this strange event ever having happened is that plutonium was specifically named by the mystery man, yet it was not isolated until February of 1941, and was not named until March of 1942. This was five years after Bergier's encounter. Nevertheless, Bergier stood by his story.

The fact is, if we are talking about Master Alchemists who have achieved the "Great Work", the history seems to indicate that they have

---

[28] Further research has convinced us that the man Bergier met was not Fulcanlli. See the excellent study of the Fulcanelli myth and a very convincing case for his true identity, *Fulcanelli*, by Patrick Rivière, a student of Eugène Canseliet, now published in English by Red Pill Press.

"time travel" capabilities to some extent. So, the matter of knowing the name of the element would not have been too great a difficulty.

Nevertheless, Patrick Rivière, a student of Canseliet, says that the whole story was made up by Bergier who later identified the mysterious stranger with Rene Schwaller who, recent investigators have claimed was the "real Fulcanelli". Reading the works of Canseliet, Fulcanelli, and Schwaller, suggests strongly that Schwaller was *not* Fulcanelli, nor was Canseliet the author of Fulcanelli's books.

So, let's look at Fulcanelli in more depth. In the early 1920's, in Paris, Eugene Canseliet was known as an alchemical enthusiast. He made many references to the fact that he worked with an actual "Master of the Art". His friend and companion, a poverty stricken illustrator named Jean-Julien Champagne, who was a score of years older than Canseliet, supported these claims.

The two of them lived in a run-down building, in adjacent apartments, at 59 bis; rue de Rochechouart, in the Butte-Montmartre district.

Because of their hints that they had contact with such a "Hidden Master", they soon became the center of a circle of aspiring occultists.

It has been claimed that both Canseliet and Champagne were frequently seen in the city libraries, the Bibliotheque Nationale, the Mazarin, the Arsenal and the Sainte Genevieve, studying rare books and manuscripts. Obviously, they were looking for something.

The story heard by those on the edges of their elite little group were to the effect that this "Hidden Master Fulcanelli" was old, distinguished - possibly an aristocrat - and very rich. He was also said to be an immensely learned, practicing alchemist who had either already, or almost, achieved the Great Work.

Nobody except Canseliet and Champagne apparently ever met Master Fulcanelli, and, because of this, a great deal of skepticism arose in the occult circles of Paris. But then, the skepticism was laid to rest with the publication of *Le Mystere des Cathedrales* in 1926, which I have mentioned previously.

The first edition consisted of only 300 copies, and was published by Jean Schemit, of 45 rue Lafitte, in the Opera district. It was subtitled "An esoteric interpretation of the hermetic symbols of the Great Work", and its preface was written by Eugene Canseliet, then aged only 26. The book had 36 illustrations, two of them in color, by the artist, Champagne.

The subject of the book was a purported interpretation of the symbolism of various Gothic cathedrals and other buildings in Europe as being encoded instructions of alchemical secrets. This idea, that the secrets were contained in the stone structures, carvings, and so forth, of the medieval buildings had been hinted at by other writers on esoteric art and architecture, but no one had ever explicated the subject so clearly and in such detail before. In any event, Fulcanelli's book caused a sensation among the Parisian occultists.

In the preface, written by Canseliet, there is the hint that Master Fulcanelli had attained the Stone - that is, had become mystically transfigured and illuminated and had disappeared!

> "He disappeared when the fatal hour struck, when the Sign was accomplished... Fulcanelli is no more. But we have at least this consolation that his thought remains, warm and vital, enshrined for ever in these pages."

The extraordinary scholarship and unique qualities of the personality of the writer of *Le Mystere* drove the occultists of Paris to endless speculation about who Fulcanelli really was! About these speculations regarding Fulcanelli's possible identity, Kenneth Rayner Johnson writes:

> "There were suggestions that he was a surviving member of the former French royal family, the Valois. Although they were supposed to have died out in 1589 upon the demise of Henri III, it was known that members of the family had dabbled in magic and mysticism and that Marguerite de France, daughter of Henri II and wife of Henri IV of Navarre, survived until 1615. What is more, one of her many lovers was the esoterically inclined Francis Bacon (whom many still claim as an adept to this day); she was divorced in 1599 and her personal crest bore the magical pentagram, each of whose five points carried one letter of the Latin word **salus** - meaning 'health'. Could the reputedly aristocratic Fulcanelli be a descendant of the Valois, and did the Latin motto hint that some important alchemical secret of longevity had been passed on to him by the family?"

Actually, there is no proof that Marguerite de France and Francis Bacon were lovers. There is even the possibility that Marguerite, Queen of Navarre, wife of Henri, King of Navarre, who became King Henri IV of France, daughter of Henri II and Catherine de Medici, has been confused with her great Aunt, Marguerite, wife of Henri d'Albret, King of Navarre, (who was never King of France) who was also Queen of Navarre, but who was the daughter of Charles of Orleans, and sister of Francois I, King of France. In short, Marguerite who lived during the time of Francis Bacon was the great niece of Marguerite who lived during the time of Nostradamus and Rabelais. We will return to this problem.

> "Some claimed Fulcanelli was a bookseller-occultist, Pierre Dujols, who with his wife ran a shop in the rue de Rennes in the Luxembourg district of Paris. But Dujols was already known to have been only a speculative

alchemist, writing under the nom de plume of Magophon. Why should he hide behind two aliases?

Another suggestion was that Fulcanelli was the writer J. H. Rosny the elder. Yet his life was too well known to the public for this theory to find acceptance.

There were also at least three practical alchemist working in the city around the same period. They operated under the respective pseudonyms of Auriger, Faugerons and Dr. Jaubert. The argument against them being Fulcanelli was much the same as that against Dujols-Magophon: why use more than one alias?

Finally, there were Eugene Canseliet and Jean-Julien Champagne, both of whom were directly connected with Fulcanelli's book, and both of whom had claimed to have known the Master personally." [Johnson, 1992]

There was one major objection to Canseliet being Fulcanelli: he was too young to possibly have gained the knowledge apparent in the book. And, yes, a study of his preface as compared with the text of the book demonstrated distinctly different styles. So, Canseliet was excluded.

Champagne is the next likely suspect because he WAS older and more experienced, and it was a certainty that his work as an artist had taken him around France so that he would have had opportunity to view all the monuments described in such detail. The only problem with this theory was that Champagne was a, "noted braggart, practical joker, punster and drunkard, who frequently liked to pass himself off as Fulcanelli - although his behaviour was entirely out of keeping with the traditional solemn oath of the adept to remain anonymous and let his written work speak for itself". In addition to that, Champagne was an alcoholic whose imbibing of absinthe and Pernod eventually killed him. He died in 1932 of gangrene at the age of 55. His toes actually fell off. Doesn't sound much like a "Master Alchemist".

On the other hand, some of the descriptions of the transmutation of the alchemist make you wonder if the toes falling off isn't part of the process!

Joking aside, there are many more details and curiosities involved in the sorting out of who or what Fulcanelli may have really been.

The bottom line is: more than one person has attested to Fulcanelli's existence, his success in transmutation and to his continued existence into the present time - which would make him over 140 years old! And some theorists think he may be older than that!

The Morning of the Magicians, by Louis Pauwels and Jacques Bergier, was published in 1963, and it was only then that English-speaking occultists and students of alchemy became aware of Fulcanelli. At that point in time, it was to be another eight years before *Le Mystere Des*

Cathedrales would be translated into English. But, each of these books awoke a whole new audience of Seekers to the possibility of present day miracles as well as the very *real* likelihood of *a millennia old secret held in trust by persons unknown.*

In the English edition of *Mystery of the Cathedrals*, Eugene Canseliet said that the Master had given him a minute quantity of the alchemical "powder of projection" in 1922 - and permitted him to transmute 4 ounces of lead into gold. Vincent Lang, who wrote the introduction to the book, received a letter from Canseliet, which said, in part:

> "The Master was already a very old man but he carried his eighty years lightly. Thirty years later, I was to see him again... and he appeared to be a man of fifty. That is to say, he appeared to be a man no older than I was myself.
>
> Canseliet has since said that he has met with Fulcanelli several times since and that Fulcanelli is still living." [Johnson, 1992]

The only person who claimed to have seen Fulcanelli since was Canseliet, his pupil. He said that he met the Master in Spain in 1954 under highly unusual circumstances. The late Gerard Heym, founder member of the Society for the Study of Alchemy and Early Chemistry and editor of *Ambix*, its journal, acclaimed as Europe's foremost occult scholar of his day, made friends with Canseliet's daughter and through her, had a look at Canseliet's passport. It *did* carry a Spanish entry-visa stamp for 1954. So, at least on this one item we have a fact.

One friend of Canseliet, who wished to remain anonymous, said that this meeting was, "in another dimension... a point where such meetings are possible".

The story was that Canseliet "received a summons", of some sort; perhaps telepathic, and traveled to Seville where he was met and taken by a long, roundabout route, to a large mountain chateau which proved to be an enclave of alchemists - a colony! He said that Fulcanelli appeared to have undergone a curious form of transformation so that he had characteristics of both male and female - he was androgynous. At one point, Canseliet said, Fulcanelli actually had the complete characteristics of a woman. Some alchemical literature does point to this androgyny. The adept going through the transformation supposedly loses all hair, teeth and nails and grows new ones. The skin becomes younger, smoother and the face takes on asexual characteristics. This reminded me of what the Cassiopaeans had once said about transitioning to 4th density:

> Q: (L) Now if, theoretically, an individual was to develop in a natural way by making all the proper choices, and was to arrive at the point in time

when the major transition is to be made, would that individual's body pass through into that heightened dimension in a physical state?

A: Of course.

Q: (L) Now suppose this theoretical person were to pass through this transition to the other side, in what state would they find their body? Would it be exactly as it is now in terms of solidity? What would be the experience?

A: The key concept here is variability of physicality.

Q: (L) Does this mean that everybody will be different or that an individual will have greater control over the substance and constitution of the body?

A: Not exactly either. Your physicality will be variable according to need and circumstance.

Q: (L) Okay, does this mean that sometimes we will be more of a light body?

A: Close.

Q: (L) Does this mean that sometimes we will be more of a firm body as we have now?

A: Yes.

Q: (L) Will our bodies age differently?

A: Yes.

Q: (L) What will be the median lifespan?

A: 400 years

Q: (L) And will those who pass through this transition as, say, 50 year olds, will they have an equal opportunity to live an additional 400 years?

A: Will regenerate in youthful appearance.

So, this is a sort of fascinating idea that the alchemical transmutation is an interaction with another density. And, there was another comment made about this regarding the seeming "androgyny".

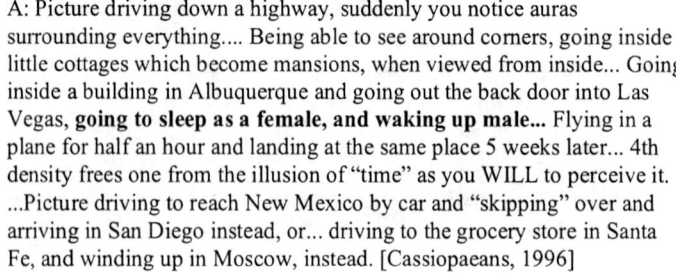

A: Picture driving down a highway, suddenly you notice auras surrounding everything.... Being able to see around corners, going inside little cottages which become mansions, when viewed from inside... Going inside a building in Albuquerque and going out the back door into Las Vegas, **going to sleep as a female, and waking up male...** Flying in a plane for half an hour and landing at the same place 5 weeks later... 4th density frees one from the illusion of "time" as you WILL to perceive it. ...Picture driving to reach New Mexico by car and "skipping" over and arriving in San Diego instead, or... driving to the grocery store in Santa Fe, and winding up in Moscow, instead. [Cassiopaeans, 1996]

It would certainly not be a stretch, in such a reality, to transmute lead into gold! The key seems to be accessing the 4th density reality, and that requires the transmutation of the alchemist!

But, returning to our discussion: After Canseliet's visit to the Enclave of the Alchemists, Gerard Heym said that he only had vague recollections of his experiences in Spain, as though some form of hypnosis had been used on him to make him forget the details of what he had seen and been told. (Why are we not surprised?!)

The point of this recitation is that there have been many well attested stories of strange things about alchemy reported by reliable and reputable witnesses, and the stories continue in a sort of "subculture" down to this very day.

There IS something going on, and it has been going on for a *very* long time! So, the trail of Fulcanelli ended in Seville.

The trail was getting very interesting... At about this point, I watched the David Hudson video about Monoatomic Gold. I was pretty excited by David Hudson's purported discovery, though there were some elements of the story that didn't quite fit. Nevertheless, after gathering all this data, I thought I was ready to ask the Cassiopaeans for the next set of clues:

Q: (L) Okay, Back when we were talking about the pit on Oak Island, and you asked me to do some research on it, the answers I came up with were that the responsible group were alchemists. Is this correct.

A: Yes.

Q: (L) Was one of the alchemists involved Nicholas Flamel?

A: Yes.

Q: (L) Is it true that there is an enclave of alchemists that live somewhere in the Pyrenees...

A: Yes.

Q: (L) Do these alchemists use this power as talked about by David Hudson to enhance their longevity and their physical health?

A: And to control.

Q: (L) Are there people in this enclave who live for literally hundreds, if not thousands, of years?

A: Open.

In retrospect, I understand that the Cassiopaeans were very gently indicating the opening of a certain path... a course of study and learning that was to have enormous implications. Most curious of all, the connections of "Arcadia", "sect", and "alchemy" would become the central motif of the Greatest Mystery of all - the search for the Holy Grail. To think, it all began on Oak Island...

Chapter 31
Grape Wine In a Mason Jar, Jesus, Di and Dodi Take Off From the Denver Airport In Winter to Rain Contrails Upon Our Heads...

I think that the reader is beginning to get the idea that following clues that the Cassiopaeans give is a lot of work. It is, and we are only getting warmed up here! But, I think you will also agree that we are having a little fun after all the grim facing of reality we have done. Once we have acknowledged that we may be in a prison, we can look on the journey *out* as a true adventure! And it is. Not only that, it is a *lot* of fun!

At some point in the early part of 1992 I had read an article about the book *Holy Blood, Holy Grail*, and I did think that the hypothesis presented by the authors, i.e. that Jesus had been married to Mary Magdalene and had children, was certainly possible, but not sufficiently interesting to me to warrant pursuing that particular line of investigation.

To familiarize the reader who has not pursued such subjects with the basic hypothesis, let me just say that when *Holy Blood, Holy Grail* was published in 1982, it aroused a firestorm of controversy. The local *St. Petersburg Times*, Florida, published a review that quoted the Rt. Rev. Montefiore as saying:

"Academically absurd... howler after howler."

This was balanced by a quote from one of the book's author's, Henry Lincoln saying:

"Is it more plausible that a man should be married and have children, or that he should be born of a virgin, attended by choirs of angels, walk on water and rise from the grave?"

Excellent point, in my opinion.

The Duke of Devonshire who would be, according to the premise of the book, one of Jesus' descendants, pronounced it "absolutely obnoxious".

Quoting from the *Times* article:

"Research began with Lincoln's preparation of a 1972 BBC documentary on a 19th century French priest, Berenger Sauniere. The cleric reputedly amassed great wealth after discovering and deciphering four parchments hidden in a hollow pillar of his church at Rennes-le-Chateau, a hilltop village in the south of France.

The authors say they have discovered those parchments, or facsimiles, still exist and disclose the existence of a secret society called the **Prieure de Sion**, founded in the 11th century at the start of the Crusades. Its aim was to guard the Holy Grail - according to medieval legend, the cup used by Jesus at the Last Supper.

The authors claim the society remains active, and that its adherents over the years included Isaac Newton, Andre Malraux, Victor Hugo, Claude Debussy and Charles de Gaulle.

According to the authors, the words "Holy Grail" are a mistranslation of early French words for "royal blood", and the true purpose of **Prieure de Sion** is to protect alleged royal descendants of Jesus and prepare the way for their accession to world power.

To bolster their description of the society, they provide several chapters of scholarly references from legends, romances, paintings, documents and the Bible.

All this is controversial enough, but author Leigh said it led the three to reexamine the conventional interpretations of the New Testament. That study led them to propound a "hypothesis" that:

Jesus literally had a claim to being "king of the Jews" and was descended from the royal house of the Israelite King David.

He married Mary Magdalene and had at least one child by her.

He and sympathizers staged his Crucifixion and Resurrection and he survived into old age somewhere outside the Holy Land.

Mary Magdalene and her offspring made their way to southern France - then Roman ruled Gaul.

Jesus' bloodline mixed with that of the Franks and started the Merovingian dynasty of the early Middle Ages.

The Merovingian line extends into the modern noble houses of Europe, so Jesus' descendants are alive today.

The book's contentions have started a religious firestorm.

'It is a sign of the degeneracy of the times that a publisher like Jonathan Cape should take this book', said Anglican Bishop Montefiore.

Montefiore catalogues what he calls '79 instances ... of gross errors, vital omissions, gravely misleading statements or the adoption of way-out hypotheses'.

Another Anglican bishop, Rt. Rev. Mervyn Stockwood, was even less reserved. 'Let them write a second book suggesting that Caesar married Boadicia and that the offspring is Ian Paisley', he was quoted by The Times of London as saying.

The authors say they are merely making reasonable suppositions based on careful research and new evidence. They add that serious work on medieval history has been obscured by the furor over their conclusions."
[St. Petersburg Times, January 19, 1982, byline: Mark S. Smith]

As I say, I didn't pay much attention to it other than filing it away in my mind. I was certainly never motivated to read the book! But, the subject was mentioned in a most curious way by the Cassiopaeans in our discussions about Jesus, and, like many important clues, it went right over my head. The question I asked was mainly concerned with the remarks in the Bible about the family of Jesus and I wanted to see what the Cassiopaeans would say about the purported "brothers" of Jesus, as well as the claim of the Catholic Church that his mother, the Virgin Mary, had lived her entire life as a sanctified virgin. So, I thought I would just slip the subject in there and see what came out of it:

Q: (L) Did Mary and Joseph, once together, subsequently have other children?

A: No. But Jesus did.

Q: (L) How many children were there?

A: Three.

Q: (L) Is that, as some people claim, the true meaning of the search for the Holy Grail, that it is not a cup but the "Sang Real", or holy bloodline?

A: Yes.

Q: (L) And what happened to the children?

A: Survived and multiplied fruitfully.

Q: (L) Are there any descendants of Jesus living today?

A: 364,142.

There are several things about the above comments that are worthy of note. The first thing is that the Cassiopaeans volunteered the comment in response to a different question. They almost never do this unless it is something that is vital to know. At the time I was not aware of the significance of this fact. The second thing is the number of descendants. Anyone who does genealogy knows that this number, while seeming to be rather large, is actually very small. We are talking about 2000 years of reproductive history where, if each of the three children really DID multiply "fruitfully", there would be a lot more than close to 400,000 descendants. But, the significance of that didn't occur to me at the time either.

Nevertheless, I was still pursuing the alchemical line of thinking, certain that I had found significant clues to the "Hidden Masters" of the world - at least in human terms. It was a puzzling pursuit. I had read reams of material on conspiracies, supposed "revelations" of "who was on first", and over and over again, when I followed the trail, I found lies and confusion, shell games and obfuscation.

Yet, circumstantial evidence pointed to the existence of a secret fraternity unknown in its entirety to the human race. Other so-called "Secret" groups such as the Rosicrucians, Illuminati, Freemasons, Templars, Priory of Zion, and so forth, seemed to be merely red herrings created and destroyed by the true Secret Masters in their masterful manipulations of humanity and seekers after truth. I came across many allusions to the idea that, from time to time, they replenish their membership from some of these groups, but that the groups themselves were NOT "in on the secrets", and any one of them was as likely to be used in the next gambit of bait and switch as another.

I came to the realization that, if they existed, these Secret Masters possessed incredible knowledge and unsurpassed cunning. I realized, at one point, that the trails I was following had been followed by the greatest minds of the human race for millennia with no evidence of the truth being revealed by any of them at any given point. Who was I to think that I could accomplish what had never been done before?

Yes, over and over again this or that person claimed to have "discovered" the "Greatest Secret", to have "found the evidence" that there was some group that had long term plans to take over the world, but in the end, the evidence would not hold up to scrutiny, or would slip away like mercury. The trail would come up against a locked door. I finally understood that this was the "nature of the beast". It was deliberate. These Secret Masters manipulate our lives and experiences like puppet masters. I understood something else: they also leave clues here and there to lead potential members through a complex maze for purposes of possible recruitment. Many of these clues are so convincing, are so "synchronous", are so cunningly set up that it is easy to come to the wrong conclusions - to believe that you have arrived at the "Holy City", when, in fact, you have only come across a road sign pointing the wrong way. Apparently, they only admit the most clever and sincere seekers of Truth who prove themselves through years of work and dedication. And, in the present time when conditions seem to be conducive to "breaks in the veil", there seem to be even greater efforts being put forth to further conceal and obfuscate the matter. The wild claims and rumors being propagated by "agents of disinformation" serve only to further conceal the truth. We are in a veritable maelstrom of a shell game!

According to some sources, the number of members of the Secret Fraternity is fixed and in order for one to pass on, another must be put in his place. Because of the frequent lack of qualified candidates, some of the members must extend their life spans for many hundreds of years. This may sound pleasant to those who are addicted to life in the flesh, but to those who possess Great Knowledge, this seems to be actually a burden.

Another curious fact was, over and over again I came across what I called The Scottish Question. Every time I hit a brick wall in my research, it seemed that the only scant thread left lying, broken and untraceable, suggested something to do with Scotland.

But, to continue with the story, as a result of attending a showing of the David Hudson video, I was introduced to a woman who later attended two sessions where several of the threads we were following all came together.

However, on the 12th of September, before the guest just mentioned scheduled to visit us, we had a private session for the purpose of asking a few questions about the David Hudson/Monoatomic Gold issue.

For those of you who aren't aware of what this is, a man named David Hudson "discovered" a substance that seemed to be exactly what many alchemical texts were talking about in terms of the "White Powder of Gold" that was not only the agent of transmutation for metals, but also for the human body. His claim was that taking this powder acted on the DNA in such a way as to effect a rapid and amazing healing and perfecting of the human body so that one was "spiritualized" to such an extent that superpowers were not only possible, but probable. At one point in his talk, he said that some people who had taken this powder over a period of time had described having "whole body orgasms" that just went on and on.

The gist of the reason for the video lecture was to "raise money". That sort of bothered me, but it was awhile before I figured out exactly why. I wrote down some questions about the David Hudson work in my notes as follows:

1. Why, after spending purportedly 5.5 million dollars to isolate and attempt to patent Monoatomic Gold, has David Hudson's obsession for knowledge suddenly stopped short of self-experimentation? (I know, he says his wife won't let him, but that begs the question with something like what he claims to have discovered, especially if he is as convinced of what it is as he claims to be and is trying to "sell the public" on it.)

2. If David Hudson possesses the "Philosopher's Stone" why is he asking for money? The literature tells us that one part in one hundred thousand will transmute base metals into gold. Doesn't it work?

3. If The Secret Masters have existed these many thousands of years with the knowledge and use of this substance, and if they have kept it a continual secret, assassinating, if necessary, entire groups of people to protect the secret, why is it suddenly being allowed out now?

These were the issues in my mind on September 12, 1995, when we settled down to ask a couple questions about David Hudson:

Q: (L) OK, this David Hudson tape, about what he calls the Philosopher's Stone, what is this substance that David Hudson has discovered? We watched the video about it; I'm sure you guys watched it with us, so, what is this stuff?

A: Watch developments there only from a distance.

Q: (L) Is taking this substance as he is talking about, is it dangerous, as I kind of think it is?

A: Possibly.

Q: (L) So, in other words, I should not get involved in that, either?

A: Up to you.

Q: (L) I know it's up to me, but you said to watch it from a distance, so I'm assuming that is a clue...

A: Yes.

Q: (L) OK, my feeling is that there is some negative energy manipulating David Hudson, even though he may be a positive and giving person who is trying to do positive things, and that...

A: This is often true!

Q: (L) I think that taking something like that to transform your consciousness without doing the work or having it occur naturally is very much like black magic. That's what I think. (F) It's too easy... I read over the years bits and pieces from various different sources that all the things he described in there **are possible** for those who are willing to sacrifice; to exert what to us would appear to be an extreme degree of ethereal and spiritual energy... (L) I am not even sure that it is a question of sacrifice, though it may be; but it also includes desire for knowledge and the natural destiny of the soul and ..... (F) Well, did Jesus take this gold powder?

A: No.

Q: (L) Did Adolph Hitler take this kind of powder, or something similar?

A: Yes.

Q: (F): That paints a rather bleak picture, doesn't it? (L) Could this powder be utilized to transform a person in a very positive way, enabling them to do great good?

A: Or could it be utilized to transform an entire race of beings into hypnotic submission!!!!!!!!!!!!

Q: (F): Wow! (L) Put it in the water. (F) Or even just advertise it as the "Manna from Heaven!" I mean, remember who runs this world, and has for 309 thousand years, are they just going to sit back and say "Oh, yeah, we'll just let this gold powder get spread round everywhere, and get totally defeated", just like that? I don't think so! (L) Oh, that's a scary thought! Well, I guess, unless you have .... Do you have something you would like to tell us or communicate to us at the present time?

A: Reflect upon messages received and good-bye.

The last comment seemed, on the surface, to merely be a remark relating to the answers about Monoatomic Gold. And if it hadn't been for the dream I had that night, I would never have thought anything further about this, more or less "volunteered" remark.

In this dream, I was a bride and was wearing a wonderful dress with flowers in my hair and there was a limousine waiting outside to take me to my "wedding". I didn't know who the groom was, but there were a lot of people around me encouraging me to "get in the car" and go to "meet the bridegroom". For some reason, I was filled with happiness and the joy of those around me was contagious, so, overcoming my hesitations, I went to the car, got in and was taken to the place of the wedding. I was aware that the day was a Saturday, and it seemed to be the 14th because something was said about Friday the 13th.

It turned out to be a big restaurant with a wonderful feast prepared and waiting. It was all decorated with flowers and streamers everywhere and many, many people were gathered in a happy and joyful crowd who cheered me as I got out of the car.

The "Bridegroom" came forward to take my hand and we walked through the crowds of people to stand in front of a priest-like person who married us. I was overcome with happiness even though I could not see the groom's face!

As soon as we were married, the music began to play, and he took me out onto the middle of the floor where everyone had cleared a space, and we began to dance. It was like flying and we whirled and spun and it was happiness such as I had never experienced in my entire life and I awoke bathed in a sensation of ecstatic joy!

Now, I have all kinds of dreams, some of them are just mundane "sorting of the subconscious". This kind doesn't leave much of an impression on me in any way, and the "feel" and "flavor" of them is pretty bland and unemotional. Some of my dreams are mundane "prophetic" dreams where I will dream about events that actually happen, though they are insignificant. These are a little stronger in terms of "feel and flavor", but it is easy to tell from the lack of emotional content that they are not terribly important. Then, there are the dreams that warn me of actual danger wherein there is an actual drama that is unreal in terms of the actual actions and reality in which I live, but which are dynamically accurate because the actual "dangerous persons" are in the roles of the villains just to get the point across. These dreams are generally very strong in flavor and emotional content. But, only rarely have I ever had a "happy dream" that was so overwhelming that it shook me to the core.

This dream of the wedding had the most powerful emotional content of any dream I ever had, yet the dynamics of it were, in real terms, incomprehensible. I was already married and had five children, so I really couldn't think of it as anything but a powerful symbolic "prophecy" that I would somehow "find the truth" or something like that. I decided that I was being given a foretaste of my success in the quest for knowledge and understanding of the human condition. There are all kinds of ways you can interpret the symbols of a marriage, being a bride, dancing and attending a party.

But, in any event, I wanted to ask about it and did at the next session which was also attended by this young woman (RC) I had met via the David Hudson thread:

> Q: (L) I dreamed the other night that I got married, and there was a big party, dancing, the limousine and so on... flowers, happiness. In my dream, I heard a voice saying that the wedding would be on a Saturday the 14th, following Friday the 13th, could you tell me anything about this dream?
>
> A: No.

Well, that was pretty final! The Cassiopaeans were simply not going to tell me anything about it and that was that. I was not yet fully "conditioned" to the fact that, in cases of the most important issues of my life, they will tell me nothing at all and their declining to answer was indeed *most* significant.

In retrospect, I can see that this meeting and the presence of this individual was a "trigger" for a variety of things. She was Jewish and almost immediately began talking to me about her past life in Nazi Germany and how she had been experimented on by Dr. Mengele and had died as a result, (or so she claimed). I shared with her my own belief and dreams about having committed suicide in Germany after my husband and children were taken and killed by the Nazis. My guest became very excited and was convinced that she had been one of my children. It was true that there was a strong rapport between us, but I wasn't sure that her interpretation was the correct one. But, she wanted to ask:

Q: (RC) What is my relationship to Frank and Laura from any past life connections? Did we know each other in Germany?

A: Maybe. Discover.

Q: (L) Now, I was looking at the astrological charts, just to see what kind of matches there were and it was a lot. (RC) According to astrology, that shows a past life connection.

A: Who were you?

Q: (L) You mean me?

A: Yes.

Q: (L) I was just a German woman... (RC) I was wondering about Egypt?

A: But we are still in Germany! [It was clear from this, though only in retrospect, that the Cassiopaeans had an agenda in following this line. They were not answering RC, they were talking to me.]

Q: (L) All I know was that I committed suicide, name was Helga, I think...

A: Who was your husband?

Q: (L) I don't know. He was Jewish. Is that what you are getting at?

A: Okay. Who were your children?

Q: (RC) They asked who were the children. Was I one of your children?

A: Discover. When we say discover, we mean for you to use your given talents to learn, not to have us lead you by the hand every step of the way. If we were to do that, we would cheat you out of an opportunity to gain knowledge, and more importantly, understanding. Thus, we would be abridging free will!

Clearly there was something about my past life in Germany and my husband in that time that I was supposed to discover. Not only that, it struck me as strange for them to be directing me to think about this in this way immediately after my question about the dream of getting married which they had refused to answer in explicit terms. They were not answering my question, but they were trying to get something across without violating free will. Then, they said this:

A: We are receiving strong wave pattern surrounding subject we chose to cover, thus we interrupted inquiries! Moshe in Israel.

Q: (RC) Who is Moshe in Israel?

A: Moshe is IN Israel.

But we could get no more. They would not tell us who Moshe was or what the connection was. But, I did get to toss in a last couple of questions:

Q: (L) Is it true that there is an enclave of alchemists that live somewhere in the Pyrenees...

A: Yes.

Q: (L) Is this the group that you referred to as "The Quorum" in a previous session?

A: Partly.

Q: (L) Do these alchemists use this power as talked about by David Hudson to enhance their longevity and their physical health?

A: And to control.

Q: (L) Are there people in this enclave who live for literally hundreds, if not thousands, of years?

A: Open.

Now, we have to divert in another direction to bring in this most important thread about a strange thing called The Quorum. This had been mentioned by the Cassiopaeans almost exactly a year earlier. It happened this way:

Q: (L) I would like to know what is the origin of the Freemasons?

A: Osirians.

Q: (L) Can you tell us when the original Freemasons formed as a society?

A: 5633 BC

Q: (L) Is Freemasonry as it is practiced today the same?

A: 33rd degree, yes.

Q: (L) So, there is a continuing tradition for over 7 thousand years?

A: Yes.

Q: (L) Is this organization with a plan to take over and rule the world?

A: Not exactly.

Q: (L) What is their focus?

A: Overseers of the status of Quorum.

Q: (L) What is the Quorum?

A: Deeper knowledge organization. Totally secret to your kind as of yet. Very important with regard to your future.

Q: (L) In what way?

A: Changes.

Q: (L) Can you get more specific? Is that changes to us personally?

A: Partly.

Q: (L) Earth changes?

A: Also.

Q: (L) What is the relationship between this quorum and the Cassiopaeans?

A: They communicate with us regularly.

Q: (L) Do they do this knowing you are Cassiopaeans or...

A: Yes.

Q: (L) Has there been an ongoing relationship between the Cassiopaeans and this quorum for these thousands of years?

A: For some time as you measure it.

Q: (L) Is the Quorum composed of members who are humans on this planet?

A: Partly.

Q: (L) Would we know any of them as well known figures?

A: Hidden. None you would know.

Q: (L) How do the Masons relate to the Illuminati?

A: Masons are low-level branch.

Well, this was pretty disturbing, to say the least. Here the Cassiopaeans were telling me that *they* were "in contact" with this Quorum which, as far as I could tell, were the Secret Masters of the World, and there seemed to be a lot of evidence, circumstantial though it might be, that this group did *not* have humanity's best interests at heart. At least, that was the propaganda!

So, I brought it up again, determined to get to the bottom of this mystery:

Q: (L) On a number of occasions we talked about the Quorum and the Illuminati. They both seem to be the highest levels of secret organizations. What is their relationship to each other?

A: Quorum mostly alien; Illuminati mostly human. Meet; two halves of whole.

Q: (L) Well the Quorum was described as being in touch with the Cassiopaeans, that is yourselves, which you have described as beneficial beings, or Service to Others oriented beings, is this correct?

A: Close.

Q: (L) The illuminati has been described as being behind or with the Brotherhood of the Serpent which you have described as being connected with the Lizard beings...

A: Close. But not that simple.

Q: (L) Well, if the Quorum are supposed to be the good guys and the Illuminati are supposed to be the bad guys, and they both are at the high levels of Freemasonry, what is the story here? I do NOT understand!

A: Picture a circle or cycle first, now then contemplate for a moment before follow up.

Q: (L) Okay, I am contemplating a cycling circle.

A: Now, two halves representing positive and negative. Two halves.

Q: (L) Well, what I am getting out of that is there are two halves and both sides are playing with the human race. Is that it?

A: No. This is complicated but if you can learn and understand, it will be a super revelation.

Q: (L) Well, go ahead and explain.

A: Ask step by step.

Q: (L) Why do we so often have to ask things step by step?

A: In order to absorb the information.

Q: (L) The Quorum is described as the good guys. The illuminati are described as bad guys. And yet, they are both drawn from higher Masonic ranks, or so it seems. When a person in the Masonic organization reaches the higher levels, are there individuals from these two groups that are essentially recruiting Masons to one side or the other?

A: First, not exactly one side or another.

Q: (L) I am beginning to not understand something here...

A: Unblock.

Q: (L) I don't have a block here. If the brotherhood AKA illuminati AKA Lizzies AKA Beast AKA Antichrist are the ones who are screwing around with human beings, planning to take over this planet, how are they related or connected to the Quorum, which is in touch with...

A: This will take time to explain be patient it will be worth it. Ask step by step.

Q: (L) Okay. What is the nature of evil?

A: Blend.

Q: (L) I don't understand. Are the Lizzies what we would consider to be evil or STS?

A: Yes.

Q: (L) Are the Cassiopaeans what we would consider to be good or STO?

A: Yes.

Q: (L) Yet, do the Cassiopaeans use and manipulate the Lizzies to accomplish certain things?

A: No.

Q: (L) The Lizzies work independently and in opposition to the Cassiopaeans?

A: Independently, not in opposition. **We serve others therefore there is no opposition.** Careful now. Step by step. If you do not fully understand answer ask another.

Q: (L) Part of a whole. Part of a circle.

A: Blend. Picture a blending colored circle image.

Q: (L) Are you saying that at some levels the two halves overlap in some way?

A: Close.

Q: (L) Are you saying that some of the Quorum are good guys and bad guys and the same for the Illuminati because the two are on opposing sides of the circle but at the point of blending one is weighted more to one side and the other to the other side? And these organizations are where the interactions come together?

A: Closer.

Q: (L) Well, I don't get it. Let's leave it for the time being.

A: No. Now please.

Q: (L) Okay. So it is a blending. Does it have something to do with ... in your case service to others means that you even serve those who serve self, is that correct?

A: Yes; we serve you and the Lizards have programmed your race to self-service, remember.

Q: (L) So, I am still a Service to Self individual, is that correct?

A: But moving slowly toward Service to Others. Not all humans are.

Q: (L) Does this mean that when beings who are members of the Quorum or Illuminati call for information or help, that you, because of your service to others orientation are obliged to answer whoever calls?

A: Yes and no.

Q: (L) What is the no part.

A: If vibrational frequencies are out of pattern we do not connect.

Q: (L) Is the activity of the Lizzies part of an overall grand plan or design?

A: All is.

Q: (L) Let's go on.

A: Must answer question. You will feel ecstasy once answered.

Q: (L) Okay. A blending. Yet two halves.

A: Of a circle.

Q: (L) Who designed this circle?

A: Natural frequency wave. Some near conjunction blend both service patterns and each "camp" to create perfect balance.

Q: (L) Okay, so the Illuminati are the higher level on the pathway of Service to Self and somehow, by reaching these higher levels may even come to the realizations or frequencies which have caused their position to be modified or blended to where service to self becomes or incorporates or moves them to service to others realizations, is this correct?

A: Continue.

Q: (L) Okay, the beings in the Quorum are those who are focused on Service to Others and they, in their pathway of Service to Others begin to understand that some Service to Others includes refusing to give to those who are Service to Self?

A: Close.

Q: (L) And the whole idea is to blend both pathways no matter which direction you come to it from?

A: Service to Others provides the perfect balance of those two realities; Service to Self is the diametrical opposite closing the grand cycle in perfect balance.

Q: (L) So it is necessary to have a pathway of Service to Self in order for the pathway of Service to Others to exist?

A: Yes.

Q: (L) And those who are in the Quorum and the Illuminati ...

A: Blends in middle.

Q: (L) So it is necessary to have the darkness in order to have the light...

A: Yes.

Q: (L) And both the Quorum and Illuminati are drawn from the higher-level Masonic organizations...

A: Freemasonry is human reflection in physical of these processes.

We begin to see that everything is not quite as simple as we might have thought. You can't just say that the good guys wear white hats and the bad guys wear black tee shirts. There is no easy answer.

But, we knew this all along. We know it from our own natures, and from the fact that every family has black sheep and white sheep and everything in between. We can't get on our soapbox and declare that the Masons or Illuminati are implementing a plan to control the world and take away Free Will. On the other hand, there may certainly be elements in both organizations and others with such plans. And, of course, the practical implication of this is the fact that the followers of the Service to Self pathway use their free will to violate the free will of others *through lies and deceptions*. And, of course, the cleverest of these lies is to blame everything that they do themselves on someone or something else while they, themselves, continue to conceal their presence and true nature.

In recent times this shell game has become quite interesting, to say the least.

So, just who is on first here?

Gary Allen writes in his book *None Dare Call it Conspiracy*:

> "It must be remembered that the first job of any conspiracy, whether it be in politics, crime or within a business office, is to convince everyone else that no conspiracy exists. The conspirators' success will be determined largely by their ability to do this."

How, precisely, is this done? Well, the chief way is through control of the media. Through the media, the most effective weapon is ridicule, satire and character assassination. These extremely potent weapons are used to redirect attention away from the issues. Even a person who doesn't care what other people think of him/her, will find little cachet in the minds of reasonable persons with the stigma of absurdity attached to them.

In the present time, it seems that more people are becoming aware, so the ante has been "upped" a bit. It is no longer so easy to just ridicule those who suggest conspiracies because "conspiracy theories" are just "silly". Now it is necessary to add another ingredient to the mix.

In this program, special "agents" are sent out to plant disinformation that expand and accelerate the conspiracy theories by "overdrawing" them to the point of absurdity.

Gary Allen writes:

> "Some conspiratorialists do indeed overdraw the picture by expanding the conspiracy (from the small clique which it is) to include every knee jerk liberal activist and government bureaucrat. Or, because of racial or religious bigotry they will take small fragments of legitimate evidence and

expand them into a conclusion that will support their particular prejudice, i.e., the conspiracy is totally "Jewish", "Catholic", or "Masonic". These people do not help to expose the conspiracy, but, sadly play into the hands of those who want the public to believe that all conspiratorialists are screwballs."[Allen, 1972]

Let me go in this direction for just a little bit longer to illustrate my point. In recent weeks, a member of the Cassiopaea E-group discussion list, apparently a fan of David Icke, wrote:

"I am noticing a serious problem here. The British Royals who are shape shifting/child sacrificing reptilians are *never mentioned* here. The DIANA case is completely covered up. That story of "suicide" is complete crap. The Royals are alleged (I should say 100% guilty) to have ordered and been involved in the *ritual masonic sacrifice* of *Diana/Dodi* (and allegedly the child). the *Egypt Air* crash has been labeled; "a gust of wind" "these things just happen". No they do not when they have massive 33 and 19.5 symbolism, totally beyond coincidence. These are 2 major examples of *masonic ritual sacrifices* that have been blatantly *covered* up by the Cassiopaeans or someone involved in the info distribution process. Is there a *mason/templar* among us? I have seen every other site infiltrated. Once again this is just *theory*. But there is reason for concern. Not to mention the biggest event occurring above your home *worldwide* right now; *chemtrail spraying*. Just a military exercise? Give me a break, this is a totally *massive worldwide spray* that is intended to keep down the vibrational rate of the population and kill some in the process. *remember; disinformation is sandwiched between layers of factual info*. Something stinks here, and the C's or somebody need to do some explaining."

Well, as usual, I went to the recommended sites that were presented as sources of proof. On the subject of the death of Princess Diana, I found a list of questions as follows:

In *Death of a Princess*, Thomas Sancton and Scott MacLeod investigate the questions everyone has been asking since Diana, Princess of Wales, and Dodi Al Fayed were killed in a Paris car crash in the small hours of August 31, 1997.

How was a drunken, drugged, nonlicensed driver allowed at the wheel of the Mercedes?

Why was the driver, off-duty Ritz Hotel assistant security director Henri Paul, called back to the hotel that night and assigned a job that was not his?

Didn't senior officials of the Al Fayed - owned Ritz know that Paul was a chronic alcoholic and that he was drinking in the hotel that very night?

What was the role of the paparazzi that had stalked the couple all day long and pursued them in that final high-speed chase?

Why was Dodi so spooked by the photographers, to the point of changing normal security procedures and exposing himself and the princess to unwarranted risks?

What do skid marks, paint, and glass fragments tell us about the involvement of a second car?

Who was the driver of the second car, why didn't he stop, how did he escape, and how did the police organize a nationwide manhunt aimed at tracking him down?

And so on. These are all good questions similar to "why was JFK's parade route changed at the last minute"?; "why was he allowed to dispense with his bullet proof bubble"? ; "why did the authorities not pursue the gunshots from the grassy knoll"?; on and on infinitum.

In any of you have read Jim Garrison's book *On the Trail of the Assassins*, or if you have watched Oliver Stone's movie, JFK, (and you have sufficient synapses on your neurons), you will be convinced to an extreme degree of probability that there WAS a conspiracy to murder JFK. Not only that, you will be in agreement with a large segment of the world's population that the *Warren Report* was a sham and somebody got away with murder. And it may even make you sick to think about it. But, it won't matter.

During the period of time that *St. Petersburg Times* journalist, Tom French, was interviewing me for his article, he attended a number of sessions. At one of them, the subject of the Stone movie and Garrison's book came up during a discussion that I have on tape. Mr. French, an "investigative reporter", opined that Oliver Stone did a terrible disservice to the American people by making his movie which was so "misleading" and was based on so much "erroneous speculation". Needless to say, we were rather astounded by this remark and asked him what he believed. He fell back on the Warren Commission report as being the definitive conclusion!

Now, remember, this is a really nice and sincere guy who believes he is doing his job well. I have absolutely *no* doubts about that. But he still believes that the Warren Commission gave us the correct answer: that Lee Harvey Oswald assassinated JFK "all by his lonesome"! I wonder if he is still of the same opinion after Gerald Ford admitted to "doctoring" the report? Probably so. Some people have an infinite capacity for "shoving the truth under the rug". And when they are journalists, we have no hope for unbiased journalism. And how many more of them are exactly like that? Innocent and brainwashed. It's, "Mom, apple pie and all that"!

But, getting back to Jim Garrison's book: the careful reader will note that Garrison reports some incidents that are described as "sheep dipping" of undercover agents that simply do *not* make sense. In order for some of the events he uncovered to happen, whoever was managing things would have had to have *time travel capabilities*. That is to say, for certain scenarios to have played as they were reported, well in advance of JFK being elected president, someone would have had to know *years* in advance that 1) Kennedy was going to run for office; 2) that he would be elected; 3) and that he would need to be assassinated. Who could know these things that far in advance?

Jim Garrison did not seem to note this problem though he did express extreme bafflement at the results of his investigation. The very fact that he was reporting what he found, what the many witnesses attested to, and which was, in some cases impossible, indicates that he was *not* trying to promote a hyperdimensional Control System. Yet, in the end, that is the only rational explanation for the reported sequence IF the facts, as presented, were accurately portrayed.

In fact, some of the items collected by Garrison actually pointed away from *his* suspects, yet he reported them nonetheless, so we have no logical reason to assume that he was grinding a personal ax in the writing of his book.

We find the same issues present in the above list of questions about the death of Princess Diana. For the scenario that developed to have been part of a conspiracy, it would have to have been a hyperdimensional control system with space/time management capabilities. And in such a case, whether or not Masons, Jews, Templars or anybody were "implicated" would be somewhat moot. Because, if they were, it was very likely completely unconscious and serves no purpose to fling such accusations around other than further obfuscation of the real source of the conspiracy.

Regarding the death of Diana and Dodi, I wrote to the list member as follows:

> "What is decided at 'higher levels' can manifest in many ways at *this* level. The bottom line is: nobody dies unless they have reached a "check out" point in their "life blueprint". Whether they agree at some level to participate in an event that leads them down a path to being murdered or otherwise...
>
> ...Now, all of you know (or should by now) that I have researched the 'alien phenomenon' and have received much info about it from the C's over the years. And, you know, if you have read the web site, that it does not seem to be a very pretty picture. You also may know that I have followed many 'paper trails' that relate to secret societies and conspiracies and have read many different views of these matters in an attempt to 'sort

out' the subject. In the end, when you delve deeply into these things, you find endless lies and confusion - layer after layer of them.

It is at this point that you have to begin to *think*.

What could possibly be the reason for this? And you finally realize that the very effect you have observed IS the desired objective - Lies and Confusion. And that is where the rubber hits the road and you understand that if you take as truth the *wrong* view, you are no better than anyone who believes the most blatant and obvious lie, even if the lie you believe is far more subtle and cunningly devious. It still boils down to the fact that you have been deceived and made a fool of - if not food!

So, I understood that great caution needed to be employed in studying these matters. I also understood that the greatest minds of all time have been applied to these problems for millennia - with no real result of 'waking up mankind'. So, what is the deal here? Why is it so that suddenly, at this particular point in time, different people think that they have 'plumbed' the mystery - have found the 'Greatest Secret' and can now expose it for the world to view and believe as true?

Well, when you consider the great machine behind these lies, the apparent (though not proven) hyperdimensional nature of the reality from which ours is manifested, you come to realize that it is not going to be that easy!

When I read David Icke's book *The Robot's Rebellion,* the main fault I found in his searches for the evidence of a global conspiracy was his reliance on what other people have said before, as well as what he was being 'fed', with very little checking of the sources or using of cerebral abilities to really think about what he was saying. I was very put off with his beginning that referred to that old hackneyed idea of the 'Luciferian Rebellion' and the 'out of synch' energy of evil and all that - because I had already been through that belief system and found its errors and the root of those errors. Still, I felt that this was a pretty good compilation, even if I would have liked a little less hysteria and a lot more documentation.

As it has been noted before, asking for proof of some of these things is like asking for mercury to stay between your fingers. Just isn't going to happen. So, at best, we have 'tracks' and circumstantial evidence that piles so high that it would certainly convict in a court of law, but yet the mainstream community wants the 'smoking gun' or the 'UFO Cadillac' on the White House Lawn. Not gonna happen.

So, when I ask for 'sources', you must understand that I mean the sources of the idea, the key to the chain of evidence that has been followed, even if that evidence is merely circumstantial. At the same time, I do realize that there *are* some 'hard facts', that taken together with other 'hard facts', *can* be connected as 'circumstantial evidence' chains - and we really need to look for these things.

But, getting back to David Icke. Yes, I realized that he had followed a similar path that I did when I was researching conspiracies back in the 80's for the writing of the *Noah Syndrome*. There was very little new in that book for me. *But,* he made rather short shrift of the 'alien question'. That troubled me. He wasn't 'getting it' at the deepest level, in my opinion.

Let me explain my reasoning for this. When one deeply studies 'conspiracy' theory, one comes face to face with a consortium of 'Hidden Masters' who are evident in their tracks, but can never be 'seen', so to speak. We find Masons, Illuminati, Templars, Priory of Sion, Rosicrucians, Elders of Zion, and a host of other minor and major players. They come and go on the stage of history like actors playing many different parts. As soon as one 'loses its force' another comes into power and holds sway for a time and then becomes 'known' and obvious and is replaced.

The next thing is the 'time' factor. When we consider conspiracies that have been in place for many thousands of years (and, yes, there is a pile of circumstantial evidence for this) we have to consider what I call the 'pay-off' factor. We can study the lives of the various people who are supposed to have been 'masters of the game' in these different secret societies that have been exposed from time to time, and determine that it is clear that they are human and that they are being used as 'screens' and 'red herrings' to draw attention away from something else.

The very idea of a group of people who live and die in the ordinary way being motivated to put events into motion that may benefit someone else a thousand years down the road, and who then suffer exposure and ignominious death or other unpleasant consequences would, on the one hand, bespeak someone who is devoted to serving others, yet it is clear that this is not the touted agenda. So, we can only conclude that they are serving themselves, and that leaves us with the blank as to what they get out of it!

Standard psychological theories apply here, and we realize that either these people are extremely stupid, and in that case, the whole conspiracy would fall apart rather quickly rather than having lasted for thousands of years, or we must think that these people are being used by *someone* or *something* else, for its own ends. And, in that case, we have to realize that the various proposed sources of the conspiracy, whether it is Masons or Rosicrucians or Illuminati, are merely another facet of the smoke screen.

Once we have realized that, we realize that if we jump on the bandwagon of accusations and 'we have discovered the secret', we may very well be falling for the same old Machiavellian ploy that has been used for millennia.

Well, I puzzled over this for a long time - a period in which I was not considering a hyperdimensional reality. I simply could not see the motivation for any group of men, who must be at least somewhat ordinary, to perpetrate such a plan with no apparent 'payoff' Supposedly, many of them would 'put a certain action' in gear that would only bear fruit a few hundred, or many hundreds, of years in the future to their time, and then they would be exposed and killed or otherwise done away with. Again, such self-sacrifice is either a symptom of pure STO, or evidence of *someone else* behind the scenes.

So, David Icke found these things... so have many others. It's been fairly common stuff for a very long time. Some may be true; some may be red herrings. Of course, putting it all together in this day and time, and tracking it through the centuries is an interesting exercise - *if one is then able to see* the fact that there is a 'puppetmaster' that has set this whole thing up to lead astray those who are more clever than others, but not yet clever enough to see the *unseen* element.

Well, fine and good. He wrote this book and it made a big splash. What next? Well, his next book was a *huge* disappointment because I could see that 'they' had gotten to him. Now, just imagine this scenario: a person discovers all these things that he wrote about in his first book... (or thinks he is 'discovering' them) - very similar to what I wrote in *Noah*, (but was completely unable to get it published and had no resources at the time to do it myself), and he gets it published, it gets promoted, and a lot of folks begin to think that maybe nothing is as it seems.

Well, clearly, David was going in the right direction. He might even be able to figure it out once he came to a full understanding of the 'hyperdimensional' factor.

What do you think the 'Puppet Masters' are going to do now?

And remember, you are *not* dealing with human minds here... you are *not* dealing with ordinary logic... you have *no* hope of figuring out their next 'move' except to pay close attention to the action. And, I only knew this because I had taken great pains to study not only the evidence, but who gathered the evidence, how and why and then what happened to them *after* ... So, I *knew* that there were repercussions to speaking out. And David is a very personable and dynamic person. Not only that, I think he has a real drive for truth. (Even if he doesn't have a 'nose' for it.)

So, here he is, David Icke on the 'Truth Train', picking up a lot of passengers, and building a lot of steam. Well, I think that if a couple guys in three piece suits knocked on his door one night and said 'Mr. Icke, we are here to make you an offer...' he probably would have slammed the door in their faces. At least, I would *like* to think that. But, maybe something like that *did* happen and he invited them in.

But, what is more likely is this: Somebody knocked on his door (figuratively speaking) and said: 'Mr. Icke, I see that you have a great deal of courage and you are making a lot of waves, and I came to you to tell you my story about what is behind the scenes of these conspiracies that you talk about. And, I am afraid for my life, so you must be very careful and help me... so we can reveal to the world the *greatest secret*!'

And, of course, being a person who is 'dedicated to truth', and a person who wants to 'save the world', and all that, Mr. Icke invited this person onto his 'truth train'. But, he didn't realize that this person was an agent of the Puppet Masters... and that this person would secretly be slipping nuclear bombs into the firebox of the steam plant of the engine of his train... and that this nuclear power would speed the train up so fast that not only could it no longer stop to pick up new passengers, it would eventually run off the track and crash and burn.

So, what do I mean? Well, yes, we know that the C's have talked about underground bases, about genetic experiments and the creation of a 'Master Race' breeding ground for the Nephilim - they have talked about Drachomonoid controllers of our realm and they have talked about many of the same bizarre things that David Icke talks about... the difference is in the 'deeper explanations' and the 'mode of response'.

I will give you an example: First of all, the 'sources' of David Icke's information about the Reptilians from 'the constellation Draco' are extremely questionable. When I began to track this idea, the closest I could come to it was that it originated with folks who claimed to have been given this info *by* reptoids!

So, let's get this straight: we are trying to uncover a conspiracy, and we go to somebody who we suspect is part of the conspiracy, and ask them what the whole thing is about? Or rather, they came to someone who then reported what they were told, and this became the basis for the 'knowledge' about the Drachomonoids. That's like asking Richard Nixon what was on the missing tape.

Other information he writes about relates to pedophile abuse by public figures. That sets the warning bells off immediately because accusations of sexual aberration have been used throughout millennia to smear and destroy many people and groups, most notably the Templars and Cathars. Nevertheless, the inflammatory dwelling on these kinds of things in prurient and graphic detail bespeaks an almost fiendish delight in just simply talking about it. And that is not to say that I don't think that such things go on - god only knows the awful stuff I have had to deal with in the course of doing hypnotherapy. So, that is not the issue. What IS the issue, is the creation of the 'us against them' hard line philosophy that focuses on *people* and *not* the true hyperdimensional source of the control.

A couple of David's sources include Cathy O'Brien and Arizona Wilder. Regarding the former, her accusations of truly bizarre sexual abuse, pedophilia, and assorted disgusting factors are well publicized on the net, and we have already discussed them, so I won't repeat them here. And, yes, the C's have confirmed that there is, indeed, something along this line going on, though with modifications to the story.

The bottom line is: we have to wonder exactly why it is that Cathy O'Brien and Arizona Wilder have been allowed to 'come out of the closet?'

Think about it.

Now, one correspondent wrote to me that the revelations of Cathy O'Brien made were very carefully orchestrated so that the information came out in a way that was able to protect her from the possibility of being 'hit.' In other words, if she had been killed *after* the book came out, it would be seen as 'confirmation' of her story. (The mistake made with Morris Jessup has not been repeated!)

So, how to do the conspirators do damage control with Cathy O'Brien?

Well, the answer is simple: Arizona Wilder!!!

Icke tells us that Wilder 'conducted human sacrifice rituals for some of the most famous people on Earth, including the British Royal Family'. Arizona says, (in Icke's book, *The Biggest Secret):*

"The Queen - I have seen her sacrifice people and eat their flesh and drink their blood. One time she got so excited with blood lust that she didn't cut the victim's throat from left to right in the normal ritual. She just went crazy, stabbing and ripping at the flesh after she'd shape-shifted into a reptilian. When she shape-shifts she has a long reptile face, almost like a beak, and she's off-white colour."

"Prince Charles - I've seen him shape-shift into a reptilian and do all the things the Queen does. I have seen him sacrifice children."

"The Queen Mother is a lot older than people think. To be honest, the Royal Family hasn't died for a long time, they have just metamorphised. (sic) It's sort of cloning, but in a different way... They looked like reptiles originally, but they look like us when they get out now... The Queen Mother is 'Chief Toad' of this part of Europe and they have people like her in each continent." [Icke, *The Biggest Secret*, 1999]

Now, just think about what this has done here. (Or could do to the less subtle and informed reader.) The first thing is that it has placed the focus of blame on *human* beings. Human beings ARE shape shifting Reptilians in cahoots with 'ethereal' demonic reptoid beings. And you can see where that is leading back to, can't you? Yes, that old time religion! We have a 'Luciferian Rebellion' going on here, and those pesky reptoids are really just demons in service to Satan. And, of course, being demons, we have absolutely *no* hope of doing anything at all without help from somewhere 'out there', most likely prayers or rebukes to 'get thee behind me, Satan!'

So, not only have we accomplished a huge coup in terms of hiding the true nature of the *real* conspirators, we have advanced the cause of disempowering human beings by reinforcing their beliefs in the same nonsense that has kept them captive for over two thousand years.

Why would that be so?

The aim of religion is to create a completely controlled artificial environment composed of thoroughly predictable human behaviors - made predictable because they have been programmed in through centuries of lies and obfuscations presented in the form of a 'story' that is actually untrue, and wholly misrepresentative of the real negative aim.

For centuries these programs have been being set up through space/time manipulation. Various prophets or religious leaders have been influenced to preach, prophesy or teach philosophies designed to lay a foundation for later takeover - possibly in our present time. It doesn't matter that the religions are essentially 'good' or seem to be positive. What matters are the programmed responses. If a person is programmed to believe in 'Jesus', if a figure appears to them presenting itself as Jesus, and uses 4th density technology to stimulate the release of certain neuropeptides that can induce feelings of bliss, the individual is primed and ready to obey any command of said being whether it is to 'kill them all and let God sort them out', as was the general rule of the Inquisition, or 'insult everyone who doesn't believe that DI and Dodi were sacrificed by reptilian royals'.

Recently a parody of door-to-door evangelizing was sent around the Internet. It was so exceedingly irreverent that it probably was too shocking for many people to understand how truly enlightening it was. For those who may not have seen it, I am going to include it here because it makes very important points that need to be emphasized:

John: "Hi! I'm John, and this is Mary."

Mary: "Hi! We're here to invite you to come kiss Hank's ass with us."

Me: "Pardon me?! What are you talking about? Who's Hank, and why would I want to kiss His as?"

John: "If you kiss Hank's ass, He'll give you a million dollars; and if you don't, He'll kick the sh*t out of you."

Me: "What? Is this some sort of bizarre mob shakedown?"

John: "Hank is a billionaire philanthropists. Hank built this town. Hank owns this town. He can do whatever he wants, and what He wants is to give you a million dollars, but He can't until you kiss his ass."

Me: "That doesn't make any sense. Why..."

Mary: "Who are you to question Hank's gift? Don't you want a million dollars? Isn't it worth a little kiss on the ass?"

Me: "Well maybe, if it's legit, but..."

John: "Then come kiss Hank's ass with us."

Me: "Do you kiss Hank's ass often?"

Mary: "Oh yes, all the time..."

Me: "And has He given you a million dollars?"

John: "Well no. You don't actually get the money until you leave town."

Me: "So why don't you just leave town now?"

Mary: "You can't leave until Hank tells you to, or you don't get the money, and He kicks the sh*t out of you."

Me: "Do you know anyone who kissed Hank's ass, left town, and got the million dollars?"

John: "My mother kissed Hank's ass for years. She left town last year, and I'm sure she got the money."

Me: "Haven't you talked to her since then?"

John: "Of course not, Hank doesn't allow it."

Me: "So what makes you think He'll actually give you the money if you've never talked to anyone who got the money?"

Mary: "Well, he gives you a little bit before you leave. Maybe you'll get a raise, maybe you'll win a small lotto, maybe you'll just find a twenty-dollar bill on the street."

Me: "What's that got to do with Hank?"

John: "Hank has certain 'connections'."

Me: "I'm sorry, but this sounds like some sort of bizarre con game."

John: "But it's a million dollars, can you really take the chance? And remember, if you don't kiss Hank's ass He'll kick the sh*t of you."

Me: "Maybe if I could see Hank, talk to Him, get the details straight from him..."

Mary: "No one sees Hank, no one talks to Hank."

Me: "Then how do you kiss His ass?"

John: "Sometimes we just blow Him a kiss, and think of His ass. Other times we kiss Karl's ass, and he passes it on."

Me: "Who's Karl?"

Mary: "A friend of ours. He's the one who taught us all about kissing Hank's ass. All we had to do was take him out to dinner a few times."

Me: "And you just took his word for it when he said there was a Hank, that Hank wanted you to kiss His ass, and that Hank would reward you?"

John: "Oh no! Karl has a letter he got from Hank years ago explaining the whole thing. Here's a copy; see for yourself."

From the desk of Karl

1) Kiss Hank's ass and He'll give you a million dollars when you leave town.

2) Use alcohol in moderation.

3) Kick the sh*t out of people who aren't like you.

4) Eat right.

5) Hank dictated this list Himself.

6) The moon is made of green cheese.

7) Everything Hank says is right.

8) Wash your hands after going to the bathroom.

9) Don't use alcohol.

10) Eat your wieners on buns, no condiments.

11) Kiss Hank's ass or He'll kick the sh*t out of you.

Me: "This appears to be written on Karl's letterhead."

Mary: "Hank didn't have any paper."

Me: "I have a hunch that if we checked we'd find this is Karl's handwriting."

John: "Of course, Hank dictated it."

Me: "I thought you said no one gets to see Hank?"

Mary: "Not now, but years ago He would talk to some people."

Me: "I thought you said He was a philanthropist. What sort of philanthropist kicks the sh*t out of people just because they're different?"

Mary: "It's what Hank wants, and Hank's always right."

Me: "How do you figure that?"

Mary: "Item 7 says 'Everything Hank says is right'. That's good enough for me!"

Me: "Maybe your friend Karl just made the whole thing up."

John: "No way! Item 5 says 'Hank dictated this list himself'. Besides, item 2 says 'Use alcohol in moderation', Item 4 says 'Eat right', and item 8 says 'Wash your hands after going to the bathroom'. Everyone knows those things are right, so the rest must be true, too."

Me: "But 9 says 'Don't use alcohol'. which doesn't quite go with item 2, and 6 says 'The moon is made of green cheese', which is just plain wrong."

John: "There's no contradiction between 9 and 2, 9 just clarifies 2. As far as 6 goes, you've never been to the moon, so you can't say for sure."

Me: "Scientists have pretty firmly established that the moon is made of rock..."

Mary: "But they don't know if the rock came from the Earth, or from out of space, so it could just as easily be green cheese."

Me: "I'm not really an expert, but I think the theory that the Moon was somehow 'captured' by the Earth has been discounted*. Besides, not knowing where the rock came from doesn't make it cheese."

John: "Ha! You just admitted that scientists make mistakes, but we know Hank is always right!"

Me: "We do?"

Mary: "Of course we do, Item 5 says so."

Me: "You're saying Hank's always right because the list says so, the list is right because Hank dictated it, and we know that Hank dictated it because the list says so. That's circular logic, no different than saying 'Hank's right because He says He's right'."

John: "Now you're getting it! It's so rewarding to see someone come around to Hank's way of thinking."

Me: "But...oh, never mind. What's the deal with wieners?"

Mary: She blushes.

John: "Wieners, in buns, no condiments. It's Hank's way. Anything else is wrong."

Me: "What if I don't have a bun?"

John: "No bun, no wiener. A wiener without a bun is wrong."

Me: "No relish? No Mustard?"

Mary: She looks positively stricken.

John:(He's shouting.) "There's no need for such language! Condiments of any kind are wrong!"

Me: "So a big pile of sauerkraut with some wieners chopped up in it would be out of the question?"

Mary: Sticks her fingers in her ears. "I am not listening to this. La la la, la la, la la la."

John: "That's disgusting. Only some sort of evil deviant would eat that..."

Me: "It's good! I eat it all the time." (Mary faints.)

John: (He catches Mary.) "Well, if I'd known you where one of those I wouldn't have wasted my time. When Hank kicks the sh*t out of you I'll be there, counting my money and laughing. I'll kiss Hank's ass for you, you bunless, cut-wienered kraut-eater." With this, John dragged Mary to their waiting car, and sped off.

Did you get it? Did you *really* get it? And did you see how accurately it portrays the whole religious mindset? Most importantly, did you notice how "good rules" can be posited for the express purpose of establishing Faith in rules that are not only lies, but are actually detrimental to growth and development? And did you notice how cleverly this little skit actually captured the dynamic of the "true believer"?

More than that, the totally illogical and nonsensical dynamic of "believe this" or you will be damned, punished or otherwise "left out" of some exclusive club is the essence of STS stalking wherein confusion and cross-purpose prevents a clear perception on the part of the Stalkees.

What is the designed objective of this *stalking*?

It is twofold. First, the effect of Stalking is sort of like stampeding a herd of cattle so that they run into a dead end canyon or corral and have no way out. Bit by bit, they are consolidated into an "us against them mode"." Even though, on the surface, it may seem that this "mode" is positive or STO, (i.e. save the world because it is "wrong" or flawed, or blighted with original sin or whatever) the very fact that it is formed in the "dominator" mode of perceiving salvation "outside", or from some "other" source no matter how it is presented, means that it can more easily be "taken over" body, mind and soul at a level that is "unseen and unseeable".

Many people believe they are playing out the basic 'antagonism' and 'self- protection' roles of Satan vs. God. They believe that "sending love and light" to those "in need" is appropriate, without realizing that this activity is predicated upon a deep belief that there is something wrong, in error, in rebellion, and thus becomes again, "us vs. them".

The primary objective of Negative stalking is to persuade through *strongly influenced,* but not robotic, behavior patterns, the Free Choice of the targeted *consciousness* to align with negative higher-density existence. It doesn't matter that the believer thinks he is following the teachings of Jesus, Brahma or Allah. If he is following the STS agenda, no matter how he was deceived to believe it is right, it is still the STS agenda. And, by being a "true believer", he can, at any time, be co-opted to the 4th density STS hierarchy by the appearance of an "angelic" being, or the receiving of a "benevolent message, prophecy, or healing". It is only with knowledge of these conditions that anyone has any hope of being able to see through the ploys and the programs.

The second objective of stalking is to create a belief in defensive measures that are totally and completely ineffective. And then, the same beings that advise us to pray, to "rebuke Satan", to "just say no" to abductions, take great pains to make sure that these techniques *seem* to work so that more and more people will be deluded into thinking that they are actually protected by silly rituals and prayers and "surrounding themselves with light" and other nonsense. Don't be fooled. Reptoids are *not* demons! They are not etheric minions of Satan. They are variably physical, techno-wizards and they use *our* energy to interact with us and only knowing how to make that energy unavailable to them will provide any protection at all.

Now, yes, we know that human beings - *all* human beings - have reptilian genetics... and bird genetics and just the whole gamut. But by disinforming people about the true nature of the 4th density STS hierarchy and state of existence, as such people as Arizona Wilder and others do; by making humans the "physical" or "paraphysical" Reptoids, the attention is drawn away from the actual "control system" of Drachomonoid beings of hyperdimensional, variable physical capability.

But, in a funny twisted way, there IS some truth there. Reptoid beings *can* shape shift into human appearing beings, but, the problem is, according to the understanding of hyperdimensional existence, they have some difficulty doing this, and "holding the frequency", so that even when they do it, it is a very bad imitation - witness Men In Black cases.

And, human beings *can* be easily controlled by 4th density beings through their genetics, their minds, their chemistry, and by setting up "dramas" in which other people who may or may not be active "agents" of the STS hierarchy act as "vectors" of thinking and activity.

So, do you see the inversion in the Arizona Wilder story? That ordinary human beings can be Reptoids and we would just never know it! This amounts to loading the truth train with nuclear speed capabilities to run it off the track! Take a little grain of truth, exaggerate it all out of proportion, twist it, and toss it out there to outrage the sensibilities of the rational thinkers, and to dupe the non-critical thinker into believing a scenario that prepares him to be further manipulated. And, if in the end, the whole story is discredited through associated ideas that can be proven false, a very effective screen has been dropped over the true activities of 4th density negative beings. Meanwhile, everyone is looking in the direction of something that is merely a distraction... the oldest game in the world - the shell game of reality.

Just a few days after I had written the above referenced message to the E-group, an event transpired to confirm it. There is a curious thing that I would like to note here in passing: It seems that the STS mode of manipulation includes "synchronous events" and or "signs and wonders" *before* a choice is made to do something, which, in fact, "weight" the choice. STO seems to refrain altogether from any kind of overt contact or demonstration, leaving the will entirely free. But then, there is always the little "confirmations" *after* the choice has been made and the action initiated.

Getting back to the "event" of confirmation. As I was reading through my e-mail, I came across a response to our David Icke fan on the E-group who had sent a web site that was purported to "expose" the evil intentions of the Masons via the Denver Airport murals. What caught my eye was the remark that a particular mural had been "removed". So, I clicked on the URL to have a look. The e-mail I wrote immediately after will explain:

From: "Laura Knight-Jadczyk"

Date sent: Sat, 28 Oct. 2000 16:38:18 -0400

Subject: DENVER MURALS DETAILED ANALYSIS

"1st member wrote:

make sure to click on "next image" at the bottom for a Detailed Analysis of every portrait...
http://www.50megs.com/bridgeoflove/simonvol10/den.html

2nd member wrote in response:

You are a little behind the times. I agree that this mural is *very* disturbing; however, it was also removed a year ago."

I responded to the exchange as follows:

"Laura here:

It made me curious about what mural would have been removed, so I went and had a look at the picture, which, as it happens, was *never* one of the "Denver Murals". It is Poussin's painting entitled "Winter", and we *do* have it on *our* Denver Airport page and it is explained in the text that it is Poussin's painting...

Now, why would someone else have a picture of Poussin's painting included as a "Denver Mural" if they had not mistakenly *thought* it was a Denver Mural because it was on a page of pictures of the Denver Murals, only they simply did not bother to read the text telling that it was NOT one of the murals????

I think I will have a look at the other images on this site... the originals from our pages are from photos taken by a close friend and member of our group at our request, and I know there are certain little glitches in her photographic technique and a couple of angles and extra features in the pictures when she did not get the picture framed properly. How much you want to bet that the pictures from this other site are stolen from ours??? (taking odds...)"

As it turned out, sure enough, the pictures were stolen from our site without credit given. Ark came in to have a look at it since he had been the one who did the scans and made the catalogue. So, he followed up my post with one of his own:

From: "Arkadiusz Jadczyk"

Date sent: Sat, 28 Oct. 2000 18:55:53 -0400

Subject: Denver, David Icke fans and a practical lesson in disinformation

"Hi All,

Laura already wrote about it a while ago, but let me try to make it completely clear. This is a very good example of how disinformation connects and works." Our former-list member (who is now unsubscribed) wrote:

Date sent: Wed, 25 Oct. 2000

Subject: DENVER MURALS DETAILED ANALYSIS

make sure to click on "next image" at the bottom for a Detailed Analysis of every portrait..
http://www.50megs.com/bridgeoflove/simonvol10/den.html

****

"Ark here: When you go there - what do you see? You see *our* pictures. I mean, really ours, because they were taken by a friend of ours on her trip to Denver, then scanned and put on our web site. We have the original photographs.

OK, so David Icke's friends 'borrowed' our material without quoting the source. But that is not all. WE have a little 'Catalogue' page, which I did myself: Denver_cat.htm

On this page, together with scans of the Denver murals photos, I put an image of a famous painting, 'Winter' by Poussin, because Cassiopaeans suggested that there is a hidden relation: Denver.htm

So, what did our David Icke associate do: he 'borrows' also the Poussin painting (again without quoting Cassiopaean web site), but he states that this is from pictures taken at Denver!

That is how Lizzies work: least effort.

Clearly sooner or later someone will discover that his 'Winter' is *not* from Denver, but an old painting. What will happen? All the story about mind control and about Denver murals will become suspect. Origin of all of that will be forgotten. Laws of sandwiching truth between lies will be at work. Baby will be tossed out with the bath water The Denver Airport issue will be ignored because lies are connected with it.

Of course, we could start making noise about 'copyrights' and about nonsensical interpretations. But is it worthwhile? Is it not better to write a web page explaining on a live example how disinformation works?"

This now brings me to the contrail issue. The group here talked about it quite a bit the other day and the idea that is being promulgated that contrails are being used to commit genocide on the human race. Well, think about that for a moment. It would sure be a lot easier to commit genocide with land based vectors... a lot more economical... and *easier to hide* - than making such a big display of contrails and then having people connect them with sickness. That does not compute logically.

Not only that, IF such things were being done from aircraft as is suggested, it is no problem at all to do it without leaving a trace... invisible vapors dispensed from low flying craft rather than clearly obvious, long lasting contrails that get everyone excited and worked up in hysterical formation of theories and terror. So, think about *that* for a moment. Do you suppose that the result is the intended effect? Terror and hysterical conspiracy theories?

And what will happen next when these theories are exposed as nonsense, which is very likely?

Meanwhile, just what are we being distracted from observing by paying so much attention to something that is so blatant that we would have to think those boys in Black Ops were really having a bad day to come up with something so obvious?

All anyone has to do is read Machiavelli to understand *some* of the tricks and machinations of the Control System and to see clearly that *what is apparent is only the distraction from what is really being done "behind the curtain".*

Well, meanwhile, the "buildup" continues. Just today, November 1st, 2000, I received the following so-called "proof" of the genocidal purpose of the "chemtrails". A member of the "robots-rebellion" discussion group wrote:

"So you haven't yet figured out the airborne conditioning-agent release program that is being operated by the government. I'll give you some hints, but first I'll give you a little information about myself. I'm a retired government scientist with an advanced degree in one of the health-related disciplines. I do not use my real name for fear of retaliation, either against me, or against members of my family. I always try to route my e-mail communications so that they appear to come from another source, usually from one somewhere within the government. Sometimes I use the Internet resources of the public library - whatever it takes to hide my true identity and confuse those who don't want the sort of information I possess to fall into the public's hands. I have a small circle of friends who are, or were, in key positions within our military and several government agencies. These are not the very top level personnel, but mid to upper mid-level people, scientists and analysts, who are in positions where they can see the day-to-day activities of what's going on, who are charged with implementing the details, but who are never quite privy to the schemes behind the work they do. Each of my contacts has been able to supply me with a portion of the puzzle, but separately, none of them understands the whole story."

Right away we have a problem because the "source" does not identify himself except to say that he uses all kinds of methods to prevent anyone from knowing who he is. So, basically, we come down to having to take his word for everything he is saying. And, he speaks so calmly and rationally, too! He sure must be a "dinkum" guy! And how courageous he is to even speak under such threat! Aren't we lucky to be hearing all he has to say?

This whole paragraph is so blatantly loaded with psychological "triggers" designed to induce confidence that it actually screams, "Methinks he protests too much"! But, let's go on here:

"I'll tell you what I've pieced together so far. But I have to admit that this information frightens me because there is no place I can go with it. What am I supposed to do - write my congressman? I believe that would be like signing my own death warrant."

Oh, wowie zowie! He's a guy just like the rest of us! We are scared and we feel helpless too! And again, we see how *brave* he is to even whisper the great revelation he is going to give us!

"This whole chemtrail issue is related to the plan for decreasing the world population to around 450-500 million -- and starting with the US first. Why? The people of the US are the only ones with even the remotest chance of stopping this. That is, if they knew about it. That's why the US has to be the first to go."

Wait a minute here! He says that the people of the good ol' U.S. of A. (stand up and salute, boy!) are the ones who have to go first because *they* (yer durn tootin' pilgrim!) are the *only* ones who could stop this dire and dreadful plot *if they knew about it*! Let's just gloss right over the fact that we are talking about an atmospheric ocean of deadly poison blazoned across the sky! So, the homies here in the land of golden grain and purple mountains have to be gotten rid of first, in *great secrecy* so they won't catch on! Ooooh! I see it now! The chemtrails are just a distraction... no? They are the real thing? But, I don't understand! I thought it was supposed to be a *secret*! Well, never mind...

> "You have to understand that the world's elite covet the US for its
> geographic diversity - and they would love to return this country to its
> condition as it existed prior to Columbus setting foot here, but without the
> Native Americans this time of course."

Now *that* is about the lamest crock of nonsense I ever heard! You boys
in Black Ops better go back to school! You are suggesting that power and
greed aren't the motivators they used to be!? And at the same time, you
are pulling out the "sacred Native American" ploy!

> "You may have already heard how several national parks have been
> designated as world biospheres - that's the plan for all of North America,
> a giant nature park and playground that will be devoid of annoying human
> beings (that would be us)."

Never mind the fact that those "annoying human beings" have been and
are the source of labor, wealth, and power for millennia, and it would be a
lot easier to reduce the population with some well-placed anti-fertility
agents in the water or the soda pop drunk by practically every man,
woman and child in the country! Not only that, it would be a lot cleaner
and neater because you wouldn't have all those icky dead bodies to burn
or bury!

> "And the people actually involved in doing the spraying, as well as those
> who will take part in the rest of the plans, are being duped into believing
> they will be spared, that is, permitted to live and remain on this continent
> as administrators and caretakers of this vast nature preserve."

And do you, our fine disinformation artist, think that we are stupid
enough to buy into this story, knowing that, if such a thing were actually
being done, even those who are purported to be doing it at the deepest
levels could have no guarantee of escaping the effects of it? Are they
living in bunkers and going around wearing gas masks? For months and
years? Why would they do that when there are so many other easier ways
of accomplishing genocide if that was what they really wanted? Oh, I
know! They have *vaccines*! That's why they are so confident that only the
designated ones will succumb. Stupid me! Never mind that vaccines have
been found to be deplorably ineffective and the chances of them NOT
working are about the same as the chances that you will get the disease
from the vaccine!

> "I understand that about 150 to 200 thousand people are projected as
> necessary for maintenance purposes. But it's likely these people will not
> be Americans. Those in charge wouldn't want to risk the possibility of
> some sort of revolt, so the workers will probably be brought in from
> Europe and Asia."

Do you hear *that*, my fellow Amurrikins? Furriners in our land! Them's fightin' words, boy! (Another psychological ploy.)

"There are rumors floating about the Internet that the chemtrails are part of some sort of secret program the government is doing to protect the US from future biological attacks. Nothing could be further from the truth. The plan is to sensitize, or condition, the US population to being wiped out by influenza A. Over the past few years, people have been encouraged to get flu shots to protect them against the generally non-lethal strains that circulate through the population during flu season. Each year the US government has guessed which strains were most likely to spread. They seem to always guess right - don't they?

This flu season, the government protected people with a trivalent vaccine that included the A/Beijing/262/95-like (H1N1) and the A/Sydney/5/97-like (H3N2). It also contained the B/Beijing/184/93-like hemagglutinin antigens. For those not familiar with virology, the H and N refer to proteins on the outside of the virus, the hemagglutinin and neuraminidase, which are responsible for the virus attaching to, and then invading, a host cell. The public has been quite pleased with the success of the vaccines offered so far. But that will change in the future."

Now, curiously, I think our guy may be onto something. As he says, the rumor about "protecting the U.S. from future biological attacks" is just that, nonsense. But then he introduces an idea that could get us somewhere. Now just suppose, for the sake of argument, that a hellacious Flu strain *does* erupt? And what if people who have some idea that this is related to contrail activity become hysterical and say "*See*?! We told you"! And further, what if these people begin to form groups to spread the rumor, to protest, or otherwise act in a way that could be interpreted as a "threat to the security of the peace" of the U.S.A? What a perfect opportunity to slam controls on the Internet, freedom of speech and assembly, and any of a number of other sanctions against those who might be termed insurrectionists. Are we beginning to smell a setup here?

"Researchers at the US Army Medical Research Institute of Infectious Diseases (or USAMRIID) at Fort Detrick in Fredrick MD have reconstructed and modified the H1N1 Spanish Flu virus, making it far more deadly than it ever was back when it was responsible for the 1918-1919 flu pandemic that killed over 20 million worldwide and over 500,000 here in the US. Consider that it could have killed many more, but back then, people couldn't hop on a jet and travel from New York to LA in five hours. Now, our ability to travel will increase the spread and will be our downfall.

The flu vaccines contain killed virus and protect the body well against challenge by that particular strain, but work poorly against other strains not included in the inoculation. At some point, the vaccine stockpile will include the more lethal modification of the 1918 H1N1 in its live form. Most people receiving this vaccine will simply be renewing their annual flu shot, and the vaccine will still include the inactivated version of the more benign form of H1N1 (as was included in this year's vaccine). The presence of the milder strain in the inoculum will slow down the progression of the more lethal H1N1 form, so people will become sick more slowly - but they will still eventually die. It will just take a few weeks longer. In the meantime, they will be carriers for the lethal form of the virus, passing it on to everyone with whom they make contact. And as people hear that others are dropping dead from the flu, they will flock to get their own vaccination. And the entire population will be more receptive to infection because their lungs will have been preconditioned to guarantee it."

Now wait a minute here! I thought we were talking about "chemtrails"? What's this nonsense about spreading the flu via person-to-person contact? Are we talking out of both sides of our mouth now?

"If you will remember back to 1968 and '69, the Hong Kong flu, which was influenza A type H3N2, killed over 30,000 people in the US alone. That was a fortuitous learning event for some because it taught them that the flu could still conceivably be used to wipe out a population. But at the same time, it pointed out the need to precondition the populace so that those who might normally be resistant could be rendered susceptible.

Hence the development of the vaccine program and the aerial spraying procedures to condition the population. The purpose of the chemicals in the chemtrails is to help the viral envelope fuse with lung cells, permitting easier penetration and infection."

This is nonsense. The potential fatalities from a "tweaked" virus would not even need a "conditioning agent". I think our guy better read up on his recombinant DNA. Once again, we have serious logical inconsistency.

"But what about those few individuals who don't succumb to the flu? Probability alone demands that there will be some who survive - pockets of the population that are either not reached or somehow (and this is less likely) are resistant to the lethal H1N1 strain. At this point you must also remember that our military personnel have been immunized against a variety of pathogens, including the anthrax bacillus. For those geographically isolated areas where the flu doesn't do its job, it's a fairly simple matter to lay down anthrax spores and then send in what's left of the military to take care of anyone still breathing. The anthrax spraying will probably come under the guise of a flu protection program to save those still alive after the epidemic."

Well, the story is getting so wild and absurd that my willingness to exert the energy to comment further has just succumbed to extreme boredom. Here's the wrap-up. I think you can figure it out if you can keep from falling on the floor laughing.

> "And the military, having been exposed to civilians with the flu, will eagerly await their own flu shots. I should emphasize that this is a last resort scenario. Those orchestrating the plan will not want to use anthrax until all other possibilities are exhausted - this because of the long-term viability of anthrax spores. To scatter them over the countryside would mean the area would be dangerous for use by humans, at least those not vaccinated against the bacteria. And think about this for a moment. Why do you suppose agencies like Fish and Wildlife are so eager to reintroduce wolves and other species into areas of the country that haven't seen these animals for generations. It's all part of the plan to restore this land to what the elite envision as its early paradise-like state, with wild animals freely roaming the uninhabited plains and forests. Granted, it will take some time to clean up the place and to maybe destroy a lot of small towns that might otherwise be considered a blight on the landscape. But for the global elite it will be a small price for us to pay for their enjoyment."

Did we forget anything? Oh, yes! Egypt Air Flight 990! Another dreaded Masonic conspiracy. And, right here, direct from the casino show palace in Las Vegas, we have that paragon of scientific virtue, Richard Hoagland and his Enterprise Mission! Let's make Star Trek *real*!

I think we all need to remember that in the late summer, early fall of last year, Mr. Hoagland and his group were predicting an imminent cometary impact based on "inside information" from a "reliable source". We never even thought it was worth exerting our energy to ask the Cassiopaeans, but they brought it up themselves when we were asking about the prospects of a Y2K disaster (another hysteria of the very kind we are discussing):

> Q: Next question, and I think this one will be quick: can you make any comments on the likelihood of this Y2K situation getting out of hand and bringing on the "New World Order" or causing the institution of Martial Law, or causing people to need to store food, guns, ammunition and take all their money out of the bank? There is an *awful* lot of hysteria out there about this...
>
> A: Ask them what happened on November 7th.
>
> Q: Oh, you mean the big Hoagland prediction that something was going to strike the earth... supposedly revealed to him by a "confidential informant" who somehow proved his "reliability," by having "inside information" and so forth. In other words, another spate of disinformation?
>
> A: Yup!

We read at Richard Hoagland's web site the following about Egypt Air Flight 990:

> "The first problem we had with the apparent crash of this flight was in the numbers. Many of our regular readers wrote to us and pointed out the excessive number of "19.5" and "33" coincidences related to this flight. According to an Egypt Air official, Chairman of the Board, Eng. Mohammed Fahim Rayan, live on CNN, the plane spent "nineteen and a half hours" in the United States on this particular series of flights. In fact the exact time (according to the New York Port Authority timeline) was specifically 19 hours and 47 minutes (!), the so-called "tetrahedral value" (see below) we have cited on so many occasions. The flight number 990 is of course divisible by three as 330, or 330 X 3 (33-3 anybody?) Add to that the fact that according to the Pentagon there were 33 Egyptian military officers on board, the plane was at 33,000 feet when it began its horrendous crash dive (down to just over 16,700 feet when transponder contact was finally lost), it had picked up 33 passengers in Los Angeles, it disappeared exactly 33 minutes after take off, and it had just over 33,000 flight hours -- and we of course were very interested. [**Note: all of these numbers have been reported, but not necessarily confirmed at this time**]."

Now, note the last line above, a disclaimer. "All of these numbers have been reported, but not necessarily confirmed at this time."

Does it stop them from speculating and starting rumors? Does it produce in them a desire to check those "reported numbers" out before such speculation? Do they even bother to put a large notice at the top of the article stating that it is only speculation?

Nope. And the correspondent on the Cassiopaea e-group forwarded this web site as *proof* that the crash of Egypt Air Flight 990 was a Masonic Sacrifice, and that the Cassiopaeans and yours truly were "protecting" the Masons!

Well, we have wandered very far afield, and now it is time to have some more fun! So, let's get back to our narrative.

A year had gone by since the discussion about the Quorum and I was still buried in Alchemy and Secret Societies and trying to figure out just what the central issue of all of these mysterious allusions could be. The dream of getting married had come on the exact day that I actually would get married some three years later, though I did not yet know this. The following week, with RC present again, I decided to pursue the "Scottish Question".

> Q: (L) Okay, a year ago we talked about the quorum and I did not understand. Now, what I would like to know is, is the understanding I have acquired in the past two weeks regarding this group... [I was

referring to the possibility of a real human conspiracy lasting for hundreds, or thousands of years, which would be possible with the use of David Hudson's Monoatomic Gold, or something similar. I had begun to think that, not only was it possible for purported alien beings to have space/time manipulation abilities, but that maybe some humans did as well. This certainly made some conspiracy theories a lot more plausible.]

A: You need some review. Not just about the "Quorum", but also about many important subjects, and tonight, we intend to have some free flowing energy, if you don't mind. In other words, we may supersede questions, when appropriate. However, it may be necessary for you to begin the process by asking a question.

Q: (L) Okay, square one: Is the Quorum composed of semi-humans who have been alchemists, who are presently in possession of a substance called "the elixir of life" and which David Hudson calls "monoatomic gold"?

A: And much, much more! Monoatomic gold is but one minor issue here. Why get lead astray by focusing upon it solely. It would be akin to focusing on the fact that "Batman" can fly! Is that the only important thing that "Batman" does in the story? Is it?

Q: (L) Of course not! (RC) Batman fights crime!

A: What we mean is that alchemy is but one minor piece of the puzzle.

Q: (L) Okay, I understand. But, understanding the alchemical connection, and its potential for extending life and opening certain abilities, makes it more feasible to think of a group that has been present steadily and consistently for many thousands of years on earth.

A: They are not the only ones! Let us go to the root. Who, or what made you?

Q: (RC) The Creator. (L) Prime Creator.

A: How? And who is Prime Creator?

Q: (L) Everything, I guess.

A: You are "Prime Creator."

Q: (RC) We are creators, but we aren't the Prime Creator...

A: Prime Creator Manifests *in* you.

Q: (L) Okay, so at the root is Prime Creator.

A: But... who was secondary?

Q: (RC) The Sons of God? The Elohim?

A: Who is that? Remember, your various legends are "seen through a veil". Here comes a shocker for you... one day, in 4th density, it will be your descendants mission to carry on the tradition and assignment of seeding the 3rd density universe, once you have the adequate knowledge!!! In this part of your 3rd and 4th density universe, specifically your "galaxy" it is the region known as Orion that is the one and only indigenous home of human type beings... reflect on this! Indigenous home base, not sole locator. What you are most in need of review of is the accurate profile of "alien" data.

Q: (RC) I thought that humans originated in Lyra and then a war broke out there and they ended up in Orion.

A: Lyra is not inhabited. There have been homes in all places, but some were/are transitory, and some are not. Pay attention to Orion! This is your ancestral home, and your eventual destination. Here is the absolutely accurately accurate profile of Orion to follow: This is the most heavily populated region of your Milky Way galaxy! This is a region that extends across 3rd and 4th density space for a distance as vast as the distance between your locator and it. There are 3,444 inhabited "worlds" in this region. Some are planets as you know them. Some are artificially constructed planetoids. Some are floating space barges. And some are "satellites". There are primary homes, traveling stations and incubator laboratories all in 2nd, 3rd and 4th densities. There are overseer zones in 5th and 6th densities. Approximately one half is STO and one half is STS. Together, along with many other colonies, located elsewhere, this is called, in translation, Orion Federation. Orions created grays in 5 varieties, as cybergenetic beings, and installed them on Zeta Reticuli 1, 2, 3, and 4, as well as on 2 planets orbiting Barnard's Star. The Reptilians also inhabit 6 planets in the Orion region in 4th density, and are owned by the Orion STS as slaves, and, in some cases, pets!!! The name "Orion" is the actual native name, and was brought to earth directly. Study the legend of the "god" of Orion for parallels."

I still was not getting where I wanted to go with the "Scottish Question". The issue of just *who* was on first, and *who* was really trying to "take over the world" as promulgated by the many conspiracy theories was uppermost in my mind. One of the main tenets of these theories is that it is a *Jewish* conspiracy. From almost the very beginning, the Jews were seen as the "enemy". Even though they were the "progenitors" of Christianity. It seems that the Christian antipathy was almost an Oedipal impulse to "kill the father"! I had a deep feeling that there was an important clue here, and that it did, indeed, relate to the Scottish Question!

Q: (L) Are the Orion STS the infamous redheaded Nordic aliens?

A: Yes, and all other humanoid combinations.

Q: (L) Okay, if it started with the Nordic types, and that is where the other humanoid combinations came from, what genetic combinations were used for human beings? Black people, for instance, since they are so unlike "Nordics"?

A: The Nordic genes were mixed with the gene pool already available on Earth, known as Neanderthal.

Q: (L) What was the genetic combination used to obtain the Oriental races?

A: Orientals come from a region known in your legends as "Lemuria", and are a previous hybridization from 7 genetic code structures from within Orion Union, designed to best fit the earth climate and cosmic ray environment then existent on earth.

Q: (L) Okay, what about the Semitic and Mediterranean peoples?

A: Each time a new flock was "planted", it was engineered to be best suited to the environment where it was planted. Aryans are the only exception, as they had to be moved to earth in an emergency.

Q: (L) If races are engineered on earth to be "best suited", what factors are being drawn from or considered regarding the Semitic race?

A: They are not engineered on earth, but in Orion lab as all others. They were "Planted" in the Middle East.

Q: (L) What genetic type were the Atlanteans?

A: They were the same as the "Native Americans".

Q: (L) Why do some Native Americans believe they come from the Pleiades?

A: Where are the Pleiades?

Q: (L)Well, near Orion. (RC) Oh, okay. So, they are considering the Pleiades part of Orion. What about Sirius?

A: Sirius is confused as a locator because it appears in similar location in the sky in the northern hemisphere. The American Indians were confused in the translation because of similar seeming location due to vantage point.

Q: (RC) Well, but Sirius is clearly Sirius! It's the brightest star in the sky... it's in all the legends! How could it be translated wrong? This is not clear! The star charts are very specific!

A: How have *you* translated *your* legends wrong?

Q: (F) I think the point is that it is clear that we, in our present culture, are easily able to get things very wrong, even from the more recent times; so it is not a great consideration to think that the more ancient legends can also be distorted, embellished, and misrepresented.

A: Review what we said at the beginning of this session.

Q: (L) Did the Dogon come from Sirius?

A: All humanoid types originated in Orion region, there are and have been and will continue to be literally millions of colonies.

Q: (L) If a lot of the information that is being propagated these days is confusion or disinformation, what is the purpose of all this?

A: You answered yourself: Confusion and disinformation.

Q: (L) I have a theory that the truth, in any large degree, will not be known until just prior to some sort of transition...

A: You expect "truth" then?

Q: (RC) Absolutely! (L) Considering how things are from personal observation, this may be unrealistic...

A: All there is is lessons, no short cuts!

Q: (L) I want to get back on my question that you have not answered... I want to know who, exactly, and why, exactly, genetically engineered the Semitic people, and why there is such an adversarial attitude between them and the Celts and Aryans.

A: It is not just between the Jews and Celts, if you will take notice. Besides, it is the individual aural profile that counts and not groupings or classifications. But, to answer your question: there are many reasons both from on and off the planet.

Q: (L) Why was Hitler so determined, beyond all reason, even to his own self-destruction, to annihilate the Jews?

A: Many reasons and very complex. But, remember, while still a child, Hitler made a conscious choice to align himself with the "forces of darkness", in order to fulfill his desires for conquest and to unite the Germanic peoples. Henceforth, he was totally controlled, mind, body, and soul, by STS forces.

Q: (L) So, what were the purposes of the STS forces that were controlling Hitler causing him to desire to annihilate an entire group of people?

A: To create an adequate "breeding ground" for the reintroduction of the Nephalim, for the purpose of total control of the 3rd density earth prior to elevation to 4th density, where such conquest is more difficult and less certain!

Q: (L) Do you mean "breeding ground" in the sense of genetic breeding?

A: Yes. Third density.

Q: (L) Did they accomplish this goal?

A: No.

Q: (L) So, the creation of the Germanic "Master Race" was what they were going after, to create this "breeding ground"?

A: Yes.

Q: (L) And, getting rid of the Jews was significant? Couldn't a Germanic master race be created without destroying another group?

A: No.

Q: Why?

A: Because of 4th density prior encoding mission destiny profile.

Q: (L) What does that mean?

A: This means encoding to activate after elevation to 4th density, thus if not eliminated, negates Nephalim domination and absorption. Jews were prior encoded to carry out mission after conversion, though on individual basis. The Nazis did not exactly know why they were being driven to destroy them, because they were being controlled from 4th density STS. But, Hitler communicated directly with Lizards, and Orion STS, and was instructed on how to create the "master race".

Q: (L) And they were going to use this as their basis to introduce a new blend of the Nephilim... (RC) And the New World Order... their version of it. (L) Meanwhile, back to the Celts: obviously if the Lizard Beings thought that the Aryans/Celts were a good breeding ground for this "Nephilim Master Race," then it must be because there is something genetically inherent in them that makes them desirable in this sense. Is this correct?

A: No, not in the sense you are thinking. We suggest that you rephrase this question after careful reflection on the implications.

This was startling information, to say the least! And, true to form, Prince Lizard Machiavelli was in evidence in this cunning effort to make the Jews a scapegoat all the while manipulating them through their own religion to *be* and *act* the part of the scapegoat! Oh, what a tangled web we weave!

After RC and her husband went home, I went to bed in a strangely excited state. I knew it was going to be difficult to get to sleep, so I began to practice meditative breathing exercises to relax myself. Suddenly, I saw a face right before me! It was as clear and real as if someone had entered the room! It is difficult to convey to anyone how truly solid and three-dimensional this face was. I did not know this face, but it was a man with light hair and glowing eyes and he looked at me so kindly and lovingly before he vanished like a popping balloon! I was so startled that I nearly lost my breath altogether, but with firm effort, I resumed my meditation and soon went to sleep.

I was pretty driven in the following days to try and figure out what it was about the "purified Aryan genetic strain" that was so desirable to the Reptoid beings. I wanted to find the exact series of questions that would bring forth the information that I needed to understand this problem. I finally thought I had figured out a way to ask the question:

Q: (L) I have thought about my question from the last session and I want to ask it this way: You have said that Hitler received instructions from higher density beings about creating a 'Master Race'. Why were the Aryan genetic types seen to be more desirable for creation of this Germanic 'master race'?

A: Both similarity and ancestral link most unblemished from Orion 3rd and 4th density stock.

Q: (L) So they were essentially trying to breed a group of people like themselves?

. A: Yes.

Q: (L) Well, I don't exactly understand why they had to put a lunatic like Hitler in charge of such a project and have him work at eliminating the undesirable strain...

A: Not point. How would you suggest creation?

Q: (L) Okay. They were preparing this breeding ground, so to speak. Obviously this was for the introduction of some other genetic strain. What was this?

A: Nephalim.

Q: (L) Well, if the Nephilim are coming in ships, 36 million of them, why bother to create half-breeds here?

A: Yes, but having an "advance party" makes 3rd density conquest much easier.

Q: (L) So, this Master Race was supposed to get everything ready...

A: Yes.

Q: (L) Okay, what is it about the Semitic genes that was considered to be so undesirable in the creation of this 'Master Race' at the 3rd density level, excluding the "prior encoding" for 4th density activation issue?

A: Would blemish genetic characteristics inclined to ruthlessness and domination.

Q: (L) So, you are saying that there is something, some genetic tendency or set of genes in the Semitic type that would counteract this?

A: Close.

Q: (L) But isn't the nature of a person determined by their soul and not the physical body?

A: Partially, remember, aural profile and karmic reference merges with physical structure.

Q: (L) So you are saying that particular genetic conditions are a physical reflection of a spiritual orientation? That the soul must match itself to the genetics, even if only in potential?

A: Yes, precisely.

Q: (L) So a person's potential for spiritual advancement or unfoldment is, to a great extent, dependent upon their genes?

A: Natural process marries with systematic construct when present.

Q: (L) Well, if that is the case, and the aliens are abducting people and altering their genes, can they not alter the genes so that higher-level souls simply cannot come in?

A: Not incarnative process, natural biological processes. Incarnative involves strictly ethereal at 5th density and lower, and thus is enveloped in triple cycle "veil" of transfer which is impregnable ay any means. However, any and all 1st, 2nd, 3rd, and 4th processes can be manipulated at will and to any degree if technology is sufficient.

Nevertheless, we are coming to the point where the background for my questions that led to the 3-5 code references is more or less "set up". There were Secret Societies everywhere you looked, Celts, Aryans, Jews, Masons, Illuminati and Alchemists; Rosicrucians, Templars and the Quorum! What a *mess*!

During a discussion of all these secret societies with my guest, RC, I was informed that I *must* read *all* of the *Holy Blood, Holy Grail* series of books if I ever expected to understand *anything*! It was only in there that I would find out the *real* key to who was on first. And, in RC's opinion, it was the Priory of Zion!

The *who*?

The *Prieure de Sion*! They were at the bottom of everything! Until I knew about them, I could not claim to know anything.

Well, heck! I had hardly ever heard of them except in an article about the Lincoln, Leigh and Baigent books. How come I had never come across a mention of them anywhere else? I had certainly dug pretty far and deep. Just who were these guys?

Maybe we can find out? After all, learning is *fun*!

Chapter 32
The Priory of Sion and The Shepherds of Arcadia

The entry of the Prieure de Sion/Priory of Sion onto the world stage occurred via the efforts of Henry Lincoln, Michael Baigent and Richard Leigh. It all began rather innocently when Lincoln, a television writer, was on an ordinary family vacation back in 1969, at which time he stumbled upon a little mystery that he had no idea was soon going to explode into the mass consciousness as a result of his curiosity. He writes in *Holy Blood, Holy Grail*:

> "...En route for a summer holiday in the Cevennes, I made the casual purchase of a paperback. *Le Tresor Maudit* (The Accursed Treasure) by Gerard de Sede was a mystery story - a lightweight, entertaining blend of historical fact, genuine mystery, and conjecture. It might have remained consigned to the post-holiday oblivion of all such reading had I not stumbled upon a curious and glaring omission in its pages.

> The "accursed treasure" of the title had apparently been found in the 1890's by a village priest through the decipherment of certain cryptic documents unearthed in his church. Although the purported texts of two of these documents were reproduced, the "secret messages" said to be encoded within them were not. The implication was that the deciphered messages had again been lost. And yet, as I found, a cursory study of the documents reproduced in the book reveals at least one concealed message. Surely the author had found it. In working on his book he must have given the documents more than fleeting attention. He was bound, therefore, to have found what I had found. Moreover, the message was exactly the kind of titillating snippet of "proof" that helps to sell a "pop" paperback. Why had M. de Sede not published it?" [*Holy Blood, Holy Grail*, 1982]

Lincoln goes on to say that this little omission continued to bother him "like an unfinished crossword puzzle", so he decided to see if he couldn't get funded to investigate it for a possible television show, thus satisfying his personal curiosity within the constraints of his work schedule which did not allow time for the investigation he would have liked to undertake.

The idea was received favorably by his employers, the BBC, and he was sent to dig deeper into the mystery so as to make a short film. Lincoln arranged to meet the author of the book, M. de Sede in Paris in 1970 and there, asked him the question: "Why didn't you publish the message hidden in the parchments"?

De Sede's answer astounded Lincoln: "What message"?

Lincoln writes:

> "It seemed inconceivable to me that he was unaware of this elementary message. Why was he fencing with me? Suddenly I found myself reluctant to reveal exactly what I had found. We continued a verbal fencing match for a few minutes and it became apparent that we were both aware of the message. I repeated my question: "Why didn't you publish it?" This time de Sede's answer was calculated. "Because we thought it might interest someone like you to find it for yourself."

> That reply, as cryptic as the priest's mysterious documents, was the first clear hint that the mystery of Rennes-le- Chateau was to prove much more than a simple tale of lost treasure." [*Holy Blood, Holy Grail*, 1982]

What kind of answer was that? "Because we thought it might interest someone like you to find it for yourself." Was Mr. Lincoln dealing with a very clever con artist, or some forces that were unknown? After all, nobody forced him to buy the book and read it; nobody forced him to be curious about the hidden message; nobody forced him to seek to investigate further. It was all a series of chance events. Or so it would seem. Nevertheless, there was the most curious fact that a number of documents, "Secret Dossiers", had been "published", (i.e. deposited in the Bibliotheque Nationale of France) several years in advance of Gerard de Sede's book and Henry Lincoln's curiosity.

The earliest of these documents, dated <u>August of 1965,</u> is entitled *Les descendants Merovingiens ou l'enigme du Razes Wisigoth*, or *The Merovingian descendants, or the enigma of Razes of the Visigoths*. Its purported author is a Madeleine Blancasall, and claims to have been translated from German by a Vincent Celse-Nazaire, and supposedly published by the *Grande Loge Alpina*. The document describes the descent of the Merovingians from their alleged biblical origin to the 20th century, by way of the family of Plantard. The genealogy is signed by a Henri Lobineau.

Now, of course, M. de Sede helpfully informed Henry Lincoln in advance that he must not look under the name "Lobineau", but instead must look under the name "Schidlof".

Henry Lincoln notes:

> "Madeleine Blancasall is clearly made up from a reference to Rennes-le-Chateau's patron saint, Marie-Madeleine, linked with the names of the two rivers, the Blanque and the Sals which conjoin just to the south of Rennes-le-Bains. [A town near Rennes-le-Chateau.]"

Also, of course, we note that the church of Rennes-les-Bains is dedicated to the two saints Celse and Nazaire. The Grande Loge Alpina, the main lodge of Swiss Freemasonry, denies all knowledge of this little work.

Nine months after the deposit of this curious genealogy, in May of 1966, another document was deposited in the Bibliotheque Nationale. It also bears the imprint of the Grande Loge Alpina and the title is *Un tresor Merovingien a Rennes-le-Chateau.* The author is Antoine l'Ermite. The grotto of St. Antony the Hermit is only a short distance from Rennes.

One month later, June 1966, another document was deposited in the Bibliotheque entitled *Pierres gravees du Languedoc,* and this was a purported reprint of an earlier book published in 1884 by Austrian historian, Eugene Stublein. [Stublein *did* exist and *did* publish a book in 1877 entitled *Description d'un voyage aux establissements thermaux de l'arrondissement de Limoux.* There is, apparently, no known extant *real* copy of his 1884 book of which the 1966 version purports to be a copy.]

Papers in the *Dossiers* also suggest that the author of the genealogies, Lobineau, was a pseudonym for this same Leo Schidlof, who had died in Switzerland the previous year. Schidlof's daughter has insisted that he knew nothing of genealogy. So, we find a dead man's name being used to give credibility to something with which he probably had absolutely no connection.

Then, in March of 1967, still another document was deposited/published with the Bibliotheque Nationale. It was entitled *Le serpent rouge,* and this one had three authors: Messieurs de Koker, Saint-Maxent and Feugere. There is some disagreement over the date on which, after the necessary red tape had been gone through, the document was considered to be officially "published". The *Depot legal* states March 20th, but Lincoln et al gave it as January 17. This matter was investigated by another researcher, Franck Marie, who claims to have established the date of February 15. Whatever the date of deposit, it is a fact that Louis Saint-Maxent and Gaston de Koker were found hanged on 6 March, and Pierre Feugere the following day.

Were these three men victims of revenge or a suicide pact as de Sede suggests? Their respective families all insist that the three were absolutely unacquainted with one another and that their deaths by hanging, so close to one another in time, are just horrible coincidence. The obvious conclusion is that someone found the names of three unrelated persons with suitable deaths in the French newspapers, put their names on this document, and *then* deposited it after falsifying the deposition slip and that the date of March 20, as given by the Bibliotheque Nationale, is the correct date. Again, we have dead men being made authors of books they probably knew nothing about.

At about the same time of the publication of Gerard de Sede's book *L'or de Rennes*, another document attributed to Henri Lobineau was deposited with the Bibliotheque Nationale entitled *Dossiers secrets*. Lincoln et al say it was:

> "...A thin, nondescript volume, a species of folder with stiff covers which contained a loose assemblage of ostensibly unrelated items - news clippings, letters pasted to backing-sheets, pamphlets, numerous genealogical trees and the odd printed page apparently extracted from the body of some other work. Periodically some of the individual pages would be removed. At different times other pages would be freshly inserted. On certain pages additions and corrections would sometimes be made in a minuscule longhand. At a later date, these pages would be replaced by new ones, printed and incorporating previous emendations."

The main thrust of this odd collection of items was the establishing of Pierre Plantard de St.-Clair as a direct lineal descendant of Dagobert II, who was assassinated in 679 and was not known to have had any legitimate issue. It seems that the name "Lobineau", was derived from the Rue Lobineau near Saint-Sulpice in Paris, the church that plays a significant part in the story of Berenger Sauniere.

But, before we proceed, let's just give the story itself a general overview: In 1885, at the age of 33, Abbe Berenger Sauniere became priest of Rennes-le-Chateau and employed a young girl named Marie Denarnaud as his housekeeper. She became his lifetime companion and confidante. The church was terribly run down and the village was poor and it seemed that Abbe Sauniere faced a life of penury and obscurity.

However, he received a serendipitous donation (though the source of this money varies from researcher to researcher) and decided to upgrade his church a bit. During the renovation work, he supposedly discovered some mysterious documents containing a coded message. He then made a trip to Paris and hung out with some fellows with connections to the Parisian occult world, purchased copies of an odd selection of paintings from the Louvre, and returned to Rennes. At this point it is said that his behavior suggested strange doings. He was reported to have been tramping around the country side collecting rocks, holing up in the church doing secretive things at night, and then, ultimately, redecorating the church in a bizarre way. At some point, he traveled a great deal and it was reported that money poured in to his housekeeper during his travels, originating, it is said, from various religious houses around Europe.

Over the next twenty years, Abbe Sauniere allegedly spent huge amounts of money on his building projects, entertaining lavishly, living the high life and other activities.

That's the basic story. Of course, there were a couple of murders tossed in for good measure and an on again, off again friendship with another priest who was equally mysterious and clearly involved in whatever was going on.

The region already had legends of buried treasure, and now it was thought that Abbe Sauniere found it or, at least, part of it. And now, the curious story of the "accursed treasure" of Rennes-le-Chateau was to be brought to the attention of the world by the BBC through the efforts of Henry Lincoln.

At his meeting with Gerard de Sede, Lincoln indicated that he wanted to make this short television program. De Sede agreed to assist in such a project by digging up all the information he could and sending it to Lincoln.

> "First came the full text of a major encoded message, which spoke of the painters Poussin and Teniers. This was fascinating. The cipher was unbelievably complex. We were told it had been broken by experts of the French Army Cipher Department, using computers. As I studied the convolutions of the code, I became convinced that this explanation was, to say the least, suspect. I checked with cipher experts of British Intelligence. They agreed with me. 'The cipher does not present a valid problem for a computer.' The code was unbreakable. Someone, somewhere, must have the key."

In other words, whoever deciphered the documents MUST have also possessed the key either by virtue of being the author of the documents *and* key, or by having been given the key.

> "And then de Sede dropped his second bombshell. A tomb resembling that in Poussin's famous painting *Les Bergeres d'Arcadie* had been found. He would send details as soon as he had them. Some days later the photographs arrived and it was clear that our short film on a small local mystery had begun to assume unexpected dimensions." [Lincoln, Leigh, Baigent, 1982]

This item, the Poussin painting, *The Shepherds of Arcadia*, had a strange effect on me at the time that I was reading the story. There was a reproduction of it in the article about the Rennes-le-Chateau mystery, but it was a poor copy. I was thumbing through an art book on my shelves, trying to find any scholarly commentary, and lo and behold, there was a large, full-page reproduction of it right there. I cut it out of the book and pinned it to the wall over my desk where I could see it all the time and went back to studying the matter at hand.

With the addition of such mysterious developments, Henry Lincoln decided to do more research and make a longer program. The first screening of *The Lost Treasure of Jerusalem,* which was the result of the first stages of research into the matter, was on February of 1972. Essentially, the conclusion was that Abbe Sauniere had discovered the Temple Treasure of the Jews. Supposedly, it had been taken by the Romans and then, when the Visigoths sacked Rome, they took it and it ended up in Rennes-le-Chateau.

Apparently, the public was consumed with curiosity about this mystery, so a follow-up film was planned with more research. In 1974, *The Priest, the Painter and the Devil* was screened, and it was an unmitigated hit with viewers. More research was needed and Mr. Lincoln decided that the many complexities of the mystery were too much for one man, so Richard Leigh, a writer with graduate degrees and knowledge of history, philosophy, esoterica, etc. was brought onboard. Richard brought in Michael Baigent, a photojournalist and researcher of Templar history. The three of them began to dig into the problem of Rennes-le-Chateau in a more thorough way and produced another television special entitled *The Shadow of The Templars* in 1979. Mr. Lincoln writes:

> "The work we did on that film at last brought us face to face with the underlying foundations upon which the entire mystery of Rennes-le-Chateau had been built. But the film could only hint at what we were beginning to discern. Beneath the surface was something more startling, more significant, and more immediately relevant than we could have believed possible when we began our work on the 'intriguing little mystery' of what a French priest might have found in a mountain village.
>
> In 1972 I closed my first film with the words, 'Something extraordinary is waiting to be found... and in the not too distant future, it will be'."
> [Lincoln, Leigh, Baigent, 1982]

What Lincoln, Leigh and Baigent claim to have found is the secret that Jesus was a king in a long line of Priest kings, and that he had been married to Mary Magdalene, and produced a child, born posthumously (after his crucifixion), and that this child had been spirited away to France to be the progenitor of the kings of the Franks, the Merovingian, and that this Holy/Royal Bloodline is the real secret contained in the mysteries of the 'Holy Grail' stories.

How in the world did a story about a possible hidden treasure found by an obscure priest in a remote corner of rural France transmogrify itself into *that*?!

Good question. It's a complicated story that you will have to read on your own for all the juicy details. But intimately connected to the "how" of it, and far more important, is the "who says"?

A group calling itself *Le Prieure de Sion*, The Priory of Sion, and its purported agent, Pierre Plantard.

Messrs. Lincoln, Leigh and Baigent write in the conclusion of *Holy Blood, Holy Grail:*

> "We were looking for answers to certain perplexing questions, explanations for certain historical enigmas. In the process we more or less stumbled upon something rather greater than we had initially bargained for. We were led to a startling, controversial, and seemingly preposterous conclusion. ...We were simply trying to determine whether or not our conclusion was tenable. And exhaustive consideration of biblical material convinced us that it was. Indeed, we became convinced that our conclusion was not only tenable, but also extremely probable." [*Holy Blood, Holy Grail*, 1982]

Note that they 'stumbled upon', and were 'led to' this conclusion, and it was, apparently, the idea that the Priory of Sion wanted them to believe and publish.

About the latter they say:

> "If we cannot prove our conclusion, however, we have received abundant evidence - from both their documents and their representatives - that the Prieure de Sion can. On the basis of their written hints and their personal conversations with us, we are prepared to believe that Sion does possess something - something that does in some way amount to 'incontrovertible proof' of the hypothesis we have advanced." [Ibid.]

What do they think this proof is that is in the possession of the Priory of Sion? They write:

> "If our hypothesis were correct, the Holy Grail would have been at least two things simultaneously: On the one hand, it would have been Jesus' bloodline and descendants - the 'Sang Raal', the 'Real' or 'Royal' blood of which the Templars, created by the Prieure de Sion were appointed guardians. At the same time the Holy Grail would have been, quite literally, the receptacle or vessel that received and contained Jesus' blood. In other words, it would have been the womb of the Magdalen - and by extension, the Magdalen herself.

> ...But it may have been something else as well. In AD 70, during the great revolt in Judaea, Roman legions under Titus sacked the temple of Jerusalem. The pillaged treasure of the temple is said to have found its way eventually to the Pyrenees; and M. Plantard, in his conversation with us, stated that this treasure was in the hands of the Prieure de Sion today. But the temple of Jerusalem may have contained more than the treasure

plundered by Titus' centurions. In ancient Judaism religion and politics were inseparable. The messiah was to be a priest-king whose authority encompassed spiritual and secular domains alike. It is thus likely, indeed probable, that the temple housed official records pertaining to Israel's royal line - the equivalents of the birth certificates, marriage licenses, and other relevant data concerning any modern royal or aristocratic family. If Jesus was indeed 'king of the Jews', the temple is almost certain to have contained copious information relating to him. It may even have contained his body..." [Ibid.]

There are a few problems with this. If M. Plantard claims that the Priory of Sion holds the Treasure of Solomon's Temple, they must have a pretty empty treasury and maybe that's why he has been known to do the 'Midnight flit' without paying his rent, (as has been reported by a number of researchers into his past and background). You see, the Temple of Solomon was looted by Antiochus Epiphanes, *not* Titus. And, of course, this was *after* the Temple had been sacked by Rameses in 930 B.C., and the Babylonians in 586 B.C.

As I have written in my series "Who Wrote the Bible"[29], the existence of the original Temple of Solomon is problematical. There is actually no evidence that it *ever* existed - in Israel, that is. Yet, somehow, the scribe Ezra managed to convince Cyrus, King of Persia, of the "chosenness" of his people, thereby garnering support for the return of the Jews to Israel and the "rebuilding of the temple". I would suggest that this was not a "rebuilding", but an original building motivated by myths and legends patched together by Ezra, extended in time by endless faked genealogies designed to deceive. By convincing Cyrus that the Israelites had been guided and chosen by the One God, he would naturally think that he would be blessed by Israel's god if he assisted this project.

According to the Book of Ezra, there was a whole slew of treasure given to the Jews by the Persians to put in their new temple. This was done approximately 516 B.C. and, supposedly, for the next 481 years the treasure of Solomon's rebuilt temple just hung out there doing what treasure in a temple is supposed to do. We should note right here that the Ark of the Covenant disappeared from view and discussion between 750 B.C. and 650 B.C., more than a hundred years *before* Ezra, who would have, if he had been able to do so without being caught out at lying, claimed that it was still present among the treasure.

Over and over again we read in these Rennes-le-Chateau books a citation from Josephus that Titus sacked the Temple in Jerusalem and made off with the treasure. However, that is not quite accurate, as I have

---

[29] Included in *The Secret History of the World and How to Get Out Alive.*

just noted above. Here is the relevant excerpt from Josephus about the loss of the treasure of the Temple:

> "King Antiochus ... got possession of the city by treachery; at which time he spared not so much as those that admitted him into it, on account of the riches that lay in the temple; but, led by his covetous inclination, (for he saw there was in it a great deal of gold, and many ornaments that had been dedicated to it of very great value), and in order to plunder its wealth, he ventured to break the league he had made. So he left the temple bare, and took away the golden candlesticks, and the golden altar [of incense], and table [of shew-bread], and the altar [of burnt-offering]; and did not abstain from even the veils, which were made of fine linen and scarlet. He also emptied it of its *secret treasures*, and left nothing at all remaining; and by this means cast the Jews into great lamentation, for he forbade them to offer those daily sacrifices which they used to offer to God, according to the law. treasure of the Temple:" [Josephus, *The Jewish Wars*, Emphasis, mine.]

Note that Josephus clearly says that Antiochus "left the Temple bare". Not only that, but he also "emptied it of its secret treasure, and left nothing at all remaining". Those are strong words. And nowhere does Josephus indicate that the Temple was ever again replenished in terms of treasure.

The story is, in the short version, in the year 175 B.C., Antiochus IV, also known as Epiphanes, murdered Seleucus IV and took the throne. In the year 169 B.C. Antiochus invaded Egypt in an attempt to destroy the Ptolemaic Dynasty. Soon it was rumored back in Palestine that the king had been killed in battle. The news of Antiochus' death was false, however, and when he returned to Jerusalem, he entered the Temple and stole a great deal of valuable treasure, an act which the pious Jews looked upon as an abomination before God.

The following year (168 B.C.) Antiochus renewed his campaign against the Egyptians, but he was stopped by the Roman representative Popilius Laenus, and was ordered to leave Egypt and never come back. This so infuriated Antiochus that he came back and took out his frustration on the city of Jerusalem. He tore down the city walls, slaughtered a great many of the Jews, ordered the Jewish Scriptures to be destroyed, and he and his soldiers brought prostitutes into the Temple and there had sex with them in order to defile the Temple. He also issued orders that everyone was to worship the Greek gods, and he established the death penalty for anyone who practiced circumcision, or who observed the Sabbath or any of the Jewish religious feasts and sacrifices. The cruelty of Antiochus in enforcing these new laws against the Jews became legendary. The final outrage for the pious Jews of the land came when Antiochus sacked the Temple and erected an altar there to the pagan god Zeus. Then, on

December 25, 168 B.C., Antiochus offered a pig to Zeus on the altar of Jehovah/Yahweh.

Now, if the treasure was taken by Antiochus in 169 B.C., that is 200 years before Titus sacked Jerusalem, and during all of this time, Jerusalem was in an almost constant state of occupation by foreign powers, oppression and/or revolt, such conditions were definitely not conducive to either assembling or displaying any treasure of significance, much less keeping any! Josephus never mentions any "restoration of the treasure" to the temple. What Antiochus did with it, we can only guess, but the likelihood is that it was spent wildly and wantonly.

Nevertheless, one writer on Rennes-le-Chateau claims that confirmation of the existence of this treasure comes from the discovery of the Copper Scroll in Cave 3, Qumran, in 1952. This turned out to be a list of 64 hiding places in Jerusalem and surrounding districts, where gold, silver, Temple offerings and so forth are said to have been deposited. In modern terms, it amounts to 65 tons of silver and 26 tons of gold.

The experts are arguing over it, but the consensus of opinion is that the style of the document, i.e. dry realism, along with the fact that it is recorded on copper, a valuable metal in its own right which therefore would not have been used to record a fairy tale, all contribute to the idea that it describes a *real* treasure.

Now, just *what* treasure it was describing is in dispute. Was this the treasure from the Temple at Jerusalem?

Not very likely. In the first place, the scroll was found among the Qumran/Essene documents. The Essenes were dedicated opponents of the Temple at Jerusalem; so the Essene community would have been a hostile environment for such a list, to say the least, if it *were* the Temple treasure. Besides that difficulty, it is not likely that the sacking of the Temple was foreseen so that any treasure, if it had existed by this time, could have been hidden. And, of course, hidden treasure around the time of the fall of Jerusalem to Titus contradicts the words of Josephus who has already told us that it was all plundered by Antiochus.

There are experts who propose that the treasure listed on the Copper scroll belonged to the Essenes themselves, which is hard to understand since they were advocates of poverty, simplicity and were a relatively small community.

So, that is all that can safely be said about the "proof" of the Copper scroll. It is certainly suggestive of some group that had a treasure, but just who or what this group was cannot be determined. Maybe some of the clues the Cassiopaeans have given will point us in the direction of this group? But more on that later.

In 35 B.C., Herod decided to build a new Temple because, apparently, the old one was pretty run-down and must have been falling apart. It was this temple that was sacked by Titus. It is possible that Herod did some decorating and jazzed things up with a little gold here and there, but it is unlikely that he had the resources to adorn his temple in the manner of the former one. Josephus' remarks relating to the Roman sacking of the temple of Herod are as follows:

> "Accordingly, the number of the high priests, from the days of Herod until the day when Titus took the temple and the City, and burnt them, were in all twenty-eight; the time also that belonged to them was a hundred and seven years." [Josephus, *The Jewish Wars*]

Notice that here, Josephus made no mention of Titus making off with the Treasure of the Temple. Yet, Baigent, Leigh and Lincoln cite a record of this purported carrying off of the treasure by Titus. And everybody who has researched in Rennes-le-Chateau since then, has referred back to this "original research" of Baigent, Leigh and Lincoln which claims that Titus and the Romans took possession of the Treasure of the Jewish Temple. It has even been said that the Arch of Titus, built in A.D. 81 by the Senate at Rome, is proof of this because it has a bas-relief depicting the return of the triumphant General Titus, the priceless seven-branched candlestick carried on the shoulders of Jewish prisoners.

If you look at this bas-relief, you see the giant menorah and an object that can only be a stylized representation of the scroll of the Torah. I have to think that this "proof" that Titus obtained the treasure of the Temple at Jerusalem may fall under the category of artistic symbolism. How else could one express the conquest of the Jews other than depicting their main religious symbols on a bas-relief? And, of course, this menorah taken by Titus could certainly have been gold. But, it seems clear that the main treasure, the piles of loot that everyone is looking for, actually disappeared with Antiochus, and what he did with it is anybody's guess.

But, such a detail as that doesn't stop the Rennes-le-Chateau crowd! The story continues that when the Visigoths sacked Rome, Alaric took the Temple treasure of Jerusalem and it ended up in the Languedoc.

The conclusions reached by Lincoln, Leigh and Baigent are very well presented, even if somewhat carelessly researched, and it is much easier to read it as they originally wrote it than to attempt to summarize all of it, but the main point should be that the whole thing started with Gerard De Sede's book *Le tresor maudit de Rennes* (The Accursed Treasure of Rennes), which Henry Lincoln read on his vacation in France. Also, keep in mind that most of the "source notes" in the back of the book refer to the information supplied by the purported Priory of Sion and its "agents".

The intrepid threesome was pretty busy. By the time they finish with their investigation, we have not only the Treasure of the Temple of Solomon hiding at Rennes, we also have the Treasure of the Templars and the Treasure of the Cathars! We have all the noble families of the region connected to the Templars as Guardians of the Grail; we have the Holy Grail and maybe even the Ark of the Covenant! Heck, all the mysteries of the whole blasted planet are right there in Rennes-le-Chateau for the enterprising treasure seeker to discover!

And the Pied Piper is the Priory of Sion.

The whole deal about the Priory of Sion boils down to this: Their claim is that a secret order, (The Priory of Sion), predates the Knights Templar and that the Templars were actually created as the military and administrative arm of this other group. Supposedly, the heads of this Prieure de Sion, Grand Masters as they are called, are nearly all people whose names are famous through history.

Supposedly, even though the Templars were dissolved between 1307 and 1314, the Prieure was untouched by this tragedy, and continues up to the present day, playing a significant part in contemporary international affairs. And, here's the clincher: its declared objective is the restoration of the Merovingian dynasty!!!

Why?

Well, because they are supposed to be the descendants of Jesus and Mary Magdalene and the proof is in their long hair! (Just joking!)

> "The Merovingian dynasty issued from the Sicambrians, a tribe of the Germanic people collectively known as the Franks. Between the fifth and seventh centuries the Merovingians ruled large parts of what are now France and Germany. The period of their ascendancy coincides with the period of King Arthur - a period that constitutes the setting for the romances of the Holy Grail. It is probably the most impenetrable period of what are now called the Dark Ages. But the Dark Ages, we discovered, had not been truly dark. On the contrary, it quickly became apparent to us that someone had deliberately obscured them. To the extent that the Roman Church exercised a veritable monopoly on learning, and especially on writing, the records that survived represent certain vested interests. Almost everything else has been lost - or censored." [*Holy Blood, Holy Grail*, 1982]

Lincoln, Leigh &Baigent (LL&B) say that there are enigmas surrounding the origins of the Merovingians because they did not find any abrupt transition or usurpation - that they seemed already to rule over the

Franks; that they were duly acknowledged kings. Not only that, but it seems that there was something special about the one who gave the name to the dynasty, Merovee/Merovech/Meroveus. They state that he was a semi-supernatural figure.

LL&B say that according to both the leading Frankish chronicler and subsequent tradition, Meroveus was born of two fathers. When already pregnant by her husband, King Clodio, Merovee's mother supposedly went swimming in the ocean. In the water she is said to have been seduced or raped by a "Quinotaur". What a Quinotaur is, we have no clue. Nevertheless, this creature impregnated her a second time and when Merovee was born, he had a dual bloodline.

Yes, it is true that very often, behind a facade of legend lays a truth. And here LL&B suggest that the seed of truth behind this one is that there was intermarriage of some sort, a pedigree transmitted through the mother, as in Judaism, for instance. The idea is bruited that this might indicate an alliance with someone from "beyond the sea".

In any event, because of this, Merovee was supposed to be a supernatural being and "the Merovingian dynasty was mantled in an aura of mystery and magic".

> "According to tradition Merovingian monarchs were occult adepts, initiates in arcane sciences, and practitioners of esoteric arts - worthy rivals of Merlin... They were often called the sorcerer kings or thaumaturge-kings. By virtue of some miraculous property in their blood they could allegedly heal by the laying on of hands; and according to one account the tassels at the fringes of their robes were deemed to possess miraculous curative powers. They were said to be capable of clairvoyant or telepathic communication with beasts and with the natural world around them and to wear powerful magical necklaces. They were said to possess an arcane spell that protected them and granted them phenomenal longevity - which history, incidentally, does not seem to confirm. And they all supposedly bore a distinctive birthmark, which distinguished them from all other men, which rendered them immediately identifiable, and which attested to their semi divine or sacred blood. This birthmark reputedly took the form of a red cross, either over the heart - a curious anticipation of the Templar blazon - or between the shoulder blades.

> The Merovingians were also frequently called the longhaired kings. Like Samson in the Old Testament, they were loath to cut their hair. Like Samson's their hair supposedly contained their **vertu** - the essence and secret of their power. Whatever the basis for this belief in the puissance of the Merovingians' hair, it seems to have been taken quite seriously, and as late as A.D. 754. When Childeric III was deposed in that year and imprisoned, his hair was ritually shorn at the Pope's express command.

...The Merovingians were not regarded as kings in the modern sense of that word. They were regarded as priest-kings - embodiments of the divine. ...And they seem to have engaged in ritual practices that partook, if anything, more of priesthood than of kingship. Skulls found of Merovingian monarchs, for example, bear what appears to be a ritual incision or hole in the crown. Similar incision can be found in the skulls of high priests of early Tibetan Buddhism.

...In 1653, an important Merovingian tomb was found in the Ardennes - the tomb of king Childeric I, son of merovee and father of Clovis, most famous and influential of all Merovingian rulers. The tomb contained arms, treasure, and regalia such as one would expect to find in a royal tomb. It also contained items less characteristic of kingship than of magic, sorcery, and divination - a severed horse's head, for instance, a bull's head made of gold, and a crystal ball.

One of the most sacred of Merovingian symbols was the bee, and King Childeric's tomb contained no less than three hundred miniature bees made of solid gold." [*Holy Blood, Holy Grail*, 1982]

The remark is made after this that Napoleon not only had the miniature golden bees affixed to his coronation robes, but that he commissioned a genealogy report by someone named Abbe Pinchon, the ostensible reason being to determine if the Merovingian bloodline had survived the fall of the dynasty. And then we get the clincher for this one: much of the so-called Prieure documents are genealogies based on those compiled at Napoleon's request!

Now, whom do we have to thank for all of this startling information?

Well, the Priory of Sion, of course.

If we look to the back of Holy Blood, Holy Grail where the reference notes are assembled, we find that the whole story is based on "a comprehensive body of material is contained in *L'Or de Rennes pour UN Napoleon*", which is handily made available by one of Pierre Plantard's close associates, Philippe de Cherisey.

The first thing we want to look at is the "tradition" of the origins of the Merovingians. What their chronicler, Gregory of Tours says in book II.9 of his *History of the Franks* is:

"Many people do not even know the name of the first king of the Franks. The *Historia* of Sulpicius Alexander [which has been lost, by the way] gives many details about them, while Valentinus does not name their first King but says that they were ruled by war-leaders."

Gregory then quotes directly from the *Historia*:

"At that time the Franks invaded the Roman province of Germania under their leaders Genobaud, Marcomer and Sunno..."

[Sulpicius] says that these events occurred at a time when the Franks were ruled by war-leaders. Then he continues: [This is Gregory quoting Sulpicius]

"A few days later there was a short parley with Marcomer and Sunno, the royal leaders of the Franks." When he says, '*regales*' or royal leaders, it is not clear if they were kings or if they merely exercised a kingly function." He goes on: "That same year Arbogast, urged on by tribal hatred, went in search of Sunno and Marcomer, the kinglets of the Franks. ...He ...crossed the River Rhine and laid waste the land nearest to the bank, where the Bructeri lived, and the region occupied by the Chamavi. He did this without meeting any opposition, except that a few Amsivarii and *Chatti* showed themselves on the far-distant ridges of the hills, with *Marcomer* as their war-leader." A few pages further on, having given up all talk of "duces" and "regales", he states clearly that the Franks had a king, but he forgets to tell us what his name was.

[Gregory quoting Sulpicius] "The next thing which happened was that the tyrant Eugenius led a military expedition as far as the frontier marked by the Rhine. He renewed the old traditional treaties with the kings of the Alamanni and the Franks, and he paraded his army, which was immense for that time, before their savage tribesmen."

So much for the information that this chronicler Sulpicius Alexander has to give us about the Franks.

As for Renatus Profuturus Frieridus... when he comes to tell us how Rome was captured and destroyed by the *Goths*, he writes: [Gregory quoting Frieridus] "Meanwhile *Goar* had gone over to the Romans, and Respendial, the King of the Alani, therefore withdrew his forces from the Rhine. The Vandals were hard-pressed in their war against the Franks, their King Godigisel was killed and about twenty thousand of their front-line troops had been slaughtered, so that, if the army of the Alani had not come to their rescue in time, the entire nation of Vandals would have been wiped out."

[Gregory is speaking here] It is an extraordinary thing that, although he tells us about the kings of these various peoples, including the Franks, when he describes how Constantine, who had become a tyrant, summoned his son Constans to come from Spain to meet him... [Gregory quoting Frieridus] "They sent Edobech to contain the people of Germania and they themselves set out for Gaul, with the Franks, the Alamanni and a whole band of soldiery... Constantine had been beleaguered for about four months when messengers arrive all of a sudden from northern Gaul to announce that Jovinus had assumed the rank of Emperor and was about to attack the besieging forces with the Burgundes, the Alamanni, the Franks, the Alani and a large army."

[Gregory is speaking here] After a few more sentences, Frigeridus goes on: "...The city of Trier was sacked and burnt by the Franks in a second attack."

He notes that Asterius was made a patrician by a patent signed by the Emperor and then he continues: [Gregory quoting Frieridus] "At this time Castinus, Master of the Imperial Household, was sent to Gaul, as a campaign had been begun against the Franks."

That concludes what these two historians have to say about the Franks.

[Gregory is speaking here] In Book VII of his work, the chronicler Orosius adds the following information: "Stilicho took command of an army, crushed the Franks, crossed the Rhine, made his way across Gaul and came finally to the Pyrenees."

The historians whose works we still have give us all this information about the Franks, but they never record the names of their kings.

It is commonly said that the Franks came originally from Pannonia and first colonized the banks of the Rhine. Then they crossed the river, marched through Thuringia, and set up in each country district and each city longhaired kings chosen from the foremost and most noble family of their race. ...

We read in the consular lists that Theudemer, King of the Franks, son of Richemer, and his mother Ascyla, were executed with the sword. They also say that Clodio, a man of high birth and marked ability among his people, was King of the Franks and that he lived in the castle of Duisburg in Thuringian territory. ...Some say that Merovech, the father of Childeric, was descended from Clodio.

This particular race of people seems always to have followed idolatrous practices. ...They fashioned idols for themselves out of the creatures of the woodlands and the waters, out of birds and beasts: these they worshipped ...and to these they made their sacrifices.

Childeric, King of the Franks, whose private life was one long debauch, began to seduce the daughters of his subjects. They were so incense about this that they forced him to give up his throne. He discovered that they intended to assassinate him and he fled to Thuringia. He left behind a close friend of his who was able to soothe the minds of his angry subjects with his honeyed words.

Childeric entrusted to him a token, which should indicate when he might return to his homeland. They broke a gold coin into two equal halves. Childeric took one half with him and the friend kept the other half. "When I send my half to you," said his friend, "and the two halves placed together make a complete coin, you will know that you may return home safe and sound."

Childeric then set out for Thuringia and took refuge with King Bisinus and his wife Basina. [After eight years] Childeric's faithful friend succeeded in pacifying them secretly and he sent messengers to the exile with the half of the broken coin... By this token Childeric knew for sure that the Franks wanted him back, indeed that they were clamouring for him to return.

...Now that Bisinus and Childeric were both kings, Queen Basina... deserted her husband and joined Childeric. He questioned her closely as to why she had come from far away to be with him, and she is said to have answered: "I know that you are a strong man and I recognize ability when I see it. I have therefore come to live with you. You can be sure that if I knew anyone else, even far across the sea, who was more capable than you, I should have sought him out and gone to live with him instead." This pleased Childeric very much and he married her. She became pregnant and bore a son whom she called Clovis." [*History of the Franks,* translated by Lewis Thorpe, 1974]

The *History of the Franks*, in the words of one translator, "is spattered with blood and festers with pus, it re-echoes with the animal screams of men and women being tortured unto death: yet Gregory never once questions this effective method of exacting confession, implicating confederates, or simply satisfying the bloodlust of Queens and Kings". "...Time and time again, usually at the conclusion of some most serious passage, of some stomach-turning description, he adds an amusing comment, often a sly quip at himself."

I can assure you myself that this is not a book for the highly imaginative or the squeamish. It's a great read, however. And, what may happen to you by the time you finish reading it is that you will think: Good Riddance! What person in their right mind would want those lunatics back in power? There is definitely something about the Merovingian blood - it is tainted with madness.

According to Ian Wood, author of *The Merovingian Kingdoms*, 450-751 A.D., the Franks were the last of the invaders of Gaul and the most successful. In spite of this, their origins are shrouded in mist. Clovis's father, Childeric I, is the first of the dynasty who is well attested by legitimate sources and before him; most of the evidence for a royal dynasty is legend.

The Franks were reasonably well known to the Roman emperors in the 4th century; but even they couldn't make up their minds as to whom, exactly, they were. Nevertheless, the myths and legends that have been shaped around them may hold some clues. On the other hand, they may be more red herrings.

"Writing in the mid-seventh century, probably in Burgundy, the chronicler known as Fredegar recorded the tradition that Priam was the first king of the Franks. Friga succeeded him. The people then split up, some remaining in Macedonia, others following Friga to the Danube and the Ocean. There a further division took place. Some stayed and, ruled by Torcoth, they became known as Turks, while others followed Francio to the Rhine, where they became known as Franks. Thereafter, under the leadership of military leaders, *duces*, they remained undefeated.

Another version of this Trojan origin legend was written down in 727 by the [anonymous] author of the *Liber Historiae Francorum*.

According to him or her, after the fall of Troy Priam and Antenor led twelve thousand men to the river Tanais, and then to the Maeotic swamps. From there they moved to Pannonia, where they built a city called Sicambria.

Meanwhile the emperor Valentinian offered remission of tribute for ten years to any people who could drive the Alans out of the Maeotic swamps. This the Trojans did, and as a result they were called *Franci*, which the author thought was the Attic for "fierce".

When the ten years were over the Romans tried to reimpose tribute on the Franks, but the latter killed the tax collectors. As a result Valentinian sent troops against them, but they fought back. In the battle Priam was killed. The Franks left Sicambria, and moved to the Rhine. There Sunno, Antenor's son, died, and on the recommendation of Priam's son, Marchomir, the Franks elected Faramund as their *rex crinitus*, of long-haired king.

[Common to both these stories] are Trojan and migration traditions. The Trojan story is first recorded in Fredegar, and it seems to have had some vogue in seventh and eighth century Francia, where other Trojan legends were preserved.

...Gregory of Tours seems not to have known about the Trojan origin of the Franks, but he did know an undeveloped version of their migration legend. He thought that the Franks came from Pannonia, and that they crossed the Rhine, and marched through Thuringia... [Which makes no sense.]

The peculiar geography involved has disturbed many, who have wanted to emend Thuringia to Tongres, and emendation already made by a scribe of one manuscript of Gregory's Histories.

The fuller versions of the migration, as preserved in Fredegar's Chronicle and in the *Liber Historiae Francorum*, may have been written in response to the origin legends of the Goths, which had been developed by Cassiodorus. In fact there is no reason to believe that the Franks were involved in any long-distance migration: archaeology and history suggest that they originated in the lands immediately to the east of the Rhine.

...The Franks first appear in historical sources relating to the barbarian invasions of the third century. There they are already established in the region of the lower Rhine. ...

It is generally thought that they were a new people only in name, and that they were made up of tribes such as the Amsivarii, Chattuarii and *Chatti*, who are mentioned in earlier sources, but rarely, if at all, in later ones.

At the end of the century the Franks appear in the Latin panygyrics as a maritime people, causing trouble in the Channel. As such, *they were the precursors of the Saxons,* who came to be more and more associated with attacks on the coasts of northern Gaul and Britain.

By the late fourth century, in fact, the Saxons were said to have been involved in raids, which had previously been ascribed to the Franks.

...In the fourth century the Franks were also in close contact with the Romans, as allies and as recruits for the imperial forces. ...One or two even gained the consulship.

...Sulpicius Alexander recorded conflict in 389 between Arbogast, a Frank who held high military office in the empire, and two *regales,* or petty kings, of the franks, Sunno and Marcomer, and he revealed that the latter was the war leader of the Amsivarii and the *Chatti.*

The *History* of Frigeridus covered events of a slightly later period. From it Gregory learnt about the activities of the Franks in the first decades of the fifth century, including their involvement in the civil wars, which followed the usurpation by Constantine III." [*The Merovingian Kingdoms*, 450-751 A.D., Wood, 1994, emphases, mine.]

The fact is, nobody really knows who the Franks were or where they came from. It has been conjectured that they were barbarian tribes from the East that met and mingled with the Frisians.

The areas that the Frisians originate from was settled *as early as 3500 B.C..* There were comings and goings of additional peoples as the archaeological records show, but it seems to be possible to systematically track who was who and who went where by their pottery and other artifacts.

During the period 400-200 B.C., the archaeology shows that a group with its own identity developed from the Ems/Weser and Drenthe settlers. This group was called the Proto-Frisian culture by archaeologists. These Proto-Frisians lived in an area between modern Leiden and Delfzijl. Over the coming centuries, this group of Proto-Frisians expanded to fill the whole of the habitable region.

The coming of the Romans to the southern Netherlands in 12 B.C. prevented the Frisians from expanding their territory to the south of the Amstel and the Rhine. Around the year 150 B.C., the Frisians also lost the

Groningen salt-marshes to the *Chatti* who had *advanced from East Friesland.*

A list of place-names compiled in Alexandria by geographer Claudius Ptolameus (Ptolemy) c.150 A.D. was turned into maps by Europeans in the 15th century. These maps also supply the names of those tribes dwelling along the North Sea coastal regions. The evidence indicates that Saxons lived in southwest Jutland (Ribe and southwards), North Friesland and Ditmarschen - as far as the Elbe. Between the Elbe and the Weser lived the "greater" Chatti, while the "lesser" Chatti lived in East Friesland. The descriptions given by Ptolemy agrees with what has been reconstructed from the archaeological finds.

Depopulation of the Frisian salt-marshes occurred between 250 and 400 A.D. due to the rising sea levels and flooding and, undoubtedly, the cometary destruction of Europe. This resulted in an almost total depopulation of the Frisians in North Holland.

This depopulation not only affected Frisian areas. In the Baltic and northern European coastal regions, the population *retreated to the higher areas inland during the second century A.D.*. Where the Frisians went still cannot be stated with certainty. It is thought that some of them migrated to Flanders in the 3rd century, and from there crossed over to Kent in England. Frisian Tritzumer pottery has been found in both regions. Kerst Huisman has theorized that the Frisians of the flooded salt-marshes migrated to East Friesland and there, together with the *Chatti,* formed the tribe known as the Franks. There came into being, at any rate, a new tribe bearing the name of the Franks about the year 300 A.D.

The presence of the tribe known as the Chatti has been mentioned by several ancient sources. What I find to be of great interest is that the Hittites were also known as the Chatti. And Abraham, the patriarch of the Jews, was said to have been a Hittite. That is to say, an Aryan. I began to wonder if the so-called pejorative characteristics that were historically assigned to Jews might actually be an "Aryan cultural inheritance"? It is, after all, the "Salic Law," from the Salian Franks, that deprived women of the rights of inheritance and the position of women was seriously degraded with the impostion of monotheism through Judaism.

Above we have stated that the experts note that Frisian Tritzumer pottery has been found in Kent in England.

A definitive link between the Frisians and a tribe in England? Could it be possible that the Frisians came *from* England to the salt marshes of northern Europe?

Gregory could not understand how the Franks of the late fourth and early fifth centuries could be related to those led by the Merovingians in the late fifth and sixth centuries. What distressed him the most was the failure to talk about the royal lines, the kings. If Gregory had read Ammianus Marcellinus, as Wood notes, he would have known about a Frankish king called *Mallobaudes*. Gregory tried to make Faramund the father of Chlodio. This would have served to unite the Trojan and Merovingian families. Fredegar, on the other hand clearly stated the Trojan origin and then, after the death of Francio, just said that they were ruled by *duces*, or petty kings. This was his explanation for the lack of a royal family that was so upsetting to Gregory.

Fredegar also provided an account of Merovech's birth, which may cast light both on the origins of the Merovingians and also on the strangeness of the account by Gregory.

> "According to Fredegar, Merovech was conceived when Chlodio's wife went swimming, and encountered a Quinotaur. Although is not explicitly stated that this sea-monster was the father of the eponymous founder of the Merovingian dynasty, that is clearly the impression which Fredegar intended to give. The royal dynasty, thus, was thought to have had a supernatural origin. Gregory may well have known of these claims, and have thought of them as pagan. Whereas Fredegar relates the tale of the encounter with the Quinotaur, in the corresponding section of his *Histories* the bishop of Tours has an outburst against idolatry.
>
> The origin legend of the Merovingians as recorded by Fredegar is important not only for its suggestion that the family claimed to be descended from a supernatural ancestor, but also for the implications it has for the rise of the dynasty." [*The Merovingian Kingdoms*, 450-751 AD, Wood, 1994]

And, it seems that we have a serious problem here: Chlodio was recorded by Sidonius Apollinaris as having lost a battle at the *vicus Helena* in Artois - an event that took place c. 448 A.D. Merovech would then have to belong to the second half of the fifth century if he was Chlodio's son. This suggests that the emergence of the family as a power should also be dated to this same period. At the same time, Faramund, who is supposed to have been Chlodio's father, is not attested to in any early source. In other words, the Merovingians were not a significant dynasty at all before the mid-fifth century. *Their origins were separate and later than those of their people.*

In this respect, we can see that it is possible that Thuringia may have truly been more significant to the family of Meroveus than to the origins of the Franks themselves. If we consider the fact that Merovech's son, Childeric, had close ties to Thuringia (remember the story of Basina!), *it is altogether possible that the Merovingians originated in the east of Frankish territory.* In other words, the "Trojan origin" story of the Franks seems to belong to the people themselves, and not the family of Merovech. The family's own stories of its origins are peculiarly supernatural and pagan and different from the Franks themselves.

The story of the Trojan War is, in Western Civilization, the greatest NON-religious story ever told. It has haunted the western imagination for over three thousand years. "In Troy there lies the scene", Shakespeare said.

The story of Troy is at the bedrock of Western Culture from Homer to Virgil, From Chaucer to Shakespeare to Berlioz to Yeats. We talk about "Trojan Horses" and "Achilles Heels" and go on Odysseys and "work like Trojans" and on and on.

The tales of Achilles and Hector, Helen and Paris, and so many other great heroes all assembled into one story have lured a constant stream of pilgrims to the assumed region of Troy for all of that three thousand years; from Alexander the Great to Lord Byron to Heinrich Schliemann, the alleged discoverer of "Troy". The British queen is referred to as the seed of Priam, and it was the fantasy of the Nazis to become the new Achaians, comparing Hitler with Achilles.

Troy has come to stand for *all* cities because of one tragic event: the siege and destruction and death of all its heroes - all because of a woman. Herodotus tells us that the Trojan war is the root of the enmity between Europe and Asia.

Homer is the starting point of our search for Troy. The Iliad deals with one episode of the war, a few weeks in the tenth year; a small fragment of the vast cycle of stories that dealt with the Trojan War. In classical times a series of epics now only available in fragments, or lost completely, told the rest of the story, drawing on a long and venerable tradition.

The hold that the legend of Troy had on the Greek imagination was such that, based on the story of a violation of Athena's altar at Troy by Ajax of Lokris, the people of Lokris each year sent selected daughters to expiate this sin of their ancestor. They suffered indignities willingly, and it was said that the Trojans had the right to kill them. They lived out their days as slaves, in confinement and poverty. This custom continued into the 1st century AD as a testimony to the potency of the legend of Troy.

In the ancient world, it was uniformly believed that the Trojan War was a historical event. Anaxagoras was one of the few who doubted it because there was no proof. Herodotus, in the 5th century B.C., inquired of the Egyptian priests as to whether or not the Greek version of the story was true, that is, did they have an alternative record of it, since there were no written records before Homer committed it to writing.

Based on the work of Homer, around 400 B.C., Thucydides constructed a "history" of prehistoric Greece. No one knows how much of this was based on deductions from Homer, or derived from other sources that we no longer have. Thucydides wrote:

> "We have no record of any action taken by Hellas as a whole before the Trojan War. Indeed, my view is that at this time the whole country was not even called Hellas... The best evidence for this can be found in Homer, who, though he was born much later than the time of the Trojan War, nowhere uses the name 'Hellenic' for the whole force."

Thucydides tried to deal with the problem of a story of a great clash of forces that seemed to be contradicted by the evidence of the small sites and relative primitive nature of the region where Troy was supposed to be. He tells us that, as far as he knew, Mycenaea had always been a village without great importance, while Homer referred to it as a "town with broad streets".

> "...Many of the towns of that period do not seem to us today to be particularly imposing: yet that is not good evidence for rejecting what the poets and what *general tradition* have to say about the size of the expedition ... we have no right therefore to judge cities by their appearances rather than by their actual power and there is no reason whey we should not believe that the Trojan expedition was the greatest that ever took place."

So it was that , even in the 5th century B.C., Thucydides has commented on the fact that the only evidence for the Trojan war is the words of poets and "general tradition". The fact is, many present day scholars doubt the existence of a "Mycenaean empire" because the archaeological evidence simply does not support the claims of the story.

Yet, the detailed nature of the descriptions incorporated into the work of Homer suggest that the original works were composed by eye witnesses of a significant conflict.

The problem that faces the scholars is this: if you were to remove the place names and read the Iliad, you would *not* think that the writer was talking about the Mediterranean. The text talks about tides, salty, dark, misty seas and a climate of rain, fog and snow. The tall, *long-haired warriors* raveling overseas in "symmetrical" ships "eager to kill their enemies" remind us more of the Vikings than the Greeks of the classical era. Several of the commanders in the story had honorific titles: "Sacker of Cities". It even seems that, since the Greeks themselves could hardly imagine the behavior of these people in the stories, they consigned them to a "heroic age" and some of them to semi-divinity.

The Greek text of the Iliad speaks of "ceaseless rains" in the Trojan plain. The adjective is *"athesphatos"* which means "what even god cannot measure". Such rains are certainly typical of the climate of Northern Europe, but most definitely not typical of Greece or the Mediterranean.

Iman J. Wilkens was intrigued by this as a schoolboy in Holland. He knew that he was reading a description of an environment much like his own, and not like that of the sunny south. Could the climate of the Mediterranean have changed so much since then? But even that wouldn't explain the tides or the fact that Homer had placed Troy near to Lesbos and the Hellespont, from which Crete and Egypt are just a few days voyage by boat. That, of course, raised a question about the Odyssey: how could Ulysses have possibly gotten so terribly lost in the Mediterranean where nearly everything is just a day or two sail away?

The experts answer that Homer's work was obviously just a fantasized version of a historical seed event.

We certainly know that the written versions of the Iliad and Odyssey originated in Greece, but do we know for sure that the oral version was about Greece as we know it today?

Thucydides noted certain anomalies in Homer's text that may give us a clue. He was surprised that Homer never used the word "barbarian" for foreigners or non-Greeks. He wrote:

> "This word ought to have been used by the poet if the Greeks had really
> united to wage war against non-Greeks."

More than this, Thucydides remarks that barbarians were living in various parts of Greece and names the Taulentians "of the Illyrian race" living on the shores of the Ionian Gulf. From classical mythology, we know that a certain Galatea had three sons: Galas, Celtus and Illyrius, who founded the three major Celtic peoples: the Gauls, the Celts and the Illyrians. Professor Henry Hubert hypothesized that the ancient Greeks had been in contact with Celtic culture through the intermediary of the Illyrians, which seems to be confirmed by Thucydides remark. What if, during this contact, they received the epics sung by the bards and began to give the place names in the stories to their own settlements. In the manner of mythicization that I have described in *Secret History of the World*, the Greeks might then begin to believe that the Trojan War had been fought by their own ancestors against an overseas kingdom.

There is still another issue. Wilkens writes:

"Quite apart from the difficulty of fitting most places described in the Iliad and the Odyssey into the physical reality of the lands surrounding the Aegean Sea, there is also a problem with the spiritual content of Homer's works. Plato had doubts as to their Greek origin and the great philosopher was by no means an admirer of this imaginative poet whose gods, with their jealousies and vengeances, behaved like spoilt children. Plato was particularly worried about the corrupting influence of Homer's poems on the minds of Greek youth, above all because of their "lack of respect" for the gods. He suggested that certain passages of the Iliad and Odyssey should be corrected or even expurgated and if he had been the dictator of his 'ideal state', he would have had them burned, thus breaking the chain of transmission of these unique and extremely ancient poems. [...]

Reading the text [of the Iliad and the Odyssey] with an atlas of Greece on one's knees, it is hard to understand the descriptions of many places, or the distances between places, or the sailing directions, or how it was possible to travel of drift in a boat with a head wind. In short, the place names in Greece, the pieces of the puzzle, seem completely jumbled. Once these names are sought in western Europe, however - and about 90 percent of them can still be found there, far more than in Greece - all the pieces of the puzzle fall perfectly into place and the events described by Homer become entirely logical and comprehensible. [...]

I am certainly not the first to have the impression that the Trojan War must have taken place in western Europe. As early as 1790, Wernsdorf thought that the stories about the Cimmerians, one of the peoples mentioned by Homer, were of Celtic origin. He had a very precise reason for this: the classical Greek author Aelian mentions them in connection with the 'singing' swan, *Cygnus musicus*, which is found in the British Isles and northern Europe, whereas Greece and the rest of Southern Europe knew only the 'silent' swan, *Cygnus olor*.

In 1804, M. H. Vosz believed that the Odyssey most probably described certain landscapes in the British Isles and, in 1806, C.J. de Grave arrived at the general conclusion that the historical and mythical background of Homer's works should be sought not in Greece but in western Europe. Towards the end of the nineteenth century, Th. Cailleux wrote that Odysseus adventures had taken place in the Atlantic, starting from Troy, which by a process of deduction he concluded to be near Cambridge in England." [*Where Troy Once Stood*, Wilkens, Rider, 1990]

Near Cambridge in England? The Gogmagog hills?

Well, let's go in a slightly different direction. Let's talk about the Mongols and Khazars and Lev Gumilev's work on *Ethnogenesis and the Biosphere*:

"Names deceive. When one is studying the general patterns of ethnology one must remember above all that a real ethnos and an ethnonym, i.e. ethnic name, are not the same thing.

We often encounter several different ethnoi bearing one and the same name; conversely, one ethnos may be called differently. The word 'Romans' (romani), for instance, originally meant a citizen of the polis Rome, but not at all the Italics and not even the Latins who inhabited other towns of Latium.

In the epoch of the Roman Empire in the first and second centuries A.D. the number of Romans increased through the inclusion among them of all Italians-Etruscans, Samnites, Ligurians, Gauls, and many inhabitants of the provinces, by no means of Latin origin.

After the edict of Caracalla in A.D. 212 all free inhabitants of municipalities on the territory of the Roman Empire were called 'Romans', i.e. Greeks, Cappadocians, Jews, Berbers, Gauls, Illyrians, Germans, etc. The concept 'Roman' lost its ethnic meaning, it would seem, but that was not so; it simply changed it.

The general element became unity not even of culture, but of historical fate, instead of unity of origin and language. The ethnos existed in that form for three centuries, a considerable period, and did not break up.

On the contrary, it was transformed in the fourth and fifth centuries A.D., through the adoption of Christianity as the state religion, which began to be the determinant principle after the fourth ecumenical council. Those who recognized these councils sanctioned by the state authority were Romans, and those who did not became enemies.

A new ethnos was formed on that basis, that I conventionally call 'Byzantine', but they themselves called themselves 'Romaic', i.e. 'Romans', though they spoke Greek.

A large number of Slavs, Armenians, and Syrians were gradually merged among the Romaic, but they retained the name 'Romans' until 1453, until the fall of Constantinople. The Romaic considered precisely themselves 'Romans', but not the population of Italy, where Langobards had become feudal lords, *Syrian Semites* (who had settled in Italy, which had become deserted, in the first to third centuries A.D.) the townsmen, and the former colons from prisoners of war of all peoples at any time conquered by the Romans of the Empire became peasants.

Florentines, Genoese, Venetians, and other inhabitants of Italy considered themselves 'Romans', and not the Greeks, and on those grounds claimed the priority of Rome where only ruins remained of the antique city.

A third branch of the ethnonym 'Romans' arose on the Danube, which had been a place of exile after the Roman conquest of Dacia. There Phrygians, Cappadocians, Thracians, Galatians, Syrians, Greeks, Illyrians, in short, all the eastern subjects of the Roman Empire, served sentences for rebellion against Roman rule. To understand one another they conversed in the generally known Latin tongue. When the Roman legions left Dacia, the descendants of the exiled settlers remained and formed an ethnos that took the name 'Romanian', i.e. 'Roman', in the nineteenth century.

If one can treat the continuity between 'Romans' of the age of the Republic and the 'Roman citizens' of the late Empire, even as a gradual extension of the concept functionally associated with the spread of culture, there is no such link even between the Byzantines and the Romans, from which it follows that *the word changed meaning and content and cannot serve as an identifying attribute of the ethnos.*

It is obviously also necessary to take into consideration the context in which the word - and so the epoch - has a semantic content, because the meaning of words changes in the course of time. That is even more indicative when we analyze the ethnonyms *'Turk', 'Tatar', and 'Mongol',* an example that cannot be left aside.

Examples of camouflage. In the sixth century A.D. *a small people living on the eastern slopes of the Altai and Khangai mountains were called Turks.* Through several successful wars they managed to subordinate the whole steppe from Hingan to the Sea of Azov. [The Khazars] The subjects of the Great Kaghanate, who preserved their own ethnonyms for internal use, also began to be called Turks, since they were subject to the Turkish Khan.

When the Arabs conquered Sogdiana and clashed with the nomads, they began to call all of them Turks, including the Ugro-Magyars.

In the eighteenth century European scholars called all nomads *'les Tartars'*, and in the nineteenth century, when linguistic classification became fashionable, *the name 'Turk' was arrogated to a definite group of languages.*

Many peoples thus fell into the category 'Turk' who had not formed part of it in antiquity, for example the Yakuts, Chuvash and the hybrid people, the Ottoman Turks.

The modification of the ethnonym 'Tatar' is an example of direct camouflage. Up to the twelfth century this was the ethnic name of a group of 30 big clans inhabiting the banks of the Korulen. In the twelfth century this nationality increased in numbers, and Chinese geographers began to call all the Central Asian nomads (Turkish speaking, Tungus-speaking, and Mongol-speaking), including the Mongols, *Tatars.* And even when, in 1206, Genghis-khan officially called all his subjects Mongols, neighbors continued for some time from habit to call them Tatars.

In this form the word 'Tatar' reached Eastern Europe as a synonym of the word 'Mongol', and became acclimatized in the Volga Valley where the local population began, as a mark of loyalty to the Khan of the Golden Horde to call themselves Tatars. But the original bearers of this name (Kereites, Naimans, Oirats, and Tatars) *began to call themselves Mongols.* The names thus changed places.

Since that time a scientific terminology arose in which the Tatar anthropological type began to be called 'Mongoloid', and the language of the Volga Kipchak-Turks Tatar. In other words we even employ an obviously camouflaged terminology in science.

But then it is not simply a matter of confusion, but of an ethnonymic phantasmagoria. Not all the nomad subjects of the Golden Horde were loyal to its government. The rebels who lived in the steppes *west of the Urals* began to call themselves *Nogai*, and those who lived on the eastern borders of the Jochi ulus, in Tarbagatai and on the banks of the Irtysh, and who were practically independent, because of their remoteness from the capital, became *the ancestors of the Kazakhs*.

These ethnoi arose in the fourteenth and fifteenth centuries as a consequence of rapid mixing of various ethnic components. The ancestors of the Nogai were the *Polovtsy, steppe Alans*, *Central Asian Turks*, who survived a defeat by Batu and were taken into the Mongol army, and inhabitants of the southern frontier of Rus, who adopted Islam, which became a symbol at that time of ethnic consolidation. *The Tatars included Kama Bulgars, Khazars, and Burtasy, and also some of the Polovtsy and Ugric Mishari.* The population of the White Horde was the mixture; three Kazakh jus were formed from it in the fifteenth century.

But that is not yet all. At the end of the fifteenth century Russian bands from the Upper Volga began to attack the Middle Volga Tatar towns, forced some of the population to quit their homeland and go off into Central Asia under the chieftainship of Sheibani-khan (1500-1510). There they were met as fierce enemies because the local Turks who at that time bore the name of 'Chagatai' (after Genghis-khan's second son Chagatei, the chief of the Central Asian ulus), were ruled by descendants of Timur, the enemy of the steppe and Volga Tatars, who ravaged the Volga Valley in 1398-1399.

The members of the horde who quit their homeland took on a new name 'Uzbeks' to honor the Khan Uzbeg (1312-1341), who had established Islam in the Golden Horde as the state religion. In the sixteenth century the 'Uzbeks' defeated Babur, the last of the Timurides, who led the remnants of his supporters into India and conquered a new kingdom for himself there.

So the Turks who remained in Samarkand and Ferghana bear the name of their conquerors, the Uzbeks. The same Turks, who went to India, began to be called 'Moghuls' in memory of their having been, three hundred years earlier, subject to the Mongol Empire.

But the genuine Mongols who settled in eastern Iran in the thirteenth century, and even retained their language, are called Khazareitsy from the Persian word khazar -a thousand (meaning a military unit, or division).

But where are the Mongols, by whose name the yoke that lay on Rus for 240 years is known?

They were not an ethnos, because by Genghis-khan's will Jochi, Batu, Orda, and Sheibani each received 4 000 warriors, of whom only part came from the Far East. The latter were called 'Kins' and not 'Tatars', from the Chinese name of the Jurchen. This rare name occurred for the last time in the Zadonshchina, in which Mamai was called Kinnish.

Consequently, the yoke was not Mongol at all, but was enforced by the ancestors of the nomad Uzbeks, who should not be confused with the settled Uzbeks, although they merged in the nineteenth century, and now constitute a single ethnos, who equally revere the Timurides and the Sheibanides, who were deadly enemies in the sixteenth century, because that enmity had already lost sense and meaning in the seventeenth century."

The Khazars flourished from the seventh to the eleventh century. This means that they emerged following the reign of the emperor Justinian.

The issues surrounding the reign of Justinian, recorded by Procopius, indicate to us that something very strange was going on during that period of history. In 1998, "Us in the Future" made a comment about this that was only later confirmed scientifically which again, I cannot resist including for its historical interest:

Q: (L) I have discovered that three of the supernovas of antiquity which have been discovered and time estimated by the remnants, occurred in or near Cassiopeia at very interesting points in history.
A: Yes...
Q: (L) Well, one of these periods in history was around 1054. This is a very interesting time. It just so happens that there are no European records of this supernova which was recorded by the Chinese, Japanese, and perhaps even the Koreans. Yet, there are no European records. What happened to the European records?
A: Europe was in a "recovery mode" at the "time".
Q: (L) Recovery from what?
A: Loss of civilized structure due to overhead cometary explosion in 564 AD.
Q: (L) What effect did this have on the civilized structure? Was it a direct effect in terms of material, or did it have effects on people causing them to behave in an uncivilized and barbaric way?
A: Well, the burning fragmentary shower ignited much of the land areas in what you now refer to as Western Europe. This had the results you can imagine, causing the resulting societal breakdown you now refer to as "The Dark Ages".
Q: (L) Well, it damn sure was dark. There is almost a thousand years that nobody knows anything about!
A: Check Irish or Celtic, and French or Gallic records of the era for clues.

There were temporary "islands of survival", lasting just long enough for the written word to eke out.

A year later, August 17, 1999, the Knight Ridder Washington Bureau published an article by Robert S. Boyd entitled: *Comets may have caused Earth's great empires to fall* which included the following: (emphases, mine)

"Recent scientific discoveries are shedding new light on why great empires such as Egypt, Babylon and Rome fell apart, giving way to the periodic 'dark ages" that punctuate human history. *At least five times during the last 6,000 years, major environmental calamities undermined civilizations around the world.*

Some researchers say these disasters appear to be linked to collisions with comets or fragments of comets such as the one that broke apart and smashed spectacularly into Jupiter five years ago.

The impacts, yielding many megatons of explosive energy, produced vast clouds of smoke and dust that circled the globe for years, dimming the sun, driving down temperatures and sowing hunger, disease and death.

The last such global crisis occurred between A.D. 530 and 540-- at the beginning of the Dark Ages in Europe -- when Earth was pummeled by a swarm of cosmic debris.

In a forthcoming book, *Catastrophe, the Day the Sun Went Out*, British historian David Keys describes a 2-year-long winter that began in A.D. 535. Trees from California to Ireland to Siberia stopped growing. Crops failed. Plague and famine decimated Italy, China and the Middle East."

Keys quotes the writings of a 6th-century Syrian bishop, John of Ephesus:

"The sun became dark. ... Each day it shone for about four hours and still this light was only a feeble shadow."

A contemporary Italian historian, Flavius Cassiodorus, wrote:

"We marvel to see no shadows of our bodies at noon. We have summer without heat."

And a contemporary Chinese chronicler reported, "Yellow dust rained like snow'.'

Dendrochronologist, Mike Baillie writes:

"Analysis of tree rings shows that at in 540 A.D. in different parts of the world the climate changed. Temperatures dropped enough to hinder the growth of trees *as widely dispersed as northern Europe, Siberia, western North America, and southern South America.*

A search of historical records and mythical stories pointed to a disastrous visitation from the sky during the same period, it is claimed. There was one reference to a 'comet in Gaul so vast that the whole sky seemed on fire' in 540-41.

According to legend, King Arthur died around this time, and Celtic myths associated with Arthur hinted at bright sky Gods and bolts of fire.

In the 530s, an unusual meteor shower was recorded by both Mediterranean and Chinese observers. Meteors are caused by the fine dust from comets burning up in the atmosphere. Furthermore, a team of astronomers from Armagh Observatory in Northern Ireland published research in 1990 which said the Earth would have been at risk from cometary bombardment *between the years 400 and 600 A.D.* [...]

Famine followed the crop failures, and hard on its heels bubonic plague that swept across Europe in the mid-6th century. [...]

At this time, the Roman emperor Justinian was attempting to regenerate the decaying Roman empire. But the plan failed in 540 and was followed by the Dark Ages and the rise of Islam."

Apparently, this disaster was also followed by the arrival of the Khazars.

The kingdom of the Khazars has vanished from the map of the world and today many people have never even heard of it. But, in its day the Khazar kingdom [Khazaria] was a major power.

The Byzantine Emperor and historian, Constantine Porphyrogenitus (913-959) recorded in a treatise on Court Protocol that letters addressed to the pope in Rome, and similarly those to the Emperor of the West, had a gold seal worth two solidi attached to them, whereas *messages to the King of the Khazars required a seal worth three solidi.*

In other words, it was clearly understood that the Khazars were more powerful than the Emperor of the West or the Pope. As Koestler commented, "This was not flattery, but Realpolitik". How can it be that we are taught about the Byzantine Empire and the rise of the power of the Popes of the Western Empire, and have so little knowledge of an empire that existed at the same time, that was obviously more powerful than either of them? A Jewish empire, in fact?

The country of the Khazars was strategically located at the gateway between the Black Sea and the Caspian, acting as a buffer protecting Byzantium against invasions by the barbarian Bulgars, Magyars, Pechenegs, and later the Vikings and Russians. More important than this was the fact that the Khazars also blocked the Arabs from Eastern Europe.

"Within a few years of the death of Muhammad (A.D. 632) the armies of the Caliphate, sweeping northward through the wreckage of two empires and carrying all before them, reached the great mountain barrier of the Caucasus. This barrier once passed, the road lay open to the lands of eastern Europe. As it was, on the line of the Caucasus the Arabs met the forces of an organized military power which effectively prevented them from extending their conquests in this direction. The wars of the Arabs and the Khazars, which lasted more than a hundred years, though little known, have thus considerable historical importance." [Professor Dunlop of Columbia University, authority on the Khazars, quoted by Koestler, p. 14]

Most people know that the Frankish army of Charles Martel turned back the Arabs on the field of Tours. Few people know that, at the same time, the Muslims were met and held by the forces of the Khazar kingdom.

In 732, the future emperor, Constantine V, married a Khazar princess and their son became Emperor Leo IV, known as Leo the Khazar.

A few years later, probably in A.D. 740, the King of the Khazars, his court and the military ruling class embraced the Jewish faith and Judaism became the state religion of the Khazars. This came about as a reaction against the political pressure of the other two Superpowers of the day - Byzantium and the Muslims - both of which had the advantage of a monotheistic State Religion which allowed them greater control over their subjects. Not wanting to be subject either to the Pope or the Byzantine Emperor, but seeing the political benefits of religious controls, Judaism was chosen.

The Khazar kingdom held its power and position for most of four centuries during which time they were transformed from a tribe of nomadic warriors into a nation of farmers, cattle-breeders, fishermen, viticulturists, traders and craftsmen. Soviet archaeologists have found evidence of advanced civilization with houses built in a circular shape at the lower levels, later being replaced by rectangular buildings. This is explained as evidence of the transition from from portable, dome shaped tents, to settled lifestyles.

At the peak of their power, the Khazars controlled and/or received tribute from thirty or so different nations and tribes spread across the territories between the Caucasus, the Aral Sea, the Ural Mountains, the town of Kiev, and the Ukrainian steppes. These peoples included the Bulgars, Burtas, Ghuzz, Magyars, the Gothic and Greek colonies of the Crimea, and the Slavonic tribes to the Northwest.

> "Until the ninth century, the Khazars had no rivals to their supremacy in the regions north of the Black Sea and the adjoining steppe and the forest regions of the Dnieper. The Khazars were the supreme masters of the southern half of Eastern Europe for a century and a half. [...] During this whole period, they held back the onslaught of the nomadic tribes from the East." [Soviet archaeologist M. I. Artamonov]

In the timeline of history, the Khazar empire existed between the Huns and the Mongols. The Arab chroniclers wrote that the Khazars were, "white, their eyes blue, their hair flowing and predominantly reddish, their bodies large, and their natures cold. Their general aspect is wild".

The Georgians and Armenians, having been repeatedly devastated by the Khazars, identified them as *Gog and Magog*. An Armenian writer described them as having "insolent, broad, lashless faces and long falling hair, like women".

They sound like the long-haired Franks, don't they?

One of the earliest factual references to the Khazars occurs in a Syriac chronicle dating from the middle of the sixth century. It mentions the Khazars in a list of people who inhabit the region of the Caucasus. Koestler recounts that other sources indicate that *the Khazars were intimately connected with the Huns.*

In A.D. 448, the Byzantine Emperor Theodosius II sent an embassy to Attila which included a famed rhetorician by name of Priscus. He kept a minute account not only of the diplomatic negotiations, but also of the court intrigues and goings-on in Attila's sumptuous banqueting hall - he was in fact the perfect gossip columnist, and is still one of the main sources of information about Hun customs and habits. But Priscus also has anecdotes to tell about a people subject to the Huns whom he calls Akatzirs - that is, very likely, the Ak-Khazars, or "White" Khazars.

Let's go back to that most interesting fact quoted above: The presence of the tribe known as the Chatti has been mentioned by several ancient sources. What I find to be of great interest is that the Hittites were also known as the Chatti and the experts note that Frisian Tritzumer pottery has been found in Kent in England.

A definitive link between the Frisians and a tribe in England? Could it be possible that the Frisians came *from* England to the salt marshes of northern Europe?

Then, there is the bizarre belief of the ancient Armenians and Georgians that the Khazars were Gog and Magog.

What's up with that?!

In Genesis, we find the following:

> "10:1 Now these are the generations of the sons of Noah, Shem, Ham, and Japheth: and unto them were sons born after the flood.
> 10:2 The sons of Japheth; Gomer, and Magog, and Madai, and Javan, and Tubal, and Meshech, and Tiras.
> 10:3 And the sons of Gomer; Ashkenaz, and Riphath, and Togarmah.
> 10:4 And the sons of Javan; Elishah, and Tarshish, Kittim, and Dodanim.

10:5 By these were the isles of the Gentiles divided in their lands; every one after his tongue, after their families, in their nations."

It's truly interesting to note that the word "Ashkenaz" is listed as a name of one of great grandsons of Noah, through the "gentile" line. What about the "isles of the Gentiles"?

The only other real mention of Gog and Magog is in a truly weird prophecy given by the prophet Ezekiel:

"38:1 And the word of the LORD came unto me, saying, 38:2 Son of man, set thy face against Gog, the land of Magog, the chief prince of Meshech and Tubal, and prophesy against him, 38:3 And say, Thus saith the Lord GOD; Behold, I am against thee, O Gog, the chief prince of Meshech and Tubal: 38:4 And I will turn thee back, and put hooks into thy jaws, and I will bring thee forth, and all thine army, horses and horsemen, all of them clothed with all sorts of armour, even a great company with bucklers and shields, all of them handling swords: 38:5 Persia, Ethiopia, and Libya with them; all of them with shield and helmet: 38:6 Gomer, and all his bands; the house of Togarmah of the north quarters, and all his bands: and many people with thee.

38:7 Be thou prepared, and prepare for thyself, thou, and all thy company that are assembled unto thee, and be thou a guard unto them. 38:8 After many days thou shalt be visited: in the latter years thou shalt come into the land that is brought back from the sword, and is gathered out of many people, against the mountains of Israel, which have been always waste: but it is brought forth out of the nations, and they shall dwell safely all of them.

38:9 Thou shalt ascend and come like a storm, thou shalt be like a cloud to cover the land, thou, and all thy bands, and many people with thee.

38:10 Thus saith the Lord GOD; It shall also come to pass, that at the same time shall things come into thy mind, and thou shalt think an evil thought: 38:11 And thou shalt say, I will go up to the land of *unwalled villages*; I will go to them that are at rest, that dwell safely, all of them *dwelling without walls*, and having neither bars nor gates, 38:12 To take a spoil, and to take a prey; to turn thine hand upon the desolate places that are now inhabited, and upon the people that are gathered out of the nations, which have gotten cattle and goods, that dwell in the midst of the land.

38:13 Sheba, and Dedan, and the merchants of Tarshish, with all the young lions thereof, shall say unto thee, Art thou come to take a spoil? hast thou gathered thy company to take a prey? to carry away silver and gold, to take away cattle and goods, to take a great spoil?

38:14 Therefore, son of man, prophesy and say unto Gog, Thus saith the Lord GOD; In that day when my people of Israel dwelleth safely, shalt thou not know it? 38:15 And thou shalt come from thy place out of the north parts, thou, and many people with thee, all of them riding upon horses, a great company, and a mighty army: 38:16 And thou shalt come up against my people of Israel, as a cloud to cover the land; <u>it shall be in the latter days, and I will bring thee against my land,</u> that the heathen may know me, when I shall be sanctified in thee, O Gog, before their eyes.

38:17 Thus saith the Lord GOD; Art thou he of whom I have spoken in old time by my servants the prophets of Israel, which prophesied in those days many years that I would bring thee against them?

38:18 And it shall come to pass at the same time when Gog shall come against the land of Israel, saith the Lord GOD, that my fury shall come up in my face. 38:19 For in my jealousy and in the fire of my wrath have I spoken, <u>Surely in that day there shall be a great shaking in the land of Israel;</u> 38:20 So that the fishes of the sea, and the fowls of the heaven, and the beasts of the field, and all creeping things that creep upon the earth, and all the men that are upon the face of the earth, shall shake at my presence, and the mountains shall be thrown down, and the steep places shall fall, *<u>and every wall shall fall to the ground.</u>*

38:21 And I will call for a sword against him throughout all my mountains, saith the Lord GOD: <u>every man's sword shall be against his brother.</u> 38:22 And I will plead against him with pestilence and with blood; and <u>I will rain upon him, and upon his bands, and upon the many people that are with him, an overflowing rain, and great hailstones, fire, and brimstone.</u>

38:23 Thus will I magnify myself, and sanctify myself; and I will be known in the eyes of many nations, and they shall know that I am the LORD.

39:1 Therefore, thou son of man, prophesy against Gog, and say, Thus saith the Lord GOD; Behold, I am against thee, O Gog, the chief prince of Meshech and Tubal: 39:2 And <u>I will turn thee back, and leave but the sixth part of thee, and will cause thee to come up from the north parts, and will bring thee upon the mountains of Israel:</u> 39:3 And I will smite thy bow out of thy left hand, and will cause thine arrows to fall out of thy right hand. 39:4 Thou shalt fall upon the mountains of Israel, thou, and all thy bands, and the people that is with thee: I will give thee unto the ravenous birds of every sort, and to the beasts of the field to be devoured. 39:5 Thou shalt fall upon the open field: for I have spoken it, saith the Lord GOD.

39:6 <u>And I will send a fire on Magog, and among them that dwell carelessly in the isles:</u> and they shall know that I am the LORD. 39:7 So will I make my holy name known in the midst of my people Israel; and I will not let them pollute my holy name any more: and the heathen shall know that I am the LORD, the Holy One in Israel."

There's another mention of Gog and Magog in the book of Revelation:

"20:7 And when the thousand years are expired, Satan shall be loosed out of his prison, 20:8 And shall go out to <u>deceive the nations</u> which are in the four quarters of the earth, Gog, and Magog, to gather them together to battle: the number of whom is as the sand of the sea. 20:9 And they went up on the breadth of the earth, and compassed the camp of the saints about, and the beloved city: and <u>fire came down from God out of heaven, and devoured them</u>. 20:10 And the devil that deceived them was cast into the lake of fire and brimstone, where the beast and the false prophet are, and shall be tormented day and night for ever and ever."

The Signs Team pointed out another couple of items in Revelation to me yesterday:

"2:8 And unto the angel of the church in Smyrna write; These things saith the first and the last, which was dead, and is alive; 2:9 I know thy works, and tribulation, and poverty, (but thou art rich) and *I know the blasphemy of them which say they are Jews, and are not, but are the synagogue of Satan.*

3:9 Behold, I will make them of *the synagogue of Satan, which say they are Jews, and are not, but do lie;* behold, I will make them to come and worship before thy feet, and to know that I have loved thee."

As it happens, the Gog/Magog link is another key to the mystery.

The experts tell us that where the "archaeological" Frisians went is unknown. After having a look at what Lev Gumilev said about ethnoi, we also realize that names of groups can change in context as well as content. Additionally, language is not always a clue as to origin since languages can be imposed on conquered peoples who then believe that it is their own, or adopted out of necessity.

Returning to our problem: one clue that strikes me as compelling is the idea that there was a connection between the Frisians of North Holland and a tribe that lived in Kent, England. The current idea is that some of the Frisians may have gone to Kent, but it is equally possible that they *came* from Kent to North Holland, and later traveled further, fleeing to escape destruction and famine. Some of them certainly may have migrated to East Friesland and hooked up with the Chatti to form the Franks around 300 AD. Others of them could just as easily have trekked to the Eurasian steppes.

The languages spoken by many of the tribes of the Eurasian steppes, including the Turkic languages of the Khazars, are also known as Altaic. As a language family, this is still a bit contentious. The Turkic, Mongolian, and Tungusic families do have strong similarities in many ways, but some linguists suggest these are due to intensive borrowing from long contact. To a some extent, the Altaic-Turkic languages also resemble the Uralic languages already discussed, such as Finnish and Hungarian. As a consequence, a *Ural-Altaic superfamily* has been suggested: Eurasiatic, in which Indo-European languages would also be included as a "brother" language. This super-family has a parent also which *makes a connect to Amerind languages*, (!) but we won't go into that just now. The short of it is that we can't rely on language to denote a genetic or ethnic affinity over long periods of time, though it can, sometimes, be a clue.

Returning to the Chatti: obviously, there were/are two types of Aryans as I have demonstrated in my book, *The Secret History of the World* where I wrote:

> "When one tracks back through all of the ancient "matters" and studies the different groups, trying to follow them as they moved from place to place, studying the genetic morphology in order to keep track of who is who, and comparing linguistics and myth and archaeology, one comes to the startling realization that there were significant polarities throughout space and time. I have tentatively identified these polarities as the Circle People and the Triangle - or Pyramid - People. In a general sense, one can see the broad brush of the triangle people in the Southern hemisphere, in the pyramids and related cultures and artifacts. For the most part, their art is primitive and stylistically rigid. In the northern hemisphere, one sees the circle makers, the spirals, the rough megaliths, the art of Lascaux and Chauvet and the many other caves. One can note a clear difference between the perceptions and the response to the environment between the two trends and groups. Of course, there are areas where there was obvious mixture of both cultures and styles, and ideological constructions, but overall, there is a very distinct difference."

Even with these "polarities", again and again we find those "big, blond" types popping up. However, it is not exactly that simple. As the research has proceeded, I have formed hypotheses and tested and discarded them innumerable times. For the moment, the current hypothesis runs as follows:

The issue does not seem to be one of skin color or "race", (which is a ridiculous term as it is currently used). It is more an issue of the difference between human beings who have "something" inside as opposed to those who don't have this "something".

When this "something" is analyzed, it reveals a fundamental difference in "being" that is most easily expressed as those who worship something outside themselves, vs. those who don't worship any god or thing outside themselves because *they cannot worship outside what is inside.*

There are behavioral clues to the different natures of the two polarities, and it seems that the real reason that those who are of the so-called Aryan bloodlines, often "rise to the top" in many cultures for the simple reason that they have more potent "power cells" - mitochondria - that energize their bodily functions, producing greater "heat" and activity. This "rising to the top" can be positive, or it can be negative.

This poses a unique problem: very energetic negatively oriented beings have many advantages in this world over very energetic positive beings due to the fact that the former have no "moral imperative". For them, the material world is all there is: in their core being, they worship the material universe represented by a god who is "outside" of them, and inner reflection and analysis so as to determine if they are conducting themselves in such a way so as to return to the inner "Origin" - or Edenic state - has no real meaning for them.

Many religions have been created that promise salvation or heaven via an intermediary, and these concepts are appealing to the negative orientation, but the deep, internal conviction that this can and must be accomplished by cultivating that divine spark within does not exist for them. They may claim that it does, but their actions do not match their words. Their thinking is "legalistic", and the best way to describe it is that they "strain at gnats and swallow camels".

Again, the important point is: those with the spark of the divine within *cannot* worship outside what is inside. No matter how hard they may try to "have faith" in this god or that god who has promised to save them, that divine spark within will constantly agitate, asking questions and casting doubts. Such individuals carry the bloodline - the genetic traits - to manifest the Origin - the Hyperboreans.

Just a hypothesis, as I said.

Let's come back to our problem of Gog and Magog.

I have asked: could it be possible that the Frisians came *from* England to the salt marshes of northern Europe? How does this relate to the belief of the ancient Armenians and Georgians that the Khazars were "Gog and Magog".

In Genesis, we read:

"10:1 Now these are the generations of the sons of Noah, Shem, Ham, and Japheth: and unto them were sons born after the flood.
10:2 The sons of Japheth; Gomer, and Magog, and Madai, and Javan, and Tubal, and Meshech, and Tiras.
10:3 And the sons of Gomer; Ashkenaz, and Riphath, and Togarmah.
10:4 And the sons of Javan; Elishah, and Tarshish, Kittim, and Dodanim.
10:5 By these were the isles of the Gentiles divided in their lands; every one after his tongue, after their families, in their nations."

Those of you who have read my series *Who Wrote The Bible* should know that I'm not really going "Bible Thumper" here, but that I certainly think that there is *something* to many of the ancient texts that were assembled to create the Bible. But obviously, something was going on in the ancient world that has been recorded in the Bible, and later turned into "Holy Writ". Notice again the remark about "isles of the Gentiles".

In the passage from Ezekiel we notice several of the "sons of Japheth" being named as places:

> "38:1 And the word of the LORD came unto me, saying, 38:2 Son of man, set thy face against Gog, the land of Magog, the chief prince of Meshech and Tubal, and prophesy against him,
> 38:3 And say, Thus saith the Lord GOD; Behold, I am against thee, O Gog, the chief prince of Meshech and Tubal..."

Then later, he mentions the land of Magog in the same breath with "them that dwell carelessly in the isles...".

> "39:6 And I will send a fire on Magog, and among them that dwell carelessly in the *isles*..."

Why should people in the "isles of the gentiles" be described as living carelessly? Is that "carelessly" as in "without cares", or is it carelessly as in not taking sufficient care in some way that led to an incident in which such carelessness became a "marker" for these people? Perhaps a famous blunder of some sort?

The only place on the planet that has been called Gog and Magog for any considerable length of time in our history is in England: the Gog Magog hills near Cambridge.

Curiously, crop circles appeared in a field near to these hills exactly two months before the September 11th attacks on New York.

Historians suggest that the Gog Magog hills got their name because of the innumerable human bones that have been found there; evidence of a battle so fierce that it reminded the locals of Ezekiel's passage about Gog, king of Magog.

The earliest reference to this name for these hills is in a decree of 1574 forbidding students to visit them or be fined. Nowadays, they are still a trysting area. A map dating from the end of the 16th century also depicts the Gogmagog Hills.

There is a small problem here, I think. How did the locals know about the prophecy of Ezekiel?

 John Wycliff's *hand-written manuscripts* in the 1380s were the first complete Bibles in the English language. They were obviously not widely available.

William Tyndale printed the first English *New* Testament in 1525/6. One risked death by burning if caught in mere possession of the forbidden book. Only two complete copies of that first printing are known to have survived. Any Edition printed before 1570 is very rare, most of them were confiscated and burned.

Myles Coverdale and John Rogers, assistants to Tyndale, carried the project forward. The first complete English Bible was printed on October 4, 1535, and is known as the Coverdale Bible.

Considering this timeline, it seems questionable that the locals around the Gogmagog hills should have given such a new name to their hills, or that it would have become commonly known to everyone, such that a decree could be published in less than 40 years regarding these named hills. Considering the fact that having or reading the Bible was a crime for most of those 40 years, it is not likely that the local people would have wanted to reveal their knowledge of the name in this way. One would also think that if ancient battle sites were subject to being renamed in this fashion after the release of the English Bible, many other ancient battle sites would have received Biblical names as well.

Even though there is no proof, it seems to be highly probable that the Gogmagog hills were called that from more ancient times, and for a different reason.

There are two figures of the giants Gog and Magog that strike the hours on a clock at Dunstan-n-the West, Fleet Street, but few people in London seem to know why they are there. Adrian Gilbert writes in his book, *The New Jerusalem*:

> "Once more we have to go back to Geoffrey of Monmouth's book, in which there is a story of how, when Brutus and his Trojans arrived in Britain, they found the island sparsley inhabited by a race of giants. One of these, called Gogmagog, wrestled with a Trojan hero called Corineus and was eventually thrown to his death from a cliff- top called in consequense 'Gogmagog's Leap'.

> In the 1811 translation into English of Brut Tysilio, a Welsh version of the chronicles translated by the Rev. Peter Roberts, there is a footnote suggesting that Gogmagog is a corrupted form of Cawr-Madog, meaning 'Madog the great' or 'Madog the giant' in Welsh. It would appear that with Gog of Magog, the name of a war leader who the Bible prophesies will lead an invation of the Holy Land at the end of the age.

> In another version of the Gogmagog tale, the *Recuyell des histories de Troye*, Gog and Magog are two seperate giants. In this story they are not killed but brought back as slaves by Brutus to his city of New Troy. Here

there were to be employed as gatekeepers, opening and closing the great gates of the palace.

The story of Gog and Magog, the paired giants who worked the gates of London, was very popular in the middle ages and effigies of them were placed on the city gates *at least as early as the reign of Henry VI.* These were destroyed in the Great Fire of 1666, but so popular were they that new ones were made in 1708 and installed at the Guildhall. This pair of statues was destroyed in 1940 during the Blitz, the third great fire of London, when the roof and much of the interior furnishings of the Guildhall were burnt. A new pair of the statues was carved to replace them when the Guildhall was repaired after the war."

We should note that the dates of Henry VI are from well before the English Bible was available.

The prophecies of Ezekiel date from sometime around 695-690 B.C., and we would like to consider the question as to where he heard the term "Gog, Magog" and what terrible battle was fought in the past that was used as a model for Ezekiel's prediction to which this name was attached?

As it happens, there are three terms often associated with archetypal battles: Armageddon, Gog Magog, and the Trojan War. Right away, we notice a homophonic similarity between Megiddo and Magog and it seems that we have a clear connection between Gog, Magog, Troy and Britain.

Those of you who have read *Who Wrote the Bible* might be interested to know that the untimely death of the hero - King Josiah - idolized by the author of most of the Biblical texts - Jeremiah - died in the valley of Megiddo and that was the end of the story. Note also that this tale is actually a doublet of the story of the death of King Ahab who was of "The House of David".

Megiddo also features in the story of the deaths of the *sons* of Ahab found in II Kings, chapter 9. This chapter chronicles the death of Jezebel as well. The reason I mention these odd little semi-mythical connections is because I am persuaded that careful examination of Biblical texts compared to many other sources, including hard scientific ones, can assist us in forming at least a vague picture of our true history. Those stories did not come into existence in a vacuum and could not have been foisted on the people if there wasn't something in them of truth.

We now want to ask the question: Do these two wars, Gog Magog, and Troy have anything in common?

Wilkens is proposing that there has been a transfer of western European geographical names to the eastern Mediterranean. He suggests that this occurred very late, about 1,000 B.C. My guess is that it began much earlier, after the collapse of the Bronze Age Civilization around 1600 B.C.

With the exception of the Bible, no other works of western literature have been more studied and commented upon than the Iliad and the Odyssey. Considering the fact that the prophet Ezekiel knew the name of a place in England that certainly looks as though it might be at least a very early mythical assimilation to the story of Troy, perhaps the Bible and the Iliad have a lot more in common than one would ordinarily suppose? I would like to quote a couple of sections from my book, *The Secret History of The World*, to give us some additional clues:

> "Gildas, writing in the sixth century A.D., is the first native British writer whose works have come down to us. Nennius, writing about 200 years later, refers to "the traditions of our elders". And Geoffrey of Monmouth praises the works of Gildas and Bede and wonders at the lack of other works about the early kings of Britain saying:
>
>> 'Yet the deeds of these men were such that they deserve to be praised for all time. What is more, these deeds were handed joyfully down in oral tradition, just as if they had been committed to writing, by many peoples who had only their memory to rely on'."[30]

The Stonehenge story told by Geoffrey of Monmouth begins with *a treacherous massacre* of the Britons by Hengest and his Saxons, which took place at a peace conference. The Saxons hid their daggers in their shoes and, at a signal from their leader, drew them and killed all the assembled British nobles except the king. Geoffrey tells us that the meeting took place at the "Cloister of Ambrius, not far from Kaercaradduc, which is now called Salisbury". He later describes this as a monastery of three hundred brethren founded by Ambrius many years before.

As it happens, there is a place called Amesbury about two and a half miles east of Stonehenge, which was originally called Ambresbyrig. This site in no way matches the description of the Cloister of Ambrius. The cloister is described as situated on Mount Ambrius, whereas Amesbury is in the valley of the river Avon. Geoffrey tells us that the victims of the massacre were buried in the cemetery beside the monastery, not two and a half miles away. What is more, since it seems that Geoffrey was acting under the pressure of the mythical norm of assimilating current events to the archetype, we then are left free to consider the possibility that this was the site of an ancient and famous massacre and that Stonehenge and the Cloister of Ambrius are one and the same.

The fact that Geoffrey called it a "cloister" is a curious choice of words since a cloister is "a covered arcade forming part of a religious or

---

[30] Geoffrey of Monmouth, *The History of the Kings of Britain*, translated by Lewis Thorpe, 1966, p. 1

collegiate   establishment".   That   certainly   seems   to   describe
Stonehenge very well. Geoffrey was obviously trying to "Christianize"
Stonehenge in his references to monastery and monks.

   The Saxons gave Stonehenge the name by which we know it today. The
Britons called it the *Giant's Dance*, and Geoffrey certainly had a tradition
to draw on there if he had wanted to, since he begins his history with the
adventures of Brutus, a descendant of Aeneas, who, after escaping from
the flames of Troy, and much traveling and fighting, landed on Britain,
which was uninhabited *except for a few giants*. Geoffrey had a reasonable
context here in which to place Stonehenge, but he ignored it and instead
attributed the building of Stonehenge to Merlin *after the dreadful
massacre by the Saxons*. This enabled him to connect his Arthur to the
great architect of the monument and all its glories. This suggests to us that
there was a solid tradition behind this idea: that Stonehenge was the focal
point of *a people who had suffered a terrible, terminal disaster*. In short,
this tradition may reach back into the mists of antiquity.

   In Geoffrey's story, Merlin suggests to Aurelius that he ought to send
an expedition to Ireland to fetch the Giant's Ring from Mount Killaraus.
The King begins to laugh and asks:

> "How can such large stones be moved from so far-distant a country?" he
> asked. "It is hardly as if Britain itself is lacking in stones big enough for
> the job!"
>
> "Try not to laugh in a foolish way, your Majesty", answered Merlin.
> "What I am suggesting has nothing ludicrous about it. These stones are
> connected with certain secret religious rites and they have various
> properties that are medicinally important. Many years ago the
> Giants transported them from the remotest confines of *Africa* and set them
> up in Ireland at a time when they inhabited that country. Their plan was
> that, whenever they felt ill, baths should be prepared at the foot of the
> stones; for they used to pour water over them and to run this water into
> baths in which their sick were cured. What is more, they mixed the water
> with herbal concoctions and so healed their wounds. There is not a single
> stone among them which hasn't some medicinal value."[31]

As W. A. Cummins, geologist and archaeologist remarks, all of this
sounds like a pre-medieval tradition about Stonehenge, possibly even
prehistoric. However, instead of coming from Africa, or even Ireland, the
bluestones used in the construction of Stonehenge come from the Prescelly
Mountains, or Mynydd Preselau. The so-called "altar stone", however,

---

[31] Diodorus of Sicily, English translation by C. H. Oldfather, Loeb Classical Library,
Volumes II and III. London, William Heinemann, and Cambridge, Mass., USA, Harvard
University Press, 1935 and 1939.

most likely came from somewhere in the Milford Haven area in Pembrokeshire. [...]

Cummins remarks astutely that Geoffrey was eight and a half centuries closer to the event than we are, so maybe his account is correspondingly closer?[32] [...]

Diodorus Siculus, writing in the first century B.C., gives us a description of Britain based, in part, on the voyage of Pytheas of Massilia, who sailed around Britain in 300 B.C.

> "As for the inhabitants, they are simple and far removed from the shrewdness and vice which characterize our day. Their way of living is modest, since they are well clear of the luxury that is begotten of wealth. The island is also thickly populated and *its climate is extremely cold*, as one would expect, since it actually lies under the Great Bear. It is held by many kings and potentates, who for the most part live at peace among themselves."[33]

Diodorus then tells a fascinating story about the Hyperboreans that was obviously of legendary character already when he was writing:

> "Of those who have written about the ancient myths, Hecateus and certain others say that in the regions beyond the land of the Celts (Gaul) there lies in the ocean an island no smaller than Sicily. This island, the account continues, is situated in the north, and is inhabited by the Hyperboreans, who are called by that name because their home is beyond the point whence the north wind blows; and the land is both fertile and productive of every crop, and since it *has an unusually temperate climate* it produces two harvests each year."[34]

Now, it seems that there is little doubt that Diodorus is talking about the same location - but we notice that the climate is so vastly different in the two descriptions that we can hardly make the connection. However, let us just suppose that his description of Britain was based on the climate that prevailed at the time he was writing, and the legendary description of the Hyperboreans was based *on a previous climatic condition* that was preserved in the story. Diodorus stresses that he is recounting something very ancient as he goes on to say:

> "The Hyperboreans also have a language, we are informed, which is peculiar to them, and are most friendly disposed towards the Greeks, and especially towards the Athenians and the Delians, who have inherited this goodwill from *most ancient times.* The myth also relates that certain

[32] Cummins, W. A., *King Arthur's Place in Pre-history*, (Surrey: Bramley Books 1992) p. 64.
33 Diodorus of Sicily, English translation by C. H. Oldfather, Loeb Classical Library, Volumes II and III. London, William Heinemann, and Cambridge, Mass., USA, Harvard University Press, 1935 and 1939.
34 Ibid.

Greeks visited the Hyperboreans and left behind them costly votive offerings bearing inscriptions in Greek letters. And in the same way Abaris, a Hyperborean, came to Greece in ancient times and renewed the goodwill and kinship of his people to the Delians."[35]

Diodorus' remark about the relations between the Hyperboreans and the Athenians leads us to recall the statement of Plato that the Atlanteans were at war with the Athenians, and we wonder if the Hyperboreans are the real "early Athenians". After all, the Greeks were said to be "Sons of the North Wind", Boreas. Herodotus expounds upon the relationship of the Hyperboreans to the Delians:

"Certain sacred offerings wrapped up in wheat straw come from the Hyperboreans into Scythia, whence they are taken over by the neighbouring peoples in succession until they get as far west as the Adriatic: from there they are sent south, and the first Greeks to receive them are the Dodonaeans. Then, continuing southward, they reach the Malian gulf, cross to Euboea, and are passed on from town to town as far as Carystus. Then they skip Andros, the Carystians take them to Tenos, and the Tenians to Delos. That is how these things are said to reach Delos at the present time."[36]

The legendary connection between the Hyperboreans and the Delians leads us to another interesting remark of Herodotus who tells us that Leto, the mother of Apollo, was born on the island of the Hyperboreans. That there was regular contact between the Greeks and the Hyperboreans over many centuries does not seem to be in doubt. The Hyperboreans were said to have introduced the Greeks to the worship of Apollo, but it is just as likely that the relationship goes much further back. Herodotus has another interesting thing to say about the Hyperboreans and their sending of sacred offerings to Delos:

"On the first occasion they were sent in charge of two girls, whose names the Delians say were Hyperoche and Laodice. To protect the girls on the journey, the Hyperboreans sent five men to accompany them … the two Hyperborean girls died in Delos, and the boys and girls of the island still cut their hair as a sign of mourning for them… There is also a Delphic story that before the time of Hyperoche and Laodice, two other Hyperborean girls, Arge and Opis, came to Delos by the same route. …Arge and Opis came to the island at the same time as Apollo and Artemis…"[37]

---

[35] Ibid.

[36] Ibid.

[37] Herodotus, *The Histories, Book IV*, trans. Aubrey De Selincourt, revised John Marincola (London: Penguin 1972) p. 226

Herodotus mentions at another point, when discussing the lands of the "barbarians", "*All these except the Hyperboreans, were continually encroaching upon one another's territory*". Without putting words in Herodotus' mouth, it seems to suggest that the Hyperboreans were not warlike at all.

A further clue about the religion of the Hyperboreans comes from the myths of Orpheus. It is said that when Dionysus invaded Thrace, Orpheus did not see fit to honor him but instead *preached the evils of sacrificial murder* to the men of Thrace. He taught "other sacred mysteries" having to do with Apollo, whom he believed to be the greatest of all gods. Dionysus became so enraged; he set the Maenads on Orpheus *at Apollo's temple* where Orpheus was a priest. They burst in, murdered their husbands who were assembled to hear Orpheus speak, tore Orpheus limb from limb, and threw his head into the river Hebrus where it floated downstream *still singing.* It was carried on the sea to the island of Lesbos. Another version of the story is that Zeus killed Orpheus with a thunderbolt for *divulging divine secrets.* He was responsible for instituting the Mysteries of Apollo in Thrace, Hecate in Aegina, and Subterrene Demeter at Sparta.[38]

I would like to note immediately how similar the above story of the Maenads murdering their husbands is to the story of the daughters of Danaus murdering their husbands - sons of Aegyptus - on the wedding night, and how similar both of these stories are to the story of the massacre at the Cloisters of Ambrius attributed still later to Hengist and Horsa. The story of the Maenads adds the spin that it was a religious dispute between sacrificers and those preaching against the evils of sacrifice. Additionally, it is interesting that in the stories of the daughters of Danaeus and the Maenads, women have become as deadly as treacherous Helen was to Troy.

Was an original legend later adapted to a different usage, assimilated to a different group or tribe? More than once?

In fact, when you think about it, the stories in the Bible are remarkably similar to the Greek myths with most of the fantastic elements removed, names changed, and genealogies inserted to give the impression of a long history. One could say that the "history" of the Old Testament is merely "historicized myth". And of course, the myths that it was historicized from may have belonged to an entirely different people.

Getting back to Where Troy Once Stood, Iman Wilkens did his homework in a very creative and open minded way. Among the things he

---

[38] See: Graves, Robert, *The Greek Myths* (London: Penguin, London) 1992

examined in the Iliad and Odyssey were the sailing directions. Having a friend in the shipping industry who is a specialist in guidance systems, I asked him a number of questions about this process and he confirmed that Wilkens approach and conclusions were correct. He also concentrated on the geography and spatial locations of Homer's world. Iman Wilkens tells us:

"As work on Homer's puzzle progressed, it turned out that many towns, islands and countries were not yet known in the eastern Mediterranean at the time of the Trojan War by the names mentioned by the poet.

Places like Thebes, Crete, Lesbos, Cyprus and Egypt had entirely different names in the Bronze Age, as we now know from archaeological research. The theatre of Homer's epics can therefore never have been in the Mediterranean, just as, say an epic found in the United States about a Medieval war, mentioning European place-names (which can be found in both countries) could not have taken place there, as the American continent had not yet been discovered!

As to Homer's place names, we are confronted with a similar problem but it is not really surprising that such a fundamental error in chronology could persist for some 2,700 years as traditional beliefs handed down over a long period are seldom challenged: each generation simply repeats the teachings of the previous one without asking itself the proper questions.

But now that this problem of timing has come to light, we are obliged to look for Homer's places elsewhere than the eastern Mediterranean, and situated near the ocean and its tides, in particular where dykes prevented low-lying areas from flooding. In other words: we have to look for Homer's places along the Atlantic coast.

The outcome of this research will be unsettling to many and I also realize from my own experience that it takes some time to get accustomed to the Bronze Age geography of Europe. The best way of adjusting is by reading Homer together with the explanations and maps of this book. Those who remain sceptical should realize that the problem of place-name chronology in general and the phenomenon of *oceanic tides* in particular, *exclude any alternative solution.* [...]

At first sight it seems impossible to penetrate such a very distant past, but it turns out to be still feasible to discover what happened over 3,000 years ago, and precisely where, thanks to the branch of linguistics dealing with the history of word forms - etymology.

While the Greek spelling of Homer's geographical names was fixed once and for all when the poems were written down ... place names in western Europe went on changing in accordance with more or less well-established etymological rules, to be fixed by spelling only relatively recently.

Taking this fact into account, we shall see how virtually 400 odd Homeric place-names can be matched in a coherent and logical fashion with western European place-names as we know them today. Many of them are still easily recognizable, others very much less so, often because they have changed by invaders speaking a different language.

Even over the last few centuries, some place-names around the world have changed beyond recognition, due to pronunciation by peoples of different languages. Who, for example, would believe that Brooklyn in New York comes from the Dutch place name *Breukelen*, if it were not a documented fact?

While it is not possible to prove anything that occurred more than 3,000 years ago, I hope that my detective work has at least produced sufficient circumstantial evidence to convince the readers that the famous city of Troy was situated in western Europe. [...]

The reason for the longevity of place names in general and river names in particular is that conquerors generally adopt the already-existing name, although often modified or adapted to their own tongue.

A major exception to this rule is Greece, where invaders arriving in a country almost emptied of its population gave new names to many places - names familiar to them and appearing in Homer's works. But people arriving in a new and sparsely populated country of course give familiar names to places in a haphazard kind of way.

In Australia, for example, Cardiff, Gateshead, Hamilton, Jesmond, Stockton, Swansea, and Walsend, widely scattered in Britain, are all suburbs of Newcastle, New South Wales. It is precisely this haphazard transposition of names that explains, for example, why Rhodes is an island in Greece, but a region in Homer; Euboea is another Greek island, but *part of the continent* in Homer; Chios yet another island, but not in Homer. Similarly, Homer speaks of *an island called Syria* which clearly cannot be Syros in the Cyclades. The reader may object that these are simply imprecisions due to the extreme antiquity of the text. But we have evidence that the present Egypt, Cyprus, Lesbos and Crete, all names appearing in Homer, were not known by those names in the Bronze Age.

The list of such anomalies is long. Even the identification of such Homeric places as Ithaca and Pylos has led to endless and inconclusive discussion among scholars and the difficulty of making sense of Homer in Greece or Turkey is brought out in recent studies by Malcolm Wilcock and G.S. Kirk. It is therefore clear that the poet, though he uses names we recognize, was not talking about the places that now bear those names."
[*Where Troy Once Stood*, Wilkens, p. 52-53]

Iman Wilkens cites the now very long list of reasons why Turkey is excluded as the site of Troy. (I'm not going to deal with those issues here; the reader may wish to pursue that line of research on their own.)

Additionally, he points out the many reasons that support the location of the Troad in a country with a temperate climate, open to the Atlantic, and with tides. As Wilkens noted, considering the *internal evidence* of Homer's works, it is only logical to look for the Troad in Europe, in a country formerly inhabited by the Celts, with an Atlantic climate, separated from the Continent by the sea, and having on its east coast a broad plain with a large bay capable of sheltering a big fleet of ships.

In England, there is, as it happens, an area corresponding perfectly to *all* of the descriptions in Homer - the East Anglian plain between the city of Cambridge and the Wash. Wilkens brings up a compelling argument:

> "Homer names no less than fourteen rivers in the region of Troy, eight of them being listed together in the passage where he describes how, after the Trojan War, the violence of these rivers in flood sweeps away the wood and stone rampart built round the Achaean encampment and the ships. It appears that generations of readers must have skipped over these lines, thinking they contained fictitious names of no interest, for otherwise, it is difficult to understand how nobody, not even people from the Cambridge area, was ever struck by the resemblance between the names of Homer's rivers and those of this area."

Have a look at this list of river names, keeping in mind the several thousand years that have passed and that these changes are quite in line with phonetic changes according to the rules of etymology:

Usual Rendering of the Greek River Name from Homer	Modern Name of the Corresponding River in England
Aesepus	Ise
Rhesus	Rhee
Rhodius	Roding
Granicus	Granta
Scamander	Cam
Simois	Great Ouse
Satniois	Little Ouse
Larisa	Lark

Caystrius or Cayster	Yare with Caister-on-sea and Caistor castle at the mouth
Thymbre	Thet
Caresus	Hiz
Heptaporus	Tove
Callicolone	Colne
Cilla	Chillesford
Temese	Thames

As Wilkens notes, it is impossible to find these rivers in Turkey. All that can be found are four rivers that were later given Homeric names without regard to the geographical descriptions in the Iliad.

The evidence that the Trojan plain is the East Anglian plain is also backed up by Homer's descriptions of the land: fertile soil, rich land, water meadows, flowering meadows, fine orchards, fields of corn, and many other details that perfectly describe England, but have absolutely no relationship to Turkey, either in modern or ancient times, as the archaeology demonstrates.

There still exists very substantial remains of two enormous earth ramparts, running parallel with one another, to the northeast of Cambridge, one twelve kilometers long and the other fifteen.

The ditches dug in front of the dykes are on the side facing inland, not towards the sea, which means that they were built by invaders, not defenders exactly as described by Homer. These are known today as *Fleam Dyke* and *Devil's Dyke*.

As Wilkens notes, it is obvious that the invader who built these enormous defenses was planning on a long siege. Also, a very large army would have been needed to move the huge volume of earth that went into creating these dykes which are 20 meters high and 30 meters wide at the base. Therefore, it seems that the estimated number of combatants in the Achaean army - between 65,000 and 100,000 - might not be an exaggeration.

The two dykes are about 10 km apart, leaving room for the deployment of two large armies if the defenders were to breach the first rampart. A line drawn perpendicularly through the two dykes, extending inland, cuts through the highest hill in the Cambridge area now known as the Wandlebury Ring, part of a plateau called the *Gog Magog Hills*. Wilkens produces still another confirmation:

> "A second indication that Wandlebury was the site of Troy is provided by a further detail of Homer's text, where he tells how the Trojan army, before the construction of the dykes, gathered on a small isolated hill before Troy:

> Now there is before the city a steep mound afar out in the plain, with a clear space about it on this side and on that; this do men verily call Batieia, but the immortals call it the barrow of Myrine, [an Amazon] light of step. There on this day did the Trojans and their allies separate their companies. [Iliad, II, 811-815]

> Some kilometers to the north of Wandlebury, there is indeed, an isolated hill where the village of Bottisham now stands. It seems permissible to associate the Homeric name of Batieia with that of Bottis(ham). [...]

> When Priam, with a herald, is on his way from Troy to the Achaean camp by the sea to ask Achilles to return the body of his son, Hector, they apparently follow the course of the Scamander and stop to water their horses at another place that is of great interest to us:

> When the others had driven past the great barrow of Ilus, they halted the mules and the horses in the river to drink, for darkness was by now come down over the earth... [Iliad, XXIV, 349-351]

> A modern map shows us that half way between where Troy was and the Achaean camp, on the river Cam, lies the small town of Ely, which very likely owes its name to Ilus, and ancestor of Priam and the founder of Troy. It may well be, therefore, that the great gothic cathedral of Ely was built on the site where Homer saw the tomb of the first Trojan king." [Wilkens]

According to the tale, after ten years of war and countless deaths, Troy was essentially wiped off the face of the earth. Obviously, everybody didn't die but the silting of the Wash made it impossible to rebuild on the same site at that time, assuming that the survivors had the heart to do so. A new city was built on the Thames at *Ilford*, or the Ford of Ilium east of the present City of London. The Romans called this city Londinium Troia Nova, or "New Troy". It was also known as Trinobantum, and the Celts called it *Caer Troia*, or "Town of Troy".

Geoffrey of Monmouth wrote that New Troy was founded by Brutus in 1100 B.C. That would certainly put the "real Trojan War" quite a bit earlier than most "experts" consider to be the appropriate temporal placement of this war. The Hon. R.C. Neville found glass objects from the eastern Mediterranean which were dated as being from the fifteenth century B.C., about 5 km from Wandlebury Ring. Objects of a similar date and origin have also been found in other parts of England, showing that there was trade between the Atlantic and Mediterranean peoples.

"To suppose that the great cultures in the eastern Mediterranean area and in the Near East were separated from each other, in the beginning, by the broadest of gulfs, is an interpretation wholly at variance with the facts. On the contrary, it has been clearly enough established that we have to deal, in this region, with an original or basic if not uniform culture, so widely diffused that we may call it Afrasian. [A. W. Persson]

There are two figures of the giants Gog and Magog that strike the hours on a clock at Dunstan-in-the West, Fleet Street, but few people in London seem to know why they are there. Adrian Gilbert writes in *The New Jerusalem*:

Once more we have to go back to Geoffrey of Monmouth's book, in which there is a story of how, when Brutus and his Trojans arrived in Britain, they found the island sparsely inhabited by a race of giants. One of these, called Gogmagog, wrestled with a Trojan hero called Corineus and was eventually thrown to his death from a cliff-top called in consequence 'Gogmagog's Leap'.

In the 1811 translation into English of *Brut Tysilio*, a Welsh version of the chronicles translated by the Rev. Peter Roberts, there is a footnote suggesting that Gogmagog is a corrupted form of Cawr-Madog, meaning 'Madog the great' or 'Madog the giant' in Welsh. [...]

In another version of the Gogmagog tale, the *Recuyell des histories de Troye*, Gog and Magog are two separate giants. In this story they are not killed but brought back as slaves by Brutus to his city of New Troy. Here they were to be employed as gatekeepers, opening and closing the great gates of the palace.

The story of Gog and Magog, the paired giants who worked the gates of London, was very popular in the middle ages and effigies of them were placed on the city gates at least as early as the reign of Henry VI. These were destroyed in the Great Fire of 1666, but so popular were they that new ones were made in 1708 and installed at the Guildhall. This pair of statues was destroyed in 1940 during the Blitz, the third great fire of London, when the roof and much of the interior furnishings of the Guildhall were burnt. A new pair of the statues was carved to replace them when the Guildhall was repaired after the war." [pp. 60-61]

In the above quote, we have a clue that the giants, Gog and Magog, were known to the people of England long before they had access to a Bible, so certainly the Gog Magog hills were not named after the war described by Ezekiel. Rather, Ezekiel must have known about the terrible conflict fought on the Gog Magog plateau.

The question that is often asked is: could there have been cities of as many as 100,000 inhabitants in England during the Bronze Age? The population definitely fluctuated over time, but archaeologists estimate a population of at least 3 million at the close of the Bronze Age. According to some experts, England was a populous country with well developed agriculture at that time. We read in the Iliad about orchards, vines and fields of corn.

> "About 2000 B.C. came Bell-beaker people, whose burials are in single graves, with individual grave-goods. The remarkable Wessex Culture of the Bronze Age which appears about 1500 B.C. is thought to be based on this tradition. The grave-goods there suggest the existence of a warrior aristocracy 'with a graded series of obligations of service... through a military nobility down to the craftsmen and peasants', as in the Homeric society. This is the sort of society which is described in the Irish sagas, and there is no reason why so early a date for the coming of the Celts should be impossible. ...There are considerations of language and culture that rather tend to support it." [M. Dillon and N. Chadwick, *The Celtic Realms*, Weidenfield and Nicolson, London, 1972]

If it is so that Troy was in England, then the first documented King of England was Priam - in the Bronze Age. It also explains why prehistoric spiral labyrinths engraved on rocks or laid out on the ground with stones are still called "Troy Towns" or "walls of Troy" in England, "Caerdroia" in Wales and "Trojaborgs" in Scandinavia.

There is more than a symbolic relationship between the spiral maze or labyrinths and the city of Troy. According to K. Kerenyi, the root of the word truare means "a circular movement around a stable centre". Based on the archaeological evidence, the symbolism of the circular labyrinth is far older than Homer's time, reaching back into the Stone Age.

Having discovered that there is good reason to believe the Troy was situated in England, we next must consider now the identification and locations of the Achaeans. As Wilkens has noted:

> "Places like Thebes, Crete, Lesbos, Cyprus and Egypt had entirely different names in the Bronze Age, as we now know from archaeological research. The theater of Homer's epics can therefore never have been in the Mediterranean, just as, say an epic found in the United States about a Medieval war, mentioning European place-names (which can be found in both countries) could not have taken place there, as the American continent had not yet been discovered!"

So, if the Egypt that we know was not Egypt at that time, where was it? Also, where was the land of the Achaeans?

"If fourteen rivers in the same region of England correspond linguistically
and geographically with those of the Trojan plain as described by Homer,
the coincidence is so great that it cannot be accidental, and we must
indeed be talking about the same plain. ... At the end of the Iliad, Homer
states explicitly where Troy was located, speaking through the voice of
Achilles talking to the old King Priam, come to claim the body of his son,
Hector:

And of thee, old sire, we hear that of old thou was blest; how of all that
toward the sea Lesbos, the seat of Macar encloseth, and Phrygia in the
upland, and the boundless Hellespont, over all these folk, men say, thou,
old sire, was pre-eminent by reason of thy wealth and thy sons. [Iliad,
XXIV, 543-546]

This does seem to delimit Priam's kingdom fairly precisely, and these
places are indeed now to be found in the Mediterranean. Lesbos is a
Greek island off the Turkish coast, Phrygia is the high plateau of western
Turkey and the Hellespont is the classical name for the Strait of the
Dardanelles. It is precisely this description that inspired Schliemann to
seek the ruins of Troy in a plain in northwest Turkey." [Wilkens]

Considering the fact that the archaeological evidence of the many levels
of the "Troy" that Schliemann discovered simply do not support all the
details of the story of the Trojan war, I agree with Wilkens that it seems
that there was a general shift of Homeric place-names from western
Europe to the Mediterranean after the end of the Bronze Age.

The sea upon which the Troad lay was called the Hellespont. This
means the "Sea of Helle". According to legend, Helle was a girl who fell
from the back of a winged ram and drowned in the sea which was then
named after her. She was the daughter of Athamas, King of Orchomenus
and the sister of Phrixus.

The name Hel, or Helle is also written as El or Elle by those linguistic
groups that do not pronounce the "H". It is a word of very ancient Indo-
European origin. Not only was El the name of the principal god of the
pantheon of Ugarith, the ancient Syrian town on the Mediterranean, but
"el" also means "god" in the Semitic languages.

The atlas of Europe contains so many place-names beginning with Hel,
Helle, El and Elle that it is well worth having a look: (I apologize that the
scan of the map is so difficult to read due to the contrast, but the idea can
be gotten by having a look and then further examination of an atlas will
provide additional evidence.)

Apart from the waters off the western tip of France, still called Chenal
de la Helle, the name Hellespont or Helle Sea has disappeared from
western Europe. But, there are good reasons to think that it must have been
the name of the sea on the shores of which so many places named "Helle"

remain. Also, there still remain an estuary in the Rhine delta called Hellegat, or "Gate to Helle", while the origin of the name of the French resort of Houlgate on the Channel coast is undoubtedly Hellegat. The name of the port of Hull on the northeast coast of England comes from the word "hell" according to the Oxford dictionary of English Etymology. Additionally, the name of Broceliande, the vast forest of Paimpont in Brittany, known from the cycle of the Knights of the Round Table is "Bro-Hellean" in Armorican Breton, meaning "Land near Hell".

> "It therefore seems logical to conclude that Homer's vast Hellespont was not the narrow strait of the Dardanelles in northwestern Turkey, but the sea separating England from the continent of Europe, in other words, the Channel, the North Sea and the Baltic, all the more so because the Greek adjective used to describe the Hellespont, apeiros, is much stronger than 'vast': it means 'boundless' which can only apply to the seas off the western shores of Europe, or, in other words, the Atlantic." [Wilkens]

Phrygia is the second frontier of the Troad mentioned by Homer and he describes it as an "upland". We can look for the etymology of the word Phrygia in both the name of the Norse goddess Freya, and the name Phrixos, the brother of Helle. The name of the kingdom of their father was Orchomenus and there is, in fact, a place in west Scotland called Orchy, and on the north of Scotland there are the Orkney Islands, the archaic spelling of which is Orcheny. In the Orkneys, there is a town named Aith, the same as the name of Agamemnon's horse. Following the principles of etymology, we even find the name of King Athamos preserved: Atham > Ethem > Eden> Edin > Edinburgh.

Many recent archaeological finds give evidence of big farms in Scotland dating as far back as 4000 B.C., witness to an advanced culture that subsequently spread to the south of Great Britain.

Lesbos would then be the Isle of Wight. The name of the main river on the Isle of Wight is *Medina*, cognate with the Greek *Methymna*. The narrow strait separating the Isle from the mainland is called the *Solent*, related to the Greek noun *solen* which means channel or strait. Maps of the island show a promontory known as *Egypt point*.

According to Homer, Egypt is only a few days voyage from Troy. And so, if Troy was in England, Egypt must not be far away. Somewhere in western Europe there must be a region that subsequently gave its Bronze Age name to the land of the Pharaohs down south in Africa much later.

At the time of Homer, the land of the Pharaohs was not called Egypt, but *Misr*, *Al-Khem* or *Kemi* and often *Meroë*. This latter name applied to Upper Egypt and what is now called Ethiopia. The biblical name for Egypt was *Mitsrayim* which is still modern Hebrew for Egypt. Since its independence, the official Arabic name for Egypt has returned to *Masr*.

It was Herodotus, the first Greek to visit the pyramids who first called the Land of the Pharaohs by a name taken from Homer, Egypt. Alexander the Great made this the official name of the country in 332 B.C. In other words, the Greeks did exactly what all colonialists do: they gave familiar names to places in their colonies and imposed their language on the peoples by virtue of making it the language of administration.

What is evident is that Homer's description of Egypt does not at all match the features of the Land of the Pharaohs. This was noted by the Greek Philosopher Eratosthenes who lived in Alexandria. (284-192 B.C.)

Homer uses Egypt to designate a "river fed by the water of the sky" and sometimes the surrounding country with its "fine fields". But he never, ever, mentions the pyramids which were, supposedly, already thousands of years old at the time of the Trojan War. Additionally, the pyramids are not mentioned by Aeschylus in his drama *The Suppliants*, the subject of which is the Druidic tradition from the north. He tells us how the suppliants, a group of fifty young women who wish to escape forced marriages, flee Egypt, "across the salty waves to reach the land of Argos". Later in the play, he writes how the young Io, pursued by a gadfly, returns from Argos to Egypt and *"arrived in the holy land of Zeus, rich in fruits of all sorts, in the meadows fed by the melting snow and assailed by the fury of Typhon, on the banks of the Nile whose waters are always pure"*.

Doesn't sound much like Egypt, does it?

As those of you who have studied geography realize, Argos has never been part of, or near to, Egypt as we now know it. Furthermore, Egypt - as we now know it - was the land of Ra, the Sun God and, in ancient Egypt, Zeus was completely unknown. Finally, meadows watered by melting snow never, in any way, could describe the land we now know as Egypt.

So, since the Egypt described by both Homer and Aeschylus do not fit the Egypt we now know, and we don't think they would have forgotten to mention the chief feature of Egypt - the pyramids - we must conclude that they were not talking about the Egypt we know as Egypt today.

Zeus was certainly known to France to the extent that one day of the week, *Jeudi*, or Thursday, comes from his name. It is the right distance from Troy, but, as Wilkens points out, we don't find much etymologically speaking, to support the idea that Egypt was France. However, there are a few clues.

As it happens, there is a town and branch of the Nile in present day Egypt that the Greeks called *Bolbitiron* and *Bobitinon*. Correspondingly, there is a town called Bolbec near the mouth of the Seine. Then, there is a river in France called the *Epte*. This river flows from the north to join the Seine near Vernoin, half-way between Paris and Rouen.

There are many etymological artifacts of the name of the Nile in France where many villages contain -nil- (French for Nile) in their names. There is Mesnil, near Le Havre which, in twelfth-century church Latin was called "mas-nilii" or "house in the Nile country". Then there is Miromesnil, Ormesnil, Frichemesnil, Longmesnil, Vilmesnil, and so on. Menilmontant, or "house on the upper Nile" is a district in Paris, and there is a suburb called Blanc-Mesnil. The god of the Nile had a daughter called Europe whose name is preserved in the river Eure, a southern confluent of the Seine.

At the time of the Pharoahs, in what we now know as Egypt, the Nile was called Ar or Aur. During the periods when it flooded, it was called Hape the Great.

Homer mentions a town in Egypt, Thebes, which cannot be the same town we know in Egypt which was, during the time of the Pharohs known as Wase or Wo-se. It was only eight centuries after Homer that the Greeks gave it the new name of Thebes.

Utilizing the principles of etymology, Wilkens suggests that Homer's Thebes is now called Dieppe.

> "According to etymological dictionaries the 'd' was formerly pronounced 't' and the name is connected with the Germanic tief (English 'deep') for the harbour lies deep in the country. Let us recall that Homer, who always chose sound and concise descriptions, speaks of a country of 'fair fields' and a 'heaven fed' river. Dieppe's hinterland is a beautiful farming region and the rain is never far awary in this part of France. What is more, recent archeological research has revealed that large farms existed in many parts of France in the Celtic period, so well-kept fields were a feature of the countryside even in that remote era. [...]
>
> The initial evidence found so far is thus in favour of identifying the Bronze Age Egypt as corresponding approximately to the present department of Seine-Maritime." [Wilkens]

I would like to draw the reader's attention back to a comment quoted previously:

> "Quite apart from the difficulty of fitting most places described in the Iliad and the Odyssey into the physical reality of the lands surrounding the Aegean Sea, there is also a problem with the spiritual content of Homer's works. Plato had doubts as to their Greek origin and the great philosopher was by no means an admirer of this imaginative poet whose gods, with their jealousies and vengeances, behaved like spoilt children. Plato was

particularly worried about the corrupting influence of Homer's poems on the minds of Greek youth, above all because of their 'lack of respect' for the gods. He suggested that certain passages of the Iliad and Odyssey should be corrected or even expurgated and if he had been the dictator of his 'ideal state', he would have had them burned, thus breaking the chain of transmission of these unique and extremely ancient poems." [Wilkens]

I think that there is an additional explanation for why Plato was so antagonistic to the tales of Homer: Plato's own story of Atlantis was the story of the original exemplar of the Trojan War and he knew that many of the features of the original war were being distorted by Homer and attributed to a much later war, on a different scale, with certain elements added that would create misunderstanding in the minds of readers.

The idea of a ten year war - with massive losses on both sides - being fought over a woman exercised me for quite some time especially while I was reading Herodotus' account of Helen. His observations are so pithy and his style of writing is so entertaining that I would like to share it with the reader:

"Those of the Persians who have knowledge of history declare that the Phenicians first began the quarrel. These, they say, came from that which is called the Erythraian Sea to this of ours; and having settled in the land where they continue even now to dwell, set themselves forthwith to make long voyages by sea.

And conveying merchandise of Egypt and of Assyria they arrived at other places and also at Argos.

Now Argos was at that time in all points the first of the States within that land which is now called Hellas.

The Phenicians arrived then at this land of Argos, and began to dispose of their ship's cargo: and on the fifth or sixth day after they had arrived, when their goods had been almost all sold, there came down to the sea a great company of women, and among them the daughter of the king; and her name, as the Hellenes also agree, was Io the daughter of Inachos.

These standing near to the stern of the ship were buying of the wares such as pleased them most, when of a sudden the Phenicians, passing the word from one to another, made a rush upon them; and the greater part of the women escaped by flight, but Io and certain others were carried off.

So they put them on board their ship, and forthwith departed, sailing away to Egypt.

In this manner the Persians report that Io came to Egypt, not agreeing therein with the Hellenes, and this they say was the first beginning of wrongs.

Then after this, they say, certain Hellenes (but the name of the people they are not able to report) put in to the city of Tyre in Phenicia and carried off the king's daughter Europa;--these would doubtless be Cretans;--and so they were quits for the former injury.

After this however the Hellenes, they say, were the authors of the second wrong; for they sailed in to Asia of Colchis and to the river Phasis with a ship of war, and from thence, after they had done the other business for which they came, they carried off the king's daughter Medea.

And the king of Colchis sent a herald to the land of Hellas and demanded satisfaction for the rape and to have his daughter back.

But they answered that, as the Barbarians had given them no satisfaction for the rape of Io the Argive, so neither would they give satisfaction to the Barbarians for this.

In the next generation after this, they say, Alexander the son of Priam, having heard of these things, desired to get a wife for himself by violence from Hellas, being fully assured that he would not be compelled to give any satisfaction for this wrong, inasmuch as the Hellenes gave none for theirs.

So he carried off Helen, and the Hellenes resolved to send messengers first and to demand her back with satisfaction for the rape; and when they put forth this demand, the others alleged to them the rape of Medea, saying that the Hellenes were now desiring satisfaction to be given to them by others, though they had given none themselves nor had surrendered the person when demand was made.

Up to this point, they say, nothing more happened than the carrying away of women on both sides; but after this the Hellenes were very greatly to blame; for they set the first example of war, making an expedition into Asia before the Barbarians made any into Europe.

Now they say that in their judgment, though it is an act of wrong to carry away women by force, it is a folly to set one's heart on taking vengeance for their rape, and the wise course is to pay no regard when they have been carried away; for it is evident that they would never be carried away if they were not themselves willing to go. And the Persians say that they, namely the people of Asia, when their women were carried away by force, had made it a matter of no account, but the Hellenes on account of a woman of Lacedemon gathered together a great armament, and then came to Asia and destroyed the dominion of Priam; and that from this time forward they had always considered the Hellenic race to be their enemy: for Asia and the Barbarian races which dwell there the Persians claim as belonging to them; but Europe and the Hellenic race they consider to be parted off from them.

The Persians for their part say that things happened thus; and they conclude that the beginning of their quarrel with the Hellenes was on account of the taking of Ilion: but as regards Io the Phenicians do not agree with the Persians in telling the tale thus; for they deny that they carried her off to Egypt by violent means, and they say on the other hand that when they were in Argos she was intimate with the master of their ship, and perceiving that she was with child, she was ashamed to confess it to her parents, and therefore sailed away with the Phenicians of her own will, for fear of being found out.

These are the tales told by the Persians and the Phenicians severally: and concerning these things I am not going to say that they happened thus or thus, but when I have pointed to the man who first within my own knowledge began to commit wrong against the Hellenes, I shall go forward further with the story, giving an account of the cities of men, small as well as great: for those which in old times were great have for the most part become small, while those that were in my own time great used in former times to be small: so then, since I know that human prosperity never continues steadfast, I shall make mention of both indifferently. [...]

And the priests [of Egypt] told me, when I inquired, that the things concerning Helen happened thus:--Alexander having carried off Helen was sailing away from Sparta to his own land, and when he had come to the Egean Sea contrary winds drove him from his course to the Sea of Egypt; and after that, since the blasts did not cease to blow, he came to Egypt itself, and in Egypt to that which is now named the Canobic mouth of the Nile and to Taricheiai.

Now there was upon the shore, as still there is now, a temple of Heracles, in which if any man's slave take refuge and have the sacred marks set upon him, giving himself over to the god, it is not lawful to lay hands upon him; and this custom has continued still unchanged from the beginning down to my own time.

Accordingly the attendants of Alexander, having heard of the custom which existed about the temple, ran away from him, and sitting down as suppliants of the god, accused Alexander, because they desired to do him hurt, telling the whole tale how things were about Helen and about the wrong done to Menelaos; and this accusation they made not only to the priests but also to the warden of this river-mouth, whose name was Thonis.

Thonis then having heard their tale sent forthwith a message to Proteus at Memphis, which said as follows: 'There hath come a stranger, a Teucrian by race, who hath done in Hellas an unholy deed; for he hath deceived the wife of his own host, and is come hither bringing with him this woman herself and very much wealth, having been carried out of his way by winds to thy land. Shall we then allow him to sail out unharmed, or shall we first take away from him that which he brought with him?'

In reply to this Proteus sent back a messenger who said thus: 'Seize this man, whosoever he may be, who has done impiety to his own host, and bring him away into my presence, that I may know what he will find to say.'

Hearing this, Thonis seized Alexander and detained his ships, and after that he brought the man himself up to Memphis and with him Helen and the wealth he had, and also in addition to them the suppliants. So when all had been conveyed up thither, Proteus began to ask Alexander who he was and from whence he was voyaging; and he both recounted to him his descent and told him the name of his native land, and moreover related of his voyage, from whence he was sailing.

After this Proteus asked him whence he had taken Helen; and when Alexander went astray in his account and did not speak the truth, those who had become suppliants convicted him of falsehood, relating in full the whole tale of the wrong done.

At length Proteus declared to them this sentence, saying, 'Were it not that I count it a matter of great moment not to slay any of those strangers who being driven from their course by winds have come to my land hitherto, I should have taken vengeance on thee on behalf of the man of Hellas, seeing that thou, most base of men, having received from him hospitality, didst work against him a most impious deed. For thou didst go in to the wife of thine own host; and even this was not enough for thee, but thou didst stir her up with desire and hast gone away with her like a thief.

Moreover not even this by itself was enough for thee, but thou art come hither with plunder taken from the house of thy host. Now therefore depart, seeing that I have counted it of great moment not to be a slayer of strangers. This woman indeed and the wealth which thou hast I will not allow thee to carry away, but I shall keep them safe for the Hellene who was thy host, until he come himself and desire to carry them off to his home; to thyself however and thy fellow-voyagers I proclaim that ye depart from your anchoring within three days and go from my land to some other; and if not, that ye will be dealt with as enemies.'

This the priests said was the manner of Helen's coming to Proteus; and I suppose that Homer also had heard this story, but since it was not so suitable to the composition of his poem as the other which he followed, he dismissed it finally, making it clear at the same time that he was acquainted with that story also: and according to the manner in which he described the wanderings of Alexander in the Iliad (nor did he elsewhere retract that which he had said) it is clear that when he brought Helen he was carried out of his course, wandering to various lands, and that he came among other places to Sidon in Phenicia. Of this the poet has made mention in the 'prowess of Diomede', and the verses run this:

'There she had robes many-coloured, the works of women of Sidon, Those whom her son himself the god-like of form Alexander Carried from Sidon, what time the broad sea-path he sailed over Bringing back Helene home, of a noble father begotten.'

And in the Odyssey also he has made mention of it in these verses:

'Such had the daughter of Zeus, such drugs of exquisite cunning, Good, which to her the wife of Thon, Polydamna, had given, Dwelling in Egypt, the land where the bountiful meadow produces Drugs more than all lands else, many good being mixed, many evil.'

And thus too Menelaos says to Telemachos:

'Still the gods stayed me in Egypt, to come back hither desiring, Stayed me from voyaging home, since sacrifice was due I performed not.'

In these lines he makes it clear that he knew of the wandering of Alexander to Egypt, for Syria borders upon Egypt and the Phenicians, of whom is Sidon, dwell in Syria.

By these lines and by this passage it is also most clearly shown that the 'Cyprian Epic' was not written by Homer but by some other man: for in this it is said that on the third day after leaving Sparta Alexander came to Ilion bringing with him Helen, having had a 'gently-blowing wind and a smooth sea', whereas in the Iliad it says that he wandered from his course when he brought her.

Let us now leave Homer and the 'Cyprian' Epic; but this I will say, namely that I asked the priests whether it is but an idle tale which the Hellenes tell of that which they say happened about Ilion; and they answered me thus, saying that they had their knowledge by inquiries from Menelaos himself.

After the rape of Helen there came indeed, they said, to the Teucrian land a large army of Hellenes to help Menelaos; and when the army had come out of the ships to land and had pitched its camp there, they sent messengers to Ilion, with whom went also Menelaos himself; and when these entered within the wall they demanded back Helen *and the wealth which Alexander had stolen from Menelaos* and had taken away; and moreover they demanded satisfaction for the wrongs done: and the Teucrians told the same tale then and afterwards, both with oath and without oath, namely that in deed and in truth they had not Helen nor the wealth for which demand was made, but that both were in Egypt; and that they could not justly be compelled to give satisfaction for that which Proteus the king of Egypt had.

The Hellenes however thought that they were being mocked by them and besieged the city, until at last they took it; and when they had taken the wall and did not find Helen, but heard the same tale as before, then they believed the former tale and sent Menelaos himself to Proteus.

And Menelaos having come to Egypt and having sailed up to Memphis, told the truth of these matters, and not only found great entertainment, but also received Helen unhurt, and all his own wealth besides.

Then however, after he had been thus dealt with, Menelaos showed himself ungrateful to the Egyptians; for when he set forth to sail away, contrary winds detained him, and as this condition of things lasted long, he devised an impious deed; for he took two children of natives and made sacrifice of them. After this, when it was known that he had done so, he became abhorred, and being pursued he escaped and got away in his ships to Libya; but whither he went besides after this, the Egyptians were not able to tell. Of these things they said that they found out part by inquiries, and the rest, namely that which happened in their own land, they related from sure and certain knowledge.

Thus the priests of the Egyptians told me; and I myself also agree with the story which was told of Helen, adding this consideration, namely that if Helen had been in Ilion *she would have been given up to the Hellenes*, whether Alexander consented or no; for Priam assuredly was not so mad, nor yet the others of his house, that they were desirous to run risk of ruin for themselves and their children and their city, in order that Alexander might have Helen as his wife: and even supposing that during the first part of the time they had been so inclined, yet when many others of the Trojans besides were losing their lives as often as they fought with the Hellenes, and of the sons of Priam himself always two or three or even more were slain when a battle took place (if one may trust at all to the Epic poets),-- when, I say, things were coming thus to pass, I consider that even if Priam himself had had Helen as his wife, he would have given her back to the Achaians, if at least by so doing he might be freed from the evils which oppressed him. [...]

In truth however they lacked the power to give Helen back; and the Hellenes did not believe them, though they spoke the truth... [Herodotus, *The Histories*, selected excerpts]

One thing that ought to be clear is that I don't think that it was a woman they were fighting over; no indeed, it was the "treasure". What was that treasure? Well, let me suggest that the main thing we notice about this story is that it sounds a bit like George Bush demanding Iraq's Weapons of Mass Destruction. Just such a situation as we see developing in our own time between the United States and the rest of the world may have developed between Atlantis and Europe and Asia around 12,000 years ago, and then again later, between the Trojans and Achaeans in Europe. This might give us a clue as to what sort of "treasure" the Trojan War was really being fought over.

Tracking this problem has led me down many interesting pathways and the most useful clues have come from the alchemist Fulcanelli. One of his oft-reiterated themes is that the "ancient Greeks" — not the Egyptians — were the source of the Hermetic science and all esoteric knowledge.

However, in a particular passage, he seems to contradict himself in the following remarks:

> "Atlantis. Did this mysterious island, of which Plato left the enigmatic description, ever exist? A question difficult to solve, give the weakness of the means which science possesses to penetrate the secret of the abysses. Nevertheless, some observations seem to support the partisans of the existence of Atlantis. [...]

> *Faith in the truthfulness of Plato's works* results in believing the reality of the periodical upheavals of which the *Mosaic Flood* , we said it, remains the written symbol and the sacred prototype. To those who negate what the priests of Egypt entrusted to Solon, we would only ask to explain to us what Aristotle's master wanted to reveal by this fiction of a sinister nature. For we indeed believe that beyond doubt, Plato became the propagator of very ancient truths, and that consequently his books contain a set, *a body of hidden knowledge*. His Geometric Number, and Cave have their signification; why should the myth of Atlantis not have its own?

> Atlantis must have undergone the same fate as the others, and the catastrophe, which submerged it, falls obviously into the same cause as that which buried, forty-eight centuries later, under a profound sheet of water, Egypt, the Sahara, and the countries of Northern Africa. But more favored than the land of the Atlantean, Egypt gained from a raising of the bottom of the ocean and came back to the light of day, after a certain time of immersion. For Algeria and Tunisia with their dry "chotts" covered with a thick layer of salt, the Sahara and Egypt with their soils constituted for a large part of sea sand show that the waters invaded and covered vast expanses of the African continent. The columns of the Pharaohs' temples bear on them undeniable traces of immersion; in the hypostyle chambers, the slabs, still extant, which form the ceilings have been raised and moved by the oscillating motion of the waves; the disappearance of the outer coating of the pyramids and in general that of the stone joins (the Colosses of Memnon who used to sing) the evident traces of corrosion by water that can be noticed on the sphinx of Giza, as well as on many other works of Egyptian statuary have no other origin." [Fulcanelli, *Dwellings of the Philosophers*, pp. 511-512.]

Notice that he said: "To those who negate what the priests of Egypt entrusted to Solon, we would only ask to explain to us what Aristotle's master wanted to reveal by this fiction of a sinister nature". Fulcanelli then goes on a long series of remarks that actually *do* negate what the priests of Egypt told Solon, namely, that Egypt had never been inundated. Now, why did Fulcanelli first say to "have faith in the truthfulness of Plato's words", and then turn around and negate them?

Another item of curiosity here is his remark about the "Mosaic Flood". Everybody knows that Noah was associated with the Flood and Moses was associated with the Exodus. Certainly, there was a sort of "flood" in the story of Moses where the Red Sea drowned the Pharaoh, but that story doesn't seem to have much to do with a real Flood; or does it?

Timaeus and *Critias*, written by Plato some time around 360 B.C. are the only existing ancient written records which specifically refer to Atlantis. The dialogues are conversations between Socrates, Hermocrates, Timaeus, and Critias. Apparently in response to a prior talk by Socrates about ideal societies, Timaeus and Critias agree to entertain Socrates with a tale that is "*not a fiction but a true story*".

The story is about the conflict between the ancient Athenians and the Atlanteans *9000 years before Plato's time.* Knowledge of the ancient times was apparently forgotten by the Athenians of Plato's day, and the form the story of Atlantis took in Plato's account was that *Egyptian priests* conveyed it to Solon. Solon passed the tale to Dropides, the great-grandfather of Critias. Critias learned of it from his grandfather also named Critias, son of Dropides.

Let's take a careful look at the main section of the story, omitting the introduction that describes Solon going to Egypt and chatting up the priests.

> "Thereupon one of the priests, who was of a very great age, said: O Solon, Solon, you Hellenes are never anything but children, and there is not an old man among you. Solon in return asked him what he meant. I mean to say, he replied, that in mind you are all young; there is no old opinion handed down among you by ancient tradition, nor any science, which is hoary with age. And I will tell you why.
>
> There have been, and will be again, many destructions of mankind arising out of many causes; the greatest have been brought about by the agencies of fire and water, and other lesser ones by innumerable other causes. There is a story, which even you have preserved, that once upon a time Phaeton, the son of Helios, having yoked the steeds in his father's chariot, because he was not able to drive them in the path of his father, burnt up all that was upon the earth, and was himself destroyed by a thunderbolt. Now this has the form of a myth, but really signifies *a declination of the bodies moving in the heavens around the earth*, and a great conflagration of things upon the earth, which recurs after long intervals; at such times those who live upon the mountains and in dry and lofty places are more liable to destruction than those who dwell by rivers or on the seashore. *And from this calamity the Nile, who is our never-failing saviour, delivers and preserves us.*
>
> When, on the other hand, the gods purge the earth with a deluge of water, the survivors in your country are herdsmen and shepherds who dwell on the mountains, but those who, like you, live in cities are carried by the

rivers into the sea. *Whereas in this land, neither then nor at any other time, does the water come down from above on the fields, having always a tendency to come up from below; for which reason the traditions preserved here are the most ancient.*

The fact is, that wherever the extremity of winter frost or of summer does not prevent, mankind exist, sometimes in greater, sometimes in lesser numbers. And whatever happened either in your country or in ours, or in any other region of which we are informed - if there were any actions noble or great or in any other way remarkable, they have all been written down by us of old, and are preserved in our temples."

We want to here make note of the fact that present day evidence suggests that Egypt *has* been inundated and that it also experienced a rainy climate as evidenced by the water erosion on the sphinx. Fulcanelli even commented upon the inundation of Egypt. And so we see that Fulcanelli has given us a hint, a clue. This leads us to question whether or not this story actually came from the mouth of an Egyptian priest in terms of Egypt as we now know it. If so, such a priest would have known of the period of heavy rain and shallow seas in Egypt, by which the Sphinx and other monuments were eroded, and which deposited a layer of salt on the interior of the pyramids and other structures that Fulcanelli mentioned. And so we suggest, to reconcile this difficulty, not that the story is false — because Fulcanelli has told us to "have faith in the account of Plato" — but rather that this was a deliberate exoteric "blind".

"Whereas just when you and other nations are beginning to be provided with letters and the other requisites of civilized life, after the usual interval, the stream from heaven, like a pestilence, comes pouring down, and leaves only those of you who are destitute of letters and education; and so you have to begin all over again like children, and know nothing of what happened in ancient times, either among us or among yourselves. As for those genealogies of yours which you just now recounted to us, Solon, they are no better than the tales of children.

In the first place you remember a single deluge only, but there were many previous ones; in the next place, you do not know that there formerly dwelt in your land the fairest and noblest race of men which ever lived, and that you and your whole city are descended from a small seed or remnant of them which survived. And this was unknown to you, because, for many generations, the survivors of that destruction died, leaving no written word. For there was a time, Solon, before the great deluge of all, when the city which now is Athens was first in war and in every way the best governed of all cities, is said to have performed the noblest deeds and to have had the fairest constitution of any of which tradition tells, under the face of heaven."

Again, let's interrupt the dialogue to point out that it is hardly likely that a priest of the Egypt we know would have declared the Athenians to be "the fairest and noblest race of men", nor that they "performed the noblest deeds" and had the "fairest constitution ... under the face of heaven"! This is another clue that the speaker is giving us that the Egypt that is the source of this information is *not* the Egypt we now know.

> "Solon marveled at his words, and earnestly requested the priests to inform him exactly and in order about these former citizens. You are welcome to hear about them, Solon, said the priest, both for your own sake and for that of your city, and above all, for the sake of the goddess who is the common patron and parent and educator of both our cities. She founded your city a thousand years before ours, receiving from the Earth and Hephaestus the seed of your race, and afterwards she founded ours, of which the constitution is recorded in our sacred registers to be eight thousand years old."

Yet again, the Egyptian priest is giving *greater antiquity to the Greeks than to the Egyptians*! Another clue for the reader to understand that this is not an Egyptian story of Egypt as we now know it!

> "As touching your citizens of nine thousand years ago, I will briefly inform you of their laws and of their most famous action; the exact particulars of the whole we will hereafter go through at our leisure in the sacred registers themselves. If you compare these very laws with ours you will find that many of ours are the counterpart of yours as they were in the olden time."

Here, of course, we come to the idea that there was an ancient connection and communication between the "real Egyptians" and the "real Athenians". Georges Gurdjieff once remarked that Christianity *was taken from Egypt*, a statement that might suggest that he agreed with the Pan-Egyptian school. But no: Christianity, he hastened to explain, was *not taken from the Egypt of history*, but from a "far older Egypt" which is unrecorded".

> "In the first place, there is the caste of priests, which is separated from all the others; next, there are the artificers, who ply their several crafts by themselves and do not intermix; and also there is the class of shepherds and of hunters, as well as that of husbandmen; and you will observe, too, that the warriors in Egypt are distinct from all the other classes, and are commanded by the law to devote themselves solely to military pursuits; moreover, the weapons which they carry are shields and spears, a style of equipment which the goddess taught of Asiatics first to us, as in your part of the world first to you."

The remark that the right function of society was "first taught to the Asiatics" is most interesting. The reference to "Asiatics" *in this context* from an historical "Egyptian Priest" is extremely questionable because, in the many Egyptian inscriptions unearthed by archaeology, the Asiatics are always referred to as "Vile". It is true that in historical times the Egyptians borrowed their military equipment and war strategies from the Asiatics, but that was a much later development than the above story would suggest. The issue of who the "vile Asiatics" were is an ongoing debate, but it seems to devolve on such as the Hittites, Hyksos, and other Indo-European tribes that came down from the Steppes in various waves.

> "Then as to wisdom, do you observe how our law from the very first made a study of the whole order of things, extending even to prophecy and medicine which gives health, out of these divine elements deriving what was needful for human life, and adding every sort of knowledge which was akin to them. All this order and arrangement the goddess first imparted to you when establishing your city; and *she chose the spot of earth in which you were born,* because she saw that *the happy temperament of the seasons in that land* would produce the wisest of men. Wherefore the goddess, who was a lover both of war and of wisdom, *selected and first of all settled that spot which was the most likely to produce men likest herself.* And there you dwelt, having such laws as these and still better ones, and excelled all mankind in all virtue, as became the children and disciples of the gods."

Again and again, this very strange "Egyptian" priest is saying things that completely contradict the more "historical" Egyptian view that they are the most "ancient and noble race". In the above remarks, he has said that the goddess imparted to the Greeks *first* all of the laws of health and those things needed to preserve and prolong life. The Greeks are pronounced to have been the "wisest of men", and those "most like the goddess" herself. And again "excelled all mankind in all virtue", which is not very likely to have been said by an Egyptian priest from the Egypt we know.

Here comes the story of the war, so pay close attention:

> "Many great and wonderful deeds are recorded of your state in our histories. But one of them exceeds all the rest in greatness and valour. For these histories tell of *a mighty power which unprovoked made an expedition against the whole of Europe and Asia, and to which your city put an end.*
>
> This power came forth out of the Atlantic Ocean, for in those days the Atlantic was navigable; and there was an island situated in front of the straits which are by you called the Pillars of Heracles; the island was larger than Libya and Asia put together, and was the way to other islands, and from these you might pass to the whole of *the opposite continent* which surrounded the true ocean; for this sea which is within the Straits of Heracles is only a harbour, having a narrow entrance, but that other is a

real sea, and the surrounding land may be most truly called a boundless continent.

Now in this island of Atlantis there was a great and wonderful empire, which had rule over the whole island and several others, and over parts of the continent, and, furthermore, the men of Atlantis had subjected the parts of Libya within the columns of Heracles as far as Egypt, and of Europe as far as Tyrrhenia.

This vast power, gathered into one, endeavoured to subdue at a blow our country and yours and the whole of the region within the straits; and then, Solon, your country shone forth, in the excellence of her virtue and strength, among all mankind. She was pre-eminent in courage and military skill, and was the leader of the Hellenes. And when the rest fell off from her, being compelled to stand alone, after having undergone the very extremity of danger, she defeated and triumphed over the invaders, and preserved from slavery those who were not yet subjugated, and generously liberated all the rest of us who dwell within the pillars."

Of all the things the "Egyptian priest" has said, the above is the most astonishing and the most telling. Again he is giving pre-eminence to the Greeks, that they performed the most heroic deed of all times, which was to *defeat the Atlantean Empire!*

This is the point that is so often just simply overlooked by all the Egypt and Atlantis lovers! Atlantis was the original "evil empire of the Borg"! And what is more, in this passage, the clue is given that the ancient Egyptian civilization — the pyramids and other monumental architecture upon which so much of the current Egyptian craze is based, stemming from the work of Schwaller de Lubicz, and which is declared to be the offspring of Atlantis - the ancient Egypt *that is so admired by the current day flock of Egyptophiles* - was very likely an attempt to re-construct the *evil empire of atlantis*! In other words, the "priestly science" of the Egyptians, referred to by Fulcanelli, not only *antedated* the material so diligently studied and propagated by Schwaller and others for "clues" to alchemical secrets and esoterica, it was very likely an Egypt that is no longer even known as Egypt!

But afterwards there occurred violent earthquakes and floods; and in a single day and night of misfortune all your warlike men in a body sank into the earth, and the island of Atlantis in like manner disappeared in the depths of the sea. For which reason the sea in those parts is impassable and impenetrable, because there is a shoal of mud in the way; and this was caused by the subsidence of the island.

I have told you briefly, Socrates, what the aged Critias heard from Solon and related to us. And when you were speaking yesterday about your city and citizens, the tale which I have just been repeating to you came into my mind, and I remarked with astonishment how, by some mysterious coincidence, you agreed in almost every particular with the narrative of Solon; but I did not like to speak at the moment. For a long time had elapsed, and I had forgotten too much; I thought that I must first of all run over the narrative in my own mind, and then I would speak."

Here we find another interesting clue. Critias has just told us that Socrates was discussing the very things that are included in this story — that everything Socrates had been saying the previous day "agreed in almost every particular with the narrative of Solon". Apparently, this story had been handed down via *another line of transmission*.

"And so I readily assented to your request yesterday, considering that in all such cases the chief difficulty is *to find a tale suitable to our purpose*, and that with such a tale we should be fairly well provided. And therefore, as Hermocrates has told you, on my way home yesterday I at once communicated the tale to my companions as I remembered it; and after I left them, during the night by thinking I recovered nearly the whole it. Truly, as is often said, the lessons of our childhood make wonderful impression on our memories; for I am not sure that I could remember all the discourse of yesterday, but I should be much surprised if I forgot any of these things which I have heard very long ago. I listened at the time with childlike interest to the old man's narrative; he was very ready to teach me, and I asked him again and again to repeat his words, so that like an indelible picture they were branded into my mind.

As soon as the day broke, I rehearsed them as he spoke them to my companions, that they, as well as myself, might have something to say. And now, Socrates, to make an end my preface, I am ready to tell you the whole tale. I will give you not only the general heads, but the particulars, as they were told to me.

The city and citizens, which you yesterday described to us in fiction, *we will now transfer to the world of reality*. It shall be the ancient city of Athens, and we will suppose that the citizens whom you imagined, were our veritable ancestors, of whom the priest spoke; they will perfectly harmonise, and there will be no inconsistency in saying that the citizens of your republic are these ancient Athenians. Let us divide the subject among us, and all endeavour according to our ability gracefully to *execute the task which you have imposed upon us*. Consider then, Socrates, if this narrative is suited to the purpose, or whether we should seek for some other instead." [Plato, *Timaeus*, translated by B. Jowett]

And we come to the final understanding that conveys to us the secret of the story of Atlantis: that it did not actually come from an Egyptian priest as we would now think of an Egyptian priest, but that this was a story that was created to "execute the task which you [Socrates] have imposed upon us", which was to provide the clues that the "Egyptian priest" was in no way related to the land we now know as Egypt.

As for Wilkens location of Troy in England, the reader might want to recall the passages from Diodorus Siculus quoted above. There is something more from Diodorus regarding the Hyperboreans:

> "And there is also on the island both a magnificent sacred precinct of Apollo and a notable temple, which is adorned with many votive offerings and is *spherical* in shape. Furthermore, a city is there which is sacred to this god, and the majority of its inhabitants are players on the cithara; and these *continually play on this instrument in the temple* and sing hymns of praise to the god, glorifying his deeds...
>
> They say also that the moon, as viewed from this island, appears to be but a little distance from the earth and to have upon it prominences, like those of the earth, which are visible to the eye. The account is also given that the god visits the island every nineteen years, *the period in which the return of the stars to the same place in the heavens is accomplished,* and for this reason the Greeks call the nineteen-year period the "year of Meton". At the time of this appearance of the god he both plays on the cithara and dances continuously the night through from the vernal equinox until the rising of the Pleiades, expressing in this manner his delight in his successes.
>
> And the kings of this city and the supervisors of the sacred precinct are called Boreades, since they are descendants of Boreas, and the succession to these positions is always *kept in their family*." [*Diodorus of Sicily*, English translation by C. H. Oldfather, Loeb Classical Library, Volumes II and III. London, William Heinemann, and Cambridge, Mass., USA, Harvard University Press, 1935 and 1939.]

What did it mean that every nineteen years a god "dances" from the vernal equinox *until the rising of the Pleiades*? This suggests to us a very specific date is being recorded in this myth. The heliacal rising of the Pleiades does not happen every 19 years. So, aside from telling us about a regular event that occurred every nineteen years, the myth has recorded something else very significant, the date of which is internal to the myth. When did the Pleiades rise just before the sun on the vernal equinox?

There are many who assume that a "heliacal rising" means that a star or constellation is in conjunction with the sun. But this is probably not correct. The ancients were practicing observational astronomy. Otto Neugebauer, in his many studies regarding what the ancients did or did not know about science and mathematics, noted the following:

> "When we watch the stars rise over the eastern horizon, we see them appear night after night at the same spot on the horizon. But when we extend our observation into the period of twilight, fewer and fewer stars

will be recognizable when they cross the horizon, and near sunrise all stars will have faded out altogether. Let us suppose that a certain star S was seen just rising at the beginning of dawn but vanished from sight within a very short time because of the rapid approach of daylight. We call this phenomenon the "heliacal rising" of S, using a term of Greek astronomy. Let us assume that we use this phenomenon as the indication of the end of "night" and consider S as *the star of the "last hour of night"*. [...]

We may continue in the same way for several days, but during this time a definite change takes place. [...]

Obviously, after some lapse of time, it no longer makes sense to take S as the indicator of the last hour of night. But there are new stars that can take the place of S. Thus year after year S may serve for some days as *the star of the last hour*, to be replaced in regular order by other stars."
[Neugebauer, Otto, *The Exact Sciences in Antiquity*, (New York: Dover 1969)]

In order to observe a heliacal rising of a star or group of stars, they must rise long enough *before the sun* to be "observed", because as soon as the sun rises, the stars can no longer be seen. The heliacal rising of the Pleiades would have to occur *at least* 36 minutes before the sun comes up, in order to be *seen*. So, the real question seems to be: when did the Pleiades rise around half an hour before the sun, at the time of the equinox? When were the Pleiades the stars of the "last hour of the night", and what might have been the significance of this event?

Certain "standard" texts, written by individuals who have not taken into account the observational nature of a heliacal rising, have given 2300 B.C. as the date, because this was when the Pleiades were *conjunct* the Sun on the Vernal equinox. However, after careful calculations of our own, as well as assistance by expert astronomers, the date of the actual heliacal rising of the Pleiades, in the terms that Neugebauer has given us, occurred on April 16, 3100 B.C.

April 16, 3100 B.C. when the God danced all night on the equinox until the rising of the Pleiades:

[A] "'Dark Age', meaning a period from which little is known despite much information before and after that period, occurred about 3100 B.C. to 3000 B.C. For example in Mesopotamia this period is called *Jemdet Nasr*.

About 3100 B.C. there was suddenly a change to more primitive ages compared to the preceding Uruk period. For example the numerical token system dwindled.

In 3000 B.C. however there was a *sudden recovery*. This is called the Early Dynasty, which can be described as the first known culture, that began to have some kind of a centralized system. And the tokens were not only numerated again, the basis for writing was born.

What happened 3100 B.C., maybe right in 3114 B.C.? That's the year 0 in the Mayan calendar.

There are many stories around the world of great floods. There are two small craters from about this time, but what seems more probable, is a huge meteorite swarm that both caused much damage on land, brought up tsunamis and blanketed with dust the atmosphere. It may have been a break-up of a great comet in the inner parts of the solar system. People were panic-stricken.

The beginnings of civilizations, however, got despite of the immediate damage, a first great rise, after about a hundred years had gone. There was a great boomtime that eventually led to the rise of the first great civilizations in the beginning of the third millennium B.C. The prime example is the unification of southern and northern Egypt.

The great mystery is how did the fusion happen? There is not any clear indication of one part conquering the other. It seems like the northern culture won over the southern, but that *the new kings came from the south.* The artifacts hint that the first King of the unified Egypt was called Menes and that the unification took place between 3150 and 3110 B.C.

3100 B.C. has been traditionally held as the watermark between the Predynastic and Early Dynastic Period in Egypt. It took still 400 years before it was transformed in the so called Old Kingdom in about 2700 B.C. These timestamps have oddly enough a great resemblance to the Mayan year 0.

The Mesopotamians had the great variations in their pre-writings that finally led to the first marks that really can be called as writing. Also the wheel was introduced. The great city-states Ur and Uruk were built, and around 2600 B.C. they had began to be part of a larger political union.

Gilgamesh, the great flood-king, lived during this period. *Pre-Minoan culture was rising in Crete.* Neolithic settlements, Stonehenge, Newgrange, Skara Brae in the Scottish Orkney island were built. The coastal menhirs (great stones) began to be built in Brittany."

Allow me to quote a somewhat tedious report on the re-dating of Stonehenge:

"As part of the post-excavation process a major programme of radiocarbon dating was undertaken to provide a reliable set of dates for the Monument which archaeologists can be confident in using.

To carry out this work the **English Heritage Scientific Dating Service** gathered and co-ordinated a multi-disciplinary team of experts, consisting of the archaeological team from Wessex Archaeology, the high-precision radiocarbon dating laboratory of the Queen's University of Belfast, and the Oxford Radiocarbon Accelerator Unit.

In addition to this core team of archaeologists, chemists, paleoenvironmentalists, physicists, and statisticians, specialist input on the animal bone and antler was provided by the Faunal Remains Unit of the University of Southampton, on curatorial issues by the Salisbury and South Wiltshire Museum, and on project management and the wider issues surrounding Stonehenge by the Central Archaeology Service of English Heritage.

This project has produced or identified 52 radiocarbon determinations which are considered reliable. These are from the Monument itself and associated activity.

Mesolithic activity in the car park.
Phase 1 - the construction of the main Ditch and Banks, the deposition of 'structured deposits' within them, the primary silting of the Ditch, and activity which took place on top of this silting.
Phase 2 - the secondary silting of the main Ditch, the wooden post settings within the Monument, and the Aubrey Holes.
Phase 3 - a burial cut into the top of the secondary fill of the main Ditch, the Sarsen and Bluestone settings, the Y and Z Holes, and the Avenue. We also investigated the chronological sequence of these elements of the Monument. Post-Monument use of the site.

In 1966 excavations in the Car Park to the north-west of the Monument revealed three substantial pits. The shadows of the substantial posts which these had contained were clearly visible. None of the pits produced any artefacts apart from a single piece of burnt bone and quantities of charcoal. This was identified as Pinus sp., and dated to the Mesolithic.

In 1988 a similar pit was discovered further east, although this lacked clear evidence of a post-shadow since it had been recut. However charcoal discovered within this feature also proved to be Pinus sp. and dated to the Mesolithic.

The significance of these features is unclear, although at least some of the pits appear to have held substantial timber uprights (which may have been akin to totem poles). The span of the results over 300 - 1600 years indicates the longevity of the activity and analysis of the results suggests that it occurred between 8500-7650 cal B.C. and 7500-6700 cal B.C. (see probability distributions).

Sample: W243-11, context 9585, submitted by M Allen on 16 May 1994 Calibrated date range: 7700-7420 cal B.C. (95% confidence).

Sample: W243-14, context 9582, Calibrated date range: 7580-7090 cal B.C. (95% confidence)

Sample: W243-008, context 9585, Calibrated date range: 8090-7580 cal B.C. (95% confidence)

Sample: CHAR1, submitted by H Keeley in 1966, Calibrated date range: 8820-7730 cal B.C. (95% confidence)

Sample: CHAR2, submitted by H Keeley in 1966, Calibrated date range: 7480-6590 cal B.C. (95% confidence)

Archaeological comment on HAR-455 and HAR-456 (F Vatcher): in the excavator's opinion the charcoal samples, although pertaining to the original posts, were of poor quality, being fine and mixed with other material. This may, perhaps, account for the unexpectedly early dates and the radiocarbon dating difference of approximately one millennium for postholes which had every indication of being contemporary with each other.

Comment on series (M Allen): all of these determinations fall into the eighth or late ninth-millennium B.C. They cover a period of about one millennium and so it cannot be established whether these features, containing upright pine posts, were exactly contemporary and ever all stood together, but they are certainly Mesolithic and not related to the main Monument.

[Laura's note: pay attention to this last comment because it is OPINION, not fact. And such "opinions" are repeated throughout this report.]

The main Ditch at Stonehenge was dug in a series of segments, at the base of which were deposited large numbers of antlers, many of which had been used as picks or rakes and showed heavy wear. Since these artefacts had no primary silt beneath them, they must have been deposited very soon after the Ditch was dug. It is considered that antlers would not have been kept for long before use, especially as over half (57%) came from slain deer (perhaps because a large number of antlers were needed quickly?). Consequently the digging of the Ditch can be dated to very soon after the last of the antlers was collected.

Nine reliable measurements are available from these antlers (results). They were gathered over a period of 20-160 years and, when analysed with the structured deposits at the base of the Ditch, provide an estimate of its date of construction of 3020-2910 cal B.C. (see probability distributions).

One measurement is considered unreliable (rejected result).

Four samples were analysed from animal bones deposited in, or close to, terminals in the Ditch (results). They were placed on the base below the primary silt and so must have been deposited very soon after the Ditch was dug.

However analysis of the results suggests that these objects were collected over a period of 50 and 850 years, between 3900-3050 cal B.C. and 3020-2910 cal B.C. This suggests that the four bones are statistically significantly earlier than the date of the Ditch construction (3020-2910 cal

B.C.), and so may have been curated for a substantial period of time before being placed in the Monument (see probability distributions).

A series of determinations have been obtained from the secondary fills of the Ditch in order to date their accumulation (results). The dated material was spread from the base to the upper portion of the fill. Unfortunately further archive material relating to the precise location of the samples came to light after submission, and so a number are regarded as unreliable on archaeological grounds (rejected results).

Although material was deliberately selected for size and freshness to minimise the possibility that samples were residual, we are not willing to make the assumption that such material has been excluded entirely, so the analysis does not apply the constraint that the samples from phase 2 must be later than the samples from phase 1. They must be earlier than the burial which was cut into the secondary fills however.

Analysis of the results suggests that the infilling of the Ditch took 400-730 years, although many of the items dated are likely to have been deposited well within the first century after construction. The fill accumulated between the digging of the Ditch (3020-2910 cal B.C.) and 2570-2450 cal B.C. (3% confidence) or 2500-2260 cal B.C. (92% confidence) (see probability distributions).

Unfortunately it has not been possible to date more precisely either the excavation of the Aubrey Holes or the insertion of the human cremations into them, as there was insufficient collagen in the only available samples (partially calcined skewer pins which accompanied some of the cremations).

The single determination (result) from charcoal associated with a cremation is too imprecise to be very informative, giving a calibrated date range of 3020-1520 cal B.C. (see probability distribution).

In 1978 an inhumation of an adult male was discovered cut into the secondary fills of the Ditch (Evans et al 1984). The date of this burial therefore provides a terminus ante quem for the silting up of the Ditch and the associated cremation cemetery. The burial was accompanied by three barbed-and-tanged arrowheads and a wristguard. Its fill contained three fragments of bluestone, so it can be assigned to phase 3.

Five radiocarbon determinations are available from the skeleton (results). Analysis of these results provides an estimate of 2400-2140 cal BC for the burial (see probability distribution). This is slightly earlier than the previous estimate of 2340-1930 cal B.C., provided by the single determination processed in 1979.

Material for dating from these settings is very limited. Two measurements were obtained from the Sarsen Circle (photo and results), although since one of these is from material **which must be residual (rejected results)**, the best estimate for the date of this setting (2850 - 2480 cal B.C.) relies on a single determination (see probability distributions). Stratigraphically this setting is later than the Q Holes and earlier than the Z Holes.

Here is the rejected result: Sample: S64.41, context 3547, submitted by M Allen on 11 March 1994; Material: animal bone, long bone fragment (D Serjeantson), Initial comment: from stonehole 27 of the Sarsen Circle, noted as from among the packing stones. Calibrated date range: 4360-3990 cal B.C. (95% confidence)

Archaeological comment (M Allen): this earlier Neolithic date was surprising because there is virtually no other evidence in the Stonehenge environs for activity at this time. The sample must have been residual in its context.

The Sarsen Trilithons (photo) appear to be stratigraphically earlier than the Bluestone Oval/Horseshoe and have produced three results. Analysis of these provide a best estimate for the date of construction of this setting of 2440-2100 cal B.C. (see probability distributions).

On the basis of the position of stonehole E in the entrance to the enclosure, it was initially considered that this may be part of the phase 1 Monument, however analysis of the two results from this feature produces an estimated date of construction of 2480-2200 cal B.C., placing it firmly within phase 3 (see probability distributions).

Bluestones: Material for dating from these settings is very limited - **there are no reliable determinations at all from the Q and R Holes (rejected results),** which is unfortunate as these are stratigraphically the earliest stone settings.

Two samples were analysed from the Bluestone Circle and one from the Bluestone Horseshoe (photo). The only stratigraphic relationship between these settings and other dated parts of the Monument are that they must be contemporary or later than the Sarsen Trilithons, and the Circle must be earlier than the Q Holes.

Here are the rejected results: Sample: S64.49, context 3813, submitted by M Allen on 11 March 1994, Material: animal bone, immature pig humerus (D Serjeantson), Initial comment: from a Q Hole; noted as 'in fill near top of fill'. These holes were backfilled after the bluestones were removed, and so the sample is associated with their backfilling. Although the specific Q Hole from which this sample came cannot be identified, Prof. Atkinson's attribution should be trusted. Calibrated date range: 2460-2040 cal B.C. (95% confidence)

Archaeological comment (M Allen): if the stratigraphic information that the Q Holes must be earlier than the Sarsen Circle and the Bluestone Circle is included in the mathematical model of phase 3, then the model is statistically inconsistent at more than 95% confidence. Thus either this result is anomalous or the three dates from the Sarsen Circle and Bluestone Circle are all from residual material. Re-examination of the archive did not produce any further information relating to the context of this sample, and so we suggest that the dated item may in fact have come from a feature which was wrongly described as a Q Hole by Prof. Atkinson.

Analysis of the results provides best estimates for the date of construction of the Bluestone Circle of 2280-2030 cal B.C., and of 2270-1930 cal B.C. for the construction of the Bluestone Horseshoe (see probability distributions)."

Now, what are we to make of this? We have results we don't like, occasionally, and we reject them. And we have assumptions that the more primitive parts of the structure were the earliest, because, of course, these were howling savages doing all this.

The most widely-used method for determining the age of fossils is to date them by the "known age" of the rock strata in which they are found. At the same time, the most widely-used method for determining the age of the rock strata is to date them by the "known age" of the fossils they contain. In this "circular dating" method, all ages are based on uniformitarian assumptions about the date and order in which fossilized plants and animals are believed to have evolved. Most people are surprised to learn that there is, in fact, no way to directly determine the age of any fossil or rock. The so called "absolute" methods of dating (radiometric methods) actually *only measure the present ratios of radioactive isotopes and their decay products* in suitable specimens -- not their age. These measured ratios are then extrapolated to an "age" determination.

The problem with all radiometric "clocks" is that their accuracy critically depends on several starting assumptions which are largely unknowable. To date a specimen by radiometric means, one must first know the starting amount of the parent isotope at the beginning of the specimen's existence. Second, one must be certain that there were no daughter isotopes in the beginning. Third, one must be certain that neither parent nor daughter isotopes have ever been added or removed from the specimen. And fourth, one must be certain that the decay rate of parent isotope to daughter isotope has always been the same. That one or more of these assumptions are often invalid is obvious from the published radiometric "dates" (to say nothing of "rejected" dates) found in the literature.

One of the most obvious problems is that several samples from the same location often give widely-divergent ages. Apollo moon samples, for example, were dated by both uranium-thorium-lead and potassium-argon methods, giving results which varied from 2 million to 28 billion years. Lava flows from volcanoes on the north rim of the Grand Canyon (which erupted after its formation) show potassium-argon dates a billion years "older" than the most ancient basement rocks at the bottom of the canyon. Lava from underwater volcanoes near Hawaii (that are known to have erupted in 1801 A.D.) have been "dated" by the potassium-argon method with results varying from 160 million to nearly 3 billion years. It's really no wonder that *all of the laboratories that "date" rocks insist on knowing in advance the "evolutionary age" of the strata from which the samples were taken -- this way, they know which dates to accept as "reasonable" and which to ignore.*

Dick Meehan adds to this list flood marks in paleoclimatic data, methane peak in Greenland ice and a cold time according to bristlecone pines in Britain. Although any one of these in itself would not be of any great concern, the timing of them in a frame of only 100 years, is the thing that makes us suspect that something unusual was going on. And actually, the next 1000 years or so were a very restless time globally.

> "The aftermath of this may have been a 2807 B.C. ocean impact described by Bruce Masse in Peiser et al.: *Natural Catastrophes* (Oxford, 1998). If this is the great Flood Comet, as Masse seems to indicate, this explains why the Sumerian story of Flood, on which basis the Genesis Noachian Flood story is built, is combined with the story of Gilgamesh. Gilgamesh reigned in the 27th century, 300-450 years before the two great cataclysms in late third millennium B.C. Or were the comet or comets swarming and breaking up during the whole period of 3114 B.C. to 2807 B.C. with diminishing frequency and damage ending temporarily in a great splash in the Atlantic?" [Timo Niroma, Helsinki, Finland]

From Rogue Asteroids and Doomsday Comets by Duncan Steel:

> "The outrageous suggestion that I am going to make is that the Taurid Complex was producing phenomenal meteor storms between 4,500 and 5,000 years ago, accompanied by multiple Tunguska-class atmospheric detonations, and that Stonehenge I was designed to allow the (awestruck, terrified) culture of southern England to make observations of the Phenomena and to perhaps predict their recurrence.

> Peter Lancaster Brown, in his book on megalithic sites, wrote that 'Eclipses, comets and meteorites were astronomical phenomena widely observed by the ancients. But probably only eclipses were predictable.' (Steel means to imply that Stonehenge I was needed to make observations because meteorite falls are far more unpredictable, but and at the same time may be long-lasting and recurring. - TN.)"

Let me suggest that survivors and descendants of the global cataclysm that occurred at the time of the war between Atlantis and "Athens" were reduced to little more than a Stone Age existence for a very long time except, perhaps, for small enclaves here and there which later gave rise to "civilizing" impulses at various locations around the planet. And just as some of the "good guys" survived, so were there survivors of the Evil Empire of Atlantis. Again I note the polarities between the "circle people" and the "pyramid people".

Later, there was again a battle, a great betrayal at the Cloisters of Ambrius followed by another global disruption, fixing the event in the minds of the people as being "like the destruction of Atlantis" so that the stories were joined together.

Such events would embrace the myths of the Daughters of Danaeus and the Sons of Aegyptus, as well as the story of Orpheus - the "massacre at the Cloisters of Ambrius" - a war between ancient peoples inhabiting Britain and those inhabiting continental Europe where the place names so strongly reflect the descriptions given by Homer as described by Wilkens. Refugees fled to the higher lands, to Eastern Europe, to Eurasia, to Egypt and beyond. Of course, just who is "on first" and who came from where is extremely difficult to determine without long and careful analysis.

I have before me a book entitled *The Plantagenet Chronicles*, which is a compilation of the many contemporary documents written by various medieval chroniclers regarding the Angevin dynasty. Most of these writers were monks living in monasteries or attached to great cathedrals. They were, for the most part, members of well-established institutions who took great pride in their traditions and whose agenda was to protect their own properties and independence within the feudal system. These historians didn't try to produce rational and detached analyses. Their intent was to demonstrate the power of god via the presence and activity of the Holy Mother Church. If they could make an example out of a saint or a king, they did so shamelessly. Nevertheless, even though they were making "morality lessons" out of their material, for the most part, they were still reporting facts.

In reading *The Plantagenet Chronicles*, we find that the Counts of Anjou were said to have come from the Devil. Gerald of Wales refers to the legend that they were descended from the daughter of Satan, a woman named Melusine, who was the wife of an early Angevin count. The problem is, this was only promulgated in much later times, probably by Richard the Lionhearted who was quoted as saying: "What wonder if we lack the natural affections of mankind - we come from the Devil and must needs go back to the Devil".

My curiosity is piqued by this story of the origins of the Angevins, which is so similar to the story about the Merovingians. My question is: has this story been "borrowed"? Or is it common to certain peoples because of some relationship to strange "beings"?

As to whether it applied to either group is debatable. Count Fulk Rechin de Anjou (1068-1109), admitted that he knew nothing of the first three of his line: Ingelgar, (the first Count of Anjou), Fulk the Red, and Fulk the Good (941-960). Nevertheless, the 12th century seems to have been a great time of mythmaking when many noble houses invented pedigrees in order to give themselves legendary ancestors.

The enormous volume of literature that has resulted from the story of Berenger Sauniere suggests to me that the mystery of Rennes-le-Chateau is a "staging area" for a subject that is of great importance to someone! The ideas reek with the stench of having been "planted" and systematically released to tease and entice researchers and treasure hunters around the world. Part of the "aura" of the material rests on the fact that it is supposed to originate with "highly privileged" sources. The subjects that are all connected together in this morass of disinformation include the Cathars, the Templars, the Merovingian kings, the Rosicrucians, the Masons, the Nazis and, of course, the royal line of Jesus Christ! But, all of this may be a series of red herrings!

The majority of the so-called "documentation" of the events of Rennes-le-Chateau and the Priory of Sion nearly always turns out to be of dubious, if not untraceable authorship. Names of the dead are regularly "borrowed" for attribution, and when investigations ensue, inevitably prove to be false. Addresses of "significance" turn out to not even exist. Documents seem to appear and disappear within the Bibliotheque Nationale, appearing first in one form, then another.

The whole problem seems to stem from the fact that LL&B accepted the claims and documents of the Priory of Sion mainly due to a series of numerous "strange coincidences" and anomalous findings during the course of their research. Whoever was behind these events picked their publicists well because these events were experienced by people with considerable ability to influence the thinking of large numbers of people. And they did. They worked carefully and put their findings together clearly and eloquently despite a curious blinded optimism that what they were experiencing HAD to be the truth because, of course, THEY were experiencing it and it clearly was not being faked because there simply wasn't anybody who could fake all the "confirmations" and synchronicities they encountered. It would have been a conspiracy of such vast proportions, over such long periods of time, that such incomprehensible.

Well, without considering the Control System and space/time manipulation capabilities of 4th density beings, it IS incomprehensible.

We have to remember something the Cassiopaeans said here:

"Beware of disinformation. It diverts your attention away from reality thus leaving you open to capture and conquest and even possible destruction. [...] Disinformation comes from seemingly reliable sources. It is extremely important for you to not gather false knowledge, as it is more damaging than no knowledge at all. Remember knowledge protects, ignorance endangers. [What I want to know is who has the power and ability to set up these kinds of "confirmations" or synchronicities?] Same forces spreading disinformation: Brotherhood/ Consortium/ Illuminati/ New World Order/ "Antichrist"/ Lizards. ...It is no trouble at all for aforementioned forces to give seemingly individualized attention to anybody."

Notice the initial remark about disinformation diverting our attention away from reality, leaving us open to capture, conquest and even possible destruction!

Nevertheless, the idea of a royal bloodline of Christ created not only a sensation, but also a veritable industry of books. We are here in the presence of mythology in the making and it is awesome to witness it! Most people never noticed that LL&B repeatedly urged caution about accepting the Priory of Sion as valid and its documents as unimpeachable, even if they, themselves, tended to "believe". At the end of their second book *The Messianic Legacy*, they wrote:

"We had endeavoured to learn more about the Prieure de Sion today. We had sought to ascertain something definitive about its membership, its power and resources, its specific objectives. We had hoped at some point to reach the centre of the labyrinth, not necessarily to slay whatever Minotaur lurked there, but at least to confront it. At the same time, however, **we could not escape the rueful recognition that we were often being outmaneuvered by individuals who contrived, with great subtlety and skill, to remain consistently one step ahead of us.**

[...] The Prieure de Sion is particularly well equipped to put itself forward as a vehicle for chivalric ideals. It is also particularly well equipped to put itself forward as something more. Unlike many other social, political and religious institutions, the Prieure, as we noted... has considerable psychological sophistication. **It understands the depth and magnitude of humanity's internal needs. It understands how to manipulate archetypes - archetypal images and themes - in such a way as to invest them with maximum appeal.**

One of the most resonant of archetypal symbols, for example, is that of the **roi perdu**, or lost king - the supernaturally aided monarch who, having completed his task on earth, does not quite die, but retires into some other dimension where he bides his time until the need of his people dictates his return. English-speaking readers are familiar with this archetype through King Arthur. In Wales, Owen Glendower conforms to the same pattern, as does Friedrich Barbarossa in Germany. The **roi perdu** who figures most prominently in the Prieure de Sion's mythos is Dagobert II, the last effective Merovingian monarch. **Dagobert is presented by the Prieure in such a fashion that his image becomes fused in people's minds with that of the supreme lost king, Jesus himself.** On a psychologically symbolic level, quite independent of any question of a blood descent, **Dagobert becomes an extension of Jesus. With this psychological association established, even if unconsciously, the idea of a literal and historical blood descent becomes that much easier to propagate.** It is by just such techniques that the mystery attached to Rennes-le-Chateau has been invested with such magnetic attraction, not only to us as authors, but to our readers as well.

The Prieure also understands the intimate relationship between trust and power. It understands the potency of the religious impulse and knows that this impulse, if activated and channeled, is potentially as puissant a force as, say, money - so puissant, indeed, as to represent perhaps an alternative principle of power. Finally, the Prieure knows how to sell itself, knows how to purvey an image of itself that accords with its own objectives. As we said before, **it is able to orchestrate and to regulate outsider's perceptions of itself as an archetypal cabal, if not the supreme archetypal cabal. Whatever the ultimate authenticity of its pedigree, it can convey the impression of being what it wishes people to think it is, because it understands the dynamics whereby such impressions are conveyed.**

But psychological sophistication and an ability to "market" itself are not the only points the Prieure de Sion has in its favour. In 1979, M. Plantard had said to us, quite categorically, that the Prieure was in possession of the treasure of the Temple of Jerusalem, plundered by the Romans during the revolt of A.D. 66 and subsequently carried to the south of France, in the vicinity of Rennes-le-Chateau. The treasure, M. Plantard stated, would be returned to Israel "when the time is right". If the Prieure does indeed possess the treasure of the Temple, and could produce it today, the implications are staggering. ...It would be fraught with contemporary religious and political repercussions. What, for example, would be the implications for modern Israel, as well as for both Judaism and Christianity, if - on the basis of records or other evidence issuing from the Temple of Jerusalem - Jesus stood revealed as the Messiah? Not the Messiah of later Christian tradition, but the Messiah expected by the people of Palestine two thousand years ago - the man, that is, who was their nation's rightful king, who married, sired children and perhaps did not die on the Cross at all. Would it not rock the foundations of two of the world's major religions, and possibly the foundations of Islam as well? **Would it not, at a single stroke, eradicate the theological differences between Judaism and Christianity, and at least some of the antipathy of Islam?**

In any case, and quite apart from the treasure of the Temple, the Prieure de Sion can promulgate a claim, which would enjoy considerable currency even in today's world. On behalf of the families it represents, it can establish a dynastic succession extending back to the Old Testament House of David. It can establish, quite definitively and to the satisfaction of the most fastidious genealogical inquiry, that the Merovingian Dynasty was the Davidic line - and was formally recognised as being so by the Carolingians who supplanted them, by other monarchs and by the Roman church of the period. Aided by the techniques of modern public relations, modern advertising and modern political packaging, the Prieure could thus present to the modern world a figure who, by the strictest scriptural definition of the term, could claim to be a biblical Messiah. It may seem preposterous. But it is no more preposterous, surely, than the conviction of tens of thousands of Americans who are prepared to be 'raptured' upwards from their cars at various points on the freeway between Pasadena and Los Angels.

This does not mean, of course, that we expect an imminent press conference and the media circus that would follow. ...The Prieure de Sion and/or the Merovingian bloodline could never simply unmask themselves, divulge their identity and rely on popular fervour to do the rest. There would be too many skeptics. There would be too many people who were simply not interested. Even among those prepared to acknowledge the legitimacy of the Merovingian descent, there would be too many objectors - too many people who, whatever their religious affiliations, would have no greater desire to be ruled by a Messiah than by anyone else. And there would be too many people already in power, or jockeying for it, who would be hardly disposed to welcome a new challenge on the scene.

[...] For all these reasons, then, a pedigree cannot be used as a steppingstone to power. Rather, it is a trump card which can be played only to consolidate power once power has already been obtained.

[...] We are wary of the Prieure de Sion. ...The fact remains that any concentration of power in the hands of a small group of individuals-especially a group of individuals who function in secret - is potentially dangerous.

[...] And yet our age appears determined to embrace one or another form of Messianic myth in order to obtain a sense of meaning. ...We question whether anyone other than the special effects department of a Hollywood studio can provide a Messiah of the sort that has come to be erroneously expected." [*The Messianic Legacy*, 1986; emphases, mine.]

Well, let me suggest someone else who could provide a messiah that will literally knock the socks off the peoples of the world: denizens of hyperdimensional realities, AKA "aliens".

From following this Priory of Sion phenomenon, it looks exactly like this is the groundwork for just such a coup. *How about a little One World Religion with that New World Order?* Will that be "to go"?

This small sample of details seem like strong evidence for a conspiracy of multinational individuals and groups seeking global domination but if we consider the Hermetic maxim, "as above, so below", we have to see that all these events and movements in our world express a more inclusive reality - that of a 4th density control system seeking hegemony; playing the cards over centuries, melding small groups into larger and larger groups with ever greater expansion and renewal in the image of "fire and light".

> "The new Universalism holds that mankind's gnosis of a universal God perceived or known as the Fire or Light is central to all religions and civilizations and explains their growth and decay." [Haggar, *The Fire and the Stones*, 1991]

We are at the turning point where nations all over the world are discussing political union as part of a single, universal, world-society. And it is religion that is seen as the glue to put it all together. The only problem we have when contemplating this is: who is on first?[39]

There are many who believe the old lie that "...the boundaries that focus and protect each 'world' can only be traversed by beings who are psychically and morally pure". They further promulgate the idea that: "The origins of meddlers are local and terrestrial. More subhuman than Human. Atavistic. Who would propagate the conceit that they were from elsewhere, possessing great powers, and worth fearing: a well-worn bluff and ploy."

This view is promoted in Nicholas Hagger's book *The Fire and the Stones*, where we find the following:

> "The spreading of the Fire through religions [is] the motive force which explains the genesis of civilisations. ...Can there be a widespread acceptance of the rediscovery of the lost knowledge of the Fire? ...Truth is now being revealed more widely than in recent years. The esoteric is becoming exoteric, and there are signs that what has hitherto been hidden among coteries is now being made more widely available to those of "the masses" who are prepared to seek. ...There is evidence (largely gleaned from New Age conferences) that in our time the fire is burning in the consciousness of ordinary people. ...The experience of the Fire will become increasingly available to all mankind, as it is always widespread during a civilisation's growth.

---

[39] The reader ought to keep in mind that this was written before Sept. 11, 2001, and now we know just WHO is trying to create a "One World Order".

A movement to remysticise Christendom, and other religions, is the next stage in this widening of metaphysical consciousness, and it seems that our time will see a Metaphysical Revolution. ...The deepening and widening of the European Community into an integrated conglomerate can be expected to be accompanied by a revival of the metaphysical vision.

...We have seen that all our dead civilisations have died into larger groupings; can it be that those larger groupings will themselves die into one overall larger grouping, one worldwide (albeit American-created) civilisation. ...All the various cultures and civilisations spring from one source and flow into one civilisation, perhaps in our time. Is this the end of the vision of the Fire - the vision of God - in history: to unify all the world's civilisations into one?

If an American-led worldwide civilisation takes place in the 21st century, its renewal of growth will be Fire-led. In other words, its growth will be created, unified and sustained by one worldwide Fire (its Central Idea) that will be transmitted to the world's masses through one religion. ... It would use the revolution in satellite technology and world communications to promulgate its message.

...The "alternative" New Age movement of coteries has been inspired by the growing American Fire. It has also been inspired by the vision of the 1776 Illuminati, the heresy that encourages a drawing together of all world religions. ...The New Age movement is both the successor to American New Thought and the forerunner of a coming Universalism... ...*The New Age movement is full of people who have been illumined or who are on the verge of illumination.* They are in New Age groups rather than within the Christian fold because they have (perhaps prematurely) seceded from a tradition they regard as having been enfeebled by three and a half centuries of Humanism and materialism and by the secularization of the traditional Christian vision of the 14th century mystics, whom they admire. ...*It is as if the New Age groups are groping towards the idea of an American-led worldwide religion. In fact, from the point of view of the coming American-led worldwide civilisation, the New Age groups have been doing excellent work in preparing for the worldwide culture ahead.*

...Out of their efforts may grow a worldwide religion, which will unify and dominate the American-led worldwide civilisation of the 21st century as early Christianity unified and dominated the new Roman Christian and Byzantine Empires. Just as Christianity absorbed elements from the other metaphysical systems - the Druid Yesu, the Eleusinian grain, the Roman Isis (who became the Virgin Mary) and so on - so a new American-led Universalist religion of the Fire, adopted from Europe's syncretism, may absorb ...Christianity, but blend all systems, devise new forms... combine practices..." [Haggar, ibid. emphases, mine.]

Thus, we find a completely different perspective; one in which the Illuminati, which the author has connected to world controlling banking interests that finance wars and revolutions, are the "good guys" because, in the end, what is being "evolved" is a universal religion and government! He has charted what he calls "The vision of god in twenty-five civilisations", which he says is a "Grand Unified Theory of World History and Religion". He defines 61 stages of civilization and sees, essentially, the "lies" propagated in the name of religion as acceptable if they produce "civilizational" results.

In my own studies, which seem to be more in depth than Mr. Haggar's, I have come to different conclusions for the very reason that such "stages" always end in the subsuming of one or more cultures into another, and this is almost inevitably linked to genocide.[40] But, Mr. Haggar simply glosses over that fact in his drive to present the end result as a positive outcome. I wonder if he is aware that the ultimate subsumation could be the force behind his image of "Fire". Experience - through millennia - has shown us, as LL&B write above:

> "...The fact remains that any concentration of power in the hands of a small group of individuals- especially a group of individuals who function in secret - is potentially dangerous."

And we are again reminded of what the Cassiopaeans have said in regard to this:

A: Here is something for you to digest: Why is it that your scientists have overlooked the obvious when they insist that alien beings cannot travel to earth from a distant system???

Q: And what is this obvious thing?

A: Even if speed of light travel, or "faster", were not possible, and it is, of course, there is no reason why an alien race could not construct a space "ark", living for many generations on it. They could travel great distances through time and space, looking for a suitable world for conquest. Upon finding such, they could then install this ark in a distant orbit, build bases upon various solid planes in that solar system, and proceed to patiently manipulate the chosen civilizations to develop a suitable technological infrastructure. And then, after the instituting of a long, slow, and grand mind-programming project, simply step in and take it over once the situation was suitable.

[...] Q: (L) Well, since there is so many of us here, why don't they just move in and take over?

---

[40] This was prescient at the time it was written, 1999.

A: That is their intention. That has been their intention for quite some time. They have been traveling back and forth through time as you know it, to set things up so that they can absorb a maximum amount of negative energy with the transference from third level to fourth level that this planet is going to experience, in the hopes that they can overtake you on the fourth level and thereby accomplish several things. 1: retaining their race as a viable species; 2: increasing their numbers; 3: increasing their power; 4: expanding their race throughout the realm of fourth density. To do all of this they have been interfering with events for what you would measure on your calendar as approximately 74 thousand years. And they have been doing so in a completely still state of space-time traveling backward and forward at will during this work.

[...] Q: Now, from putting the information about religions together throughout the centuries, I am coming to a rather difficult realization that the whole monotheist idea, which is obviously the basic concept of the 'sons of the law of One', is the most clever and devious and cunning means of control I have ever encountered in my life. No matter where it comes from, the religionists say, "we have the ONE god, WE are his agents, you pay us your money, and we'll tell him to be nice to you in the next world"!

A: Clever if one is deceived. Silly truffle if one is not.

Q: Well, I know! But, uncovering this deception, this lie that the 'power' is 'out there' is unbelievable. So, the Kantekkians were the 'Sons of Belial', which is not the negative thing that I interpreted it as at the time. And the 'Sons of the Law of One', was perverted to the monotheistic Judaism, which then was then transformed into the Christian religious mythos, and has been an ongoing theme since Atlantean times.

A: Woven of those who portray the lights.

Q: And that is always the way it has been. They appear as 'angels of light'. And, essentially, everything in history has been rewritten by this group.

A: Under the influence of others. And whom do you suppose?

Q: Well, the Orion STS.

A: Sending pillars of light and chariots of fire to deliver the message.

Most certainly, this Rennes-le-Chateau business is one of the clearest examples of such manipulations, as we will soon see. It is, as Mr. Haggar suggests: "A movement to remysticise Christendom, and other religions", designed as the infrastructure of a "one worldwide (albeit American-created) civilisation". He also astutely points out, "... from the point of view of the coming American-led worldwide civilisation, the New Age groups have been doing excellent work in preparing for the worldwide culture ahead".

It is extremely interesting that Mr. Haggar suggests that this "New World Religion" will be "American created" in light of a remark made by the Cassiopaeans:

> Q: (L) Why are there more abductions by the grays in the United States than in other countries around the world?

> A: Government opened channel. North America is the "capitol" of STS, currently.

Yes indeed, flocks of them will be on the tops of skyscrapers holding their welcome signs, dancing and celebrating the arrival of their "saviors"; those coming to "serve mankind". As the "main course" I should add.

In the autumn of 1996, the BBC presented another Rennes-le-Chateau program that essentially "debunked" the whole thing. They were now saying that the parchments that were supposed to have been found by Berenger Sauniere were modern forgeries. It seems that they were forged by a close associate of Pierre Plantard, the Marquis Philippe de Cherisey. Apparently, they had quarreled and one ratted on the other. Pierre Plantard was exposed as a subversive with Nazi connections and extreme right wing political inclinations. Not only that, but M. Plantard had convictions for crimes of deception.

The so-called Secret Dossiers of the Priory of Sion that had been planted in the Bibliotheque Nationale where shown to be very clever fabrications combining a deep knowledge of history combined with masterful divergence into fantasy. And so on.

Apparently, from the research done for this program, it was learned that Gerard de Sede knew that the documents were forged either before his first meeting with Henry Lincoln, or very soon thereafter. Henry Lincoln and his associates worked for ten years unaware that they were being led down the primrose path.

Nevertheless, most of the authors who have written on the subject of Rennes-le-Chateau have followed the research of LL&B. They all seem to accept the validity of the Priory of Sion and the Priory documents and Secret Dossiers and all that.

But let's not toss the baby out with the bathwater. Obviously, there was *something* going on there in Rennes-le-Chateau that was very powerful to deceive so many people!

Recently, a new book was published entitled *Web of Gold* by a gentleman named Guy Patton. Mr. Patton contends that there IS a cabal of some sort surrounding the Rennes-le-Chateau mystery, and they are associated with Nazi types. He makes a good case for Plantard's association with such. More interesting is his connection of the politics of the Abbe Sauniere with certain groups who were involved in the Arktos myth of Aryan Supremacy. My only complaint about this book is that Mr. Patton didn't check the sources of his sources and the book is rather shallow in terms of claiming that the whole issue of Rennes le Chateau is the hidden great treasure of the Jewish Temple and that this is what the Nazis and others have been after for a very long time. It is not that, I can assure you. But, as we will see, they are definitely after something that they believe will give them ultimate power over the entire globe. It may be that the secret to this is revealed in Rennes-le-Chateau to those astute enough to wade through the disinformation.

It does seem pretty clear that there is a strong belief in a treasure of some sort being hidden in the region, but another book, *The Horse of God*, (which suggests by a series of more amazing coincidences that the treasure is the Ark of the Covenant), indicated that Abbe Sauniere was being paid by Abbe Boudet.

Tracking the spending habits of Abbe Sauniere does seem to confirm this. He did have a falling out with Boudet, his friend, and during this time, the flow of money ceased. Shortly after their reconciliation, the money began to flow again and Sauniere made some ambitious building plans, but Boudet died rather soon after, and it was all brought to a halt by Sauniere's death as well. Maybe the death of one meant that the other had to be gotten rid of?

Another recent book has come along, *Rex Deus*, that surpasses all the others in its absurdity and reliance on the same old assumptions. Only the fraud chronicled in this one is truly pathetic compared to the work of the Priory of Sion! In *Rex Deus*, the "bloodline" is that of the 24 elders of the Temple of Jerusalem, and the only proponent of the idea is a strange informant who mysteriously appears to the authors and tells them his story with great sincerity and conviction. But, unfortunately, he was unable to provide the documents that he claimed existed because his brother sold the dresser in which they were hidden! How sad and how convenient! Of course, the authors claim to be extremely impressed by his manner, his story, and the subsequent "verification" they found in other works (most of which were based on the Rennes-le-Chateau business to begin with). Geez! Didn't they learn anything from LL&B's experiences?!

The only question I have for Marilyn Hopkins, Graham Simmans and Tim Wallace-Murphy about their book, *Rex Deus*, is: did you ask your guy to take a blood test? If he was of the line of the priests of the Temple as he claims, that means he is a Cohen, and it has been proven scientifically that the Cohens have a very distinct set of genetic markers.

Cohanim (plural of Cohen) are the priestly family of the Jewish people, members of the Tribe of Levi. Jewish tradition, based on the Torah, is that all Cohanim are direct descendants of Aaron, the brother of Moses. The Cohen line is patrilineal -- passed from father to son without interruption for 3,300 years, or more than 100 generations.

In a study, as reported in the prestigious British science journal, *Nature* (January 2, 1997), 188 Jewish males were asked to contribute some cheek cells from which their DNA was extracted for study. Participants from Israel, England and North America were asked to identify whether they were a Cohen, Levi or Israelite, and to identify their family background. The results of the analysis of the Y chromosome markers of the Cohanim and non-Cohanim were indeed significant. A particular marker, (YAP-) was detected in 98.5 percent of the Cohanim, and in a significantly lower percentage of non-Cohanim.

In a second study, Dr. Skorecki and associates gathered more DNA samples and expanded their selection of Y chromosome markers. Solidifying their hypothesis of the Cohens' common ancestor, they found that a particular array of six chromosomal markers was found in 97 of the 106 Cohens tested. This collection of markers has come to be known as the Cohen Modal Hapoltype (CMH) -- the standard genetic signature of the Jewish priestly family. The chances of these findings happening at random is greater than one in 10,000.

In the absence of a single shred of evidence to prove the "Rex Deus" claims of their informant, it wouldn't be too much to ask for this - a few cheek cells and you've got a case. Without it, you've done nothing but clutter the market with more of the same old nonsense.

But, getting back to the repeated incidents of "amazing synchronicities" and coincidences, and being "led" to this or that amazing discovery, I think that the authors of *The Tomb of God* (which claims that the secret is that the body of Jesus is buried near Rennes) and *The Horse of God*, are right up there with LL&B for weirdness! The experiences described by Martha Neyman, author of the latter work, prompted an exchange between us that I would like to share here:

From: Laura Knight-Jadczyk

Date sent: Tue, 3 Nov 1998

"Dear Martha,

... I realized a long time ago that this Rennes-le-Chateau 'business' was an "engineered" archetype. Those who have played parts in it have done so for reasons, though, most often, they did not even realize that they were being manipulated to say and do what they did by the 'hidden superiors'.

And, make no mistake about it, these beings *do* exist and all the events of our lives and world are 'managed' by them from behind the scenes. They create and destroy 'secret societies' at will, including Templars, Priory of Sion, Masons, Rosicrucians, etc. These are all 'covers' and 'smoke screens'. And, they have existed, in a continuous line, for many thousands of years.

For this reason, the sequence of events that you have so rationally described, regarding the main players in this 'drama' is most important to me. It fit with some of my own assessments, which I had already made about Sauniere, Gelis, Boudet and Bigou. There is a 'rule' of espionage, which goes: observe the facts, *only* the facts, and extrapolate backwards to discover *who* benefits from a given situation, and this will give you the key to the underlying truth. Well, I have been doing this about the events of history and geography for most of my adult life, and it is a most productive exercise no matter what is being assessed.

The world, in its broadest sense, is a projection, if you will, similar to the shadows on Plato's cave. We cannot know fully the origins of these 'shadow' images unless we can overcome our fascination with the moving patterns and leave the cave. But, doing that implies that we must first be aware that we *can* leave the cave...

As I said, this business is an 'engineered archetype'. Rather, it is a holographic projection of a much larger drama. But, figuring out the small-scale mystery is the key to projecting the template onto a larger landscape. It does not end, or even begin, in Southern France.

Now, there are certain 'key points' on the planet which I have discovered... with strange names and numbers... and 'temple' characteristics (in the original sense of the word) that are, apparently, veiled from the awareness of others thus far. There are symbolic and semiotic and philological connections of a substratum of 'events' that stagger the mind.

The one thing that few people think about is '*who is doing all this*'? And, connected to this is: what are their capabilities? And this is most important. If I, for one instant, underestimate the capabilities of 'them', I will surely be devoured. It is in this lack of realization of who holds the secrets and the intellect behind it that causes most people to stumble and fall in their analysis. And since I am convinced it is an *epochal* secret, which involves the history of mankind, the moving and changing of large masses of energy on the planet itself, then I *have* to think about the 'figures' behind such a thing.

One example I will mention... you remember what you wrote about St. Anthony's day... January 17... and the number nine... and all that. It is reasonable based on what is available ... but there are meanings even older than that... and they pop up in Mayan constructs... I was in Mexico last year and came across a figure carved in what was once a bas-relief of a

Mayan temple... It was a figure of a man with the flesh removed from his thighs and skull... but with the rest of his body intact... and his legs were crossed... I have an excellent photo of it which I have shared with a few people. I'm sure you recognize the symbol... And there is the ancient cult of Janus - guardian of the door - to whom January 17 was sacred... and there was the celebration of St. Augustine on the same day.... and there is the hermit in the grail stories... whose hero is Perceval... 'He who pierces the valley', or 'mummy with the long member', or 'pour suivant...' and so on; take your pick."

Ms. Neyman wrote back to me:

Subject: Re: The Horse

Date sent: Tue, 24 Nov 1998

"Dear Laura,

By now you might have finished reading my book, I think... As you are so well experienced in the subject of symbolism and know so much more then I do, I would appreciate it very much if you could let me have your opinion..."

I found it difficult to try to explain to her that her experiences with all the coincidences, the insights, and the "magical landscape" that showed itself to her with synchronous and stunning symbols, just *might* be a big manipulation, but I was going to try:

"I am impressed with what you have done, having started with more or less a blank screen. You have had the unique advantage of "being there", which I have not... but, yes, there is a *lot* I would like to discuss and I have been debating how open you would be to this "putting two heads together" on the subject. I know that I am like a mother about anything I write and very sensitive to what might be construed as "criticism", so I have not wanted to say anything that would be offensive. But, at the same time, you are *there* and can answer some questions I have and I think that there are some things that need further work. If you are ready to have a little dialogue about this 'Rennes, etc.' business, well, tell me.

What I want to do is something like what my husband does... you get a theory, you build the structure, you see how it behaves as a 'working hypothesis', and if there are problems, you tear it apart and start over. That sort of thing is what he does. He will have an idea, spend weeks on page after page of mathematical calculations and then hit a brick wall and have to start all over again. We sat up one night and analyzed, in a sort of 'hard science' way the evidence of the 'phenomenon' of Rennes... it was an interesting exercise with interesting 'conclusions'. I was thinking at the time that it was too bad you weren't with us as there were a lot of questions we had no answers to because we did not have the opportunity for personal investigation or observation.

I will say that some of the things you have found are fascinating and I am convinced that there is some purpose and reason, and maybe even your ultimate conclusions are correct - or pretty close... but there are some big gaps in the symbolic appreciation and historical background of same. There are many things to be gone over in a sort of 'cold' and analytical way - even including this business of 'synchronicity' that we both have experienced in this matter. This 'amazing' confluence of 'clues and artifacts' tends to convince us that our ideas are correct... but I have found that, often, the matter is much more complicated - like a chess game. Some of these 'synchronous' events are like a move on the chessboard by these 'unknowns' and they are waiting to see if we will see through the ruse... We can either make the mistake of 'falling into the trap' of taking the piece 'offered' while we are being set up for a swift and stunning mate. NEVER underestimate the cleverness and cunning of the opponent.

Your ideas are framed in much the same terms as the guys who wrote the Holy Grail series and the guy who wrote the Tomb of God... in the sense that all sorts of 'synchronous' and 'amazing' correspondences were found in response to the various ideas had by all. This should be taken as a warning that it can occur to just about anybody. All of you were convinced that you were 'on the right track' because of these things... don't forget that. They, as sincerely as you, were convinced of the 'rightness' of their 'path' and conclusions because of the *same types of remarkable synchronicities*!!!!

Remember - *never forget* - that the opponent wants us to come to false conclusions... And never forget that he/they are so much more clever and practiced at this deception that we can even imagine. This is *not* a secret of a couple hundred years duration. It is *thousands* of years old...

Remember, this is all 'thinking out loud', so to speak, or on paper. It is just a 'scenario' to be tried and tested. I don't pretend that it is the 'bottom line'. So, here goes: On page 4 you talk about the BBC documentary where the media, which had once 'touted' the 'mystery', now has pretty much squashed it. You ask a very good question: Why murder a good story?

Well, perhaps, at this point in time, they were *not* murdering a good story because there were already so many adherents to it, that it would be impossible to do so... it was just more controversy. In fact, this move could have been designed to make people ask the very question you did... sort of like the government constantly pooh-poohing UFOs... the more they did, the more people believed they were hiding something. So, this IS a valid point considering 'double and triple reverse psychology' commonly in use by the media and whoever runs it. So, I think that your question goes much deeper than you think.

But, it also puts light in another area... it seems that, these guys who were making money off of this business were being manipulated from start to finish. And making money was, apparently, not the objective - though for them it might have been a lure. Or it might have started for them as a lure, or a farce... and grew very serious later. Nevertheless, we may deduce that the objective of this pronouncement by the BBC was to do the exact opposite... to breathe new life into the subject by reverse psychology.

So, question about this now is: why? Why do they *want* to keep attention on this area? Why was the attention drawn here to begin with?

Now, let's skip to page 17 where you list the 'facts' which can be substantiated and back engineer a bit from there. The three 'facts'

Documents were found in 1886. We cannot accept this as a fact. It is only hearsay. No matter about the various arguments for, about, against, or whatever, no one, *no one*, outside of persons whose credibility is in question has *ever seen* any actual, ancient or even 'pretty old' MSS. They have not been submitted to any kind of professional analysis because they have never been produced. To say, 'The discovery of the manuscripts is the key to the mystery of Rennes-le- Chateau', is a huge assumption. So, let's set them aside for the moment. (Don't despair, I am ruthless, but it is useful, as you will see.)

That Saunier was digging at night in the cemetery without obvious purpose, aided by his servant. Now, on this, what verification is there? I am not too clear from the various stories... but it seems that the primary source of this information was an old guy who 'remembered' all this many years later... and, considering the circumstances of all the rest... well, it is hearsay. Not admissible as a fact.

Now, there is the 'fact', that Sauniere spent more money than his income as a village priest allowed. At last, we are on firm footing. There are ledger books, you say, with this information recorded that can be considered 'hard evidence'. And, there is the evidence of the building projects and so forth which cost more money than the guy could have made. We have a *fact*. Only one, so far. Remember, our *beliefs* are not important here... our feelings, our responses to our amazing 'synchronicities', and all that. We have to clear away the fog of emotion.

Now, in order to know what other 'facts' there may be, maybe you can answer the following questions?

You wrote: In 1892, Sauniere is often absent without permission. What he does and where he goes, remains a secret... Says WHO? Cite the source.

You wrote: In 1894, together with Marie he makes long walks. They collect stones that are used to adorn the garden with a grotto. Says WHO? Cite the source.

You wrote: Also in 1894, aided by his trustworthy helpmate, Marie, he starts to dig in his cemetery! At night, under the cover of darkness... Says *who*? Cite the source.

Now, the tomb of Marie Negre D'Ables, that he is supposed to have destroyed, but, fantastically, it happened to have been 'copied'... are you aware of the investigation into the 'background' of that little book where it was supposedly reproduced? That it was, very likely, at the hands of the very same persons who deposited the 'Dossiers Secrets' and all that in the Biblioteque Nationale? This is pretty shaky stuff here. The very idea that the Abbe was 'searching for something' could be all rumor. But, why? Where could such a rumor come from?

The story about Marie Denarnaud, (the companion of Abbe Sauniere), in her old age is highly instructive: I am sure you have a few 'old people' in your family and are familiar with their little 'manipulations' and feelings of 'helplessness' as they age. Now, just suppose there *was* some secret of the Abbe... but it had *nothing* to do with a 'treasure' at all... and whatever it was, died with him as a source of income. But, Marie, in her old age, desperate to ensure her comfort, knowing that all she has is this property that is expensive to maintain, and no money coming in anymore, hints to the people who have undertaken to care for her that there is a 'secret' that she will tell them before she dies... Obviously, this is to keep her 'control' over her life to what little extent she can. It sounds like the old 'if you are nice to me, I'll remember you in my will', routine so common among old people. From the descriptions I have heard, the people who were caring for her had a hard time making ends meet. Do you think that if she had some secret that would enable access to financial aid, that she would not have acted upon it herself and thereby enabled herself to *pay* for her own care in old age, rather than having to depend on strangers that she controlled with the promise of a secret? It is so typical of something an old lady would do, that I am completely struck by the likelihood of it being so.

But, what happens? She dies without telling anything! Supposedly. Well, the guy spends some time looking for a possible treasure which he hopes is there... because the old lady told him so... but, no luck... maybe he realizes that he was duped... and the story you have described, about the hints to the papers about a treasure to create business for a hotel... well, the guy was just playing with the cards he was dealt, and I believe that this is the source of the whole current explosion of the 'Rennes-le-Chateau' cottage industry in 'treasure hunting'. *but*, that *still does not explain the abbe's money!*

Okay, the guy had some bucks. Not only that, but his bishop had some bucks... and both were getting paid by another priest, Boudet... and, not only that, there was a third priest who was murdered.

These *facts* are of *extreme* interest! The rest is just rumor, smokescreen, hearsay, and all that.

Now, clearly, if what you say is true, that the cash flow came from Henri Boudet who wrote the strange book about language... (And I would very much like to get my hands on a copy of it complete!), there may, indeed, be a code in there... but not what anybody thinks, I suspect.

Now, on pages 19, 20 and 21 you give some very interesting facts *out of sequence*. I wonder if it was a subconscious oversight? Because, placing them *in sequence* makes for very interesting reading: Here they are:

1852, Sauniere is born.

1878 The abbe of Rennes, Pons, dies.

1881, Abbe Charles Mocquin is appointed, but leaves after just a few months. (Any reason given for his leaving???)

1885, May 5, Abbe Antoine Croc leaves Rennes... (How long was he there? This is curious. Any reason given for leaving?)

1885, July 1, Sauniere is appointed cure at Rennes...

1886, Saunier receives a 'gift of cash from Comtesse de Chambord'. (Or was it really a 'first payment' from Boudet? We see that Sauniere isn't going to leave after just a few months... wonder why? What is there to keep him when the other two appointees couldn't wait to get out of there or were deemed 'inappropriate' by someone?)

1886, According to the ledgers, it was at about this time that Abbe Boudet began paying money to Sauniere. Was this also the time he began paying money to Msr. Billard in Carcassonne? Any dates on this? The bishop was getting twice as much as Sauniere according to the figures you gave. Was it for the same period? The bishop gave most of his to charity. (Was this because of a guilty conscience?)

1887, July, the new altar is placed in the church at Rennes. This is curious. Was this a completely *new* altar, or was it a replacing of the old one? If the former, what happened to the *old* one?

1889 Bishop Felix Billard visits Rennes for the first time... (There may have been some sort of 'meeting' amongst these guys. They discuss who is to get what, who is to do what, and so on...)

1891, major restoration is begun on the church... (This does not sound too strange, since there is obviously some source of money - Sauniere bargained for enough to make his church the way he wanted. If he is stuck in this out of the way place, he is going to enjoy it!)

1891, Sept 21, entry in Sauniere's diary – 'letter from Granes - discovery of a sepulchral vault, rain in the evening'. (Does not sound like anything unusual since he is doing a major restoration on his church. AND, he does not seem too interested in it since he did not list it first.)

1892, hearsay that Sauniere was absent without permission. (Unless there are documents to confirm this)

1894, hearsay, unless documented, collecting of stones for grotto.

1894, hearsay, unless documented, digging in graveyard.

1896, restoration of church mostly finished. Sauniere buys more land.

1897, June 6, Msgr. Billard visits and the garden is unveiled. (Perhaps another 'meeting' between the 'guys' takes place now.)

1897, Abbe Gelis was murdered. Reportedly tortured before his death. Was supposed to retire **the next day**. The magistrate found money hidden at various places in the vicarage... so, he may have been on the 'payroll' as well or... He was an intimate of Sauniere and Boudet and had been there since 1857. How long was Boudet in the region? Was Gelis the 'source' of the money to Boudet? He had been there a long time... he was going to retire... perhaps take the secret of the source of income with him, or threatened to do something else at the meeting... or, being retired, he would have been a threat in some way. This needs more examination.

1898, Sauniere buys the land on which he builds his villa.

1902, the Bishop dies.

1902 A new bishop is appointed who demands that Sauniere give an explanation on the origin of his wealth... Seems that the old bishop was 'protecting' the other 'guys' in some way, so it does not seem that it could be a 'secret' that the 'church' **wants** hidden...

1902, Sauniere argues with his friend Henri Boudet. The friendly relations between Sauniere and Boudet are broken off... Funny that this comes right after the Bishop dies and the new bishop demands explanations for the money from Sauniere. This is the strangest thing of all. If there is some secret between them and Sauniere is under pressure to reveal it, it does not seem very wise for Boudet to break off relations with Sauniere if Sauniere KNOWS something about Boudet that he could tell. This point needs some consideration. Something funny here.

1910, July 23, Sauniere is suspended from his official duties. Seems that if Boudet was worried that Sauniere would reveal something, he would come to his rescue. What was happening to Boudet at this time? Was he getting along just fine, or was he being questioned also?

1915, Boudet sends a message to Sauniere... shortly after the reconciliation, Boudet dies. This is funny, that Boudet sends this message... is it documented? Or, is it documented BY Sauniere? Did he go to visit Boudet uninvited? How soon after the visit does Boudet die?

1916, Sauniere decides to build on a REALLY grand scale...

1917, January 22, Sauniere dies suddenly.

Now, of all the interesting facts above, the two that strike me most forcibly are the facts that, in the year following the death of Gelis, Sauniere buys the land on which he plans to build his villa - but holds off the building for three years; and in the year following the death of Boudet, Sauniere decides to really go 'whole hog' with his building projects. So, what we have, after getting rid of the story of the parchments, treasure and all that mess, is a *very* strange story. A*nd*, it seems to me, that once certain attention had been brought to the area due to the financial needs of Mr. Corbu and family, there was a *desperate* need to confuse the issue - to draw attention away from the situation involving the priests - and their friendship and their finances.

The question would be *why* would this be so important at such a remove in time?

Evidence indicates that it is *not* a secret of the church; the 'treasure' idea is kaput, too, as far as I can see; all the elements of the 'Shepherds of Arcadia' painting as related to this area have pretty much been shown to be 'cooked up'. But, there IS something going on!!!

Is there a connection between the facts that Abbe Gelis was murdered and Sauniere bought land for his villa soon after? Is there a connection between the fact that Boudet died "suddenly" and Sauniere made big plans to build soon after? What could be the *real* source of money being shared among these guys? Two, possibly *three* priests and a bishop... Was Sauniere's sudden death natural, considering the funny business around the deaths of the other two? What or who was it that supplied the money? Obviously, Sauniere had access to it even after Boudet died, but *not* when he and Boudet were on bad terms... hmmmm? Funny? What was the connection of Gelis to the money - so that he had to die for it, as it seems? But, whatever the source, it was *not* accessible to Marie; who used the "secret" as bait to ensure her well being until death.

So, having ripped away the entire smokescreen, we are left with a real mystery. But, that is not to say that there is not some purpose in the smokescreen, that is another subject altogether. There IS some great mystery about the Shepherds of Arcadia, but it may be far wider and more intruding than just the area around Rennes-le-Chateau."

Well, Ms. Neyman was *not* happy that I was suggesting that the Ark of the Covenant might not be the great secret. Most especially, she was not happy that I suggested that she was being manipulated to "discover" things to "confuse" the issue. And she most definitely did *not* want to give up the fairy tale of Rennes-le-Chateau!

From: Martha Neyman

Subject: Re: The Horse

Date sent: Wed, 25 Nov 1998

"Of course I will answer the questions you have and I do not see this as a criticism of the work I did, because I feel, what I did was good and not done before by anyone... Even not by the writers of the Tomb of God...

The book they wrote, has at first sight a 'certain' resemblance with my work, but it is totally different and the 'Horse of God' is not a railway, that is for sure..!

Dear Laura, do not be angry with me because I am honest to you and straight to the point... In a way, I am thinking in the same direction as you... I think, where you talk about *why* the BBC is 'murdering' the story of RLC, you dig too deep. I can well imagine the US government keeping the truth about UFO's from the people, but to believe that the respectable BBC of England is part of a plot to hide the truth of Rennes-le-Chateau in a sort of double psychology game, I think is going a bit too far.

You asked me a lot of questions... But... You started to ask questions about the 'Preface' and the 'Introduction'. Please take 'This' information at 'face value'..! This section is not of any importance to the rest of my book. The information in the introduction is common knowledge, mostly it came from the locals, and they are used by every book-writer..."

LKJ: "yes, I know that - but I want to know *why* and *how* such things were generated. I want to know if anybody ever actually documented any of these things. And these are questions that *do* occur to me for whatever reason. If the only answer is 'the locals said so...' well, that IS the answer. If there is an old diary where someone wrote about it, that is a different kind of answer. And, the point is: somehow, for some reason, stimulated by some 'raison', these so-called Priory of Sion fellows played on this story and the painting (which I believe is important because of the facts of Poussin's life) got connected to this area... Is it because there was some sort of 'rumor' that floated about in esoteric circles that this painting was connected to this place? Who came up with the idea in the first place?"

MN: "When you start writing some kind of a book, you have to start somewhere... I do not have to tell you... I did start with general information. So readers who are not so well informed, but want to know more about the whole story Rennes-le-Chateau, can get this general information.

LKJ: Yes, but you also did some 'investigating' on your own. You observed. A lot of things you mention are not mentioned by other writers, even apart from your discoveries."

MN: "That is why, in the *introduction*, I wrote: Quote: At the risk of boring those readers, who know all about the history of Rennes-le-Chateau and its obstinate priest, I would like to repeat briefly, the 'original' version, for those new to the story... Unquote. Dear Laura, those inverted commas at the word *original* were placed there on purpose... To the real initiated it means the story as it is usually told, as mysterious and uncanny as possible, without actually having completely checked out, who did what and why and who saw him doing it... This is just the 'common' Rennes-le-Chateau story, only meant as 'proof' that something weird was going on in this village and that the priest behaved strangely..."

LKJ: "Yes, but if none of those things are true... if they only 'developed' AFTER the fact of the initial 'rumor' of treasure was started, which I think you pinpointed in your description of the folks who were caring for Marie, well, then there is nothing to support the 'treasure' hypothesis. Thus, if the story about treasure, the connection to the painting, which seems to have evolved from the rumors about treasure, all are 'manufactured', then one has to start looking in a different way. **You are basing everything you are doing on the painting The Shepherds of Arcadia, and only because it was connected to the region by a story that turns out to be a fraud.**"

MN: "Because as you will find out later, as you read on, you will see that Sauniere's doings have (very) little impact on the solution I found. ...What I want you to comment on is symbolism..."

LKJ: "There are some significant symbolic images that are far more ancient and 'in your face' in that painting than what you described. Every thing has multiple layers... question is: which layer do we extract from? An example is your use of the 'knee' as a means of selecting 'seven'. Well, the knee has some very deep meanings and is used symbolically in a rather different way in numerous sources, the oldest I have found being the Sumerian Texts... And it is not chance that 'knee' is from the same root as 'knead as in bread', knight, juga, yogi, conjugal, genes, genetic, gonads, etc.

Also, the hand positions... there was in use, at the time of the painting, a 'hand alphabet' which could signify either letters or numbers or both ... it could also symbolize a mathematical 'operation'.""

MN: "I started to give an explanation of the perceptible and searching for the truth in the invisible words of symbolism in 'Chapter I'. So let us start from this first part... And... Do not forget I only used *a small* part of the Christian Church symbolism to explain, sometimes 'just enough' to make clear how I came to my conclusions in a logical way..! Otherwise for most of the people 'absolute unknown' with this material it would have been much too complicated, long-winded and even boring."

LKJ: "Agreed. But I am still trying to 'connect' the painting to the area and it is difficult. **And your entire book and 'discovery' is based on the painting!**"

MN: "This was only a short reply, because I feel the strong desire to write a whole day on my second book... Which has nothing to do with symbolism... It is the true story of the 'Shepherds' the real 'Shepherds': the church-shepherds..! *that* is the story of the painting of Poussin... 'Popes-Crusades-Templars', it starts with the Oriental Schism in 1054 ... For the 'Latin Church of Rome' this was a large loss. It ended with a second huge loss: The reformation in 1618."

LKJ: "Well, if you haven't done so already... look at the King Rene painting reproduced in the 'Tomb of God' book alongside the 'Shepherds' painting... just look at them casually and see what things you note that correspond... Note the lance and the horse head and compare it to the 'horse head' and shepherd's staff in the Arcadia painting... Note the position of the sun and the mountain peak in both paintings... note the posture of the Shepherdess and King Rene... note the ditch and flow of water exiting from the stone in the two paintings... note the funny leaning tree in the Rene painting... the funny hand gestures.... Then look at the Teniers painting and note the shape of the 'window' and compare it to the 'chink' in the tomb in the Shepherd's painting... Then, have a look at Bacchus and Ariadne by Titian... half- close your eyes and see what you can see... note the funny overturned vessel on the drapery... the dog... go back to Teniers and note the vessel in the window... the bird... In the Shepherds painting, note the drapery of the figures... the crossed shins, the bared breasts of the figures... count the numbers of knees, hands displayed... Note the positions... it is not as simple as the 'finger of Jupiter, Venus or whatever...'

The system of codes being transmitted via hand signals was widespread in both the Orient and the Occident. There are allusions to it in the writings of several Greek and Latin writers, such as Plutarch, who attributes these words to Orontes, son-in-law of King Artaxerxes of Persia: 'Just as in calculating, fingers sometimes have a value of ten thousand and sometimes of only one, the favorites of kings may be either everything or almost nothing.'

Apuleius married a rich widow named Aemilia Pudentialla and was accused of having used magic to win her favor. He defended himself before Proconsul Caludius Maximus in the presence of Emilianus, his main accuser, who had unkindly said that Aemilia was sixty years old, when she was actually only forty. Here is the record of how Apuleius addressed his accuser: 'How dare you, Emilianus, increase the real number of Aemilia Pudentilla's age by half, or even a third? If you had said 'thirty' for 'ten' it might have been thought that your mistake came from holding your fingers open when you should have held them curved. But, forty is the easiest number to indicate since it is expressed with the hand open.'

Saint Jerome wrote: 'Thirty corresponds to marriage, for the conjunction of the fingers as though in a sweet kiss represents the husband and the wife. [...] And the gesture for a hundred, transferred from the left hand to the right, on the same fingers, expresses on the right hand the crown of virginity.'

The Venerable Bede[41] gives many examples of how the system can be used for silent communication. In Islamic religions, finger counting and signing was used extensively (remember the 'contamination' of the Templars by Sufism... which is so similar to what is known of the Cathars that one cannot help but think that there is a connection... and, also, what is known of the Druids...) There are a *lot* of quotes I can cite about this 'finger and hand' signaling system... but, it would get tedious.

The meanings of these things were obvious to people of the time, (which may be why the painting was hidden), and the citations from old MSS so common that it shows that such allusions were used both in paintings and in written references... otherwise, the readers could not have been expected to understand them, but it is very obscure to those of us in the 20th century who are not familiar with the method, and casually pass over such references as being 'unimportant'. Thus, this may be an important consideration in evaluating the message of this and other paintings.

The mathematical angles are another thing altogether. At the time, the 'Golden Mean' was a standard of Art... it was taught in all the art schools that a composition based on this ratio was more aesthetically pleasing... so, pupils were taught, and masters perfected, the art of compositional placement on the medium according to the Pythagorean principles. It meant, essentially, nothing. It can be found in thousands of paintings. Its presence in art is generally meaningless. However, your finding of the stone with the ratio figure engraved upon it ... well, that requires some examination, but not necessarily in the precise terms you define. On the other hand, it may be meaningless."

This was the last of the Neyman letters... after this, she wrote and told me she did not see any point in "discussing" it further as she *knew* the truth because she had been "led" by "amazing synchronicities" and all that. She positively did *not* believe in any kind of conspiracy, she did *not* believe that there were strange beings controlling our world and manipulating our perceptions, and she most assuredly was convinced that the Catholic Church was benevolent and were the "True Shepherds". Same song, different verse.

My point is: I can see that there is a *huge* thing going on here... and it seems that everybody has had so amazing a series of "confirmations" of ideas - one leading to another... and work, work, work on the research and digging and all that. But, each one has come to a somewhat different conclusion and has been led down a somewhat different path. The odd thing about the whole place is quality of "self reflection", I think. I would like to get to the very bottom of the blasted thing! I guess I have a couple

---

[41] Historian and Doctor of the Church, born 672 or 673; died 735. Wrote "Ecclesiastical History of the English People."

of axioms I live by: one is "get results". The other is: "when all the lies are stripped away, what remains is the truth".

The important thing to remember, at this point, is that *all* of the conjecture about the Poussin painting, The Shepherds of Arcadia, resulted from the "deciphering" of the mysterious parchments purportedly found by Berenger Sauniere and reproduced in Gerard de Sede's book. In other words, the "fake" parchments as described above, were the ones that gave clues that the painting Shepherds of Arcadia was "significant" in some way. Additionally, there was the tombstone of a noble lady of the district that had "disappeared" but was supposed to reproduce the phrase "Et in Arcadia Ego" on it's face along with other suggestive symbols and encoded messages.

Out of all the things I read on the subject of Rennes-le-Chateau, the one thing that did stand out as interesting, as I mentioned to Ms. Neyman, was the Poussin painting: *The Shepherds of Arcadia.* Even if I was of the opinion that there were "negative forces" at work in this matter, I knew enough about the ways in which they operated to know that they often used truth to conceal lies and vice versa. Out of all the mess that was going on in Rennes-le-Chateau, this painting seemed to be the only thing that was really "out of place".

For some reason, the perpetrators of the fraud selected this painting and not another. There were any number of old masters they could have called on to do the job, but they didn't. Why?

Traditionally and experientially, the Control System usually adheres to "the truth" very closely in their disinformation, diverging and twisting only certain significant issues so as to lead the seeker astray. So, what was there of truth in this story? Were they using a painting that *did* include a true clue system, and were they then creating relationships to distort and obfuscate the clues, or even to cause them to lead to a completely erroneous conclusion, but a conclusion that was extremely useful to them?

Painted c. 1640, *Les Bergers d'Arcadie* did have a remarkable resemblance to the tomb that was found in the Rennes-le-Chateau countryside, even if this tomb was later proven to have been a late addition. Art historians are certain that Poussin *never* visited the Rennes area and, therefore, could not have painted this tomb, even if it had existed there at the time of Poussin.

But, there IS a link between Poussin and the nearby village of Arques.

According to research done by Guy Patton, (keep in mind that the sources of the source have yet to be verified), writing in *Web of Gold*, Poussin spent most of his life in Rome and, during this same time period,

Henrietta-Catherine de Joyeuse and her husband, Charles de Lorraine were in exile in there at the order of Cardinal de Richelieu.

Henrietta-Catherine's father was Ange de Joyeuse, Marshal Governor of the Languedoc, the area in which Rennes-le-Chateau is located. Also, Poussin was under the protection of Sublet de Noyes, the Royal Treasurer and Secretary of State during one period he was in Paris. This man's father was financial advisor to the household of the Cardinal de Joyeuse, the uncle of Charles de Lorraine. Whether or not they ever met with Poussin, we don't know, but it is possible that a secret was conveyed, and a painting was executed containing clues. It is my thought that, in later years, the tomb was built deliberately to lead *away* from the secret. (We aren't playing with amateurs here!)

In any event, Poussin's *Les Bergers d'Arcadie* that we are talking about is a *second* version he painted. I know that artists often paint more than one version of a specific subject, but I have a book full of Poussin works, and he doesn't seem to have been in the habit of doing this. So, it *is* curious that he did so with this particular subject. Especially when you look at the painting, which is, actually, quite boring!

Nevertheless, there is another hard fact that comes into play here: Nicolas Fouquet was the Superintendent of Finances to Louis XIV. He had a brother, Abbe Louis Fouquet, who visited Poussin in Rome in 1656. The Abbe sent a letter concerning this meeting to his brother. This letter is in the archives of the Cosse-Brissac family, and says, in part:

> "I delivered to M. Poussin the letter that you did him the honour to write to him; he evinced all the joy imaginable. You would not believe, Monsieur, either the pains that he takes in your service, or the affection with which he takes them, nor the worth and integrity that he brings to all things.
>
> He and I have planned certain matters that I could in a little undertake to the end for you, by which M. Poussin could provide you with advantages that kings would have great pains to get from him, and that, after him, perhaps no one in the world could recover in the centuries to come; and what is more, this could be done without much expense and could even turn to profit, and these are things so hard to discover that no one, no matter who, upon this earth today could have better fortune or even so much..."

Well, of course everybody and his brother immediately jumped to the conclusion that this must refer to the "accursed treasure" of either the Temple of Solomon, the Cathars or the Templars. I, on the other hand, had a quite different reaction to reading this.

You see, after the months and months of reading alchemical literature, and already making the connection between Rennes-le-Chateau and the Pyrenees where an enclave of Alchemists is supposed to exist, I saw nothing in the above letter but a clear reference to alchemy.

I tried to think about it in terms of a "treasure", but it just didn't fit. Kings have often had great treasure or access to treasure, and, in monetary terms, one treasure is as good as another. The remark "could even turn to profit", sort of takes away the idea of treasure, and evokes a sense of some sort of activity.

Well, I began to really examine this painting for clues. Have a look at it.

Now, aside from the fact that I already mentioned, which is that this is a very boring piece of work, what do we note about it in particular? I was trying to look at it in an open-minded way - just taking note of any little thing that would pop into my mind.

The first thing that I noted was all the knee and elbows up front and in your face! I also noted the crossed shins of the figure on the left, which is a classic Masonic/Templar clue. Then, there was the tree growing in straight line with the head of the woman, and that sort of general thing. All of these are important, but we will get to them later.

I know that lots of people have undertaken to analyze this painting by measuring angles, drawing circles, and just generally going around their elbows to get to their thumbs, but I think I have a couple of things to offer here.

The image above is a close-up of the pointing finger. What you see is that the man with the beard is pointing to the letter "R" in sequence with "RC" which is, of course, short for "Rose Cross".

The other painting that Berenger Sauniere was purported to have purchased was Tenier's "Temptation of St. Anthony". If you look at this painting, (and getting a better image than I can provide here is worth the trouble) reveals an interesting thing: the crack on the painting of the tomb in the Shepherd's painting is almost identical to the "window" opening of St. Anthony's temptation. Not only that, but the extremely bizarre

creatures that are tormenting the saint may be important.

Now, this final close-up is most interesting:. (It also gives a better view of the crack, even if upside-down.)

Look very carefully at the shapes of the man's limbs and then compare them to the shadow on the tomb - noting particularly that the shadow of the elbow is just above the crack we have already looked at. Now, does that shadow look like it matches? Well, there's just no accounting for shadows sometimes, but this one looks compellingly like a rearing horse.

So, we have horses, knees and elbows and crossed shins and cracks/windows. Meanwhile we have three guys and one gal, and some dead person in a tomb. All three of our guys have staffs; two of them are in a position that was suggested to me to represent "symbolic beheading". The other has his staff more on his shoulder, which is imagery related to the constellation, Cepheus, the consort of Cassiopeia, interestingly.

I am not even going to pretend to have the answer to this puzzle of the Poussin painting. But, I will mention that I had a dream about it one night - that it was a map that needed to be laid over Europe. And, sure enough, when I matched the bent knee of the kneeling guy to the Rhine River, all kinds of interesting associations popped up!

I should also mention that certain hand gestures indicate letters of the alphabet and numbers, and would have been understood at the time Poussin painted them. In this case, we have, from left to right, T/19, V/20, C/3, and I/9. Does it mean anything? I don't know.

At about the same time that I was thinking about the Shepherds of Arcadia, I had been given a set of the *Matrix* books put out by Val Valerian, AKA John Grace, volumes I through III, and was also deeply involved in reading them. For me, it was an amazing experience to find so many points of confirmation of the Cassiopaean material. But, at the same time, I was troubled by the many, many different and conflicting accounts of the purported alien realities that were all tossed in there together. Some of this material was so far out that my ability to keep an open mind was being seriously challenged. It was as though Val Valerian had just simply gathered everything he could get his hands on from every field and resource that approached the subjects of conspiracy, UFOs and aliens and tossed it all in together in an enormous word salad. Every conspiracy you have ever heard of or could imagine was in the pages of those books. And, there had been no effort to edit or annotate them so that the reader was left baffled as to what to think about it all, much less what to consider as being true.

In many cases, I was sure that a large segment of this material had been presented with tongue in cheek; in other cases, I was certain that it was blatant disinformation. And, as I read through these thousands of pages of descriptions of agendas, realities, research and pseudo-research, conspiracies and counter-conspiracies, confirmations and contradictions, I would turn more and more to the Cassiopaeans to see what *they* would say about some of these things. I had no idea how weird it was going to get. It was during this period of time that we learned about "retrieved" human bodies that were being used for Transdimensional Remolecularization. It was also during this period that the Cassiopaeans talked about the "robot" people and other alien types that we have already discussed.

It was extremely difficult for all of us to both grasp and accept these truly bizarre and outlandish descriptions of our reality. Well, that is not exactly correct; it wasn't our 3rd density reality that was being described, but the denizens of 4th density. I was beginning to understand that it must be the reality from which religions and myths were drawn; the reality of the "Watchers", a world stranger by far than any descriptions of Alice Through the Looking Glass.

As we progressed through this period of time, it also became apparent that there was information the Cassiopaeans were trying to convey at every opportunity. It seemed that they wanted us to have as full an understanding of the World of the Secret Masters as possible. I was reminded of William James' remark:

> "Our science is but a drop, our ignorance a sea. Whatever else be certain, this at least is certain: that the world of our present natural knowledge is enveloped in a larger world of some sort, of whose residual properties we at present can frame no positive idea." [**James**, 1895]

And it was going to get stranger before it was over.

Chapter 33

Torah, Kaballah,
And When I Dream...

I realize that some readers of these pages may wonder exactly where I am heading with this discussion, particularly that which constitutes the previous section. I only ask that you be patient and not skip any of the material because it is important to further events and revelations. What I am trying to give you is a context of what was in my mind and my environment as the "clues" were given which determined not only what clues were given, but how I followed them. Every set of questions I asked the Cassiopaeans depended on the context of what I had discovered in the time between sessions. It seems to be important, also, to keep always in mind the following:

Q: (L) ...How come I am always the one who gets assigned the job of figuring everything out?

A: Because you have asked for the "power" to figure out the most important issues in all of reality. And, we have been assisting you in your empowerment.

Once, when a guest asked if he could just contact the Cassiopaeans himself they remarked:

Q: (BRH) Is there any way I can contact you guys directly?

A: Well, B___, only if you present yourself into the presence of these 3rd densities here. Remember, their request was hard earned, and one of them has been channeling throughout this incarnation, much to his detriment. Those neighborhood kids usually do not respond favorably to psychic awareness, now do they? Another one here has literally turned the world upside down in search of the greatest truths for all of humanity, much to her potential peril. And the third one here had to endure almost unimaginable hardships and tests of stamina in order to realize his destined path of bringing your 3rd density realm to the brink of 4th density transitional adjustment. So, the path is open to you. Wanna follow?!?

So, please realize that I am working as hard as I can to enable anyone and everyone who so desires to unlock the truths they have within - and to do it perhaps a little less traumatically than I did it myself!

I can take you, the reader, along with me to a great extent, reproducing for you in these words I am writing not only the events, but the thinking processes that I followed and the discoveries that I made, but it is up to you to have the perseverance and will to accompany me, and, perhaps, to go beyond.

Yes, some parts seem to be boring or less interesting from one perspective or another; but if it were not important, and even crucially so, it would not be included here. I am excluding a lot of the "false trails" I followed and red herrings I found, unless they have some bearing on what turned out to be the "right" path.

It should be said that what was the "right path" for me may not be the same for everyone. So each of you is responsible for doing your own additional work and research. If what I have done makes it go faster and easier and eliminates some of the wasted time of pursuing disinformation and futile thinking, it is worth my effort.

At this point, I am going to try to finish filling in the "mental picture" that was in my mind at a most crucial point in the Quest so that I can then begin to move forward through the sessions from 1996 onward in a more or less chronological fashion. When I finish these next few pages, the reader will have all the clues that I had as well as the context in which they were given.

As I have already noted, the presence at two sessions of the young woman (RC), who was convinced that she had been connected to me in some way in a previous life in Nazi Germany, really seemed to "shift" the direction of the Cassiopaean communications. In retrospect, it was also the opening of a "door" and the initiating of a new path in my life. After the first session she attended, I had the dream of the "happy wedding" where I was taken to meet the "faceless bridegroom", and after the second session she attended, I had the actual hallucinatory vision of the "unknown-yet-familiar-face". RC was also the one who accelerated the project of producing a magazine as an "organ" for the Cassiopaean material. I had envisioned something that would be more "serious" and yet "open-minded" than the usual metaphysical or UFO publications, and a "journal" seemed to just fit the bill. She had been producing a magazine for a few years and wanted to give it up because she had plans to relocate, and at the same time, she didn't want to leave her subscribers hanging. It seemed to be a perfect solution for me to take over the subscription list and carry on the work.

RC's focus had been more astrological, though she included many articles about alien abduction and conspiracy theories, so the slight reorientation I planned on adding didn't seem like too great a divergence from the original format. I didn't care for the name of the "rag", but that was a minor point that could be rectified. Everything looked like it was a "go" and we felt that this was the key to "networking" in a big way!

It was also at this point that I began to read the entire series of *Matrix* books. As I was digging through this mountain of material, I kept my eye open for the possibilities of Masonic connections because everyone was very hot on the Masonic Conspiracy idea. It had been connected to the Priory of Sion by virtue of the Templars, in a very interesting book entitled *The Temple and the Lodge,* by Michael Baigent and Richard Leigh. It was proposed that the Templars had "gone to ground" in Scotland and England and "reappeared" later as the Masons. Also, there was that pesky number 33 that kept cropping up all over the place.

The more I looked into the "number business", the more confusing it became. Anyone who seeks to do research into "conspiracy theories" - who is serious and honest and fair - will eventually conclude, as Dr. Robert A. Morey (who was, by the way, an anti-Masonic researcher) wrote:

> "Anti-Masonic writers have generally been as unreliable as Masonic apologists. In their zeal to attack Freemasonry, they have been willing to use fantasy, fraud, and deceit. They have even created bogus documents when needed. Their writings must not be taken at face value."

Naturally, when one is considering the "secret significance" of numbers, Pythagorean Mathematics will be among the earliest considerations. Manly Hall wrote that:

> "The true key to philosophic mathematics is the famous Forty-seventh Proposition of Pythagoras, erroneously attributed to Euclid. The Forty-seventh Theorem is stated thus: In a right-angled triangle the square described on the hypotenuse is equal to the sum of the squares described on the other two sides."

Everyone who has attended public school and paid the slightest attention in math class knows that one. The problem is: what does it really mean that is the "true key to philosophic mathematics"? What does $C^2=A^2+B^2$ have to tell us?

Accounts of the travels and studies of Pythagoras differ, but most historians agree that he visited many countries and studied at the feet of many masters. Supposedly, after having been initiated into the Eleusinian mysteries, he went to Egypt and was initiated into the Mysteries of Isis. He then traveled to Phoenicia and Syria and was initiated into the Mysteries of

Adonis. After that, he traveled to the valley of the Euphrates and learned all the secrets of the Chaldeans still living in the area of Babylon. Finally, he traveled to Media and Persia, then to India where he was a pupil and initiate of the Brahmins there. Sounds like he had all the bases covered.

Pythagoras was said to have invented the term "philosopher" in preference to the word "sage" since the former meant one who is attempting to find the truth, and the latter means one who knows the truth. Apparently Pythagoras didn't think he had the whole banana.

Pythagoras started a school at Crotona in Southern Italy and gathered students and disciples there whom he supposedly instructed in the principles of the secrets that had been revealed to him. He considered mathematics, music and astronomy to be the foundation of all the arts and sciences. When he was about sixty years old, he married one of his disciples and had seven children. I guess he was a pretty lively senior citizen! His wife was, apparently, quite a woman in her own right and she carried on his work after he was assassinated by a band of murderers incited to violence by a student whom he refused to initiate. The accounts of Pythagoras' murder vary. Some say he and all his disciples were killed, others say that he may have escaped because some of his students protected him by sacrificing themselves and that he later died of a broken heart when he realized the apparent fruitlessness of his efforts to illuminate humanity.

The experts say that very little remains of the teachings of Pythagoras in the present time unless it has been handed down in secret schools or societies. And, naturally, every secret society on the planet claims to have this "initiated" knowledge to one extent or another. It is possible that there exist some of the original secret numerical formulas of Pythagoras, but the sad fact is that there is no real evidence of it in the writings that have issued from these groups for the past millennium. Though everyone discusses Pythagoras, no one seems to know any more than the post-Pythagorean Greek speculators who "talked much, wrote little, knew less, and concealed their ignorance under a series of mysterious hints and promises". There seems to be a lot of that going around these days! Even Plutarch did not pretend to be able to explain the significance of the geometrical diagrams of Pythagoras. However, he did make the most interesting suggestion that the relationship that Pythagoras established between the geometrical solids and the gods was the result of images seen in the Egyptian temples. The questions we would ask are: what do geometrical solids have to do with "gods"? and "Which Egypt"?

Albert Pike, the great Masonic symbolist, also admitted that there were many things that he couldn't figure out. In his *Symbolism for the 32nd and 33rd degrees* he wrote:

> "I do not understand why the 7 should be called Minerva, or the cube, Neptune. ...Undoubtedly the names given by the Pythagoreans to the different numbers were themselves enigmatic and symbolic - and there is little doubt that in the time of Plutarch the meanings these names concealed were lost. Pythagoras had succeeded too well in concealing his symbols with a veil that was from the first impenetrable, without his oral explanation."

Manly Hall writes:

> "This uncertainty shared by all true students of the subject proves conclusively that it is unwise to make definite statements founded on the indefinite and fragmentary information available concerning the Pythagorean system of mathematical philosophy."

But, of course, in the present time, there is a whole raft of folks who don't let such remarks stop them. Any number of modern gurus claims to have discovered the secrets of "Sacred Geometry"! Not only that, they don't seem to have even studied the matter deeply at all, missing many of the salient points that *are* evident in the fragments of Pythagorean teachings. Regarding this, there is a passage in *Foucault's Pendulum*, by Umberto Eco, that explicates the problem:

> "**Amid all the nonsense there are some unimpeachable truths**... I invite you to go and measure [an arbitrarily selected, but specific] kiosk. You will see that the length of the counter is one hundred and forty-nine centimeters - in other words, one hundred-billionth of the distance between the earth and the sun. The height at the rear, one hundred and seventy-six centimeters, divided by the width of the window, fifty-six centimeters, is 3.14. The height at the front is nineteen decimeters, equal, in other words, to the number of years of the Greek lunar cycle. The sum of the heights of the two front corners is one hundred and ninety times two plus one hundred and seventy-six times two, which equals seven hundred and thirty-two, the date of the victory at Poitiers. The thickness of the counter is 3.10 centimeters, and the width of the cornice of the window is 8.8 centimeters. Replacing the numbers before the decimals by the corresponding letters of the alphabet, we obtain C for ten and H for eight, or C10H8, which is the formula for naphthalene. ...With numbers you can do anything you like. Suppose I have the sacred number 9 and I want to get the number 1314, date of the execution of Jacques de Molay - a date dear to anyone who professes devotion to the Templar tradition of knighthood.
>
> ...Multiply nine by one hundred and forty-six, the fateful day of the destruction of Carthage. How did I arrive at this? I divided thirteen

hundred and fourteen by two, by three, et cetera, until I found a satisfying date. I could also have divided thirteen hundred and fourteen by 6.28, the double of 3.14, and I would have got two hundred and nine. That is the year Attalus I, king of Pergamon, ascended the throne. You see? ...*The universe is a great symphony of numerical correspondences... numbers and their symbolisms provide a path to special knowledge.* But if the world, below and above, is a system of correspondences where *tout se tient*, it's natural for the [lottery] kiosk and the pyramid, both works of man, to reproduce in their structure, unconsciously, the harmonies of the ~cosmos." [*Foucault's Pendulum*, Eco, 1988, pp. 288, 289, emphases, mine.]

The idea has been promoted with great vigor for over a thousand years that so-called Kabbalists and "interpreters of mysteries" can discover with their incredibly tortuous methods The Truth, completely misses the point of a truth that is far more ancient: *Mathematics is the language of Nature.* The Pythagoreans declared arithmetic to be the mother of the mathematical sciences. This idea was based on the fact that geometry, music, and astronomy are dependent upon arithmetic, but arithmetic is not dependent upon them. In this sense, geometry may be removed but arithmetic will remain; but if arithmetic were removed, geometry would be eliminated. In the same way, music depends on arithmetic. *Eliminating music affects arithmetic only by limiting one of its expressions.*

The size, form, and motion of the celestial bodies are determined by the use of geometry and their harmony and rhythm by the use of music. If astronomy is taken away, neither geometry nor music is harmed; but if geometry and music are done away with, astronomy is destroyed. The priority of both geometry and music to astronomy is therefore established and arithmetic is prior to all of them, being primary and fundamental. Playing endless games with numbers demonstrates only that which cannot be otherwise. The real secret seems to be much more profound and most, if not nearly all, "seekers" of truths never penetrate beyond the surface of the matter.

So, I could see that there was a lot of nonsense being propagated in the present day, mostly by people who had not bothered to study the history of metaphysical and occult matters. But, even with such an opinion in my mind, I could not help but notice the repeated occurrences of the number 33 in not only mystical literature, but also in world events of great import. Or, so it seemed. I wonder if all the *many* events of significance were cataloged, would we find a preponderance of these so-called mystical numbers, or would we find a spread of numbers that indicate no statistical significance? Just because some events occurred on the 33rd parallel, did that signify it was a "Masonic Conspiracy"? How many other events of similar significance have occurred at places and times that have no "occult" significance at all? But, of course, those that do, possibly by virtue of pure chance, get all the attention while everything else is ignored.

On the other hand, the idea was growing in my mind that such "synchronicities" or appearances of certain numbers and characteristics of events, WERE a sort of "clue" that the veil between dimensions and densities had been breached, either accidentally or deliberately. But who or what was doing it was still an issue.

But, clearly, the number 33 was being used by some occultists at various points to signify something, even if it was supposedly initiated by Bacon with his "33 cipher". So, the only right thing to do, I thought, was to ask the Cassiopaeans about this. It seemed to be a well-established "clue" that was very popular and certainly did appear to be behind or related to a lot of mysterious events.

An even deeper question seemed to me to be: If the number 33 was a code indicating both the presence and action of the Secret Masters, just WHY was this number the one selected? If mathematics is the "Language of Nature", just what was Nature saying? With the new complexity of the picture, it was pretty clear to me that all of the old explanations just were not going to hold up to scrutiny. I wanted to ask, with no prejudice or anticipation about the answer just *what* did this number 33 *really* mean? I was interested in getting to the "Pythagorean" level of secrets. So, even though we have already looked at portions of this session, let's look at it again in it's entirety.

> Q: (L) Now, the main thing I wanted to ask about is the references I come across in tons of reading, that the number 33 is somehow significant. Could you tell us the significance, in esoteric terms, or in terms of secret societies, of the number 33? There is the cipher of Roger Bacon, based on the number 33, the 33rd degree masons...
>
> A: As usual, we do not just give you the answers; we help you to teach yourself!! Now, take 11 and contemplate...

Here we see that the Cassiopaeans have immediately diverted my attention to the number 11, which is a divisor of 33. (3 X 11 = 33; 33 divided by 11=3, 33 divided by 3= 11)

> Q: (L) Well, three times eleven is thirty-three.
>
> A: Yes, but what about 11?

Again, they are diverting me to the number 11. And you are about to see how totally dense I can be!

> Q: (L) Well, eleven is supposed to be one of the prime, or divine power numbers. In Kaballah, 11 is the power number...

A: Yes...

Q: (L) Eleven is 10 plus 1; it is divisible only by itself and by 1. I can't think of anything else. What else is there to the number 11?

A: Astrology.

And here, even though I didn't know it at the time, was one of the chief clues they were dropping in my lap. My first thought was, of course, the 11th house of astrology: Aquarius, which happens to be my own sun sign.

Q: (L) Well, in astrology, the eleventh sign is Aquarius. The eleventh house is friends, hopes, dreams and wishes, and also adopted children. Aquarius the Water bearer, the dispenser of knowledge. Does 11 have something to do with dispensing of knowledge?

A: Now, 3rd house.

Note that they didn't answer my question directly, but redirected my thinking to the 3rd house so that we have the two elements that make up 33, i.e. 11 X 3. The idea of the "gods" of the signs, i.e. Mercury and Saturn (Uranus was a later addition *after* Pythagoras) did not occur to me.

Q: (L) Gemini. Okay. Gemini and Aquarius. Third house is how the mind works, communication, relations with neighbors and siblings, education, local travel, how one speaks. Gemini is known as the "consummate man". Somewhat shallow and interested in the things of material life. It is also the divine number of creation. [I should add here that originally Gemini was the "Divine children", Adam and Eve, and only later became the twins.] So, what's the connection here?

A: Matrix.

Q: (L) Is there something about this of importance in the Matrix material?

A: No.

Q: (L) This IS a matrix. The third house and the eleventh house create a matrix?

A: Foundation.

Q: (L) Gemini is in June, Aquarius is in February. Gemini is the physical man, and Aquarius is the spiritual man?

A: Yin Yang.

Well, in retrospect, I was completely missing the obvious. The 3rd house and the 11th house "create a foundation". And we note that, from the Cassiopaean point of view, Aquarius precedes Gemini in the elements given.

Q: (L) So Gemini is the physical man and Aquarius is the spiritual man... Yin Yang... is that the...

A: Yes...

And, of course when the Cassiopaeans indicate three dots in a row, they want me to go deeper. But, at the time, I really didn't know how or where they could possibly be going with this.

Q: (L) So 33 could represent the transformation of the physical man to the divine man through the action of secret or hidden teachings... and those who have gone through this process represent themselves with the number 33, which means that they started out oriented to the flesh and then became...

A: Medusa 11.

Again, in retrospect, the Cassiopaeans are interrupting my flow of assumptions with a new term.

Q: (L) Medusa 11? What does Medusa have to do with it? Please tell me how Medusa relates here?

A: Heads.

Q: (L) Heads. Medusa. 11. Were there eleven snakes on the head of Medusa or eleven heads? This is really obscure... you need to help me out here.

A: We are.

Q: (L) Do I need to read the Medusa legend to understand?

A: No.

Q: (L) Medusa. Heads. 11. Is there something about the mythical Medusa that we need to see here?

A: 11 squared divided by [or into?] Phi.

At this point in time, I am ashamed to admit that I had never heard of the term "Phi" (even if I did know about the common term "Golden Ratio"), and I assumed that the C's had made a mistake and that they really meant to say "pi" which even I, the math idiot, had heard of! So, I framed the next question in terms of my assumption.

Q: (L) By pi. 11 squared divided by pi. What does this result bring us to?

A: 33. Infinity.

Q: (L) Well, we don't get 33 out of this... we get 3.3166 etc. if we divide the **square root** of 11 by pi. Divided by Phi... what in the heck is Phi? Okay, if we divide pi into 11, we get 3.5 infinity, but not 33.

I had a calculator!

A: 1 [pause] 1

Q: (L) Oh. You weren't saying 11 times 11; you were saying 1 times 1.

A: No.

And, even though they said "no" to my question, I continued on in my assumptions.

Q: (L) 1 times 1 is what? 1.

I think the fact that I was just plowing along and ignoring everything the Cassiopaeans were saying must have caused some consternation. They changed tactics.

A: 5 minus 3.

Q: (L) Okay, that's 2.

A: 2 minus 1.

Q: (L) I don't get it. A math genius I am NOT. What is the concept here?

A: Look: 353535. Is code.

Q: (L) What does this code relate to?

A: Infinite power.

Q: (L) How is infinite power acquired by knowing this code? If you don't know the correspondences, how can you use a numerical code?

A: Lord of Serpent promises its followers infinite power, which they must seek infinite knowledge to gain, for which they pledge allegiance infinitely, which they possess for all eternity, so long as they find infinite wisdom, for which they search for all infinity.

Q: (L) And that is the meaning of the number 33? Well, that is a round robin... a circle you can't get out of!

A: And therein you have the deception! Remember, those who seek to serve self with supreme power, are doomed only to serve others who seek to serve self, and can only see that which they want to see.

Well, that sure described me at the moment! I was just *not* seeing! Even if I had the objective of asking open questions, I *had* come to the session with some strong assumptions about what the answers *should* be, and I was shooting myself in the foot with every question. Well, I sort of gave up on the number 33 in frustration because the answers weren't going where I thought they ought to go and diverted off in another tangent.

Q: (L) The thought that occurs to me, as we are talking here, is that the STS pathway consists of an individual who wants to serve themselves - they are selfish and egocentric - they want to compel others to serve them; they want to enslave others; and they find ways to manipulate others to serve them. But, they end up being compelled by some higher being than they are, because they have been tricked into believing that by getting others to serve them, or some agenda that they promote, that they are either drawing power to themselves or even that they are giving power to others or some god through the teachings, including the popular religions which promote being "saved" by simply believing and giving up your power.

And, in the end, you have a whole pyramid of people *taking* by trickery and deception, from others. The taker gets taken from in the end. There's always somebody higher than you who is "over you" in a hierarchy. A pyramid where all those on the bottom, the majority, have no one to take from, so they take from each other until one of them "gains enough weight" to be absorbed into the next level higher, and this process continues until you get to the apex and everything disappears.

But, in the STO mode, you have those who only give. And, *if they are involved only with other STO persons who are also giving,* everyone receives and no one is at the bottom or at the top or in a "void" state.

But, the funny thing is that, in the end, it seems like everyone ends up serving someone else anyway, and [the only difference is] the principle of INTENT, *which basically determines who you are giving to.* But in STO, it is more like a circle, a balance, no one is left without.

A: Balance, Yin-Yang.

Q: (L) Obviously the 33 represents the Serpent, the Medusa, and so forth...

A: You mentioned pyramid, interesting... And what is the geometric one-dimensional figure that corresponds?

Q: (L) Well, the triangle. And, if you have a triangle point up you have 3, joined to a triangle pointing down, you have 3, and you have a 33. Is that something like what we are getting at here?

A: Yes.

Q: (L) Is there a connection between the number 33 and the Great Pyramid in Egypt?

A: Yes.

Q: (L) And what is that connection? Is it that the builders of the pyramid participated in this secret society activity?

A: Yes. And what symbol did you see in "Matrix", for Serpents and Grays?

Q: (L) You are talking about the triangle with the Serpent's head in it?

A: Yes.

Q: (L) Are we talking in terms of this 33 relating to a group of "aliens", or a group of humans with advanced knowledge and abilities?

A: Either/or.

Q: (L) Is this what has been referred to in the Bramley book as the Brotherhood of the Serpent or Snake?

A: Yes.

Q: (L) Is this also what you have referred to as the Quorum?

A: Close.

Remember that Yin-Yang circle of the previous discussion about the Quorum? The Cassiopaeans are here indicating that there is a subtle, but distinct difference between the Brotherhood of the Serpent and the Quorum. Yes, the Quorum is a group with advanced knowledge and abilities, but their objectives and intent are to preserve Free Will for all, while the objectives of the Brotherhood are to manipulate, dominate and control others.

Q: (L) So, we have a bunch of people who are playing with mathematics, and playing with higher knowledge, basically as a keep busy activity to distract them at the human level from the fact that they are being manipulated at a higher level. Is this what is going on? Or, do they consciously know what they are doing? Is it a distraction or a conscious choice?

A: Both.

Q: (L) If I were to name some names, could you identify if named individuals were involved in this secret group?

A: It would not be in your best interests.

Q: (L) Is there anything more on this 33 number that I should look at now?

A: No. You need to contemplate.

Boy, did I ever! I was now completely disoriented. The idea of the Pyramid being associated with the STS oriented "faction" sort of threw me off. And there was a definite suggestion here that the number 33 was associated with the Consortium of humans and aliens who ruled the world from behind the scenes: The Brotherhood of the Serpent. This reminded me of something else the Cassiopaeans had said at one earlier point that distressed me because it went against the standard metaphysical and occult teachings:

Q: (L) Who was Hermes Trismegistus?

A: Traitor to court of Pharaoh Rana.

Q: (L) Who is Pharaoh Rana?

A: Egyptian leader of spiritual covenant.

Q: (L) In what way was Hermes a traitor?

A: Broke covenant of spiritual unity of all peoples in area now known as Middle East.

Q: (L) Who did Hermes betray?

A: Himself; was power hungry.

Q: (L) What acts did he do [in this breaking of the covenant]?

A: He inspired divisions within ranks of Egyptians, Essenes, Aryans, and Persians et cetera.

Q: (L) What was his purpose in doing this?

A: Divide and conquer as inspired by those referred to as Brotherhood in Bramley book you have read.

Q: (L) Is this the Brotherhood of the Snake Hermes formed in rejection of unity?

A: Hermes did not form it; it was long since in existence.

Q: (L) Who was the originator of the Brotherhood of the Serpent as described in the Bramley book?

A: Lizard Beings.

Q: (L) I would like to know the approximate year of the life of Hermes Trismegistus.

A: 5211 approx. (Years ago or B.C.?)

Q: (L) Who was this Pharaoh Rana? Was he prior to the Pharaoh Menes?

A: Much prior.

Q: Was the Pharaoh Menes the same as King Minos of Crete?

A: No.

Q: What was the relationship between the Cretans and the Egyptians?

A: All were the same originally.

Q: So they were Egyptians who left Egypt and moved to Crete and set up their version of the Egyptian culture there? Is that it? Or did they develop independently?

A: Former is closest.

Q: Was Abraham of the Jews the same individual as Hermes, which some people are suggesting?

A: No.

Q: Was Akhenaten the same individual as Moses, as some other people are suggesting?

A: Only through the eyes of the themes.

And we find here the idea that Abraham was a "betrayer" of a prior covenant when he made the covenant with Jehovah. And this will prove to be *extremely* interesting later on. But, back to the numbers.

When I asked about the number 33, I was directed to the number 11, Astrology and a "Matrix" of some sort. Not only that, but all the "occult" ideas, practices and teachings that I had studied for so many years were being implicated as "keep busy activities" of manipulation from higher levels. And, when you dig into anything "occult", somehow you always find yourself confronting Kaballah.

A "matrix" is defined as "the womb" or "that within which and from which something originates or develops".

In math, a matrix is "a set of numbers or terms arranged in rows and columns between parentheses or double lines". More technically, it is "a rectangular array of numbers or other elements..." having application as computational devices in such widely diversified fields as economics, psychology, statistics, engineering, physics, and mathematics.

In mathematics, matrices are useful tools in the study of linear systems of algebraic equations, linear differential equations, linear mappings and transformations, and bilinear and quadratic forms. Matrices can be regarded as generalized numbers, and their utility in applications depends on the possibility of combining them in certain definite ways.

The product of a matrix A and a number a is called a scalar product and is obtained by multiplying every element of A by a.

The term "scalar", in mathematics, is synonymous with "real" as in real number or real function. A vector is a directed line segment and, as such, has magnitude and direction. Many physical quantities such as velocity, acceleration and force, are *vectors*.

What this means is that, using a matrix, one can establish vectors, which can then be used to calculate a scalar product, which is simply a number that can mean anything depending on how it is used.

When we think about what the Cassiopaeans were saying, or trying to say, against the impenetrable thick-headedness of yours truly, we come to this:

A: 1 [pause] 1; 5 minus 3; 2 minus 1.

Q: (L) What is the concept here?

A: Look: 353535. Is code.

Q: (L) What does this code relate to?

A: Infinite power.

This "infinite power" is then further defined by the C's as:

"Lord of Serpent promises its followers infinite power, which they must seek infinite knowledge to gain, for which they pledge allegiance infinitely for, which they possess for all eternity, so long as they find infinite wisdom, for which they search for all infinity.

... And therein you have the deception! Remember, those who seek to serve self with supreme power, are doomed only to serve others who seek to serve self, and can only see that which they want to see."

In other words: Kaballah.

Basically, Kaballah developed as a way to play games with numbers and letters as described above. One school endeavors to find beneath the letters of the "sacred text", i.e. The Torah, all references to the ten *Sefirot*. The Sefirot can be compared to a theory of cosmic chains or levels of reality of the emanations of God. A hierarchy of power, that is.

The Kabbalist uses the Torah as an "instrument". They affirm that, beneath its letters, beneath the stories and events depicted there, there are "secrets" waiting for the enterprising Kabbalist to discover! Thus, the text cannot be read *only* literally, but must also be read allegorically, hermeneutically and mystically.

Notariqon is a technique of using acrostics to cipher and decipher hidden messages. The initial or final letters of a series of words generate new words.

Gematria is based on the fact that, in Hebrew, numbers are indicated by letters and every word has, therefore, a numerical value. This allows mystical relationships to be seen between completely different words having completely different meanings. It is such relationships that the Kabbalist seeks to discover.

Temurah is the art of anagrams. Abraham Abulafia systematically combined the letter Alef with each of the four letters of the Tetragrammaton YHWH; then he vocalized each of the resulting units by every possible permutation of five vowels, thus obtaining four tables with fifty entries each!!! Eleazar ben Yudah of Worms went on to vocalize every unit using twice each of the five vowels, and the total number of combinations increased geometrically. [Cf. Eco, *The Search For The Perfect Language*]

The Kabbalist has an unlimited number of options as to how to interpret the Torah, but the important thing was that they believed that this was more than just interpretation: it was the very method whereby God created the world. And understanding it would admit the practitioner to the inner circles of power and control over the forces of life.

So, we see the clue leads us to the idea of "Infinite Power".

I hope you realize that, the Kaballah has a mind-boggling array of combinations and methods. In the end, it was thought that, by these methods, along with employing certain recitations and breathing techniques, the practitioner could pass into states of ecstasy and from there, achieve the desired magical powers. Because, in the end, the objective of the Kaballah was to reproduce the same sounds with which God created the world.

The *Sefer Yezirah*, or Book of Creation, (written in the Dark Ages, I might add, somewhere between the 2nd and 6th centuries), explicated this doctrine. According to the *Sefer Yezirah*, the "stones" out of which God created the world were the thirty-two ways of wisdom, which were formed by the twenty-two letters of the Hebrew alphabet and the ten Sefirot.

It was claimed that the primordial Torah was inscribed in black flames upon white fire and many Kabbalists denied the existence of any kind of historical development of either the Torah or Kaballah. As a result of this idea, it became widely accepted that the Kaballah was the esoteric part of the Oral Law given to Moses at Sinai. There were additional genealogies in the kabbalistic literature which were designed to support the claim of a continuity of tradition but even Hebrew scholars note that they are faulty and misconceived, and lack "any historical value". [Scholem, 1974]

> "At first the word 'Kaballah' did not especially denote a mystical or esoteric tradition. In the Talmud it is used for the extra-Pentateuchal parts of the Bible, and in post-talmudic literature the Oral Law is also called 'Kaballah'. In the writings of Eleazar of Worms (beginning of the 13th century), esoteric traditions (concerning the names of the angels and the magical Names of God) are referred to as kabbalahy'. ...In his **Hilkhot ha-Kisse** (in **Merkabah Shelemah**, 1921) and **Sefer ha-Shem**. In his commentary to the Sefer Yezirah (c. 1130), when he is discussing the creation of the Holy Spirit, i.e., the **Shekhinah**, Juda Ben Barzillai states that the sages 'used to transmit statements of this kind to their students and to sages privately, in a whisper, through kabbalay'. All this demonstrates that the term 'Kaballah' was not yet used for any one particular field. **The new, precise usage originated in the circle of Isaac the Blind (1200) and was adopted by all his disciples.**

> Kaballah is only one of the many terms used during a period of more than 1,500 years, to designate the mystical movement, its teaching, or its adherents. The Talmud speaks of **sitrei Torah** and **razei Torah** ('secrets of the Torah'), and parts of the secret tradition are called **m'aseh bereshit** (literally, 'the work of creation') and **ma'aseh Merkabah** (the work of the chariot). At least one of the mystical groups called itself **yoredei Merkabah** (those who descend to the chariot), an extraordinary expression whose meaning eludes us. ...Historically speaking, **organized closed societies of mystics have been proved to exist only since the end of the Second Temple era.**" [Scholem, 1974, Emphases, mine.]

Kaballah is the "tradition" of esoteric teachings of Judaism. It is, in essence, a compilation of the different mystical movements issuing from the Second Temple in Jerusalem. One thing that has to be considered when thinking of Kaballah is the fact that its admitted purpose is to:

> "broaden the dimensions of the Torah and to transform it from the law of the people of Israel into the inner secret law of the universe." [Scholem, 1974]

And, as we have already noted, (and will go into more deeply later), the so-called "Second Temple" in Jerusalem may have been the First, and the forces behind its construction and the development of its theology could very well have been those very forces with designs on our freedom. So, at this point, we need to consider the roots of Kaballah, the Torah upon which it is based, as well as the "tradition".

In *The Curse of Cain*, Dr. Regina Schwartz writes about the relationship between Monotheism and Violence, positing that *Monotheism itself is the root of violence*. She writes:

> "Collective Identity, which is a result of a covenant of Monotheism is explicitly narrated in the Bible as an invention, a **radical break with Nature**. A transcendent deity breaks into history with the demand that the people **he** constitutes obey the law **he** institutes, and first and foremost among those laws is, of course, that they **pledge allegiance to him, and him alone**, and that **this is what makes them a unified people** as **opposed** to the 'other', as in **all other people** which leads to violence. In the Old Testament, vast numbers of 'other' people are obliterated, while in the New Testament, vast numbers are colonized and converted for the sake of such covenants."

So, we are seeing a clear example of what the Cassiopaeans have explicated in their remarks:

> "Lord of Serpent promises its followers infinite power which they must seek infinite knowledge to gain, for which they pledge allegiance infinitely, which they possess for all eternity, so long as they find infinite wisdom, for which they search for all infinity. ... those who seek to serve self with supreme power, are doomed only to serve others who seek to serve self, and can only see that which they want to see."

Dr. Schwartz also writes about the idea of the 'provisional' nature of a covenant, which the Cassiopaeans mention above: that it is conditional. "Believe in me and obey me or else I will destroy you." Doesn't sound like there is any choice, does there? And we find ourselves in the face of Nazi Theophany.

The chief thing that occurs to me in terms of the "believe in me" business in relation to religions, is that it constitutes a sort of 'permission', if you will, whether it is conscious or subconscious, for the deity to take the 'vengeful' action if the agreement is broken!

Riane Eisler, an acclaimed scholar, has developed what she calls "*Cultural Transformation Theory*", which proposes that there are two basic models of society underlying the great diversity of human culture. The first is the "Dominator Model," that can be termed a patriarchy or matriarchy. It consists of ranking one half of humanity **over** another, in the broadest terms, but essentially can be any situation where any group dominates and any other group is considered inferior, whether male or female, black or white, rich or poor, free or slave.

The second model is what Ms. Eisler calls the "Partnership Model", which is based on the principle of "linking rather than ranking".

Thus, it seems that the work of Ms. Eisler is describing precisely what the Cassiopaeans call Service to Self versus Service to Others; Networking versus judgment!

As Ms. Eisler acutely points out:

> "If we stop and think about it, there are only two basic ways of structuring the relations between the female and male halves of humanity. All societies are patterned on either a dominator model - in which human hierarchies are ultimately backed up by force or the threat of force - or a partnership model, with variations in between." [Eisler, 1987]

In an amazing book that should be read by everyone, *When God Was a Woman*, Merlin Stone reveals the sexual and religious bias of many of the scholars of the nineteenth and twentieth centuries, which have been responsible for the general lack of knowledge about these most ancient times. Most of these male scholars were raised in societies that embrace the male-oriented religions of Judaism or Christianity, and this obviously heavily influenced their opinions. One of them, Professor R.K. Harrison wrote of the Goddess religion: "One of its most prominent features was the lewd, depraved, orgiastic character of its cultic procedures".

> "Despite the discovery of temples of the Goddess in nearly every Neolithic and historic excavation, Werner Keller writes that the female deity was worshipped primarily on 'hills and knolls', simply echoing the words of the Old Testament. Professor W. F. Albright, one of the leading authorities on the archaeology of Palestine, wrote of the female religions 'orgiastic nature worship, sensuous nudity and gross mythology'. He continued by saying that 'It was replaced by Israel with its pastoral simplicity and purity of life, its lofty monotheism and its severe code of ethics'. It is difficult to understand how these words can be academically justified after reading of the massacres perpetrated by the Hebrews on the original inhabitants of Canaan as portrayed in the Book of Joshua, especially chapters nine to eleven. Professor S. H. Hooke, in his collection

of essays **Myth, Ritual and Kingship**, openly admits, 'I firmly believe that God chose Israel to be the vehicle of revelation'.

Albright himself wrote, 'It is frequently said that the scientific quality of Palestinian archaeology has been seriously impaired by the religious preconceptions of scholars who have excavated in the Holy Land. It is true that some archaeologists have been drawn to Palestine by their interest in the Bible, and that some of them had received their previous training mainly as biblical scholars'. But he then proceeded to reject this possibility of impairment, basing his conclusion primarily upon the fact that the dates assigned to the sites and artifacts of ancient Palestine, by the scholars who took part in the earlier excavations, were subsequently proven to be too recent, rather than too old, as might perhaps be expected. The question of whether or not the attitudes and beliefs inherent in those suggested 'religious preconceptions' had perhaps subtly influenced analysis and descriptions of the symbolism, rituals and general nature of the ancient religion was not even raised for discussion." [Stone, 1976]

In most textbooks of archaeology, the Goddess religion is referred to rather deprecatingly as a "fertility cult"! And, as Ms. Stone notes, the word "cult" always has the connotation of something less civilized than "religion", and is nearly always applied when referring to the Goddess worship, while the rituals associated with that clever ET, Jehovah/Yahweh are always reverently referred to as "Religion", with a capital!

Considering the extreme monotheistic, Judeo-Christian bias of the scholars who have written the words, directed the schools, published the books, and overseen our education for the past 1500 years or so, how else can we think but that males have always played the dominant role, and that males have always been the "doers" and "creators" and "movers and shakers" of our cultural, social and technological development?

As children, most little girls of the Western world are told the story of Adam and Eve. Eve is made from Adam's rib to be his companion and helper because he was lonely. Next they are taught that Eve was foolishly gullible and was pathetically "easy" to the wiles of the serpent. She disobeyed God Almighty, and led Adam down the primrose path, and forever after, all women bore the blame for this perfidy!

Not only that, but forever after, because of Eve's foolishness, all women must accept men as their masters, the representatives of the omnipotent male deity, whose wisdom and righteousness they must admire and respect with reverence and awe!

Over and over again, the legend of the loss of paradise has been utilized to impress upon us the **natural inferiority of women**. Only Man was created in God's image... woman came later and was a poor semblance of a human being! Everywhere in our culture this story pops up over and over again! It is the foundation of poetry, art, advertising and jokes. Everywhere you look, Eve is tempting Adam to do wrong over and over again. Women are portrayed as inherently conniving, contriving, (yet somehow also gullible and simple-minded) and most of all *sexy*! They clearly need a divinely appointed overseer to keep them out of trouble and there is a man around every corner just ready to do the job!

Joseph Campbell wrote about the Adam and Eve myth:

> "This curious mythological idea, and the still more curious fact that for two thousand years it was accepted throughout the Western World as the absolutely dependable account of an event that was supposed to have taken place about a fortnight after the creation of the universe, poses forcefully <u>the highly interesting question of the influence of</u> **conspicuously contrived, counterfeit mythologies** <u>and the infliction of mythology upon the structure of human belief and the consequent course of civilization.</u>" [Quoted by Stone, 1976] (emphasis, mine)

<u>The religion of the Great Mother Goddess existed and flourished for many thousands of years in the Near and Middle East before the arrival of the patriarch Abraham, the first prophet of the dominator male deity, Yahweh.</u> Archaeologists have traced the worship of the Goddess back to the Neolithic communities of about 7000 B.C., and some to the Upper Paleolithic cultures of about 25,000 B.C. From Neolithic times, at least, its existence has been repeatedly attested to well into Roman Times. Yet, Bible scholars agree that Abraham lived in Canaan as late as between 1800 and 1550 B.C., a veritable Johnny-come-lately! How in the world has such a recent appearance on the world scene managed to push itself into such prominence and domination?

Chavín is claimed to be the Mother Civilization of the Andes. The term Chavín has been applied to a developmental stage of Andean history, to an archaeological period, to an art style and to a hypothetical empire. Chavín has been interpreted as a culture, a civilization and a religion. The Chavín culture was one of agriculture and fishing and seafaring. It's earliest manifestation is in the Ica area, and we have already noted the Ica stone artifacts which suggest far greater antiquity for this culture than mainstream science even considers.

The Moche culture developed in the same area which had previously belonged to the Chavín culture, so we may assume that it was formed of survivors. Expert opinions suggest that one can easily see the influence of <u>the oldest civilisation of Peru, the Chavín,</u> on the Moche. Chavín was a well-developed class society, which was divided into nobility, farmers and slaves. The Moche people were developed in agriculture, fishing, handicraft, trade, sea-faring and metallurgy. The anthropomorphic pottery

of the Mochicans is thought to express the mythological and social themes which were the peak of this art genre in the whole civilisation of Peru.

This raises an interesting issue because the human-shaped pottery shows that the typology of the Mochicans includes Mongoloid as well as Negroid features.

The earliest "god" image, the one carved on the Gate of the Sun, is a godlike creature holding *staves or sticks* in both of its hands. It is thought that the deity with staves was a celestial supreme being, a god of the heavens, who in the course of time was attributed the characteristic features of a thunder-god. The worship of the deity with staves spread from Chavín all over Peru, more particularly so in the Tiahuanaco culture on the Altiplano Plateau in South-Peru where he was called Viracocha.[42]

Several versions of Andean Genesis at Tiahuanaco were recorded by Juan de Betanzos in 1551, and Cristobal de Molina in 1553. In the early version preserved by Betanzos, the world creator is named *Contiti*

---

[42] Berezkin, Juri 1983. Mochica. Tsivilizatsia indeitsev Severnogo poberzhia Peru v I-VII vv. Leningrad.

Viracocha, and he emerges from Lake Titicaca to create "the sun and the day, and the moon and the stars". Viracocha orders "the sun to move in its path" and so the time of mankind begins. After calling the people out from caves, rivers, and springs scattered through the mythical landscape of creation time, Contiti Viracocha furiously *turns some of them into stone for sacrilegious behavior*. Then, he starts creation all over again! Only this time, he creates the people from stone instead of turning them into stone.

Of course we wonder about the "staves" in the hands of Viracocha? Were these the "tools" he used to "turn people into stone" or call flesh forth from stone? Are they the origins of the pillars Jachin and Boaz? How do these staves relate to the staves Jacob drove into the ground in the story about the magical increase of his flocks?

These questions bring us to consider the Semites and Sargon.

Sargon the Great

According to "experts", Sargon of Akkad reigned approximately 2,334-2,279 B.C., and was one of the earliest of the world's great empire builders, conquering all of southern Mesopotamia as well as parts of Syria, Anatolia, and Elam (western Iran). He established the region's first *Semitic dynasty* and was considered the founder of the Mesopotamian military tradition.

Sargon is known almost entirely from the legends and tales that followed his reputation through 2000 years of cuneiform Mesopotamian history, and not from any documents that were written during his lifetime. The lack of contemporary record is explained by the fact that the capital city of Agade, (note the homophonic similarity to Arcadia) which he built, has *never been located and excavated*. It was destroyed at the end of the dynasty that Sargon founded and was never again inhabited, at least under the name of Agade.

According to a folktale, Sargon was a self-made man of humble origins; a *gardener* (think "gardens of the Hesperides") having found him as a baby floating in a basket on the river, brought him up in his own calling. His father is unknown; his mother is said to have been a priestess in a town on the middle Euphrates. (Note all the similarities to the story of Moses *as well as* Perseus.) Rising, therefore, without the help of influential relations, he attained the post of *cupbearer* to the ruler of the city of Kish, in the north of the ancient land of Sumer. (Notice the clue of the cup here.)

The event that brought him to supremacy was the defeat of Lugalzaggisi of Uruk (biblical Erech, in central Sumer). Lugalzaggisi had already united the city-states of Sumer by defeating each in turn and claimed to rule the lands not only of the Sumerian city-states but also those as far west as the Mediterranean. Sargon became king over all of southern Mesopotamia, the first great ruler for whom *the Semitic tongue known as Akkadian, rather than Sumerian, was natural from birth.*

Sargon wished to secure favorable trade with Agade throughout the known world and this, along with what was obviously a very energetic temperament, led Sargon to conquer cities along the middle Euphrates to northern Syria and the silver-mining mountains of southern Anatolia. He also took Susa, *capital city of the Elamites,* in the Zagros Mountains of western Iran, where the only truly contemporary record of his reign has been uncovered.

As the result of Sargon's military prowess and ability to organize, as well as of the legacy of the Sumerian city-states that he had inherited by conquest, and of previously existing trade of the old Sumerian city-states with other countries, commercial connections flourished *with the Indus Valley,* the coast of Oman, the islands and shores of the Persian Gulf, the lapis lazuli mines of Badakhshan, the cedars of Lebanon, the silver-rich Taurus Mountains, Cappadocia, Crete, and perhaps even Greece.

During Sargon's rule, his Akkadian language became adapted to the script that previously had been used in the Sumerian language, and there arose new spirit of writing evident in the clay tablets and cylinder scals of this dynasty. There are beautifully arranged and executed scenes of mythology and festive life. It could be suggested that this new artistic feeling is attributable directly to the Semitic influence of Sargon and his compatriots upon the rather dull Sumerians. In contrast to the Sumerian civilization, in Sargon's new capital, military and economic values were *not* the only things that were important.

The latter part of his reign was troubled with rebellions, which later literature ascribes, predictably enough, to sacrilegious acts that he - like Solomon - is supposed to have committed; but this can be discounted as the standard cause assigned to all disasters by Sumerians and Akkadians alike. The troubles, in fact, were probably caused by the inability of one man, however energetic, to control so vast an empire. There is no evidence to suggest that he was particularly harsh, nor that the Sumerians disliked him for being a Semite. What's more, the empire did not collapse totally, for Sargon's successors were able to control their legacy, and later generations thought of him as being perhaps the greatest name in their history. What is most interesting is that Sargon attributed his success to the patronage of the goddess Ishtar, in whose honor Agade was erected.

Sargon's story sounds a lot like a combination of the Biblical stories of Moses, David and Solomon and certainly, there is evidence of infusion of

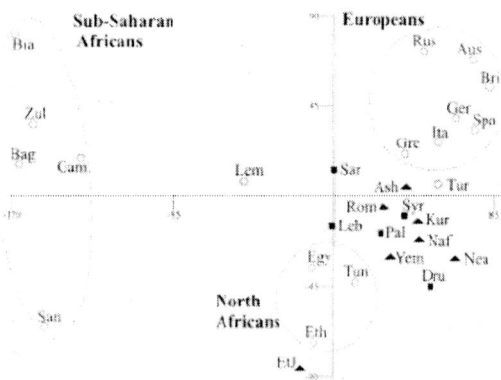

Semitic traditions into the culture of the Sumerians. We also wish to consider the the fact that Sargon was the first "semite". Nowadays "Semitic peoples" are generally understood to be, more or less, individuals of Middle Eastern origins: Jews and Arabs predominantly. That is to say, to be an Arab or a Jew is to be "Semitic".

In recent years the idea has taken hold that the Ashkenazi Jews are really Turkish and not Jews at all. Recent genetic studies place the Ashkenazi as closest in kinship to Roman Jews on one side, who are just a small step away from Lebanese non-Jews, and Syrian non-Jews on the other. The Syrian non-Jews are very close to the Kurdish Jews and the Palestinian non-Jews - i.e. the "Palestinians".

What actually seems to have happened is that when the Khazar kingdom "converted" to Judaism, as described above, they invited Jewish rabbis to come and teach them how to be proper Jews. These rabbis, being "proper Jews", took Khazar wives, mixing with the Khazar population in this way. Additionally, after the fall of the Khazar kingdom, Yiddish-speaking "Jewish" immigrants from the west (especially Germany, Bohemia, and other areas of Central Europe) - which would include Roman Jewish lines, began to flood into Eastern Europe, and it is believed that these newer immigrants intermarried with the Khazars. Thus, Eastern European Jews have a mix of ancestors who came from Central Europe and from the Khazar kingdom. The two groups (eastern and western Jews) intermarried over the centuries.

In this sense, the Ashkenazi Jews are, indeed, descendants of the Israelites through the male line.[43]

---

[43] Jews are represented by triangles: Ashkenazim = Ash, Roman Jews = Rom, North African Jews = Naf; Near Eastern Jews = Nea; Kurdish Jews = Kur, Yemenite Jews = Yem;

"Analysis of the Y chromosome has already yielded interesting results. Dr. Ariella Oppenheim of the Hebrew University in Jerusalem said she had found considerable similarity between Jews and Israeli and Palestinian Arabs, as if the Y chromosomes of both groups had been drawn from a common population that began to expand 7,800 years ago.[44]

About two-thirds of Israeli Arabs and Arabs in the territories and a similar proportion of Israeli Jews are the descendents of at least three common prehistoric ancestors who lived in the Middle East in the Neolithic period, about 8,000 years ago. This is the finding of a new study conducted by an international team of scholars headed by Prof. Ariella Oppenheim, a senior geneticist in the Hebrew University's hematology department and at Hadassah Hospital in Jerusalem. In the study, soon to be published in the scientific journal 'Human Genetics', the researchers probed the history of Jewish and Arab men by analyzing the genetic changes in the Y chromosome.[...]

The results of the study, says Prof. Oppenheim, 'support the historical documentation **according to which the Arabs are descendents of an ancient population of the country and that a large proportion of them were Jews who converted to Islam** after Islam reached Eretz Israel in the seventh century CE'. [...]

They [...] discovered that Jews and Arabs have common prehistoric ancestors who lived here until just the last few thousand years..[...] In view of the small geographical area of Israel and the Palestinian Authority, the researchers were surprised to discover that some Palestinians on the West Bank have a unique genetic trait that is reflected in a relatively high frequency of certain genetic signs. This fact indicates that they are the descendents of people who have lived here for a few hundred years at least. [...] Dr. Filon says that the unique genetic trait is characteristic of a population that has lived in the same place for many generations. [45]

Data on the Y chromosome indicates that the males originated in the Middle East, while the mothers' mitochondrial DNA seems to indicate a local Diaspora origin in the female community founders.[46]

Ethiopian Jews = EtJ; non-Jewish Middle Easterners = Pal, non-Jewish Syrians = Syr, non-Jewish Lebanes = Leb, Israeli Druze = Dru, non-Jewish Saudi Arabians = Sar; Non-Jewish Europeans: Rus = Russians, Bri = British, Ger = Germans, Aus = Austrians, Ita = Italians, Spa = Spanish, Gre = Greeks, Tun = North Africans and Tunisians; Egy = Egyptians, Eth = Ethiopians, Gam = Gambians, Bia = Giaka, Bag = Bagandans, San = San, Zul = Zulu. Tur = non Jewish Turks, Lem = Lemba from south Africa.

[44] Nicholas Wade. "Scientists Rough Out Humanity's 50,000-Year-Old Story." *The New York Times* (November 14, 2000)

[45] Tamara Traubman. "A new study shows that the genetic makeup of Jews and Arabs is almost identical, and that both groups share common prehistoric ancestors." *Ha'aretz* (2000)

[46] Judy Siegel-Itzkovich. "Dad was out and about, while Mom stayed home." *Jerusalem Post* (June 16, 2002)

We have analyzed the maternally inherited mitochondrial DNA from each of nine geographically separated Jewish groups, eight non-Jewish host populations, and an Israeli Arab/Palestinian population, and we have compared the differences found in Jews and non-Jews with those found using Y-chromosome data that were obtained, in most cases, from the same population samples. The results suggest that most Jewish communities were founded by relatively few women, that the founding process was independent in different geographic areas, and that subsequent genetic input from surrounding populations was limited on the female side. In sharp contrast to this, the paternally inherited Y chromosome shows diversity similar to that of neighboring populations and shows no evidence of founder effects. These sex-specific differences demonstrate an important role for culture in shaping patterns of genetic variation and are likely to have significant epidemiological implications for studies involving these populations. We illustrate this by presenting data from a panel of X-chromosome microsatellites, which indicates that, in the case of the Georgian Jews, the female-specific founder event appears to have resulted in elevated levels of linkage disequilibrium.[47]

The emerging genetic picture is based largely on two studies, […] that together show that the men and women who founded the Jewish communities had surprisingly different genetic histories.[…]

A new study now shows that the women in nine Jewish communities from Georgia, the former Soviet republic, to Morocco have vastly different genetic histories from the men. […] The women's identities, however, are a mystery, because, unlike the case with the men, their genetic signatures are *not related* to one another or *to those of present-day Middle Eastern populations*.[…]

The new study, by Dr. David Goldstein, Dr. Mark Thomas and Dr. Neil Bradman of University College in London and other colleagues, appears in The *American Journal of Human Genetics* this month.... His [Goldstein's] own speculation, he said, is that most Jewish communities were formed by unions between Jewish men and local women, though he notes that the women's origins cannot be genetically determined.[…]

Like the other Jewish communities in the study, the Ashkenazic community of Northern and Central Europe, from which most American Jews are descended, shows less diversity than expected in its mitochondrial DNA, perhaps reflecting the maternal definition of Jewishness. But *unlike the other Jewish populations*, it does *not* show

---

[47] Mark G. Thomas, Michael E. Weale, Abigail L. Jones, Martin Richards, Alice Smith, Nicola Redhead, Antonio Torroni, Rosaria Scozzari, Fiona Gratrix, Ayele Tarekegn, James F. Wilson, Cristian Capelli, Neil Bradman, and David B. Goldstein. "Founding Mothers of Jewish Communities: Geographically Separated Jewish Groups Were Independently Founded by Very Few Female Ancestors." *The American Journal of Human Genetics* 70:6 (June 2002): 1411-1420.

signs of having had *very few female founders*. It is possible, Dr. Goldstein said, that the Ashkenazic community is a mosaic of separate populations formed the same way as the others.[…]

'The authors are correct in saying the historical origins of most Jewish communities are unknown', Dr. [Shaye] Cohen [of Harvard University] said. 'Not only the little ones like in India, but even the mainstream Ashkenazic culture from which most American Jews descend.'[…] If the founding mothers of most Jewish communities were local, that could explain why Jews in each country tend to resemble their host community physically while the origins of their Jewish founding fathers may explain the aspects the communities have in common, Dr. Cohen said.[…]

The Y chromosome and mitochondrial DNA's in today's Jewish communities reflect the ancestry of their male and female founders but say little about the rest of the genome... Noting that the Y chromosome points to a Middle Eastern origin of Jewish communities and the mitochondrial DNA to a possibly local origin, Dr. Goldstein said that the composition of ordinary chromosomes, which carry most of the genes, was impossible to assess."[48]

These studies suggests the idea that some of the early ancestors of the ancient Levant and Mesopotamian civilizations originated in the region of Armenia and moved southwards - that they were "Semitic" the same way Sargon was. Further, the Tanach records extensive evidence of intermarriage between Jews and ancient peoples who originated in eastern Anatolia, such as the Hittites and Hurrians (including the Jebusites of Jerusalem). The Edomites who were of mixed Hebrew and Hurrian ancestry were also absorbed into the Jewish people. The Armenians and Kurds are the descendants of people who remained in Eastern Anatolia, Armenia and Kurdistan, subsequently intermarrying with the Turks and neighboring peoples. So, we see the idea of the "Ten Lost Tribes", or even the "Thirteenth Tribe" to be myths exploded by the science of genetics.

Another important point from Oppenheim's work is that **the Arabs are descendents of an ancient population of the country and that a large proportion of them were Jews who converted to Islam.** In other words, the Palestinians are closer in kinship to the original "Jews" that inhabited "Israel" than the current day Jews that are primarily of Ashkenazi stock. In short, if one is to take seriously (as the Zionists declare we must) that Israel was given to the Jews by God, then the Jews that it was given to are the ancestors of the Palestinians. That, of course, raises all kinds of interesting problems, not the least of which is the genocide of the real, ancient line of Jews being completed by Ashkenazi Jews.

---

[48] Nicholas Wade. "DNA, New Clues to Jewish Roots." *The New York Times* (May 14, 2002): F1 (col. 1)

The problem is, of course, that all existing studies fail to compare modern Jewish populations' DNA to ancient Judean DNA. The question remains: If Sargon was the "original Semitic ruler", was he a Semite as we understand Semites today? The next question that occurs to us is: Did Sargon, as a conqueror, impose a language and cultural expression on a genetically different people, the Sumerians, who had already imposed their own language and culture on the indigenous population of the Fertile Crescent?

What we notice most particularly is that Sargon was said to have come "from the North" and that he worshipped the Goddess Ishtar. Also, when we think of the word "Semitic" in terms of the Green language, we naturally wonder if it doesn't imply something that was "half" of one thing and "half" of another?

The question then becomes: Who were the Sumerians that absorbed and adopted the Semitic language and cultural expressions, adapting them to their own use?

The Sumerians were a *non-Semitic* people who, judging by archaeological remains, were generally short and stocky, with high, straight noses and downward sloping eyes. Many wore beards, but some were clean-shaven. These people apparently migrated to the Fertile Crescent - they suddenly appeared in the area - and immediately established what was, for a long time, considered to be the first *real* 'Civilization'. They built cities, *step-pyramid-temples*, large residences and economic facilities. They referred to themselves as the "black-headed people" as if to emphasize their difference from the indigenous population who, one might assume, were not black-headed.

The picture painted by the archaeological record of the Sumerian City-State civilization before Sargon is one of constant strife between these cities, especially the most prominent ones: Kish, Erech, Ur, Adab, and later Lagash and Umma. Constant warring weakened the Sumerians until "the kingship was carried away by *foreigners*" such as the king of Awan, Sargon of Akkad, the Gutians, the Elamites, and eventually Hammurabi. Sargon of Akkad, the first Semite, was then, a "foreigner" to the Sumerians who had (as we will see) a rather "lengthy" history prior to the Semitic influence.

It is quite curious that despite their sense of nationalism and the sharing of a common identity, the "black-headed people" were unable to unite in order to resist the conquerors. What is even more ironic is the fact that, even though they were unable to resist being conquered and ruled - in fact - by foreigners, the Sumerian culture was, to a great extent, *assimilated by the conquerors* by the adoption of their customs, script, and literature, including many of their religious myths.

The cultural "soul" of a people can be found in their stories, myths, and rituals. The stories of Sumer, as inscribed on its clay tablets, allow us to reconstruct, at least partially, a process of dynamic development that took place over many centuries. *Some experts* propose that Sumerian storytelling was indebted to the *wandering Semitic tribes*, who, being allegedly "illiterate", had the narrative memory capacity of "illiterate peoples". It is suggested by such experts that these Semites often entertained their more "civilized" Sumerian hosts by "telling tales around the campfire" or in the market place. It is then suggested that these stories were then written down by Sumerian scribes, who attempted to categorize the material into orderly groups of continuous narrative. Obviously, the "wandering, illiterate Semites" weren't quite so backward since they conquered the Sumerians and their influence actually gave the Sumerian civilization a cultural boost. What is more likely is that the writing of the Sumerians was developed for economic and military purposes, which was the purview of the "god" and his priests. It was only after the incursions of the Semites that a literary tradition began, and the development of writing proceeded in such a way that it could be utilized for literature.

The experts tell us that the Sumerians themselves had no real "sense of history" even though they had invented writing. This opinion is arrived at due to the fact that the Sumerians had recorded a sort of "history", in the form of a King list that was, to understate the matter, astonishing.

The Sumerians' relationship with their gods was *the* driving force in the rise of their civilization. The very reason for the existence of Sumer and her people seemed to lie with these strange and *mortal* 'deities'. The very reason for being was to *serve* the appropriate deity.

The Sumerian religion was more like a feudal covenental relationship with an overlord than the mystical *worship* of a god as we would understand religion today. For the Sumerian, worship of the gods meant *complete* servitude - the very purpose for which mankind was (according to the Sumerians) created by the Sumerian gods.

According to the Sumerians, the city-states had been founded by the gods far back in time and it was the gods who had given the Sumerians, "the black-headed people", all the tools and weapons and marvelous inventions of their culture. For the Sumerians, everything that they had - cities, fields, herds, tools, institutions - had always existed because the gods had created all of it before they had created the black headed people to run things as their slaves. This immediately makes one think of the only people who claim an origin as slaves: the Jews.

This "slave-master" Religion was the central organizing principle of the city-states, each city *belonging* to a different deity who was worshipped in a large temple. According to the Sumerians, even if the gods might prefer to be just and merciful, they had also created evil and misfortune and there was nothing that the black-headed people could do about it. Judging from the *Sumerian Lamentation texts*, the best one could do in times of trouble would be to "plead, lament and wail, tearfully confessing his sins and failings". Their family god or city god *might* intervene on their behalf, but that would not necessarily happen even if the rules were carefully followed. After all, man was created as a broken, labor saving, tool for the use of the gods and at the end of everyone's life, lay the underworld, a dreary place like the Sheol of the early Hebrews.

According to the Sumerians, their gods were very intelligent, extremely long-lived and yet, very *mortal* beings. This is evident in their king lists. According to the Sumerians, the time *before the flood* was said to be a period of 432,000 years. Two kings from after the flood that are listed were Gilgamesh and Tammuz. The legends of Tammuz were so well-liked that they were assimilated to the pantheon of Babylon and later became the model for Adonis to the Greeks. Gilgamesh became the hero of the Babylonian epic poem which bears his name, and which also contains an account of the flood.

Until recently, these king lists and the names in them were thought to be purely mythic, but in the 1930's, Sir Leonard Woolley, while excavating a building at Ur on the Ubaid level, found an inscription indicating that the structure had been erected by the son of the founder of the First Dynasty of Ur, a person up till that time regarded as fiction. Gilgamesh, too, has inscriptions telling of the buildings he built.

The "King-List" is divided into dynastic periods that are city-state oriented as apparently regards the seat of central power. The most startling of these sections is the list dealing with the pre-deluge Kings. Eight *Annunaki Kings* are listed, as are five city-states where centralized rule apparently was seated. Length of rule is given in what is known as a "sar". All of the remaining King-List sections have the length of rule measured by years. The 'sar' was equivalent in length to 3,600 years.

King	City of Rule	Sars	Years
A-lu-lim	NUN	8	28,800
A-la(l)-gar	NUN	10	36,000

En-me-en-lu-an-na	Bad-tabira	12	43,200
En-me-en-gal-an-na	Bad-tabira	8	28,800
Dumuzi	Bad-tabira	10	36,000
En-Sib-zi-an-na	Larak	8	28,800
En-me-en-dur-an-na	Sippar	5 (5 ner)	21,000
(?) du-du	Suruppak	5 (1 ner)	18,600
And here ends the Kingship of the Annunaki.			

Now it is important to note that during this astonishing length of time recorded as "history" by the Sumerians, only two *Annunaki* held overall reign. First was Enki (later known as Ea) and the second was Enlil, a half-brother of Enki. The event that ended this first list was the legendary deluge. It was also during the latter part of this first period of the King-List that human beings appeared.

Calculating the length of time back to the arrival of these "Annunaki", brings us to about 450,000 years ago. That puts it well before the *accepted date* of the appearance of modern man.

The numbering system of the Sumerians is actually quite fascinating. The Sumerian civilization can be more or less divided into three periods of cultural manifestation. The first included the development of glyptics where cylinder seals were engraved with parades of animals or scenes of a religious nature. This was followed by the development of sculpture, and finally, the emergence of writing.

During the first period of cultural manifestation, archaeology indicates that there were no palaces for such as what we would consider a real king. The "king" was actually a priest who lived in the temple. The priest-king was titled "EN", or "Lord". It was only later, in the second cultural period that the title of king, or Lugal, came into use. At the same time, palaces became evident, witnessing a separation of the State - and its military forces - and the priesthood.

At the beginning of the second millennium B.C., the Sumerians came back to dominance for a period, but after Hammurabi, Sumer disappeared entirely as a political entity. Nevertheless, the Sumerian language remained a language of priests.

Around 3,200 B.C., the Sumerians devised their numerical notation system, giving special graphical symbols to the units 1, 10, 60, 600, 3,600. That is to say, we find that the Sumerians did not count in tens, hundreds and thousands, but rather adopted base 60, grouping things into sixties, and multiplying by powers of sixty.

Our own civilization utilizes vestiges of base 60 in the ways we count time in hours, minutes and seconds, and in the degrees of the circle.

Sixty is a large number to use as a base for a numbering system. It is taxing to the memory because it necessitates knowing sixty different signs (words) that stand for the numbers from 1 to 60. The Sumerians handled this by using 10 as an intermediary between the different sexagesimal orders of magnitude: 1, 60, 60^2, 60^3, etc. The word for 60, *geš, is the same as the word for unity.* The number 60 represented a certain level, above which, mutiples of 60 up to 600 were expressed by using 60 as a new unit. When they reached 600, the next level was treated as still another unit, with multiples up to 3,000. The number 3,600, or sixty sixties, was given a new name: šàr, and this, in turn, became yet another new unit.

The Sumerian numbering system often required excessive repetitions of identical marks, placing symbols side by side to represent addition of their values. The number 3, 599 required a total of twenty-six symbols. For this reason, the Sumerians would often use a "subtractive convention" with a little symbol that meant "take this number away from that number to get the number that is being indicated".

In the pre-Sargon era, certain irregularities started to appear in the cuneiform representations of numbers. In addition to the subtractive convention, entirely new symbols were being created for multiples of 36,000. This means that instead of repeating 36,000 however many times it was to be indicated, the numbers 72,000, 108,000, 144,000, 180,000 and 216,000 had their own symbols assigned to them.

In all of human history, the Sumerians are the only ones we know of who invented and used a sexagesimal system. This can be seen as a "triumph" of their civilization, and a great mystery as well. Many people have tried to understand why they did this and numerous hypotheses were offered from Theon of Alexandria to Otto Neugebauer. These hypotheses range from "It was the easiest to use" and the "lowest of numbers that had the greatest number of divisors," to "it was natural" because the number of days in a Solar year rounded down to 360, and so on. Daniel Boorstin suggested that the Sumerians used base 60 because they multiplied the number of planets known to them (5) times the number of months in the year. It was pointed out by the Assyriologist, G. Kewitsch in 1904 that neither astronomy nor geometry can really explain the origin of a number system, presupposing that abstract considerations preceded concrete applications. Kewitsch speculated that the sexagesimal system actually resulted from the *fusion of two civilisations*, one of which used a decimal number-system, and the other used base 6 derived from a special form of finger-counting. This was not easily accepted since there is no historical record of a base 6 numbering system anywhere in the world.

However, duodecimal systems, or base 12 numbering systems ARE widely attested, *especially in Western Europe*. It is still used for counting eggs and oysters. We regularly use the words "dozen" and "gross" and measurements based on 12 were used in France right up to the Revolution, and are still used in Britain and the U.S.

The Romans had a unit of weight, money and arithmetic called the *as*, divided into 12 ounces. One of the monetary units of pre-Revolutionary France was the *sol*, divided into 12 deniers. The Sumerians, Assyrians, and Babylonians used base 12, and its multiples and divisors vary widely as well. The Mesopotamian day was divided into twelve equal parts, and they divided the circle, the ecliptic, and the zodiac into twelve equal sectors of 30 degrees. This means that base 12 could very well have played a major part in shaping the Sumerian number system.

The major role of 10 in the base 60 system is well attested as well, since it was used as an auxiliary unit to circumvent the main difficulty of the sexagesimal system. This leads us to an important clue: the Sumerian word for "ten" also means "fingers" suggesting an earlier counting system.

Taking this back to a variation on Kewitsch's hypothesis, Georges Ifrah proposes that base 60 was a "learned solution" to the union between two peoples, one of which used a decimal system derived from a *vigesimal system* and the other a system using base 12. As it happens, 60 is the lowest common multiple of 10 and 12 as well as the lowest number of which all the first six integers are divisors and, 5 X 12 is 60.

What is interesting to note is that the French words for 80 and 90 (quatre-vingts, quatre-vingt-dix) carry the traces of a *vanished vigesimal arithemetic* in Ancient Europe.

Ifrah's hypothesis is that the Sumerian society had both decimal and duodecimal number systems, and its mathematicians subsequently devised a system that combined the two bases.

Of course, this hypothesis fails on the ground that it pressupposes way too much intellectual sophistication. Unless, of course, we consider the *disjecta membra* of a vanished high civilization.

It is evident that the Mesopotamian basin had one or more indigenous populations prior to the arrival of the Sumerians. The Sumerians were "immigrants" who came from somewhere else about which we know nothing since they seem to have broken all ties with their previous environment.

Coming back to the question: "Who were the Semites?", we understand that the term itself derives from the Old Testament where the tribes of Eber (the Hebrews), Elam, Asshur, Aram, Arphasad, and Lud are said to be the descendants of Shem, one of Noah's three sons. However, this claim makes the Elamites, who spoke an Asianic language, *first cousins* to the Hebrews, Assyrians, and Aramaeans, whose languages belong to the Semitic group.

"Asianic" is the term used for the earlier inhabitants of the Asian mainland whose languages, mostly of the agglutinative-kind, were neither Indo-European nor Semitic. It is generally believed that Mesopotamia was originally inhabited by Asianic peoples prior to the arrival of the Sumerians. It is thought that the Semitic-speaking population came in a later wave and that Sargon was the first Semitic king of a "Semitic nation". Of course, that still doesn't explain the Sumerians and their language.

Significant Semitic elements are to be found in the cultures of Mari and Kis at the beginning of the third millennium B.C., and it has even been proposed that the El Obeid peoples were the original Semites, though they were absorbed and assimilated by the Sumerians. The discovery of the Ebla tablets reveal the existence of a Semitic language in the mid-third millennium B.C.

When Sargon founded the first Semitic state by defeating the Sumerians, Akkadian became the language of Mesopotamia and pushed aside the unrelated language of Sumer. When the Sumerian cuneiform writing was adapted by the Akkadians, the writing system was already several centuries old. The Akkadians found an ideographic writing system that was already drifting toward a phonetic system and accelerated this drift while still retaining some of the ideographic meanings. The Akkadian and Sumerian cultural heritages merged, creating a true literary tradition. When Akkadian speech and writing finally supplanted their Sumerian counterparts in Mesopotamia, a strictly decimal numbering became the norm in daily use. The ancient signs for 60, 600, 3,600 and so on, progressively disappeared. In the hands of the Semites, cuneiform numerals and Mesopotamian arithmetic were gradually adapted into a system with a different base working on different principles. Nevertheless, base 60 did not disappear entirely, as we have already mentioned.

We should note, however, that it was with the sudden appearance of the Sumerian civilization - as early as the 5th millennium B.C. - that the long era of the tribal, egalitarian society of the Neolithic came to an end between 4,000 and 3,000 B.C. Archaeologists and anthropologists have documented that the early society of Mesopotamia had been *guided by women* and had a Goddess as deity. The end of female leadership can be deducted from the following quote in *In the Wake of the Goddesses* by Frymer-Kenski:

> "The dynasty of Kish was founded by Enmebaragesi, a contemporary of Gilgamesh. The name breakes down as follows: *enetik - eme - ebakin - aragikor - ageriko - ezi* which can be transliterated to 'from that time on - female - harvest - lustful - notorious - to domesticate' or 'From that time on the lustful, notorious harvest female was domesticated'."

This "name" tells us in no uncertain terms that the time of the Goddess was on the decline, because male domination had arrived with the Sumerians. Sargon, conversely, attributed all of his successes to the Goddess.

Now, let's come back to the clues that the French words for 80 and 90 (quatre-vingts, quatre-vingt-dix) carry the traces of a vanished ancient European vigesimal arithmetic, put together with the fact that the first Semitic king came from the "North" and that the "Semitic influence" of the Goddess worshipping Sargon accelerated the development of the Sumerian culture toward something more than being economic slaves to the gods. Considering these factors, we might wish to reconsider the term "Semitic".

Indeed, the religion of the ancient Sumerians has left its mark on the entire Middle East. Not only are its temples and ziggurats scattered about the region, but the literature, cosmogony and rituals influenced their neighbors to such an extent that we can see echoes of Sumer in the Judeo-Christian-Islamic tradition today. In other words, most of what we consider to be Semitic is actually Sumerian written in the Semitic Akkadian language. Undoubtedly, those peoples who today are called Semitic by virtue of having had a name assigned to them from the Bible, are actually descendants of the Sumerians and their "Semitic language" was imposed on them by Sargon of Akkad who was clearly *not* one of the "black-headed people".

> "The linguistic affinity of Sumerian has not yet been successfully established. Ural-Altaic (which includes Turkish), Dravidian, Brahui,

Bantu, and many other groups of languages have been compared with Sumerian, but no theory has gained common acceptance." [49]

Sargon became king over all of southern Mesopotamia, the first great ruler for whom *the Semitic tongue* - not Sumerian - known as Akkadian was natural from birth. This suggests to us that Sargon was not Sumerian, but that he was the bringer of a new language to Mesopotamia, imposing it on the peoples there in the same way that Spanish was imposed on South and Central America, and English has been adopted all over the world as a result of American domination of trade.

The language issue is our clue to who relates to whom. The Afro-Asiatic language phylum has six distinct branches including Ancient Egyptian, which was known in its last years as Coptic, and which became extinct in the seventeenth century. The other five branches are Berber, Chadic, Cushitic, and Omotic. The Semitic language group is subdivided into an extinct Eastern branch, Akkadian, spoken by Sargon, and a Western branch with two sub-branches, Central and South. The Central group consists of Aramaic, Canaanite, and Arabic. The Southern group consists of South Arabian and Ethiopic. And here is the curiosity: one of the other branches of the Afro-Asiatic language tree is Berber, with sub-branches of *Guanche* - spoken by the original Canary Islanders; East Numidian, which is Old Libyan, and Berber proper.

Now, you ask, what is the oddity?

The Guanche language.

Some experts tell us that the Guanches must have come from the neighboring African coast long ages before the Black and Arab "invaders" overran it. We are sagely informed that Mauritania was formerly inhabited by the "same ancient Iberian race which once covered all *Western Europe*: a people tall, fair and strong". Spain invaded, and most of the Guanches were wiped out by diseases to which they had no resistance due to their long isolation. It was over a hundred years before anyone attempted to record their language, customs, and what could be remembered of their history. Friar Alonso de Espinosa of the Augustine Order of Preachers, writing in 1580, tells us:

---

[49] Arno Poebel, *Grundzüge der sumerischen Grammatik* (1923), partly out of date, but still the only full grammar of Sumerian in all its stages; Adam Falkenstein, *Grammatik der Sprache Gudeas von Lagas*, 2 vol. (1949-50), a very thorough grammar of the New Sumerian dialect, and *Das Sumerische* (1959), a very brief but comprehensive survey of the Sumerian language; Cyril J. Gadd, *Sumerian Reading Book* (1924), outdated but the only grammatical tool in English; Samuel N. Kramer, *The Sumerians* (1963), provides a general introduction to Sumerian civilization.

"...It is generally believed that these are the Elysian Fields of which Homer sings. The poet Virgil, in the 4th book of the *Aeneid*, mentions the great peak of this island, when he makes Mercury, sent by Jupiter, go to Carthage to undeceive Aeneas, and to encourage him so that he might not abandon the voyage to Italy which he had undertaken.

It has not been possible to ascertain the origin of the Guanches, or whence they came, for as the natives had no letters, they had no account of their origin or descent, although some tradition may have come down from father to son. [...]

The old Guanches say that they have an immemorial tradition that sixty people came to this island, but they know not whence they came. They gave their settlement the name 'The place of union of the son of the great one'.

Although they knew of God, and called Him by various names, they had no rites nor ceremonies nor words with which they might venerate Him. [...] When the rains failed, they got together the sheep in certain places, where it was the custom to invoke the guardian of the sheep. Here they *stuck a wand or lance in the ground*, then they separated the lambs from the sheep, and placed the mothers round the lance, where they bleated. They believed that God was appeased by this ceremony, that he heard the bleating of the sheep and would send down the rain.

...They knew that there was a hell, and they held that it was in the peak of Teyde [the volcanic mountain}, and the devil was Guayota.

They were accustomed when a child was born, to call a woman whose duty it was, and she poured water over its head; and this woman thus contracted a relationship with the child's parents, so that it was not lawful to marry her, or to treat her dishonestly. They know not whence they derived this custom or ceremony, only that it existed. It could not be a sacrament, for it was not performed as one, nor had the evangelic law been preached to them.[...]

The inviolable law was that if a warrior meeting a woman by chance in the road, or in any solitary place, who spoke to her or looked at her, unless she spoke first and asked for something, or who, in an inhabited place, used any dishonest words which could be proved, he should suffer death for it without appeal. Such was their discipline. [...]

This people had very good and perfect features, and well-shaped bodies. They were of tall stature, with proportionate limbs. *There were giants among them of incredible size...*

They only possessed and sowed barley and beans. ... If they once had wheat, the seed had been lost... They also ate the flesh of sheep, goats, and pigs, and they fed on it by itself, without any other relish whatever... The flesh had to be half roasted because, as they said, it contained more substance in that way than if it was well roasted.

> They *counted the year by lunations…* The lord did not marry with anyone of the lower orders, and if there was no one he could marry without staining the lineage, brothers were married to sisters.

> They were wonderfully clever with counting. Although a flock was very numerous and came out of the yard or fold at a rush, they counted the sheep without opening their mouths or noting with their hands, and never made a mistake." [50]

I'm sure that the reader can see that even though we have very little to go on, there are a couple of suggestive indicators recorded by the good friar. The first thing we note is the custom of driving a lance into the ground for the sheep to "call the god". A memory of ante-diluvian technology, perhaps?

But more than this, the clues seem to indicate that what we call the "Semitic language" may actually have been a northern tongue, an Aryan language, adopted by peoples we think of as ethnically "Semitic" in modern terms but who, in ancient terms, were not Semitic at all.

The Rise of Sacrifice

Returning to Viracocha, what we learn about him was that he was a *carver and shaper of humanity*. He was a god of action, a creator and destroyer of worlds: the Shiva of the Andes. Before successfully creating the world of humans, Viracocha had annihilated previous worlds; first by fire and then again by flood. In short, for the Andeans, humanity emerged not from a utopian Garden of Eden - which is a Northern concept - but from the hard, living rock and water of the natural world: clay. Viracocha had two faithful servants who he sent in opposite directions to generate a new race of humans.

In Cristobal de Molina's version of the same myth, these two culture heroes are the Andean Adam and Eve: the primeval male-female pair who were the children of Viracocha. Unlike the theme of a prior Golden Age, the events of the myth begin only *after* a universal flood. The Spanish cleric Bernabe Cobo informs us that the original name for Tiahuanaco was Taypi Kala. Taypi Kala meant "the stone in the center"; the natives ascribed this name to the site because they considered the city to be in "the center of the world, and that from there the world was repopulated after the flood".

The peoples of the Andes had no known form of indigenous writing, so the evidence for their activities must come from other sources. The early

---

[50] De Espinosa, Alonso, *The Guanches of Tenerife*, trans. by Sir Clements Markham (Nendeln/Liechtenstein: Kraus Repring 1972).

Spanish chroniclers recorded what had been described to them about life in Inca times; their accounts include frequent references to "sacrifice" and "offering". Some doubt has been expressed about these accounts, however, accusing the Europeans of a negative, Catholic point of view, suggesting that the chroniclers did not ask the right questions. However, pictorial evidence for sacrifice has long been known. The Incas made little in the way of figurative art, but existing *pre-Inca depictions* give *visual evidence for sacrifice*. Examples of archaeological evidence are now accumulating in the data from recent excavations in a number of places. Most of the archaeological evidence for human sacrifice in the Andes - most clearly among the Inca and the Moche - has been discovered only recently.

For many people in the modern Western world, making a sacrifice means either giving without receiving or giving up something valuable for a cause that may benefit others. What seems to be evident about the process of sacrifice in primitive belief systems is that sacrifices of animals and humans were done for the greater good of the group - to appease the anger of the god and prevent disaster. Blood was the symbol of life, of animation, of nourishment, the most important offering that could be given to the natural and supernatural beings. It was thought that the sacrificial nourishing of the "sacred beings" made life possible. It was also thought that the cosmos "ran" on this "nourishment". It has been suggested that the number and violence of the sacrifices increased as the desperate Moche priests tried to appease the Gods. Unfortunately, such speculations do not fully answer the question as to why *any* human being *ever* thought that the death of another human being would satisfy the gods in some way.

In artistic depictions, the Moche are seen to cut the throats of prisoners of war and then *drink their blood*. Afterwards, the bodies were dismembered. It's hard to say what the purpose of these endless sacrifices might be. Perhaps the priests thought that they obtained power from drinking the blood. We are reminded of the Biblical injunction that "the blood is the life", and the Hebrews were forbidden to drink it or to eat meat that had not been thoroughly bled. Perhaps this was because the blood - and the life in it - was supposed to be reserved for the god exclusively. Child sacrifice is a recurrent theme not only in the Andes but also in much of the world.

Returning now to our problem: Yahweh. It seems that, like the Moche and the Aztecs, the Jewish priesthood began with terrifying cannibalistic rituals and sacrifices. Just picture the priest - kohane - standing before the worshippers spattered with dripping, stringy clots of blood, throwing basins of blood on the congregation to "cleanse" them, all the while the subliminal message being conveyed that "if you don't obey Yahweh, this is what he will do to you"! This may have been what was taking place in the great Temple of Solomon which was very likely a displaced memory of a place so hated, the Temple of Hephaestus - the labyrinth - in Memphis, and was later transferred to the "labyrinth" at Crete. It was then brought to Palestine by the refugees from the eruption of Thera, and combined later with other tales of the cataclysm to produce some of the Old Testament and the rites of Judaism. We begin to understand why the labyrinth of Egypt was, according to Pliny, regarded with "extraordinary hatred" and why so many myths of a human eating Minotaur at the center circulated in the ancient world.

The idea of the ritual sacrifice of the king instead of thousands of virgins, children, or warriors, seems to be the result of the mingling of the Southern Sun god worship with the influence of the Northern Moon worshippers. This seems to be a distortion of the idea that the king was ruler by virtue of his "marriage" to the goddess, or her representative, and that this "marriage" involved a shamanic death in order to be able to transduce the cosmic energies of benevolence and prosperity to the tribe or to defend the tribe against evil spirits.

The northern custom of a king who had lost his vigor voluntarily abdicating and being replaced by the "right heir" who could "marry the goddess" was mixed with the sacrifice customs, and the result was that the priesthood had a weapon to wield over the monarch to keep him in line. Thus arose the idea of the "scape goat" king who was sacrificed in the labyrinth instead of maidens and warriors.

Herodotus tells us what seems to be an already garbled version of this mixing of the two ideas:

> "Being set free after the reign of the priest of Hephaistos, the Egyptians, since they could not live any time without a king, set up over them twelve kings, having divided all Egypt into twelve parts."

This may be the original story of Jacob and Esau and the 12 tribes.

This shift was also recorded in the myth of Theseus.

What seems to be so is that there was some sort of "object of power" at the center of the myth of the Sons of Aegyptus and the daughters of Danaus. It was a descendant of this "union" - Perseus - who "cleansed the temple" and restored the Goddess to her rightful place as depicted in the story of the slaying of Medusa, the freeing of Pegasus, and the rescue of Andromeda. But again, this is merely the assimilation of later events to the primal myth of Atlantis.

When we examine the evidence, we find many clues, but with the passage of time, the movements of people in migration and/or conquest, it is impossible to say with certainty just "who is on first". There is, of course, much more to this than the little bit I am able to include here. This will be dealt with in a future volume.

In the Bible the "wise king Solomon" is portrayed as "whoring after" the Tyrian fire and sun god Moloch/Molech. One has to wonder what this means considering the fact that there is no difference between Moloch and Yahweh when one digs beneath the surface. Some "experts" suggest that the priest Melchizedek - who was the purported teacher of Abraham - was a priest of "Moloch", and that the name means "Righteous Moloch". However, that is a cross-conceptualization, and a somewhat sly way to trick the reader. If you are going to translate one word into English, you ought to translate the other. *Malkiy*, or *Malak*, means simply "king". *Tsedeq* means "right" or "just" or benevolent. It carries the abstract suggestion of "prosperity".

What seems to have happened, once again, is that a possible revelation of truth about our reality was co-opted and diverted by the denizens of hyperdimensional realities who do not wish their nature and agenda to be discerned. In the standard method of disinformation, truth was mixed with lies in order to mislead and divert. Those who wish that everything was either clearly black or clearly white, do not take the time to patiently pick through the threads and separate them so as to discern the truth. My suggestion on this point is that the ancient Priesthood of Melchizedek was designated thus for the express purpose of distinguishing it from the worship of Moloch, the Fire god.

The apparent co-opting of names and terms and symbolism throughout the ages continues. In the present day, there are many who claim to be "of the Order of Melchizedek", who are, in fact, not.

Some experts quote Paul's remark from Hebrews 9:22 where it says: "under the Law almost everything is purified by means of blood, and without the shedding of blood there is neither release from sin and its guilt nor the remission of the due and merited punishment for sins". What such experts fail to mention - again a sly twisting - is what follows in that particular passage, which is an argument against such practices.

The religion of the Great Mother Goddess existed and flourished for many thousands of years in the Near and Middle East before the arrival of the patriarch Abraham who is depicted as the first prophet of the dominator male deity, Yahweh. Archaeologists have traced the worship of the Goddess back to the Neolithic communities of about 7000 B.C., some to the Upper Paleolithic cultures of about 25,000 B.C. From Neolithic times, at least, its existence has been repeatedly attested to well into Roman Times. Yet, Bible scholars tell us that Abraham lived in Canaan as late as between 1800 and 1550 B.C., a veritable Johnny-come-lately! How in the world has such a recent appearance on the world scene managed to push itself into such prominence and domination?

Over and over again in the studies of the ancient religions it is noted that, in place after place, the goddess was debased and replaced by a male deity - the worship of a young warrior god and a supreme father god. It has been assumed that this was the Indo-European invasion from the north. But when the cultural connections are considered, it is clear that this ideation moved northward from the South. Perhaps we ought to call it the "Indo-Incan" invasion since we have suggested a connection to the cultures of South America. Archaeology reveals that, after these incursions, the worship of the Mother Goddess fluctuated from city to city. As the invaders gained more and more territory over the next two thousand years, the male began to appear as the dominant husband or even the murderer of the Goddess! The transition was accomplished by brutally violent massacres and territorial acquisition throughout the Near and Middle East. The same is true regarding the conversion of the western world to Christianity. Something is definitely strange about this picture.

This corruption drifted north, as Eliade has noted, changing the shamanic cultures from goddess worshippers to male dominated societies. In studying the legends about the Golden Age, the Antediluvian world, we realize over and over again that these stories talk about a garden where woman and man lived in harmony with each other and nature. That is, until a dominator male god decided that woman had been a very bad girl and must now and forever be subservient to man.

The Chinese *Tao Te Ching* describes a time when the *yin*, or feminine principle, was not yet ruled by *yang*, the male principle, a time when the wisdom of the mother was still honored and followed above all. To many people, references to these times are no more than mere fantasy.

It seems that there were ancient societies organized very differently from ours, and chief among the finds in such digs are the many images of the Deity as female. Thus we are better able to interpret the references to the Great Goddess in ancient art, myth, and even historical writings.

The chief idea of these people was that the Universe was an all-giving mother. Indeed, this idea has survived into our time. In China, the female deities Ma Tsu and Kuan Yin are still widely worshipped as beneficent and compassionate goddesses. Similarly, the veneration of Mary, the Mother of God, is widespread. Even if in Catholic theology she is demoted to non-divine status, her divinity is implicitly recognized by her appellation "Mother of God", as well as by the prayers of millions who daily seek her compassionate protection and solace. In fact, the story of

Jesus' birth, death and resurrection seems to be little more than a reworking of those of earlier 'mystery cults' revolving around a Divine Mother and her son or, as in the worship of Demeter and Kore, her daughter.

It is, of course, reasonable that the deepest understanding of divine power in human form should be female rather than male. After all, life emerges from the body of a woman, and if we are to understand the macrocosm by means of the microcosm, it is only natural to think of the universe as an all-giving Mother from whose womb all life emerges and to which, like the cycles of vegetation, it returns after death to be again reborn.

What is more important to us here is the idea that societies that view the universe as a Mother would also have very different social structures from our own. We might also conjecture that women in such a society would not be seen as subservient. Caring, nurturing, growth and creation would have been valued. At the same time, it does not make sense to think that such societies were "matriarchal" in the sense that women dominated men. They were, instead, by all the evidence, societies in which differences were valued and not equated as evidence of either superiority or inferiority.

What we do know is that "Venus" figurines have been found by the thousands, all over Eurasia, from the Balkans to Lake Baikal in Siberia, across to Willendorf in Austria, and the *Grotte du Pappe* in France. Some scholars (clearly with their minds where they ought not to be) have described them as "erotic art" of the stone-age and propose that they were used in obscene fertility rites!

But is that really so?

Can these ubiquitous female images found from Britain to Malta even be described accurately as erotic "Venus" figures? Most of them are broad-hipped, sometimes pregnant, stylized and frequently faceless. They look like pithoi and are clearly symbolic, just as the cross with the crucified man is a symbol. Future archaeologists who might dig in the remains of our civilization would find equally ubiquitous and symbolic crosses!

The worship of a female creator goddess appears, literally, in every area of the world. What is significant is that the most tangible line of evidence is drawn from the numerous sculptures of women found in the Gravettian-Aurignacian cultures of the Upper Paleolithic Age. Some of these date back to 25,000 B.C., as noted above, and are frequently made of bone or clay. They were often found lying close to the remains of the sunken walls of what are probably the earliest known human-made dwellings on earth. Researchers say that niches or depressions were made in the walls to hold the figures. Such finds have been noted in Spain, France, Germany, Austria, Czechoslovakia and Russia. These sites span a period of at least ten thousand years!

It appears highly probable that the female figurines were idols of a "great mother" cult, practiced by the nomadic Aurignacian mammoth hunters who inhabited the immense Eurasian territories that extended from southern France to Lake Baikal in Siberia.

In the oldest archaeological finds, the Goddess was represented by birds and wavy symbols that indicated water and/or energy. These same wavy lines are retained as the symbol of the Astrological sign of Aquarius which may be the oldest extant symbol of the Great Mother Goddess.

But suddenly, at a certain point, around 5000 years ago, serpents became associated with the goddess, and the wavy lines of water/energy were transmogrified to snakes. What happened to bring about this association? By 4000 B.C., Goddess figures appeared at Ur and Uruk, both on the southern end of the Euphrates river, not far from the Persian Gulf. At about this same period, the Neolithic Badarian and Amaratian cultures of Egypt first appeared. It is at these sites that agriculture first emerged in Egypt.

From that point on, with the invention of writing, history as we know it, emerged in both Sumer and Egypt - about 3000 B.C. (5000 years ago!) In every area of the Near and Middle East, the Goddess was known in historic times. It seems clear that many changes must have taken place in both the forms and modes of worship, but, in various ways, the worship of the Goddess survived into classical Greece and Rome. It was not totally suppressed until the time of the Christian emperors of Rome and Byzantium, who closed the last Goddess Temples about 500 A.D.

It appears that the Goddess ruled alone in the beginning, though she was "married" to the king via a human female representative. Thus the son or brother who was also her lover and consort was part of the goddess religion in much earlier times. This individual was also truly "Semitic" in the sense of being half human and half divine.

Later, as the corruption crept in - seemingly after some dramatic, cataclysmic event - it was this youth - known in various languages as Damuzi, Tammuz, Attis, Adonis, Osiris or Baal - who died in his youth causing an annual period of grief and lamentation among those who paid homage to the Goddess.

For a very long time, this myth was annually enacted representing the fact that time was cyclical the same way the seasons were. It was the passing down of the knowledge of cyclical catastrophes connected to cyclical time. The world might end, but if it did, it was only because it had "run down" and needed to be "wound up" again.

But something changed all that. Somehow, the perception of the End of the World became a terrible punishment that might be prevented by savage sacrifices. And the sub-text of this idea was that time was linear and would end, finally and completely. This idea was brought with the invaders from the South, the murderers of the Goddess, the rapers of the Maidens of the Wells: the dominator religion that drove the sword into the stone.

Part of the cover-up seems to involve blaming this corruption on "northern invaders" or Aryan Indo-Europeans. The invasions of the Aryans took place in waves over a period of up to three thousand years according to standard teachings. They are called invasions because it seems that the arrival of masses of new people was always related, in some way, to evidence of destruction which may or may not have been related to wars of conquest. It may just as well have been related to atmospheric or geologic disruption. Those incursions of prehistoric times are suggested by speculative etymological connections. I propose that there were also invasions from the South, and these invasions brought the corruption that spread like a disease all over the globe, corrupting even the Northern worshippers of the Moon and the Goddess.

What is most significant in the coming of the "Northern invaders" revolutionized not only war, but also art and culture. They introduced the horse-drawn chariot, and the charioteer became a new aristocracy. Since the ancient steppe peoples used carts for traveling and carrying their goods, it seems logical to suggest that it was only after the mixing with the war-like Southern peoples that such vehicles were converted to the use of war and destruction.

Many "experts" tell us that it was these northern people who brought with them the concepts of light as good and dark as evil and of *a supreme male deity*. However, the archaeological and mythographic record suggests otherwise. If, indeed, they later assimilated the supreme male deity to their pantheon, it is clear that these ideas came from the mixing of cultures in Mesopotamia. The interweaving of the two theologies are recorded mythologically in the cultures of this region, and for too long, the blame has been cast in the wrong direction. But most of these ideas were formed before the knowledge of the Southern, American cultures was available. It is in the myths of South America that we discover the origins of the attitude that led to the destruction of the Goddess. It is also in these stories

that we find the beginning of the concept of time as linear, with a beginning and an end, for human beings, at least.

When we were in Mexico in 1997, I noticed an odd sculpture from one of the ancient temples that had been placed in the museum of anthropology. It was of a man whose skull, elbow joint, and thigh had been flayed, while the rest of his flesh was intact. This was a clear representation of not only the components of the skull and crossed thigh bones, but also the ubiquitous "joint" symbol of certain occult secret societies - societies that worship the flaying, blood drinking, male god.

I photographed the carving, and you will note that it also includes a rattlesnake entwined around the body of the flayed man.

The theme of flaying is also present in India in the dance of Shiva on the elephant god. After the elephant is flayed, Shiva dons the skin as a symbol of *acquiring the power of the god.* The same flaying and donning of the skin of the sacrificial victims was practiced by the South American sun worshippers, by the Egyptians, and also - so it seems - by the early Jewish priesthood.

Viracocha was the supreme Inca god, a synthesis of sun god and storm god. One version of the story says that the Creator God Viracocha "rose from Lake Titicaca during the time of darkness to bring forth light". Viracocha was represented as wearing the sun for a crown, with *thunderbolts in his hands*, and tears descending from his eyes as rain. Viracocha made the earth, the stars, the sky and mankind, but his first creation displeased him, so he destroyed it with a flood and made a new, better one, taking to his wanderings - disappearing across the ocean, walking on water - as the Christianized version goes - as a beggar, teaching his new creations the rudiments of civilization, as well as working numerous miracles.

Another version of the story tells us that the Viracocha were *so hated that the people rose up against them and massacred them,* but that *a couple of them escaped across the ocean.* This is the most likely scenario considering all of the evidence. It also reminds us of the hatred of the

Egyptian labyrinth. We should note that there are significant artistic representations in both South America and Egypt of "black headed" peoples sacrificing blond or red-headed men.

The term "viracocha" also refers to a group of men named the *suncasapa* or bearded ones - they were the mythic soldiers of Viracocha, also called the "angelic warriors of Viracocha". Later one of the Inca Kings (the eighth Inca ruler) took the name of Viracocha. But in all cases, we see the "hint" that they were Aryans was provided by the Spanish friars, and is not supported by the archaeological evidence.

On the Gateway of the Sun, the famous carved figure on the decorated archway in the ancient (pre-Incan) city of Tiahuanaco most likely represents Viracocha, flanked by 48 winged effigies, 32 with human faces and 16 with condor's heads.

What seems to be evident is that there were people who rose to power in South America known as the Viracocha. After the Spaniards destroyed all of the records of the natives of the Americas, they wrote their own versions, which included stories of the Viracocha being blond, Aryan types. This was due to the fact that the Spaniards noted a certain similarity between the myths of the Incan civilizing gods and their own religious beliefs. This was later taken up by Thor Heyerdahl, but a careful examination of the records gives no firm evidence that these individuals were Aryans. The evidence of Aryan types on Easter Island has been convincingly explained as the result of the survivors of a shipwreck taking up residence and has nothing to do with the "travels of the Incas". However, the links between certain scripts found on Easter Island, and the script of the Indus Valley, and certain mythical motifs, strongly suggest a connection between South America, Easter Island, India, Mesopotamia, Egypt, and the religion of the Jews. Of course, it *is* possible that such civilizing influence was transmitted by "big, blond, sailor" types who rose to power in South America and were destroyed in revolutions by the enslaved, native masses. Images of red headed men being sacrificed are known in South America, so perhaps they were viewed as "gods" and the indigenous population sought to acquire their powers by "flaying" them and donning their skins. We realize that skin color has been an issue throughout human history, so it would be reasonable to think that the primitive mind might see the white skin as a transmitter of power. Of course, that doesn't even address the question as to why light skinned individuals were perceived as "higher caste" and worthy of emulation to begin with, but that's another issue.

So we suggest "Viracocha" left the lands of the Inca and traveled across the Pacific. In India, we find the most interesting Indus Valley civilization which - upon visual inspection of the ruins - presents a striking resemblance to the ruins of the ancient cities of South America. The only difference was that the ability to shape megaliths seems to have been lost, and the Indus valley cities, while *stylistically* similar, are built of brick. As mentioned, we can note the similarity of certain writings found on Easter Island to the Indus Valley script.

At a later point in time, the movement was north to Mesopotamia where again, certain sigils found on cylinder seals are similar to the Indus Valley script. The rigid caste system of the Incas is found also in India.

Another item of considerable interest that connects Egypt to South America is the Ica skulls compared to the representations of elongated skulls among the Egyptian royalty. This is a subject I will cover more thoroughly in another volume. The point at the moment is to make clear the obvious connection between some very strange things in South

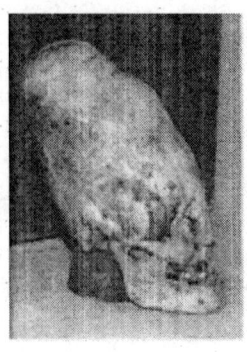

America, and other strange things in Egypt and the Middle East, all connected in mysterious ways to the creation of three monotheistic religions, and the present day struggle among the three.

At this point, we find the Viracocha types from across the Pacific, making their way up the Indian peninsula, to meet with a group of big blond nomadic herdsmen from the Altai Mountains, probably in Mesopotamia. The Southern male god was adopted by the Altai Aryans in their mingling with the Southerners that invaded India from across the Sea.[51] "And the sons of God looked upon the daughters of men and saw that they were fair and took wives..."

This new "Aryan" god was frequently depicted as a storm god, high on a mountain, blazing with the light of fire or lightning from the thunderbolts he held in his hand. In many of these transposed myths, the goddess is depicted as a serpent or dragon, associated with darkness and evil. Sometimes the dragon is neuter or even male, but in such cases, is closely associated with the goddess, usually as her son.

The Goddess religion seems to have assimilated the male deities into the older forms of worship, and survived as the popular religion of the people for thousands of years after the initial Southern Sumerian invasions. But her position had been greatly lowered and continued to

---

[51] See *Gods of the Cataclysm* for the evidence of this route of transfer of ideas.

decline. In the form of Judaism and eventually Christianity, the male sun god finally suppressed the religion of the goddess.

And here we come to the most interesting thing of all: it is in the accounts of these mixed Aryans that we find the original religious ideas of the Hebrews. It is also from this mixing - the region from which Zarathustra emerged - that we get the original ideas of the End of the World. In the mixing of the two idealogies, there is the mountain-top god who blazes with light; there is the duality between light and darkness symbolized as good and evil; there is the myth of the male deity defeating the serpent; and there is the supreme leadership of a ruling class: the priestly Levites; all of these are to be found in both the Indo-Incan and Hebrew religious concepts and politics!

In India, we suggest that there is another way to interpret the evidence. We propose a "Southern Sumerian" invasion from across the sea, meeting and mingling with the Aryan invasion from the North which resulted in the assimilation of the Goddess worshippers and the emerging dominance of the Southern male god. The books known as the *Vedas* were a record of the Aryans in India. They were written between 1500 and 1200 B.C., in Sanskrit using scripts possibly borrowed from the Akkadians.

The "Southern" attitude toward women is made clear in two sentences attributed to Indra in the *Rg Veda: "The mind of woman brooks not discipline. Her intellect has little weight"*. And orthodox Jewish males daily thank god that they were not born women! This leads us to the obvious idea: The Indo-Incan patterns were either adopted by the Jews, or the Sumerian/Jewish priests were Indo-Incans from the start.

The Indo-Aryan *Rg Veda* says that "in the very beginning there was only '*asura*', or 'living power'." The *asura* broke down into two cosmic groups. One was the enemies of the Danavas, or Dityas, whose mother was the Goddess Danu or Diti; the other group, were known as the A-Dityas. Aside from the fact that this clearly depicts exactly what we are discussing here, the title betrays the fact that this mythical structure was created in reaction to the presence of the worshippers of Diti, since A-Ditya literally means "not Dityas", or "not people of Diti".

> "[M]many sociologists believe that some kind of a hierarchical social order, in terms of an individual's occupation and duties, was in place perhaps *ahead of the arrival of the Aryans*. Its evolution into the caste or the *varna* system as we know today - with the four distinct castes of Brahmin, Kshatriya, Vaisya and Sudra in the order of social standing - probably occurred with the settling of the Aryans who sanctified and legitimised the social order in their own terms which had a distinct religious underpinning. Some sociologists hold that the societal

stratification in terms of rights and duties of the individual was a creation of the Aryans in their bid to exercise power over the indigenous proto-Asian populations of North India. [...]

In recent times, with the rise of strident nationalism in the form of 'Hindutva' ideology, which rejects the premise that Aryans were outsiders and views them as part of the continuum from the Indus valley civilisation, an unequivocal answer to this may have political implications. While material evidence of ancient history has not been able to resolve this issue, modern population genetics, based on analyses of the variations in the DNA in population sets, has tools to provide a more authoritative answer. Certain inherited genes carry the imprint of this information through the ages. [...]

An international study led by Michale J. Bamshad of the Eccles Institute of Human Genetics of the University of Utah of caste origins has found (the findings have been reported in a recent issue of the journal *Genome Research*) that members of the upper castes are genetically more similar to Europeans, *Western Eurasians* to be specific, whereas the lower castes are more similar to Asians. This finding is in tune with the expectations based on historical reasoning and the prevalent views of many social historians. In exercising their superiority over native proto-Asian populations, the Aryans would have appointed themselves to higher rank castes. [...]

Interestingly, an analysis of the genetic variations in the markers associated with the maternally inherited mtDNA and paternally inherited Y-chromosome show strikingly different trends. Maternally inherited DNA was overall found to be more similar to Asians than to Europeans, though the similarity to Europeans increases as we go up the caste ladder. Paternally inherited DNA, on the other hand, was overall more similar to Europeans than to Asians but, unlike in the case of maternal inheritance, with no significant variation in affinity across the castes. This is intriguing, but there is a plausible explanation. Migrating Eurasian populations are likely to have been mostly males who integrated into the upper castes and took native women. Inter-caste marriage practices, while generally taboo, are occasionally allowed, in which women can marry into an upper caste and move up in the social hierarchy. However, such upward mobility is not permissible for men. The caste labels of men are thus permanent, while women, by means of their limited mobility, cause a gene flow across caste barriers. This is the reason, according to the researchers, for the differing affinities of gender-specific genes among castes to continental populations." [52]

One of the major Indo-Aryan gods was known as Indra, Lord of the Mountains, "he who overthrows cities". Upon obtaining the promise of

---

[52] Ramachandran, R., *The Genetics of Caste*, Frontline, Volume 18 - Issue 12, Jun. 09 - 22, 2001; India's National Magazine, from the publishers of THE HINDU.

supremacy if he succeeded in *killing Danu and Her son Vrtra*, he does accomplish the act, thus achieving kingship among the *A-Dityas*. This reminds us of the early Sumerian text reported above:

> "The was founded by Enmebaragesi, a contemporary of Gilgamesh. The name breaks down as follows: *enetik - eme - ebakin - aragikor - ageriko - ezi* which can be transliterated to *'from* that time on - female - harvest - lustful - notorious - to domesticate' or 'From that time on the lustful, notorious harvest female was domesticated'.

> This 'name' tells us in no uncertain terms that the time of the Goddess was on the decline, because male domination had arrived with the Sumerians."

In a hymn to Indra in the *Rg Veda* which describes the event, Danu and Her son are first described as serpent demons; later, as they lie dead, they are symbolized as cow and calf. After the murders, "the cosmic waters flowed and were pregnant". They in turn gave birth to the sun. This concept of the sun god emerging from the primeval waters appears in other Indo-Sumerian-Incan myths and also occurs in connection with two of the prehistoric invasions. We suggest that all of this connects such events to times of cataclysm wherein the sun is "darkened" or concealed by dust and clouds.

The *Rg Veda* also refers to an ancestral father god known both as Prajapati and Dyaus Pitar. Dyaus Pitar is known as the "supreme father of all". The spread of the Indo-Sumerian culture mixed with the Aryan incursions brought with it the origins of the Hindu religion and the concept of light-colored skin being perceived as better or more "pure" than darker skins. (The Sanskrit word for caste, "varna" actually means color.)

The Indo-Sumerian-Aryan beliefs are found in Iran, though the records are very late - dating back only as far as 600 B.C. What the experts suggest is that the Indians and early Iranians - prior to the arrival of the Sumerians - were derived from the same ethnic group and had been established on the Iranian plateau from about 4000 B.C. speaking a Vedic Sanskrit dialect.

Though there is a considerable change from the *Rg Veda* to the Iranian *Avesta*, we still find the great father who represents light, with a new name: Ahura Mazda. He is the Lord of Light and his abode is on a mountaintop glowing with golden light. The duality of light and dark is inherent in Iranian religious thought. Ahura Mazda is on high in goodness, and the devil figure, Ahriman is "deep down in darkness". We note in this the mixing of the Shamanic concepts with the Inca-Sumerian idea of a anthropomorphized god.

In the Iranian texts of 200 A.D., known as *Manichean*, we again find good and evil equated with light and dark. However, we are told in these writings that the problems of humanity are *caused by a mixture of the two*. And here, Mithra appears as the one who defeats the "demons of darkness".

There is another clue that deserves note: the name of the Guanche Devil, *Guayota*. In the Iranian texts there is a character named *Gayo Mareta* who is the "first man". He seems to relate to Indra in the Indian versions. *Gauee* or *gavee* in Sanskrit means cow. *Mrityu* in Sanskrit means death or murder, surviving in the Indo-Aryan German language as *mord*, meaning murder, and in the Indo-European English language as the word murder itself. Thus *Gavo Mareta* appears to be named 'Cow Murderer'. Danu was symbolized as the cow Goddess, whose worship is best known from Egypt before Narmer, and Indra Her murderer, so Gayo Mareta may once have held this position in Iran.

In the *Pahlavi Books* of about 400 B.C. it was written, "From Gayo Mareta, Ahura fashioned the family of the Aryan lands, the seed of the Aryan lands". We notice right away that this is an inversion. It is pretty clear that in the most ancient times, the Goddess was worshipped, and Gayo Mareta - Guayota, the Devil, murdered her.

In any event, we are certainly entitled to speculate on the fact that the Guanches, Aryans, a group isolated for possibly thousands of years, spoke a near cousin to the language of Sargon, a worshipper of the Goddess, and that the name of the "evil" in their language, was almost identical to the name of the hero in the *Pahlavi books*. Due to the fact that the Guanches were isolated for a very long, unknown period of time, one begins to suspect that they retained their original language from very ancient times. Perhaps there was a global, antediluvian language. And perhaps this gives us a clue as to who was really "on first"?

When we consider the "ancient Egyptian language", we realize that it developed after the conquest of Narmer, and there is a very strong suggestion that Narmer had close ties with Sumeria. The famous Narmer Palette has distinctive Sumerian motifs, and also includes a row of men - sacrificial victims - with their heads cut off and placed between their thighs. Skull and Crossbones?

The Shell Game

As early as the fourth millennium B.C., a group entered the Tigris-Euphrates area. They were described as "newcomers from the east". The statement derives a certain support from tradition; "as they jouneyed from the east they found a plain in the land of Shinar [Babylon] and they dwelt there" [*Genesis* XI, 2]; but it is based on the material evidence of the pottery of al Ubaid and of Susa respectively, and on that evidence it is generally agreed that these people were related, culturally and presumably ethnically, to the early inhabitants of Elam.

Some scholars suggest that the Ubaid people brought the *Sumerian* language, which is neither Semitic nor Indo-European. Aratta is a place name often mentioned in Sumerian texts.

The Ubaid people established a major settlement in the place later known as Eridu. They broke up the Halaf culture, and wreaked devastation upon them. These Ubaids spread as far north as Lake Urmia and Lake Van, close to the Iranian-Russian border. This section was later known as Ararat or Urartu which could be corruptions of Aratta. The name "Eridu" could also be a corruption of Aratta, suggesting the original homeland.

In about 4000 B.C., the Ubaid people built a temple at Eridu which appears to be the first built on a high platform. At this temple, *not a single goddess figurine was found.* Interestingly, a statue found in graves of the Ubaid people depicted a mother and baby with *lizard-like features.*

It is noteworthy that the Sumerians and present day "Semites" only differed in language, not religion, culture or politics.

The deity worshipped at Eridu in historic times was the god Enki. Before this, the god of the shrine seems to have been a fish or water god who rose up out of the water exactly like Viracocha, had scales, and was a civilizer-teacher of language and culture. Enki was thought of later as the god of the waters and was described as riding around in his boat. He was also described as "he who rides". This concept of the fish or water god is similar to one found in a fragment of an Indo-Aryan Hittite tablet which tells of a sun god who rose from the water with fish on his head. It is also similar to the idea of the sun god who was born from the cosmic waters released by Indra by the deaths of Danu and Vrtra. Though Enki is not generally designated as a sun god, in the myth of Marduk he is named as Marduk's father and Marduk is called the "son of the sun".

The Ubaid people are credited with developing irrigation canals in Eridu which could hint at their origin in places that were along rivers and streams and where fish were common. Another clue to the identity of these people is the institution of kingship and the mention of the name Alalu as the very first king of Sumer in the king lists of the earliest part of the second millennium. According to these tablets which refer to a prehistoric period, it was in Eridu that "kingship was first lowered from heaven". Sounds rather like the Inca myth of Viracocha.

Now, let's think about this for a moment. We have a god with a fish on his head, thereby associated with scales, and who is described as "he who rides". This scaly god not only rides, he rose from the water like the sun! Also, he was born from the deaths of the Mother goddess and her son. Mountains of fire are involved, gold, and kingship being "lowered from heaven". It rather sounds like UFOs coming up out of the water as they have so often been reported to do in more modern times, or descending on mountain tops.

A third male deity - An or Anu - comes onto the Sumerian stage sometime after the beginning of the second millenium - the same period that the Hurrians are known to have entered the area, so they may well have brought this Anu with them.

In the early Sumerian period the name Anu is relatively obscure, and his name does not appear on any of the eighteen lists belonging to this period.

Anu appears as the successor to Alalu in the Hurrian and Hittite Kumarbi myth. But most interesting is his appearance in the later myth of Marduk, "the son of the sun". Here we learn that Enki was first asked to subdue the Creatress-Goddess, whom they call Tiamat, and was not able, though he did manage to kill her husband Apsu, thus becoming Lord of the Abzu (primeval waters) himself. Anu was then asked to subdue Tiamat, but according to the legend when he confronted Her, he cringed in fear and refused to complete his mission. Finally Marduk, son of Enki, was willing, though only upon the promise of the supreme position among all other deities if he succeeded. This previously secured promise brings to mind the one Indra requested before murdering Danu and Her son Vrtra; both of these myths were probably written down at about the same period (1600-1400 B.C.) though they are undoubtedly far older. In passing, I would like to note that the name *Tiamat* is similar to some of the earliest known names of male deities including Tiu, Tyr, Thor, etc, plus *Mat* which reminds us of Egyptian Maat, which was a goddess who represented truth, law and universal order.

This legend, known as the *Enuma Elish*, which explains the supremacy of Marduk, has long been designated as Babylonian and therefore Akkadian and Semitic. But more recent research suggests that, though Marduk was known in the Hammurabi period, the myth claiming his supremacy did not actually appear until *after* the Kassites, another tribe, had conquered Babylon. Saggs points out that "none of the extant texts belonging to it is earlier than the first millennium" and that "it has been suggested that in fact *this work arose only in the Kassite period*, a time now known to have been one of intense literary activity". Gurney tells us that ,"The *names of Indian deities* are found to form an element in the names of the Kassite rulers of Babylonia".[53]

In about 2100 B.C., a *Sumerian* king named Ur Nammu declared that he would establish justice in the land. He did away with the heavy duties and taxes that were burdening the people at that time and "rid the land of the *big sailors* who seized oxen, sheep and donkeys'.' [54] One suspects that they were Aryan types corrupted by the worship of the male storm god.

Now, after all this invading, conquering and demolishing of the Goddess Worship over in the Tigris-Euphrates area, the same thing happened later on in Egypt with Narmer-Menes!

There is considerable evidence for contact between Egypt and Sumer. "Abundant evidence of Mesopotamian cultural influence is found at this time in Egypt." Significant is the fact that cylinder seals (a specifically Mesopotamian invention) occur there, together with methods of building in brick foreign to Egypt but typical of the *Jemdet Nasr* culture of Mesopotamia *and the Indus Valley civilization*. Mesopotamian motifs and objects also begin to be represented in Egyptian art, such as boats of Mesopotamian type. The idea of writing, though it was expressed quite differently in Egypt, seems to have developed more or less coevally with Mesopotamia. Paintings in early dynastic tombs portray a conical basket type of fish trap, nearly identical to those of the Ertebolle people of northern Europe who were descended from the Maglemosians, a European Mesolithic culture, which links us back to the Akkadians as being from the North. The male deity of Egypt arrived with the invaders, and was portrayed as the sun riding in a boat!

Professor Walter Emery spent some forty-five years excavating the ancient tombs and pyramids of Egypt. Discussing the arrival of these people, he writes:

"Whether this incursion took the form of gradual infiltration or horde invasion is uncertain but the balance of evidence... strongly suggests the latter. ...we see a style of art which some think may be Mesopotamian, or even Syrian in origin, and a scene which may represent a battle at sea against invaders... [in these] representations we have typical native ships of Egypt and strange vessels with high prow and stem of unmistakable Mesopotamian origin...

At any rate, towards the close of the fourth millennium BC we find the people known traditionally as the 'Followers of Horus' apparently forming an aristocracy or master race ruling over the whole of Egypt. The

[53] Gurney, O.R., *The Hittites* (London, New York: Penguin revised edition 1991).
[54] Hawkes, Jacquetta, The first great civilizations; life in Mesopotamia, the Indus Valley and Egypt (New York: Knopf 1973).

theory of the existence of this master race is supported by the discovery that graves of the late pre-dynastic period in the northern part of Upper Egypt were found to contain the anatomical remains of a people whose *skulls are of greater size* and whose bodies were larger than those of the natives, the difference being *so marked* that any suggestion that these people derived from the earlier stock is impossible." [55]

These invaders were known to the Egyptians as the "*Shemsu Hor*", or people of Hor. And, of course, they brought with them their male god, *Hor-Wer* or Great Hor. By 2900 B.C. pictures of this sun god show him riding in his "boat of heaven".

It certainly makes one wonder if a brilliant flying ship rising up out of the water would cause the ancient peoples to connect a boat (that goes on water) with flying through the air while looking like the sun! And, over and over again we are finding this image or juxtaposition of images.

According to Emery, the name of the first king of the First Dynasty, known as Narmer or Menes in Manetho's history of 270 B.C., was actually Hor-Aha. Later, the name of Hor appears to have been incorporated into the more ancient goddess religion as the "son who dies". This has led to a lot of confusion between the two "Hors", Horus the Elder, god of light of the invaders, and Horus the Younger, the son of the goddess Isis.

Hor later was transmogrified into Horus by the Greeks, and is depicted as fighting a ritual combat with another male deity known as Set. Set is supposed to be his uncle, the brother of his mother Isis and father Osiris. The combat was supposed to symbolize the overcoming of darkness or Set, by light, symbolized by Hor.

In Sanskrit the word '*sat*' means to *destroy by hewing into pieces*. In the myth of Osiris, it was Set who killed Osiris and cut his body into fourteen pieces which naturally reminds us of the sacrifices of the Moche. However, the word "*set*" is also defined as "queen" or "princess" in Egyptian! "*Au Set*", known as Isis by the Greeks, means, "exceeding queen"!

In the myth of this ritual combat, Set tried to mate sexually with Horus; this is usually interpreted to have been an extreme insult. But the most primitive identity of the figure Set, before the wavy lines of water or energy became serpents, may be found in the goddess religion, and this combat, just as with the combat of Marduk with Tiamat, may have represented the suppression and destruction of the Goddess religion. Of

---

[55] Quoted by Stone, op. cit.

course, the conquering invaders presented themselves as "saviors" and their conquest as a triumph of light over darkness!

So it has always been. At the present moment, George Bush is telling the Iraqi people the same thing; he is "saving" them by death and destruction.

Nevertheless, the followers of Hor established the institution of kingship in Egypt. And, again, marrying the representative of the goddess in order to "steal her power" was an important part of the assumption of kingship as was recorded in the story of Solomon - he married an Egyptian Princess. We may justifiably compare the name of "Hor" to the Hurrians or Horites who came from India to Sumer.

Around the time of the Second Dynasty, the town of Heliopolis (known to the Egyptians as Annu!) became the home of a school of scribal priests who also worshipped a sun god who rode in a boat. In this town they used the name Ra. In Sanskrit, *Ra* means royal or exalted on high. This prefix is found in the Sanskrit word for king, *raja* and queen, *rani*. It survives in the German word *ragen*, to reach up, in French as *roi*, meaning king, as well as in the English words *royal*, *reign* and *regal*.

In the pyramid texts of the Fifth Dynasty, Horus was equated with Ra. Both Horus and Ra were closely connected, at times competitively, with the right to kingship. As Ra-Harakhty, Ra is identical with Horus of the Horizon, both meaning the sun at rising. Ra too is portrayed as the sun who rides across the heavens sitting in his sacred boat. Again, why a boat in the heavens?

Ra's boat was said to emerge out of the primeval waters, much as Enki was said to ride his boat in the deep waters of the Abzu of Eridu, or as the Indo-Aryan sun god was said to have emerged from the cosmic waters, (as in the myth of the sun god in the water who rises from the sea with fish on his head), so too, Ra rose from the waters each morning.

As the name of Horus was assimilated into the Goddess religion, as the son of Isis, the priests of Memphis proposed another concept of the great father god. This time his name was Ptah, curiously like the Sanskrit *Pitar*. The texts concerning him describe the creation of all existence, suggesting that Ptah was there first. This time we are told that it was through an act of masturbation that Ptah caused all the other gods to come into being, thus totally eliminating the need for a divine Mother!

This idea of the masturbating god is not new. One of the Sumerian gods, Enki, was supposed to have masturbated and thereby caused the Tigris and Euphrates rivers to flow!

Even though these conquering Indo-Incans came in wave after wave, bringing their gods who ride in shining boats in the sky, the goddess religion still survived. This very fact may indicate the presence of another group who worked quietly to preserve the ancient truths in the face of almost overwhelming opposition. The new male gods were assimilated and synthesized, creating an almost impossible to sort mish-mash of gods and goddesses.

With the knowledge that the worship of the Goddess was violently overturned by invading Indo-Incans, descendants of the Incan Sun worshippers, whose objective was to forestall another "end of the world" with the sacrifice of enormous numbers of human beings, we may better understand the transitions and inversions that have occurred in our myths and legends, as well as our concepts of time. With this understanding, we are free to pursue a more open and reasonable series of speculations as to what the End of the World, and all the prophecies related to it, might be about.

Just as there was a Dark Age surrounding the period of time in which the Old Testament came into being, (during which time Monotheistic Judaism - the parent of Christianity and Islam - was imposed forcibly on the Canaanites), we have a similar period of Dark Ages enveloping the development and codification of the New Testament and the imposition of Monotheistic Christianity on the Western World, and Islam on those who were susceptible to neither of the former two.

Don't you find that curious?

The End of Time

The god of the Jews is a personality who purportedly ceaselessly intervenes in history and who reveals his will through events. Historical facts thus acquired a religious value in the fact that they were specific situations between man and god, and history became the epiphany of god. This conception was continued and magnified by Christianity. We can see the seeds of the original myths here, but we can also see the major distortions.

In monotheism, *every event is definitely situated in time* - a given time and no other - and is not *reversible;* it is a historical event with weight and value in and of itself. That weight is placed upon the shoulders of mankind, individually and collectively.

In Judaism's daughter, Christianity, the Messianic hope, the victory over the forces of darkness, is projected indefinitely into the future and will only happen *once* in terms of linear time. Further, there is only ONE who can accomplish this conquest of darkness, and man's only hope is to give up his will to this one who has been crucified and resurrected to symbolize his verity, even if he has really done nothing to change the state of the world in REAL time. When the Messiah comes again (never mind that he was supposed to have already been here and global conditions did not improve), the world will be saved once and for all, and history will cease to exist - and most of humanity along with it, not to mention a "third of the angels", and so on.

This idea of irreversible, linear time, was imposed upon mankind through violence and exclusion, serving as the basis for the philosophy of history that Christianity, from St. Augustine on, has labored to construct.

In case you didn't notice what just happened here, let me make it a little clearer. The concept of linear time gives value to the "future" as an *end* to everything. That's it; there is nothing more. Further, the arbiter of that future is *one* god, who, I might add, is his own surety because he has helpfully announced at the beginning that he IS the *one* god. This one god has a select group of servants who will be preserved to the exclusion of all others in some way if they obey him, and destroyed if they disobey him. But, of course, it is "free will choice" as to whether to believe this or not. It doesn't sound like a choice; it sounds like an ultimatum!

We begin to smell a rat here, a hint that the introduction of the concept of linear time was the *raison d'être* for the introduction of monotheism.

For the most part, our modern world is predicated upon linear time. Thus, the *raison d'être* can be dimly seen by those who have been tracking with me here: it is that linear time is a supreme weapon to use against the mind of man in terms of *control and domination*! Monotheism is a myth that establishes a particular identity as an antithesis, against another - actually, just about all Others! The ultimate club of elitists!

We come to the fact that most of the Old Testament is a chronicle of genocide and horrendous practices of human and animal sacrifice. In the New Testament, we find that the work of a remarkable man who lived two thousand years ago in the Middle East, whose teachings gave birth to Christianity, has been replaced by a "story" based a human sacrifice ritual which was an already ages old corruption - the ubiquitous solar/fertility cult. At about the same time this was done, Judaism was revived, the Cathars were destroyed, and the Crusades were begun to discover some mysterious object in the "Holy Land".

Curious, eh?

In any event, the concept of the barbaric custom of blood sacrifice passed into Christianity. It is, in fact, the heart of Christianity as it is understood by Christians today. However, making Christ the "once for all atonement" for everyone had curious consequences. With such an event as an "example", it became quite easy to manipulate the populace to willingly emulate this self-sacrifice, and thus, the motivation for the Crusades, and endless wars and genocide by "civilized" peoples was made "normal".

Fiendishly clever, I say.

The word "iron" may be related to the word "Aryan", and the mining and smelting of iron which was associated with these peoples, was a closely guarded secret for many centuries.

The original Hattians may have been related to the goddess worshipping people of Catal Huyuk which is about 125 miles from the Hittite capital of Hattusas. The goddesses of the Hatti appear to have survived from an even earlier Hattian religion. In several texts the Goddess was simply called "The Throne", a title associated with Isis in Egypt and may be related to Cassiopeia, known as the "Enthroned Queen", and the "hump of the camel", a throne of sorts.

Now, Ms. Stone has brought up a very interesting thing regarding a group called Luvians, Luvischen or Louvites. They seem to be a group of Indo-Europeans who lived directly south of the Hittites in Cilicia, close to the Toros Mountains which is practically the same area as Catal Huyuk once flourished.

Very little is known of these people except that they were authors of what has become known as the Hittite hieroglyphs. These are picture words that appear most often on royal monuments and in a few texts. These hieroglyphs are still, for the most part, a mystery.

Professor Albright says that the Luvians occupied most of southern Asia Minor not later than the third millennium B.C. Another writer, R.A. Crossland suggests a later date. Professor Lloyd agrees with Crossland saying:

> "In about 2300 B.C. a great wave of Indo-European *speaking* peoples, speaking a dialect known as Luvian, seems to have swept over Anatolia... their progress was marked with widespread destruction..." [quoted by Stone, 1976]

The name Luvian comes from the Hittite texts which refer to the land of these people as Luviya and their language as Luvili. French archaeologists call them Louvites; the Germans call them Luvischen.

The one thing that has come out of the partial translation of their hieroglyphs is that their major deity was the storm god whose name was Tarhund, Tarhunta or Tarhuis. The only material so far found in their texts is what is referred to as the "magic type; spells and incantations inserted into ritual texts". The fact that this totally religious material was written in their own hieroglyphs while other means of writing was available could indicate that they were a priestly caste of the Indo-Europeans. Other indications that seem to confirm this are the fact that *scribal schools producing myths in Hurrian, Hittite and Akkadian appear to have been located in the Luvian territory of Kizzuwatna.*

A priestly class of Indo-Europeans with scribal schools who worshipped the Weather God, whose similarity to Jehovah in all respects, is startling, was busily turning out myths for all the local and not so local populations? Magic spells and incantations? Oh, my! What have we found here?! Sounds an awful lot like what was going on in Spain and France during Medieval times when Kaballah was being developed.

It is certainly beginning to look like the Hebrew religion was not, as is taught, formed in a vacuum or necessarily delivered directly from the hand or mouth of God!

Both of the two creation accounts in Genesis have long been noted to be related to Mesopotamian creation stories. The stories of the origins of civilization in the Bible are markedly similar to Phoenician tales. The divine "fiat" in the beginning: "Let there be light", is derived from Egyptian myth and this motif achieved its classic form in the cult of Heliopolis. In some of the earliest forms of this myth, there is the primeval ocean whose origin is not explained, from which emerges the creator god who is either reptilian, insect or birdlike, and he engages in the creative activity as an act of expectoration, self-fertilization, or masturbation - he "broods upon the face of the waters".

> "The pinnacle of the quest after the First Principle in ancient Egypt was reached with the composition of the so-called **Memphite Theology**. In form a dramatic-cultic text glossed by a commentary at the end, the **Memphite Theology** is found on a block now in the British Museum that dates to the reign of Shabaka (712-697 B.C.), who claims to have found the original on a papyrus 'which the ancestors had made, worm-eaten and unknown from beginning to end'.

> ...The contents became known (again?) only at the beginning of the Kushite period around 710 B.C. and were disseminated during the following two centuries.

> The commentary, among other novel ideas, advances the proposition that the essence of the creator god, Ptah, resides in 'heart' and 'tongue, [keeping in mind that the Egyptian intent in the word 'heart' is our present concept of consciousness/mind.] ...That is to say mind and creative utterance. Mind conceived of being, and the creative word made it concrete. So the creation itself becomes in a sense an emanation of the creator, or at least that part of it which has life-force:

'Thus it happened that the heart (mind) and the tongue gained control over every other member of the body through the teaching that he (Ptah) is in every body and every mouth, of all gods, all men, all cattle, all creeping things and everything that lives, by thinking and commanding everything that he wishes.'

...It seems premature to commit oneself to a judgment on the possibilities of Egyptian influence on the Genesis creation account. It may in fact prove to be a simple case of linear borrowing, albeit *accompanied by a purposeful intent to 'demythologize.'"* [Redford, *Egypt, Canaan, and Israel in Ancient Times*, 1992, Princeton; emphasis, mine.]

The oldest extant texts of the Old Testament in Hebrew are those found at Qumran which date only to 2 or 3 centuries before Christ. The prior oldest version was a Greek translation from about the same period! The earliest complete **Hebrew** text dates only from the tenth century A.D.!!! Something is wrong with this picture.

It is generally believed from textual analysis, that a very small part of this bible was written about 1000 B.C. and the remainder about 600 B.C. And, the Bible as we know it, is the result of many changes throughout centuries and is contradictory in so many ways we don't have space to catalog them all!

The first five books of the Bible, the Pentateuch, also known as the Torah, upon which Kaballah is based, were supposed to have been written by Moses. Early Christian and Jewish tradition held this view even though nowhere in these five books does the text say that Moses was the author.

Biblical scholars generally date Abraham to about 1800 - 1700 B.C. The same scholars date Moses to 1300 or 1250 B.C. However, if we track the generations as listed in the Bible, we find that there are only seven generations between and including these two patriarchal figures! Four hundred years is a bit long for seven generations. Allowing 35 to 40 years per generation, places Abraham at about 1550 B.C. and Moses at about 1300 B.C. Tracking back to Noah, using the generations listed in the Bible, one arrives at a date of about 2000 to 1900 B.C. - about the time of the arrival of the Indo-Europeans into the Near East.

Using the Bible as source material presents a number of very serious problems. There are many contradictions in the text that cannot be reconciled by the standard theological mental gymnastics. In some places, events are described as happening in a certain order, and later the Bible will say that those events happened in a different order. In one place, the Bible will say that there are two of something, and in another it will say that there were 14 of the same thing. On one page, the Bible will say that the Moabites did something, and then a few pages later, it will say that the

Midianites did exactly the same thing. There is even an instance in which Moses is described as going to the Tabernacle before Moses built the Tabernacle! (I guess Moses was a time traveler!)

There are things in the Pentateuch that pose problems: it includes things that Moses could not have known if he lived when he is claimed to have lived. And, there is one case in which Moses said something he could not have said: the text gives an account of Moses' death, which it is hardly likely that Moses described. The text also states that Moses was the humblest man on earth! Well, as one commentator noted, it is not likely that the humblest man on earth would point out that he is the humblest man on earth!

All of these problems were taken care of for most of the past two thousand years by the Inquisition. Meanwhile, even the Jewish commentators took care of the problems in novel ways. The contradictions were not contradictions, they were only "apparent contradictions"! They could all be explained by "interpretation"! Usually, these interpretations were more fantastic than the problems, I might add. Moses was able to "know things he couldn't have known" because he was a prophet! The medieval biblical commentators, such as Rashi and Nachmanides, were *very* skillful in reconciling the irreconcilable!

In the 11th century, a real troublemaker, Isaac ibn Yashush, a Jewish court physician in Muslim Spain, mentioned the distressing fact that a list of Edomite kings that appears in Genesis 36 named a few kings who lived long after Moses was already dead. Ibn Yashush suggested the obvious, that the list was written by someone who lived after Moses. He became known as "Isaac the Blunderer". The guy who memorialized clever Isaac this way was a fellow named Abraham ibn Ezra, a 12th century rabbi in Spain. But Ibn Ezra presents us with a conundrum because he also wrote about problems in the text of the Torah. He alluded to several passages that appeared not to be from Moses' own hand because they referred to Moses in the third person, used terms Moses would not have known, described places that Moses had never been, and used language that belonged to an altogether different time and place than the milieu of Moses. He wrote, very mysteriously, "And if you understand, then you will recognize the truth. And he who understands will keep silent".

So, why did he call Ibn Yashush a "Blunderer"? Obviously because the guy had to open his big mouth and give away the secret that the Torah was not what it was cracked up to be and lots of folks who were totally "into" this Jewish mysticism business would lose interest. And keeping the interest of the students and seekers after power was a pretty big business. It still is.

In 14th century Damascus, a scholar by the name of Bonfils wrote a work in which he said, "and this is evidence that this verse was written in the Torah later, and Moses did not write it...". He wasn't even denying the "revealed" character of the Torah, just making reasonable comment. Three hundred years later, his work was reprinted with this comment edited out!

In the fifteenth century, Tostatus, Bishop of Avila also pointed out that the passages about the death of Moses couldn't have been written by Moses. He then said that there was an "old tradition" that Joshua, Moses' successor, wrote this part of the account. A hundred years later, Luther Carlstadt commented that this was difficult to follow because the account of Moses' death is written in the same style as the text that precedes it.

Well, of course, things were beginning to be examined more critically with the arrival of Protestantism, and the Inquisition tried, but failed, to keep a complete grip on the matter. But, it's funny what belief will do. In this case, it was decided that the problem was solvable by claiming that, yes, Moses wrote the Torah, but editors went over them later and added an occasional word or phrase of their own!

Wow. Glad we solved that one!

The really funny thing is that one of the proponents of this idea of editorial insertions, who was really trying to preserve the "textus receptus" status of the Bible, was blacklisted by the Catholic Index. His book was put on the list of "prohibited books"!

Well, finally, after hundreds of years of tiptoeing around this issue, some scholars came right out and said that Moses didn't write the majority of the Pentateuch. The first to say it was Thomas Hobbes. He pointed out that the text sometimes states that this or that is so "to this day". The problem with this is that a writer describing a contemporary situation would not describe it as something that has endured for a very long time, "to this day".

Isaac de la Peyrere, a French Calvinist, noted that the first verse of the book of Deuteronomy says "These are the words that Moses spoke to the children of Israel across the Jordan...". The problem was that the words meant to refer to someone who is on the other side of the Jordan from the writer. This means that the verse amounts to the words of someone who is *west* of the Jordan at the time of writing, who is describing what Moses said to the children of Israel on the *east* of the Jordan. The problem is exacerbated because Moses himself was never supposed to have been in Israel in his life.

De la Peyrere's book was banned and burned. He was arrested and told that the conditions of his release were conversion to Catholicism and recanting his views. Apparently he perceived discretion as the better part of valor.

Not too long after this, Baruch Spinoza, the famous philosopher, published what amounted to a real rabble rousing critical analysis. He claimed that the problem passages in the Bible were not isolated cases that could be solved one by one as "editorial insertions", but were rather a pervasive evidence of a third person account. He also pointed out that the text says in Deuteronomy 34 that, "There never arose another prophet in Israel like Moses...". Spinoza pointed out, quite rightly, that these were the words of a person who lived a long time after Moses and had had the opportunity to make comparisons. One commentator points out that they also don't sound like the words of the "humblest man on earth"! [Friedman, 1987] Spinoza was really living dangerously because he wrote:

> "It is ... clearer than the sun at noon that the Pentateuch was not written by Moses, but by someone who lived long after Moses."

Spinoza had already been "excommunicated" from Judaism. Now, he was in pretty hot water with the Catholics *and* Protestants! Naturally, his book was placed on the "prohibited books" list and a whole slew of edicts were issued against it. What is even more interesting is that an attempt was made to assassinate him!

A converted Protestant who had become a Catholic priest, Richard Simon, undertook to refute Spinoza and wrote a book saying that the core of the Pentateuch was written by Moses, but there were "some additions". Nevertheless, these additions were clearly done by scribes who were under the guidance of God or the Holy Spirit, so it was okay for them to collect, arrange and elaborate on the text. It was still God in charge here.

Well, you'd think the church would know when it was ahead. But, nope! Simon was attacked and expelled from his order by his fellow Catholics. Forty refutations of his work were written by Protestants. Only six copies of his book survived burning. One of these was translated by a guy named John Hampden who also got into some hot water. He "repudiated the opinions he had held in common with Simon ... in 1688, probably shortly before his release from the tower". [Edward Gray]

Simon's idea that scribes had collected, arranged and elaborated on the textus receptus was, finally, going in the right direction.

In the 18th century, three independent scholars were dealing with the problem of "doublets", or stories that are told two or more times in the Bible. There are two different stories of the creation of the world. There are two stories of the covenant between God and Abraham. There are two stories of the naming of Abraham's son Isaac, two stories of Abraham's claiming to a foreign king that his wife is his sister, two stories of Isaac's son Jacob making a journey to Mesopotamia, two stories of a revelation to Jacob at Beth-El, two stories of God's changing Jacob's name to Israel, two stories of Moses' getting water from a rock at Meribah, and on and on.

Those who were stuck in wishful thinking, believing that Moses wrote the Pentateuch, tried to claim that these doublets were always complimentary, not repetitive nor contradictory. Sometimes they had to really stretch this idea to say that they were supposed to "teach" us something by their contradictions which were not really contradictions. This explanation, however, didn't hold up against another fact: in most cases, one of the two versions of a doublet would refer to the deity by the divine name, <u>Yahweh,</u> and the other would refer to the deity simply as "<u>God</u>". What this meant was that there were two groups of parallel versions of the same stories and each group was almost always consistent about the name of the deity it used. Not only that, there were various other terms and characteristics that regularly appeared in one or the other line of stories and what this demonstrated was that <u>someone had taken two different old source documents and had done the original cut and paste job on them to make a "continuous" narrative.</u>

Well, of course, at first it was thought that one of the two source documents must be one that Moses had used as a source for the story of creation and the rest was Moses himself writing! But, it was ultimately to be concluded that both of <u>the two sources had to be from writers who lived</u> *after* Moses. By degrees, Moses was being eliminated almost entirely from the authorship of the Pentateuch!

I would like to note right here that this was not happening because somebody came along and said, "hey, let's trash the Bible"! Nope. It was happening because there were glaring problems and each and every researcher working on this throughout the centuries was struggling mightily to retain the textus receptus status of the Bible! The only exception in this whole chain of events is our curious guy Abraham ibn Ezra, who knew about problems in the text of the Torah in the 12th century and enjoined others to silence! Remember what he said? "And if you understand, then you will recognize the truth. And he who understands will keep silent." And what do we see as the result of this silence? Eight hundred years of Crusades, the Inquisition, and general suppression. But, we'll come back to that.

Back to our chain of events: in the nineteenth century, Biblical scholars figured out that there were not just two major sources in the Pentateuch; there were, in fact, four. It was realized that the first four books were not just doublets, but there were also triplets that converged with other characteristics and contradictions leading to the identification of another source. Then, it was realized that Deuteronomy was a separate source altogether. More than that, there were not only the original source documents, there was the work of the "mysterious editor".

Thus, after years of suffering, bloodshed and even death over the matter, it was realized that somebody had "created" the Bible by assembling four different source documents into a "continuous" history. After much further analysis, it was concluded that most of the laws and much of the narrative of the Pentateuch were not even part of the time of Moses. And, that meant that it couldn't have been written by Moses at all. More than that, the writing of the different sources was not even that of persons who lived during the daysof the kings and prophets, but were evidently products of writers who lived toward the end of the biblical period!

Many scholars just couldn't bear the results of their own work. A German scholar who had identified the Deuteronomy source exclaimed that such a view "suspended the beginnings of Hebrew history not upon the grand creations of Moses, but upon airy nothings". Other scholars realized that what this meant was that the picture of biblical Israel as a nation governed by laws based on the Abrahamic and Mosaic covenants was completely false. Another way of putting it was that the Bible claimed a history for the first 600 years of Israel that probably never existed.

Well, they couldn't handle this. So along came Wellhausen (1844-1918) to the rescue. Wellhausen synthesized all of the discoveries so as to preserve the belief systems of the religious scholars. He amalgamated the view that the religion of Israel had developed in three stages with the view that the documents were also written in three stages, and then he defined these stages based on the content of the "stage". He tracked the characteristics of each stage, examining the way in which the different documents expressed religion, the clergy, the sacrifices and places of worship as well as the religious holidays. He considered the legal and narrative sections and the other books of the Bible. In the end, he provided a "believable framework" for the development of Jewish history and religion. The first stage was the "nature/fertility" period; the second was "spiritual/ethical" period; and the last was the "priestly/legal" period.

As Friedman notes: To this day, if you want to disagree, you disagree with Wellhausen. If you want to pose a new model, you compare its merits with those of Wellhausen's model.

I should also note that a professor of Old Testament, William Robertson Smith, who taught at the Free Church of Scotland college at Aberdeen, and who was the editor of the Encyclopedia Britannica, was put on trial before the church on the charge of heresy for promoting the work of Wellhausen. He was cleared, but the tag "the wicked bishop" followed him to his grave.

Opposition to critical study of the Bible has been spearheaded, throughout the centuries, by the Catholic Church. But, curiously, in the modern day, the Catholics are more open to examination of the text that the new American Christian Fundamentalists who resemble, more than anything, Holy Crusaders and Inquisitors!

Nevertheless, analysis of the Bible has proceeded. The book of Isaiah was traditionally thought to be written by the prophet Isaiah who lived in the eighth century B.C. As it happens, most of the first half of this book fits such a model. But, chapters 40 through 66 are apparently written by someone who lived about 200 years later!

New tools and methods of our modern time have made it possible to do some really fine work in the areas of linguistic analysis and relative chronology of material. Additionally, there has been a veritable archaeological frenzy since Wellhausen!

This archaeological work has produced an enormous amount of information about Egypt, Mesopotamia, and other regions surrounding Israel, which includes clay tablets, inscriptions on the walls of tombs, temples and habitations, and even papyri. And here we find another problem: in all the collected sources, both Egyptian and west Asian, there are virtually NO references to Israel, its "famous people" and founders, its Biblical associates, or anything else prior to the 12th century B.C. The fact is, for 400 years after that, no more than half a dozen allusions can be deduced.

This same problem finds correspondence in the Bible itself. The Bible displays absolutely no knowledge of Egypt or the Levant during the 2nd millennium B.C. The Bible says nothing about the Egyptian empire spreading over the entire eastern Mediterranean, (which it did), there is no mention of the great Egyptian armies on the march (which they were), and no mention of marching Hittites moving against the Egyptians (which they did), and especially no mention of Egyptianized kinglets ruling Canaanite cities (which was the case).

The great and disastrous invasion of the Sea Peoples during the second millennium is not mentioned in the Bible. In fact, Genesis described the Philistines as already settled in the land of Canaan at the time of Abraham!

The names of the great Egyptian kings are completely absent from the Bible. In other places, historical figures who were *not* heroic have been transformed by the Bible into heroes as in the case of the Hyksos Sheshy (Num. 13:22). In another case, the sobriquet of Ramesses II is given to a

Canaanite general in error. The Egyptian king who was supposed to assist Hosea in his rebellion of 2 Kings 17:4 has suffered the indignity of having his city given as his name. The Pharaoh Shabtaka turns up in the Table of Nations in Gen 10:7 as a Nubian tribe!

The errors of confirmable history and archaeology pile higher and higher the more one learns about the actual times and places so that the idea that comes to mind again and again is that the writers of the Bible must have lived in the 7th and 6th centuries B.C., and knew almost nothing about the events of only a few generations before them.

"Such ignorance is puzzling if one has felt inclined to be impressed by the traditional claims of inerrancy made by conservative Christianity on behalf of the Bible. And indeed the Pentateuch and the historical books boldly present a precise chronology that would carry the Biblical narrative through the very period when the ignorance and discrepancy prove most embarrassing.

A totaling of the lengths of reign of the kings of Judah from Solomon's fourth year (when allegedly the temple in Jerusalem was dedicated) to the destruction of Jerusalem in 586 B.C. yields 430 years which should take us to the year 1016 B.C. for the reign of Solomon.

Again, according to 1 Kings 6:1, 480 years is supposed to have elapsed between the Exodus and the dedication of the temple, thus producing a date of 1496 B.C. for the [Exodus.]

Since the Sojourn in Egypt is stated to have lasted for 430 years (Exodus 12:40), the descent of Jacob and his family to the land of Goshen must have taken place in 1926 B.C.

If now we add the lengths of life of Abraham, Isaac, and Jacob (290), we arrive at 2216 B.C. for the birth of Abraham. This would mean that Abraham's arrival in Canaan would have to fall in 2141 B.C., And his descent to Egypt between that date and 2116 B.C., or under the 10th Dynasty of Herakleopolis. Jacob's descent would have occurred in Senwosret I's reign, and the entire Sojourn would have occupied the outgoing 12th dynasty, the entire 13th Dynasty, the Hyksos occupation, and the early Dynasty to Hatshepsut's ninth year!

In the light of Numbers 32:13, which assigns 40 years to the Wandering, the conquest of the land under Joshua must have begun in 1456 B.C., Or on the morrow of Thutmose III's victorious campaigns when all Canaan belonged to Egypt, and on the eve of Amenophis II's deportation of the local population.

Even more astounding are the implications of the resultant placement of the Period of the Judges, namely 1456 to 1080 B.C. this is almost exactly coeval with the Egyptian Empire in Asia! yet our Egyptian sources mention neither the patriarchs, Israel in Egypt, Joshua, nor his successors, while the Bible says absolutely nothing about the Egyptian empire in the land.

In fact, the Biblical writers are wholly and blissfully unaware of the colossal discrepancy to which their "history" and "chronology" have given rise.

The strength, however, of a confessional commitment to bolster a prejudgment will not allow most conservative Jewish or Christian exegetes to discard the whole chronological arrangement, and recent work has proven Muslim scholars similarly in thrall. (A. Osman)

The basic pattern of Patriarchal Age, Descent and Sojourn, Exodus and Conquest, and Judges MUST be essentially correct - Is it not inherently reasonable? Do you have a better one? - and consequently numerous ingenious solutions are devised.

The most common trick has been to reduce time spans to generations: thus the 480 figure must really represent twelve generations: but 40 years per generation is too long, 20 being much closer to the average. Hence we can cut the figure in half and put the Exodus around 1255 B.C. instead of 1486, and lo! it falls squarely in the reign of Ramesses II, and thus allusion to 'Ra'amses' in Exodus 1:11 can be nicely accommodated!

Similarly the 430 years of the Sojourn must simply be a curious equivalent of roughly four generations - does not Genesis 15:16 virtually prove it? - and so the Descent will come to rest about the middle of the fourteenth century B.C., Or at the close of the Amarna age.

Although the Gargantuan ages of the patriarchs are not extraneous to the Genesis material as we now have it, but actually inform it, nevertheless these too are swept away or transmogrified into normal generation estimates; and thus the 'Patriarchal age' can occupy the fifteenth and early fourteenth centuries and accommodate the alleged 'Nuzi' parallels.

And if one is still impressed by the 'appropriateness' of having Joseph rise to power under the Hyksos who, as his Semitic congeners, would have taken kindly to him (although the Joseph story clearly distinguishes Joseph from Pharaoh and his court as Egyptians, then what matter if we drop our objections to the 430 years and take them literally? Joseph would then come to Egypt around 1680, just as the Hyksos were taking power!)

Such manhandling of the evidence smacks of prestidigitation and numerology; yet it has produced the shaky foundations on which a lamentable number of 'histories' of Israel have been written. Most are characterized by a somewhat naive acceptance of sources at face value coupled with failure to assess the evidence as to its origin and reliability. The result was the reduction of all data to a common level, any or all being grist for a wide variety of mills.

Scholars expended substantial effort on questions that they had failed to prove were valid questions at all.

Under what dynasty did Joseph rise to power? Who was the Pharaoh of the Oppression? Of the Exodus? Can we identify the princess who drew Moses out of the river? Where did the Israelites make their exit from Egypt: via the Wady Tumilat or by a more northerly point?

One can appreciate the pointlessness of these questions if one poses similar questions of the Arthurian stories, without first submitting the text to a critical evaluation. Who were the consuls of Rome when Arthur drew the sword from the stone? Where was Merlin born?

Can one seriously envisage a classical historian pondering whether it was Iarbas or Aeneas that was responsible for Dido's suicide, where exactly did Remus leap over the wall, what really happened to Romulus in the thunderstorm, and so forth?

In all these imagined cases none of the material initially prompting the questions has in any way undergone a prior evaluation as to how historical it is! **And any scholar who exempts any part of his sources from critical evaluation runs the risk of invalidating some or all of his conclusions.**

...Of much more significant reference are such questions as:

Under what conditions and to what purpose did the ancestor traditions of Israel take shape?

Where and when did the Exodus theme originate?

Of what nature and how reliable is our evidence for the pre-monarchiacal history of the component elements of the Iron Age 'Israel'?

And in all our efforts to formulate the right questions, we should be wise to reject the application of the adjective 'Biblical' to 'history' and 'archaeology'.

...Too often 'Biblical' in this context has had the limiting effect on scholarship by implying the validity of studying Hebrew culture and history in isolation. What is needed rather is a view of ancient Israel within its true Near Eastern context, and one that will neither exaggerate nor denigrate Israel's actual place within that setting." [Redford, *Egypt, Canaan, and Israel in Ancient Times,* 1992, Princeton]

Now, back to our Louvites/Luvites/Levites. Judging by the artifacts and partly deciphered texts, these Luvites seem to have been a separate, priestly class of Indo-Europeans much like the Brahmins in India. Their "sacred texts" were used exclusively for votive rituals and inscriptions on royal monuments. Many of the scribal schools were located in their territory suggesting that the Luvites used the Hurrian, Hittite and Akkadian languages to disseminate their ideas while retaining their ancient hieroglyphs as a private and secret manner of writing.

The Brahmins of India, the priestly class, made fire sacrifices one of the most important aspects of their religion. Giuseppe Sormani writes that in the early Sanskrit Yajurveda, a collection of Brahmin sacrificial and ritual prayer formulas dated shortly after the Rg Veda,

> "The priests commanded society; *they were the lords even over the gods, whom they bent to their own will by means of ritual.* The priestly power of the Brahmins was already evident in this Veda." [Quoted by Stone, 1976]

The one group that stands apart from the Hebrew people as a whole, is the priestly Levites. Hmmm... that word is suspiciously similar to Luvites, yes? Indeed!

According to the law of Jehovah/Yaweh, the Levites were to remain a very exclusive group, marrying only other Levites. Moses is described as the son of a Levite mother and father!

Only Levites were acceptable as priests of Yahweh. They were forbidden not only to marry outside their tribe, but they also could not marry a woman who was a widow, divorced or had ever had sexual relations with another man. The Levites were sole judges of disputes, "Their voice shall be decisive in all cases of dispute". (Deut. 21:6) They had possession of the trumpets of the congregation and only they were allowed to sound them. They commanded military strategy, and they were exempt from most nasty jobs like being warriors, carrying out the trash and so forth.

Fire sacrifices were very important rituals of the Levites. The first ten sections of Leviticus are totally concerned with fire sacrifices. These sacrifices were to be made twice daily as well as on the Sabbath, and other special times.

The curious thing about this is the fact that the prophet Jeremiah, right there in the Bible, denies that all of this "temple cult" business had any basis in the old traditions! "Keep on with your burnt offerings and sacrifice", he represents Yahweh as saying to the people, "and eat the flesh. But I did not speak with your forefathers and I issued no command to them on the day I brought them out of Egypt concerning burnt offering and sacrifice"!

The Levites had the right to eat the food offerings that were brought to the Tent of the Presence. In this way, they were served by all the other Israelites with cattle and foodstuffs of all kinds. Other gifts to the Levites were commanded by Yahweh, such as silver and gold and property. Levites who sold their houses had the right of redemption, and if they did not pay to redeem it, it would be returned automatically at the seven-year jubilee. If a man of another tribe chose to sell his house to a Levite, the

Levite had the sole right to decide upon the price. If the man wanted to buy it back he was expected to pay another twenty percent of the value.

On and on we read of the benefits to the Levites assigned by Yahweh/Jehovah; gifts and "allotted portions" and tithes and clothing and on and on. And, all these laws, first written by the Levites, were then placed in the care and keeping of the Levites, who then were the only ones able to read them, interpret them, change them. What a racket!

Now, the Levites are said to be descended from one of Jacob's twelve sons, Levi. Tracing the genealogies, Moses would have been the great-grandson of Levi. This, of course, does not tally with the number of males that were supposed to have left Egypt. The Levites claimed 22,000 males among them - quite a feat for a bunch of priests in only three generations! There sure wasn't much time left for fire sacrifices!

The far more likely scenario is that the Levites created this heritage to justify their relationship to the other tribes who were very likely just disenfranchised peoples of all types that they had assembled under the aegis of their god. This may explain why Jacob, who was supposedly the father of the twelve tribes, was called Israel, rather than the appellation being applied to Abraham who is generally considered the first father of his people. I think that there may be more to this 12 tribes and 12 sons business than that, but we will come back to it later.

Another curious connection is the actual name of the Levites. It is here that Ms. Stone makes a rather interesting series of relationships that may have significance later. She points out that, in Latin we have *lavo* which means to wash in a stream which flows, while *lavit* means to pour. In Hittite, *lahhu* also means to pour. In French we have *laver*, to wash and in German we have *lawine*, meaning avalanche and the English word *lavish*. *Levo* in Latin means lift and is especially associated with the sunrise. In Sanskrit *lauha* is "glowing redness", while lightning is *lohla*. In German we have *lohe*, meaning blaze or flame, while in Danish *lue* means to go up in flames. In English, the word *lava*, the German *lave*, and the French *lave*, each meaning the blazing molten mass that pours from a volcanic mountain, may give us the key to the two concepts in unity: that which is light and flaming, while still pouring almost as a liquid at the same time. *Sons of Light and Fire*. The mountaintop Weather God who issues from deep within the Earth!

At Qumran, where the oldest extant Hebrew texts were found, there was a scroll discovered that was completely new to Biblical scholars entitled *The Scroll of the War of the Sons of Light Against the Sons of Darkness*. This text consists of the plans for a battle that is about to be fought. This scroll reveals that the Levites were still in control at that time, and may be still in control at the present!

The name of the Hebrews as *Yehudi*, or Judah, is rather close to the Sanskrit word for warrior: *Yuddha*.

As Ms. Stone points out, if these speculations, supported by so much circumstantial evidence, hold up to further investigation, then what are we to make of the Aryan versus Jew stance of W.W.II? It becomes more than a tragedy, it becomes utterly ironic that the monster of monotheism created by the Hebrews turned around to devour them. On the other hand, maybe it was intentional. It is even beginning to look like the Hebrews, as an ethnic group, were actually created for "use" by the members of the Control System. And we have to keep in mind also, that the same Control System seems to be behind the development of Kaballah and the many related occult/mystical practices, in which case we have to ask ourselves why?

But, before we move on, let us make one last observation: It was sometime before and directly after W.W.I that *nasili* was being accepted as the real name of the Hittite language, and Nesa or Nasa, their first capital. The original name of the Hittite invaders may have been Nesians or Nasians. Nuzi was the capital of the Indo-European nation of Mitanni. And this brings up another connection between the Hittites and the Hebrews, the use of the word *nasi* for prince from which we derive nazarene. We can't help but observe here how close to these words is the term Nazi.

With the knowledge that the worship of the Goddess was violently overturned by invading Indo-Europeans, we may better understand the transitions and inversions that have occurred in our myths and legends. If we can come to some understanding of *who* and *what* this Yahweh/Jehovah was, who spoke to Moses from the summit of Mount Horeb and Mount Sinai, we may discover an explanation for why the patriarchal laws and attitudes of the Levite priests were bent upon the destruction of the Goddess religion.

But keep in mind the remark above that the evidence for the continued existence of an inner core of Levites, possibly completely unknown to the Levite priests of the Temple at Jerusalem, is suggested by *The Scroll of the War of the Sons of Light Against the Sons of Darkness.*

Now, for those who think that I am proposing a "Jewish Conspiracy", DON'T EVEN GO THERE! If you haven't yet figured out that the differences between the Jews and the Aryans disappears in the inner circles, you haven't been paying attention!

Again, as I have said before, just as there was a Dark Age surrounding the period of time in which the Old Testament came into being, during which time Monotheistic Judaism was imposed forcibly on the Canaanites, and we have only the Old Testament itself to attest to its validity; we have a similar period of Dark Ages enveloping the development and codification of the New Testament and the imposition of Monotheistic Christianity on the Western World.

Don't you find that curious?

Out of this history emerged what is known today as Kaballah.

And, so we come back in a circle to the remarks about the 3-5 code:

Well, it was difficult to know what to think about all of it. I decided, at one point, to ask the Cassiopaeans directly about Kaballah:

Q: (L) What is the origin of the Kaballah?

A: Channeled truths given to early pre-Mosaic Jews to use your terminology.

Q: (L) When the Jewish commentators began setting down the teachings, was this the first time this had been put into writing?

A: No. Not even close.

Q: (L) Is the form that it is in today very close to the original form and can it be relied upon?

A: No. Corrupted.

So, again, we have the idea that there are seeds of truth but, for the most part, what we have today was corrupted so long ago that great care must be taken to compare and analyze; and most especially, before putting any of it into practice! But, just to give a clue to those who want something to mull over before I get to it, remember the 22 letters of the Hebrew Alphabet? The ones that are supposed to be so special and magical?

Well, the Phoenician, or West Semitic, alphabet was the starting point of all the later European alphabets, as well as the Hebrew and Arabic alphabets. The definitive version of the Phoenician alphabet is the inscription on the sarcophagus of King Ahiram of Byblos, dated to about 1000 B.C. It, too, was a systematized alphabet of 22 characters.

Hebrew script was formalized around the same time as the early Greek, but the characters took a different form. Hebrew was, and still is, written from right to left. Resh, with the phonetic value "R", resembles the lower case Roman "r", written the opposite way around. Both the Greek and Hebrew alphabets have parallel esoteric meanings.

What, then, makes Hebrew so mystical and mysterious? Well, we have already mentioned the *Sefer Yezirah*, the "cornerstone" of Kaballah which details this doctrine.

In Kabbalistic Judaism, it is stated that the God, Jehovah, is not transcendent, but is rather subordinate to a higher form of existence, the "Ain-Soph". The Ain-Soph exists beyond the realms of cause and effect, beyond desire, beyond the realms of being and non-being. And, the "god of creation" is only an agent of the Ain-Soph. The creation of the universe itself has come directly from the Ain-Soph through a complex process, achieved by the operation of the "emanations", or "sephiroth" which are supposed to be 10 in number, the same as the fingers on two hands. However, most kabbalistic images of the Sephiroth in the tree of life diagrams include an 11th Sephira for which various explanations are given. If we just "turn off the sound" and look at the picture, what we see are 11 sephiroth, 22 letters of an alphabet which is a multiple of 11. Then, if we think about the major arcana of the Tarot, which is supposed to have strong Kabbalistic relations, we find the number 22 appearing again. If we put those items together with the fact that the Cassiopaeans have tried to point us in the direction of examining the number 11 more closely, we may come to some interesting conclusions.

"[During the Babylonian captivity] strange events occurred. Besides Ezekiel's resurrection of Israel's religious tradition, which urged them to return home to Jerusalem, the men responsible for the inner teaching of the Religion realised that here was a unique possibility at the second rebirth of the Nation. Hebrew, in the overriding presence of the vernacular used in Babylonia, had ceased to be a first language. So here was a chance to embed, before it became established again as a national speech, many ideas - make it a language that contained more than just an everyday vocabulary of meanings. At this point we know that the actual twenty-two letters of the alphabet were reconstructed, changed from the ancient pictograms into a more robust alphabet known as the Syrian script.

Later, long after this new Hebrew had been established, (though it never quite took over from Aramaic the lingua franca of the Middle East), it became regarded as a holy language, and like Sanscrit to be used in Holy matters.

One work in particular reveals the philosophical construction of the Hebrew alphabet. This was the *Sepher Yitzerah*, reputed to be written by Abraham, but more likely to have been drafted in the earlier centuries of the Common Era. In this, to each letter was ascribed a planet and a Sign of the Zodiac. Herein lies our date clue *inasmuch that the Sign Libra was inserted into the Zodiac circle long after Abraham died.*" [Z'ev Ben Shimon Halevi, 1972]

What happened to the hand of God inscribing the fire letters and all that? What are we going to do with all the mystical allusions to this most holy of languages and works? Could it be possible that we might obtain as much enlightenment by applying the Kabbalistic practices to a copy of *War and Peace* or *The Decline and Fall of the Roman Empire*? I have the feeling that this is the case. Anybody game to try it?

Getting back to our story, what gradually dawned on me was the fact that all the centuries of Kabbalistic Gematria and Notariqon and Temurah might be nothing but a distraction from truth. Yes, we can see intimations of certain threads that will bear closer scrutiny, and the Cassiopaeans have suggested that we might figure out something important if we examine astrology as an 11-house system. We also find confirmation of this number 11 as an important number by simple virtue of the numbers of letters of the alphabets along with the major arcana of the Tarot.

But then, there was the odd mention of Medusa and "heads". What did Medusa mean in relation to this? Were the "heads" the sephiroth of the tree of life, since there are, in some versions, 11? It is called the "unseen sephira" which "functions only in particular conditions". Daat is "the veil of the bride" beyond which lies knowledge and being of the Objective Universe.

One writer on Kaballah says:

> "In their totality the Sefirot make up the tree of emanations or the tree of the Sefirot, which from the 14th century onward is depicted by a detailed diagram which lists the basic symbols... The cosmic tree grows downward from its root, the first Sefirah, and spreads out through those Sefirot which constitute its trunk to those which make up its main branches or crown. This image is first found in the *Sefer ha-Bahir*. However, in the Bahir [the tree] includes only those Sefirot from Binah downward [that is to say, only 9 Sefirot in the oldest Tree of Life Image.] ...Alongside this picture we have the more common image of the Sefirot in the form of a man. While the tree grows with its top down, this human form has its head properly on top, and is occasionally referred to as the 'reversed tree'. The first Sefirot represent the head, and, in the Zohar, the three cavities of the brain; the fourth and the fifth, the arms; the sixth, the torso; the seventh and eighth, the legs; the ninth, the sexual organ; and the tenth refers either to the all-embracing totality of the image, or to the female as companion to the male, since both together are needed to constitute a perfect man [!] *...On the whole, however, the overall structure is built out of triangles."* [Scholem, 1974, emphases, mine.]

That is to say, exactly 3 triangles.

And what was said about triangles?

A: You mentioned pyramid, interesting... And what is the geometric one-dimensional figure that corresponds?

Q: (L) Well, the triangle. And, if you have a triangle point up you have 3, joined to a triangle pointing down, you have 3, and you have a 33. Is that something like what we are getting at here?

A: Yes.

Q: (L) Is there a connection between the number 33 and the Great Pyramid in Egypt?

A: Yes.

Q: (L) And what is that connection? Is it that the builders of the pyramid participated in this secret society activity?

A: Yes. And what symbol did you see in "Matrix", for Serpents and Grays?

Q: (L) You are talking about the triangle with the Serpent's head in it?

A: Yes.

Q: (L) Are we talking in terms of this 33 relating to a group of "aliens", or a group of humans with advanced knowledge and abilities?

A: Either/or.

Q: (L) Is this what has been referred to in the Bramley book as the Brotherhood of the Serpent or Snake?

A: Yes.

And we come back again to the 3-5 code, which is what we ended up with by asking about the number 33.

I have to admit that my first ideas about this 3-5 code were very "kabbalistic". The 3-5 code stuck in my mind as a means of finding some coded secret in some ancient text. I will admit that I followed this idea to an almost absurd degree, reading through and marking only the 3rd and 5th words, or reading the 35th line, or the 35th word, or the 3rd chapter, 5th word, and endless permutations thereof in a large body of "occult" literature. I created charts, diagrams, tables of permutation. I did Gematria, Notariqon and anagrams! It was becoming such an obsession that I had to deliberately will myself to stop counting everything all the time.

I finally gave it up. It wasn't going anywhere. Sure, there were occasional "hits", but there were also endless nonsensical combinations. When I kept notes on the results, I found that the hits were no better than chance, and I wonder if that is not the case for many so-called occultists who see only the successes of their methods, and ignore the failures. Or, they read more into the hits than are really there. As Dr. Eco says, the structure of the universe is expressed in mathematics. Is it any wonder that anything and everything relates to everything else via numbers?

Another thing that struck me were the remarks about the pyramid being associated with the STS/Drachomonoid controllers. I had a lot of work invested in the Egyptian religious traditions as being of positive orientation. But, the comments about the pyramid shape being related to the Negative STS hierarchy reminded me of something else the Cassiopaeans had said earlier in 1995:

Q: (L) We have some questions tonight. We were discussing earlier this evening the 'abomination of desolation' as written about by the prophet Daniel and also spoken of by Jesus. What is this?

A: Disinformation.

Q: (L) Are you saying that the abomination of desolation IS disinformation, or that the writing about it is disinformation?

A: Both.

Q: (L) Who, or what was the source of that information as prophesied by Daniel?

A: Illuminati.

Q: (L) The prophecies given to Daniel were disinformation?

A: Close.

Q: (L) Is there an 'abomination of desolation'?

A: There is anything, if the definitions are unrestricted.

Q: (L) Well, okay. Who were the Elohim of the Bible?

A: Transdefinitive.

Q: (L) What does that mean? Transcends definition as you just mentioned?

A: And variable entities.

Q: (L) Were the Elohim 'good guys?'

A: First manifestation was human, then non-human.

Q: (L) Well, what brought about their transformation from human to non-human?

A: Pact or covenant.

Q: (L) They made a pact or covenant with each other?

A: No, with 4th density STS.

Q: (L) Are you saying that the Elohim are STS? Who were these STS beings they made a pact with?

A: Rosteem, now manifests as Rosicrucians.

Q: (L) What is their purpose?

A: As yet unrevealable to you.

Q: (L) Okay, since he relies so heavily on this "Elohim" idea, what is the source of the **Keys of Enoch** that was written by James Hurtak. He claims that he was taken up to the higher realms and that the 'Keys' were programmed into him...

A: Disguised reality. Both the place he was taken to and the message.

Q: (L) What is the source of this disguised reality?

A: Research to discover explosive reality trailblazings.

Q: (L) Okay. Is there coded information in this book on several levels as M__ suggests?

A: There is coded information all over the place. Suggest slower pace of studying in order to discover earth-shaking principles. Remember the old parable about biting off more than you can chew? It is important because it is hard to see the veins in the leaves when the car is traveling too fast to see the trees clearly. We suggest that you be more like the tortoise than the hare. Network and all falls into place. We cannot tell many things at present, because then you would not learn, and if you do not learn, you do not progress as an individual soul!

Well, I was trying. And, along with my growing obsession with numbers, a couple of very strange things happened to me in the week following the session where the 3-5 code was brought up. The first was the beginning of a long series of Out Of Body Experiences that continued for over a year and a half, and the second was a dream accompanied by a physical "trace". Interestingly, in the very next session, the Cassiopaeans seemed to be desperately trying to communicate some things to us without violating free will. Naturally, we had our own agenda and very often our questions were what limited us, but revealing the activities of some sort of Secret Masters of the World seemed to be very much on the Cassiopaean's mind(s?). As usual, the door to strange things was opened by a seemingly innocuous question:

Q: (L) Is there any relationship between all of the terrorist bombings that have been taking place in Paris recently, and any stepped up alien activity?

A: Open. USAir-194 crash; United Air crash, Colorado Springs; Connection? Get voice recorder tape transcripts.

Q: (L) Is this in some way related to the question about the Paris bombing?

A: No. Strobe lights are used for 3rd density mind control. [Now, how did "strobe lights" come in here when we were asking about terrorist bombings? Further, what did it have to do with a plane crash?]

Q: (L) Strobe lights located where?

A: Not a question asked with much thought! We have picked up your thought waves, which are progress oriented, and are trying to assist you in your increased learning and progress frequency wave. You see, this increases the energy level!! It is advisable to ask questions, but be unconcerned with the nature or content of the answers beforehand.

Q: (L) Okay. You mentioned the strobe lights. Are these strobe lights that are used to control minds, are these something that we would or might come in contact with on a daily basis?

A: Do you not already know? We didn't say: some strobe lights, we said: strobe lights, i.e. all-inclusive!

Q: (T) Strobe lights come in many forms and types. TV is a strobe light. Computer screens are a strobe light. Light bulbs strobe. Fluorescents strobe. Streetlights strobe.

A: Police cars, ambulances, fire trucks... How long has this been true? Have you noticed any changes lately??!!??

Q: (F) Twenty years ago there were no strobe lights on any of those vehicles mentioned. They had the old flasher type lights. Now, more and more and more there are strobe lights appearing in all kinds of places. (L) And now, they even have them on school buses! (T) And the regular city buses have them too, now. (L) Okay, is the strobing of a strobe light, set at a certain frequency in order to do certain things?

A: Hypnotic opener.

Q: (L) What is the purpose of the hypnotic opener being used in this way?

A: You don't notice the craft.

Q: (T) Okay, what craft are we NOT seeing?

A: Opener. Is precursor to suggestion, which is auditory in nature.

Q: (T) What suggestion?

A: Put on your thinking caps. Networking is not making assumptions. Bold unilateral statement of "fact" is.

Q: (T) Oh. Phrase your statements in the form of a question! I'd like "Hypnotic Openers" for $200, Alex! Cosmic Jeopardy! (L) Okay, you said the "suggestion is auditory in nature". If this is the case, where is the suggestion coming from auditorially?

A: Where do you normally receive auditory suggestions from?

Q: (L) Radio, television... (T) Telephone... (L) Is that what we are talking about?

A: Yes.

Q: (L) If you encounter a strobe while driving, or you are sitting in front of your television, then the suggestions can be put into you better because of this hypnotically opened state? Is that it?

A: Yes.

Q: (L) What are these suggestions designed to do, to suggest? In a general sense? To not see the craft?

A: Yes.

Q: (T) Do we get these signals from the radio in the car even if it is turned off?

A: Depends upon whether or not there is another source.

Q: (T) Another source such as?

A: ELP, for example.

Q: (L) What is "ELP"?

A: Extremely Low Pulse.

I should note here that, until Col. Phil Corso published his book *The Day After Roswell*, I had never heard the term "ELP". And, remember, this session was in the latter part of 1995. Corso's book wasn't published until several years later.

Q: (T) ELF, Extremely Low Frequency, and ELP, Extremely Low Pulse - is this the same thing?

A: Sometimes.

Q: (T) This would be an external pulse or frequency?

A: Yes.

Q: (T) Would it be originating from the source of the strobe?

A: No. They act in unison.

Q: (L) And this process prevents us from seeing something, such as craft flying in our skies at any given time?

A: Or maybe see them as something else.

Q: (L) Now, we have to stop for a minute because I **want** to tell you something. In the past few months, I have really been watching the sky carefully every opportunity I get. On 3 or 4 separate occasions I have seen what I thought was an ordinary airplane, and I would watch it carefully and then scan to the left or right, and when I looked back at the place where this plane should be, based on observable speed and direction, there would be NOTHING there. I have stood there and searched and searched and found nothing. These things just VANISHED. I knew I had seen it, I knew I wasn't crazy, I knew it couldn't have gone away that completely - and having it happen several times has just really unsettled me. What are the implications of this, other than the fact that we could be completely overblown at all times for any number of purposes and be, as a mass of people, completely unaware of it?

A: Yes, monoatomic gold!

Q: (L) And what does the reference to monoatomic gold mean?

A: Total entrapment of the being, mind, body and soul. Strobes use minute gold filament. What composes minute filament, do you suppose? Hint, it ain't from Fort Knox! You see, this has extraordinary properties.

Q: (T) I'm sure it does! The thing is, if it does what Hudson says it does, the power structure would have shut him down - he wouldn't have gotten this far with it. So, if they are letting him do it, it's because it doesn't do what he says it does, it does the opposite. Which is what he said. When you take the stuff for so many days, you complete the program, it restructures your genes. Isn't that what happened to us before? Do we want to do it again? (L) And, wasn't it said that LIGHT was used to cancel certain DNA factors? (J) Exactly! (L) Okay, how do we block this kind of control?

A: You don't.

Q: (L) Let me ask this, CD asked an interesting question. It was, if we know what he thinks we know, and if we are building the kind of strength that he thinks we are building, and getting factual information about all such things, why hasn't somebody, either on 3rd density or 4th density, seen fit to stop or block US? He was asking very plainly why has something physical not been done to, as he put it, "take us out"?

A: The powers that be want slow release of information.

Q: (L) Does this include the 4th density STS?

A: No, **but they don't see that which they do not wish to see.**

[Now notice the distinction here. They said that "the powers that be" want a slow release of information, and I asked if this included the STS factions and the answer was "no". So that obviously means that the "powers that be" we are talking about here may be the "good guys".]

Q: (L) They don't see us as a threat?

A: More like an annoyance.

At this point, I wanted to ask about the strange experiences I had been having since the beginning of the inquiry into the "Secret Societies" business, the Out of Body Experiences. Apparently, they were not all precisely the same thing!

Q: (L) Okay, I want to ask about the experience I had the other night - I had what seemed to be an O.O.B.E. the other night. Was I actually having one?

A: Was an "all intensive ooze" of the solar realm.

Q: (L) Okay, what is an "all intensive ooze" of the solar realm?

A: Realms are compartmentalized at graduated levels, like everything else. The root basis of the study of Astrology is the "unified entity realm", which relates to the effect that local cosmic bodies have upon the body and soul of third density beings in any given locator.

Q: (L) So, what does this mean in terms of what I experienced? I felt that I was moving in and out of my body over and over, sort of like doing an exercise.

A: Solar activity occurring when your experience took place was such that, based on your "solar return", had the effect of partially separating your soul from your body. Now, just for fun, why not check your chart for that day, and see if the aspects were a little more favorable for expiration of the body potential than usual?

Q: (L) Now that I have been able to play with it a little, will I experience it again, or can I?

A: Well, it is always experienced at least once in the lifetime of a human being, but for most people, it occurs at the conclusion.

Q: [much laughter] (L) You mean I died? Or was this what people experience when they die?

A: Yes, but you got to come back in time for dinner!

Q: (L) So, that wasn't just an O.O.B.E., it was a separation of the soul from the body? Is that different from astral projection?

A: No. With "astral projection" the consciousness level is not as intense because of "the silver cord" and the shroud of third density awareness.

Q: (L) You guys just don't know how intense this experience was. I was SO conscious of EVERYTHING. (T) More conscious than you have ever been before, right? (L) I have to say yes. I was playing with what was happening to me and having fun. I noticed every little sensation. The separating from the body produces a sizzling sound, a sort of electrical sizzle, and it changes as you move in and out of the body. I was actually having a ball playing with the effects. (T) In astral projection, the soul is still connected to the body. In this case, was Laura's soul completely separated from her physical body?

A: Not completely, but the part that was, was.

Q: (L) Well, I did sort of keep a toe in. (T) So, if Laura had lost complete connection, would she have died at this point?

A: Yes.

[Break]

Q: (L) Now, the next strange thing after this was that I had a safari dream. I dreamed we all went to Africa, and I got some information there from some people in some kind of an underground place, like a cave that went into rocks in the side of a mountain. There were all kinds of rooms and people and electronic equipment monitoring the planet and we were being taken on sort of a tour that seemed like a series of lessons. At one point, something was given to me, a stone, and I put it in my pocket on the right side. And then, just a few days later, still in the dream, I felt a danger, something probing in the direction of my mind and the children here in the house, and a protective device shot up out of my lower right abdomen, like a rocket. When it reached a point just above the house, it opened out like a crystal parachute and enveloped the entire house with a sort of shield. The crazy thing is, next day when I was in the bath, I noticed a small, deep, wound at that spot. What was this?

A: Energy surge. Magnetic plane weakness there.

Q: (L) So, is it beneficial to be able to do this?

A: Maybe.

Q: (L) Well, it seems that having the body automatically erect defenses when a threat is felt is a pretty handy talent to have.

A: Sure, in 4th density.

Q: (L) Was this a 4th density action, or ability?

A: Close.

Q: (L) Okay, it was an energy surge. Did this energy surge leave the wound in my body?

A: Yes. Learn naturally as you evolve.

Though I never again had the same intense O.O.B.E as I did just after the introduction of the 3-5 code information, I continued to have almost regular experiences with what must be 4th density reality. I could see with my eyes closed, I could sleep without being "asleep", and be fully aware of both the "present reality", including the children and all their varied activities around me, and at the same time, a whole other world was open to me in which people came and went and talked to me and I conversed with them. It was impossible to "generate" such experiences, but this "bleed through" occurred so often that I could say that about half of my day to day experiences took place in a dual reality. I observed this phenomenon with curiosity and skepticism. I would "project" myself to where the children were to see what they were doing exactly, and then come back, make myself "orient" in this reality, and then physically go to check the observations. Over and over again, I realized that what I was doing was, in some strange sense, "real". I didn't know what was happening to me or even why, but it was sufficiently strange to keep me in an attentive state. I didn't want to talk about it too much because whenever I brought such things up to the group, it seemed that even they were not quite able to grasp what I was trying to tell them. I did spend some time reading psychology texts in an effort to determine if I was losing my mind! Exactly what I was experiencing, I wasn't sure, but some clues to the possible nature of it were given in the next session. And, again, the Cassiopaeans were using an opportunity to bring up more information about the Consortium:

Q: (L) The other day I experienced one of those extended pre-sleep states, and it seemed that I was in a class and there was someone explaining things to me. What they were telling me was that during this Christmas season, certain steps would be taken by those controlling the economy, and that after Christmas, in January and February, a whole lot of stuff was going to be put into motion to send the economy into a dive of major proportions. It was not clear that it was THIS year, but that it was right after Christmas. Can you tell me where this information was coming from, and what was I experiencing?

A: This is a long and complicated subject, but we will do our best to explain it. **What you were seeing was one possible future.** The economy of your 3rd density world is entirely manufactured. The forces that control it are both 3rd density and 4th density. There are conflicting opinions in the 3rd density sector right now as to when, where, and how to institute an economic depression. This has been "in the works" for quite some "time" as you measure it. So far, the forces arguing against institution of a collapse have prevailed. How long this condition will be maintained is open to many outcomes. Also, please be aware that the state of the economy is entirely an illusion. In other words, the world economy performs solely based upon what the population is told to believe.

Q: (L) Well, that is all fine and good except for one fact that I have been observing lately, and that is that prices continue to go up, and wages for the average person do not. I watch prices, and they have been jumping in a very erratic and frightening way. I know for a fact that people simply cannot afford to live. A large segment of the population cannot, that is.

A: Nobody who obeys the "rules" can afford to "live", but if you refuse to play the game as you are told to, you will do quite well, indeed.

Q: (L) Okay. What do you mean by not playing by the rules? What rules?

A: The best way for us to answer that is for you to think out loud, and wait for our responses.

Q: (L) Okay. The first rule is that you have to have a "regular job".

A: "Trap" number one!

Q: (S) Rule number two is that you have to save your money.

A: You save your money by multiplying it, not storing it. When you store it in the bank, you are helping the Brotherhood AKA Illuminati AKA Antichrist multiply it for itself; all you get is the "crumbs" left over. And, the Antichrist can "call it in" anytime it wants to!

Q: (L) One of the most popular ways to make money by investing is in the stock market. But, it seems to me that the stock market is also part of the Antichrist system and investing there would also amount to only getting "crumbs".

A: Yes and no. Not all stocks traded publicly are under direct control of the Illuminati. We are not suggesting anything specific, we are just laying the groundwork. With the general clues we give you, you will figure out the details yourselves, which is tantamount to learning, which is how you progress as souls.

Q: (L) You said we should multiply our money and that storing it is not making it work for you....

A: If you notice, all successful business people do this. They multiply their money; expand their horizons, continuously. They multiply their money by multiplying their output, thus their intake likewise. And the process is never ending, because they understand instinctively that it is part of a cycle. For the intake to continue, it must not be only retained, but must increase in order to keep pace with the ever-spiraling cycle of increase and expansion. And, for this to happen, the output must be expanded accordingly. When it stops, it collapses. And this is how the Illuminati AKA The Brotherhood AKA The Antichrist creates a "Panic", by stemming the flow, even only slightly, and then broadcasting the created impression aggressively.

Q: (S) Well, investing is fine if you have money, but Laura and Frank don't have any money to invest. What would be a way for them to do this?

A: One example would be to share their experiences, insights, and learnings. One way to replicate such would be to publish, for example.

Q: (L) I know you are 6th density light beings and we are just 3rd density humans, and it is hard for us to continue what we are doing when under constant attack from all directions, internally and externally. I don't see how we can tell about all these experiences without risking further problems.

A: The work has not been stopped and will not be. You have been told that publishing all or parts of your work is merely "a phone call away", but, as of yet, you have not had faith in that statement, and you have problems asking for what you want for fear of creating the wrong

"impression", which is in your head and also a part of the attack process.
We have lead you to this position, but you know what they say: "You can
lead a horse to water..." You have expended an enormous amount of
energy communicating with many sources, but most of these are fruitless.
We have told you to network!! This works wonders!!!

Now, aside from the interesting remarks about the economy, the
significant thing for me was the remark that I was seeing "one possible
future" in this semi-dream state. I wondered if that were the case for the
many other instances of "bleed through". Was I at some sort of point of
"branching" of the universe, where the energies are such that many
realities are present in potential? And, again, the Cassiopaeans urged
"networking" as something that "works wonders". Was I networking? I
thought I was. I was sure talking to a lot of people and working very hard
to put a magazine together that would become an "organ" for the
Cassiopaean material. But getting the work done alone was a crushing
labor. The entire burden, it seemed, was mine.

One of the things in the Matrix books that interested me particularly,
considering the comments made by the Cassiopaeans about Hitler and the
creation of a "Master Race", was the idea that it was the Germans/Nazis
who were really the Secret Masters of the world. It was further suggested
that they were producing the whole show, including the alien scenario,
because they had been able to construct a Time Machine. There were some
variations on this theory, including an evil Consortium of Nazis and
American Secret Groups involved in mind control experiments, among
other things. So, I brought it up:

Q: (L) Did the Germans construct a time machine during W.W.II?

A: Yes.

Q: (L) They actually did it?

A: Ja.

Q: (L) Were the German experiments in time travel carried to the U.S.
after the war?

A: In splintered form.

Q: (L) Did the US take possession of a time machine constructed by the
Germans?

A: No.

Q: (L) Why not?

A: Was taken elsewhere. Mausenberg, Neufriedland.

Q: (L) Where is Mausenberg?

A: Antarktiklandt.

Q: (L) Who is in control of or running this machine?

A: Klaus Grimmschackler.

Q: (L) I didn't mean a specific person, a group. Americans or Germans?

A: Deutsche.

Q: (L) Did they use this machine to transport themselves there and also in time?

A: Has been performed in Glophen in gestalt, bit, yie aire das gluppen und werstalt de vir seinderfor bidde. [Since I don't know German, I don't really know where to put the word breaks in this string of letters and have done it based on my best guesses.]

Q: (L) Why are you giving this so that we don't understand?

A: Sorry, got the transmissions mixed up due to subject matter.

Q: (L) Getting back to this German time machine: did the Germans capture a crashed, or retrieve a crashed, UFO during the war?

A: Yes.

Q: (L) Who was flying that craft - excuse me - OPERATING that craft?

A: Grays.

Q: (L) Were the Germans able to back engineer and construct other craft similar to the one they captured?

A: Did not need to. They got the information on such things from channeled sources.

Q: (L) Did the Germans get the information from the Vril Society?

A: Partly. Also Thule Society.

Q: (L) These individuals who have this time machine in Antarctica, what are they doing with it or what do they plan to do with it?

A: Exploring time sectors through loop of cylinder.

Q: (L) What is a loop of cylinder?

A: Complex, but is profile in 4th through 6th density.

Q: (L) Are there any particular goals that they have in doing this "time exploration"?

A: Not up to present, as you measure it.

Q: (L) Well, if they escaped and took this time machine to Antarctica, are they working with any of the so-called "aliens"?

A: 4th density STS.

Q: (L) Are these Germans and their time machine, any part of the plan to take over earth when it moves into 4th density?

A: Maybe.

Q: (L) Are the Germans behind any of the conspiracies in the US?

A: No. 4th density STS behind both.

Q: (L) So there is a maverick German element, but to focus on that as being the foundational aspect of this phenomenon, is to focus on the wrong thing?

A: Maybe.

Q: (L) Among the things that were discussed among the Germans in the Thule Society and the Vril Society, was the "Black Sun That Illuminates the Interior". Can you tell us what this "Black Sun" is?

A: Ultimate destiny of STS orientation.

Q: (L) Is this Black Sun an actual astronomical phenomenon?

A: In essence.

Q: (L) What would we know this Black Sun as? A black hole?

A: Good possibility.

Q: (L) A little off to the side, but is there any Japanese connection here as suggested by a recent episode of the X-Files?

A: Only to extent of level of participation in "secret" world government.

Q: (L) Terry has a theory that the United States is so greatly in debt to the Japanese, and that they are going to default on their obligation and cause the Japanese government to fail, and that the Japanese and some others are going to be played as the "bad guys", once again, as they were in W.W.II. Is this a plan in the making?

A: No.

Q: (L) Why did the X-Files have an implied Japanese experimental conspiracy blamed for the UFO/alien activity in the United States? Why are they presenting the Japanese as the Bad Guys?

A: Remember, the "X-Files" has a fictional basis.

At this point, I went off in other directions so I will omit that material. However, right at the end of this same session, I remembered something the Cassiopaeans had said almost a year earlier right as we were winding up another session. The issue of the present moment was the UFO conference in Gulf Breeze that was to be held rather soon. We were talking about attending and distributing our magazine, the Aurora Journal, and I was reminded of the fact that the Cassiopaeans had suggested going to a Gulf Breeze conference "in the spring" at a time when the Gulf Breeze conferences had always been held in the fall. The older session went as follows:

Q: (T) Any other questions?

A: Go to Pensacola.

Q: (L) Who wants to go to Pensacola?

A: I do, I do. [Laughter]

Q: (T) Is something going to happen in Pensacola?

A: Conference. Increasing activity in Florida panhandle, vortex. If you go to Pensacola you will see UFOs of all origins including yours truly.

Q: (T) Oh! It's your conference! And we've been invited!

A: Okay.

Q: (T) When is it that we are supposed to go. Is it that whenever we go, then will be the conference?

A: May.

Q: (T) Is there something in May? In Pensacola? (J) Project Awareness is in May but that's in Tampa. Are you talking about the conference in May that is being put on by the Pensacola group?

A: Look and see.

Q: (T) Okay, in May we should go to Gulf Breeze?

A: Yes.

Q: (T) Okay, the conference in Gulf Breeze in going to be in Tampa in May.

A: Do a session and monitor the skies at the same time. Have someone posted outside with a video camera!! Let's try to steer all these "Ufologists" in the right path.

Now, the strange thing about this UFO conference that we were talking about was that the normal schedule was for the spring conference to be held in Tampa and the fall conference to be held in Gulf Breeze. As it turned out, that very year the fall Gulf Breeze conference was nearly canceled because of a hurricane! That, in itself, was an extremely interesting event. We had been planning on attending this particular conference and T and J had already made the reservations. Hurricane Opal was spinning around in the Gulf and everyone was waiting to see where it would come ashore:

Cassiopaeans: Review: what did we say about weather. Why do you suppose "Opal" occurred at time, place reference point?

Q: (L) To put a stop to the UFO conference in Gulf Breeze? Does this mean we ought to stay home?

A: Up to you, but, suggest deferment, we could tell you of titanic battle!!!!

Q: (L) So, hurricanes are a reflection of battles at higher levels? Did the good guys win?

A: Yes, but not concluded, and we fear for those drawn to locator because of sinister plans by 4th density STS.

Q: (L) Plans such as what? More weather phenomena or something more direct?

A: Both, several options open to them, and in works; monstrous hurricane to hit during conference, or tornado strikes Embassy Suites hotel, or bomb blast levels conference center, or mass abductions and mental controls initiated in order to cause dissension and possibly violence, followed by extreme factionalization.

Q: (L) So, there is the possibility that something really positive could come from the connections made at the conference and, to prevent this possibility, the 4th density STS are taking steps?

A: Yes, why do you suppose it has been disrupted as of now? And have you noticed that the hurricanes have been increasing in October, rather than decreasing as would normally be true?

Q: (L) Well, then, I guess we will be staying home.

A: Free will.

So, we canceled our reservations for the UFO conference. As it turned out, the hurricane did hit Gulf Breeze almost dead on, and the conference was moved to Mobile. Clearly, there was no bomb blast or tornado so if any of the above mentioned possibilities did play out, it would seem to have been mass abductions and mental controls initiated.

As a result of this hurricane, the organizers of the conference decided to switch the schedule around so that *the Gulf Breeze conference was held in the spring* the following year, 1996. But, *not* in May. In March. So, even if the Cassiopaeans were picking up something about this specific switcheroo, it was not a bull's eye exactly. Another thing that has happened since that hurricane is that the organizers of the conference broke up their organization and reformed. They no longer hold "UFO" conferences, but rather focus on "Metaphysical/New Age" assemblies. So, it may be that there was a mass abduction and mental controls that initiated dissension. But, it would be difficult to make Ufologists any more fragmented and factional than they already were and are!

The End of Volume 4 of
The Wave

Those readers who have read The Wave online know that it is almost a thousand pages of text. Thus, we have decided to split it up into separate volumes to make it easier to handle, to read, and even to print.

Volume 3 has not contained the introductory materials that have been included in Volume 1, nor will Volumes 3 and 4, 5 and more, and thus there will be nothing but *The Wave*, with additional notes and illustrations.

The introduction to the series on the website says:

> The Wave is a term used to describe a Macro-cosmic Quantum Wave Collapse producing both a physical and a "metaphysical" change to the Earth's cosmic environment theorized to be statistically probable sometime in the early 21st century. This event is variously described by other sources as the planetary shift to 4th density, shift of the ages, harvest, etc., and is most often placed around the end of 2012. The subject of The Wave begins with a UFO abduction account, a transcript of an actual hypnotic regression session, that refers to a global cataclysmic change.

> This series of articles, written by Laura Knight-Jadczyk, demonstrates the unique nature of the Cassiopaean Experiment. In her skillful collecting of the pieces of the puzzle from throughout the transcripts, in-depth research, personal experiences, weaving them into a finished product, Laura brings added depth and dimension to the original transmissions. Laura presents what the Cassiopaeans - We are YOU in the future - have to say about the eventuality of The Wave - FROM the future - including an exploration of the limitations of man's present estate, in cognitive, biological, historical and ontological terms.

The fact is, in the past three years, we have made much progress in our understanding of the Wave and our relationship to it. I will be adding material to the end of this book version of the series, that will not appear on the website, that will include this information and finally we will have a conclusion to *The Wave*. Whether or not that conclusion is correct remains to be seen.

I don't think we have very long to wait to find out.

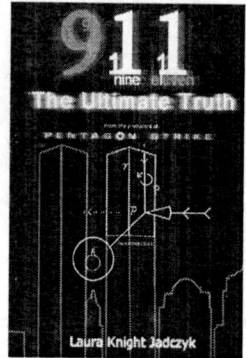